高等教育“十二五”系列教材

国际市场营销

International Marketing

（修订本）

主　编　高　杰
副主编　王志华　谢印成　刘　凡

北京交通大学出版社
·北京·

内容简介

本书采用英文撰写，主要服务于各高校市场营销专业和国际贸易专业学生的双语课教学。教材内容涵盖了近年来国际营销的相关理论，罗列了大量国际营销的实践案例，并结合我国企业的国际营销实践对相关问题进行了探讨，为配合教学工作的开展，在每个章节的开始部分给出了章节的主要内容，在每个章节的结束部分给出了相关的案例、总结以及需要学生进行练习的习题，从内容上讲基本上覆盖了国际营销的主要方式以及操作国际营销所需要具备的主要条件和操作过程中需要解决的主要问题，并给出了相关的策略和方法，力图使学生在学习了本门课程以后可以掌握一种操作国际营销的技能。

图书在版编目（CIP）数据

国际市场营销=International Marketing：英文 / 高杰主编. —北京 ：北京交通大学出版社，2013. 1（2022. 1 重印）

（高等教育“十二五”规划教材）

ISBN 978-7-5121-1348-0

Ⅰ. ① 国… Ⅱ. ① 高… Ⅲ. ① 国际营销-双语教学-高等学校-教材-英文 Ⅳ. ① F740. 2

中国版本图书馆 CIP 数据核字（2013）第 011530 号

国际市场营销

GUOJI SHICHANG YINGXIAO

责任编辑：韩　乐　　助理编辑：严慧明

出版发行：北京交通大学出版社　　电话：010-51686414　　http：//www. bjtup. com. cn

地　　址：北京市海淀区高梁桥斜街 44 号　　邮编：100044

印 刷 者：北京虎彩文化传播有限公司

经　　销：全国新华书店

开　　本：185 mm×260 mm　　印张：23. 5　　字数：587 千字

版 印 次：2013 年 1 月第 1 版　　2017 年 9 月第 1 次修订　　2022 年 1 月第 4 次印刷

书　　号：ISBN 978-7-5121-1348-0/F · 1137

印　　数：4 501～5 000 册　　定价：49. 00 元

本书如有质量问题，请向北京交通大学出版社质监组反映。对您的意见和批评，我们表示欢迎和感谢。

投诉电话：010-51686043，51686008；传真：010-62225406；E-mail：press@bjtu. edu. cn。

前　言

在经济全球化背景下，企业经营活动的国际化日益成为一种广泛的现象，企业要想在激烈的市场竞争中博得一席之地，参与国际市场营销将成为一种必然趋势。特别是信息和交通技术的高度发展使得国家、企业的经济活动跨越国界成为常态，并形成了超越民族国家地理疆域的全球大市场。国际市场营销在解决国内市场容量相对饱和、企业经营规模扩大、产品生命周期缩短等重大企业经营问题过程中具有不可替代的重要作用。

此外，在当今世界政治和社会环境复杂多变、世界金融危机远未消除的背景下，也迫使企业经营活动向国际化发展。一方面，政治和社会环境复杂性的增加要求将企业经营分散在许多国家进行，以分散企业风险，避免因某一国环境的剧变导致企业蒙受重大损失；另一方面，环境的复杂性要求企业深入各国市场，充分研究了解各国市场环境，紧密结合当地市场情况进行生产和销售。这样才能保持其在各国的市场地位，避免或减少由于各国政策变化给企业带来的负面影响。由此可见，参与国际市场营销是当今世界经济、市场和企业发展的必然要求。企业只有进入国际市场，进行国际市场营销，才能不断降低产品成本，保证企业利润；才能保持企业竞争优势；才能保持并扩大企业的市场，企业也才能生存和发展。

本书阐述了国际市场营销的基本理论、基础知识和操作方法，由国际市场营销概述、国际市场营销环境分析、国际市场营销战略、国际市场营销策略组合四个部分共 12 章内容构成，重点阐释普遍适用于各国或地区的国际市场营销分析框架，突出国际市场营销跨文化环境分析，增添了全球环境分析、区域环境分析及东道国环境分析框架和方法。随着中国经济的快速成长以及中国经济对世界经济发展的影响力日益扩大，本书强调从中国视角分析国际市场营销问题，探讨国际企业在中国市场的营销策略组合，以增强读者对中国企业国际市场营销的认识和思考。

本书主旨在于训练国际市场营销基本分析框架及思维路径的形成，同时服务于高校的双语教学，因为采用全英文形式编写，可以使学生在参与本课程的学习中不仅学到专业知识，同时通过教师的英文讲解和阅读教材内容提高自己的英文水平。本书强调理论性与实践性相结合，适合作为高等学校国际经济与贸易、市场营销、工商管理等专业本科生、研究生 MBA 教材，也适合作为政府、企业相关人员，尤其是外贸人员的培训教材。

参与本书编撰的作者长期从事经济科研和双语教学工作，一直希望编撰一部适合我国高校本科生英文水平的双语课程教材，以提高双语课程教学质量，经过数年的艰苦努力终于完成了这项工作。本书共分为13章，其中第1章和第2章内容由高杰编写，第3至第6章内容由刘凡编写，第7至第9章内容由谢印成编写，第10至第12章内容由王志华编写，全书的校对及总撰工作由高杰负责。

本书获得江苏技术师范学院教材基金资助。在本书的写作和出版过程中，得到保罗·金森教授和北京交通大学出版社编辑郭碧云女士的指导和支持，在此表示感谢！本书参阅了大量国内外教材、著作、报刊及各类媒体报道，如有遗漏未列出的参考文献，敬请作者谅解，并在此表示感谢！对于多年来一直给予我们支持和帮助的老师、学生、领导、朋友、同事及家人，表示感谢！

编者
江苏技术师范学院商学院
2012年10月

Contents

Chapter 1 International Marketing Overview

Concept preview

After reading this chapter, you should be able to

1. Appreciate: the concepts of market and marketing.
2. Understand: the significance of the globalization for multinationals.
3. Distinguish: the differences between domestic marketing and international marketing.
4. Comprehend: the characteristics of world-famous companies.
5. Describe: how the Chinese forces influence international marketing.

By now, the integration of the global economies has become an irresistible trend and multinational companies are playing a more and more important role in the real world. All countries pay more attention to the export and import, foreign investment, labor cooperation, technology transfer and other international economic activities. And all of the countries including developed and developing countries try their best to occupy the foreign resources to promote their economic growth. As one of the most important methods, international marketing has become the major way for most companies to take up the global division and most of the countries have harvested the huge benefits through taking international marketing. Especially, one of the most important reasons for China to make the great economic achievement is the Reform and Openning-up Policy.

However, it is a question for lots of the Chinese companies to use their advantages to develop foreign markets. As a matter of fact, most of the Chinese companies lack enough experience and marketing skills when they want to develop foreign markets. This is why they have to study the relavent knowledge about international marketing. With the world's economic development, various global resources are integrated by multinationals and governments. "Going global" and finding new marketing opportunities in the global market have become a very important measures for lots of companies to expand their business. It is inevitable for the Chinese companies to utilize the international market to develop their business if they want to be famous enterprises of the world. So it is very necessary for us to study how to develop the international market and how to defeat our competitors in the global market.

In this book we will discuss some questions about the international marketing and try to tell the readers how to integrate various resources when they take international marketing.

1.1 Concept analysis

As the change to a new discipline, international marketing was formed in the 1960s, improved in 1970s, and established its international position in 1980s. Since 1970s, business colleges in America began to take international marketing as their major course and the systematic study about the international marketing became one of the most important subjects for economists. With deep research, the theoretical system of international marketing was formulated gradually.

Before discussing the questions about international marketing, we should understand "what is market" first. The word "market" derives from the Latin *mercari* meaning "to buy or trade" and the infinitive finds its roots in *merx*, which means "goods".

The "market" lies in which goods or services may be sold or traded. Nowadays, it can range from a simple open-air exchange of farm products to a description of a huge economy entity, like the European Market, or a nebulous commercial functions like stock market or future market. The term also covers specific ethnic, cultural, religious, national, political, or social groups. People may purposefully group themselves together as market (e. g., NAFTA) or they may come together by circumstantial default (e. g., adults 21 to 30 years old). And all markets can be subdivided or segmented into smaller and smaller groups.

However, as a new word, marketing is very different from market and lots of people define the concept based on different ideas. For example, some people think "marketing" is the process that the companies get profits using their resources, others think "marketing" is the process that the enterprises beat their competitors in the real world, and Philip Kotler said "Marketing is the sum of all of the social relationships.

The authors think it is not very important to give an exact definition for "marketing", especially for businesspeople, an accurate concept is not significant for their business in the real world. But we should understand the characteristics of the concept and this is the foundation for us to understand international marketing.

1. Marketing is the activity of innovation

This means marketing needs the marketers to use their ability and wisdom to make profits for the company and it is impossible for any companies to dominate or occupy the market for a long time if they don't take any innovation in the fields of production, promotion, price or distribution. All of the famous and outstanding companies in the world base their market position on innovation without exception.

For example, Dell has become the famous IT company because it has created the direct-sell model; Haier has become the most famous home appliance brand in China depending on its service system, Nokia has become the first brand in the mobile phone for a long time because it introduced at least 3 types of new mobiles in just one month and Apple can beat Nokia to become the first brand mobile phone in today's market just because of its advanced technology. So marketing is a creative activity, it is impossible for any companies to defeat their competitors if they don't take innovation. Moreover, the international market is more complex than domestic market. It requires the managements to take innovation in all of the aspects of marketing.

2. Marketing is the process to satisfy the demand of consumers

All managements must understand that the goal of every company is to make profits, and if you want to reach it, the first question you have to face is how to satisfy the demand of your consumers and it is the only way for you to make money in the real world.

With social and economic development, the consumer's demands change constantly, and the basic mission for the managements is to study your consumers and make your products or services satisfy their demands. Of course, it is not very easy, especially when you want to study the foreigner's consumption habits or other factors influencing their behaviors, you have to face different languages, different income level, different regulations, etc. This is why international marketing is more complex than domestic marketing.

3. Marketing is the process of the management

Management plays the most important role in any marketing process, and all the realization of the target markets is dependent on various management ways, including the resource integration, product manufacture, product sales, promotion, and the study of market environments. Excellent management is essential for any companies to win the market, especially for multinational companies. Any success in marketing is based on the outstanding management. For example, as one of the most famous multinationals, GE is the most successful company in the world, and the most important reason is that it occupied the world market with the strong management resources.

4. Marketing is the bridge between the society and enterprises

The goal of marketing is to make money for the companies. Marketing is a process, any companies must sell their products or services to their consumers to achieve their value. However, it is not very easy, because manufacturers have to try their best to persuade consumers to buy, and all of the products should be supervised by the authorities and public. That means the managers not only have to contact the consumers and show the advantages of their products to them, but also have to understand the relevant policies and the public value. At the same time, they have to utilize various media to introduce their products or establish the brand name in consumer mind. All of the above require the managers to take various marketing methods to reach the goal. This is why marketing is the bridge between the society and enterprises.

5. Marketing is the unique activity for human beings

Adam Smith said: "Nobody saw two dogs were exchanging their bones in the world." The sentence means only people can take marketing activities and if you want to win the market, you have to deal with different relationship and analyze different situations of society. Another important content for marketers to study is the "demand" of consumers. As a matter of fact, the consumer's demand is the greatest force to lead the market; the excellent companies always pay more attention to demand than supply, and it is another reason for them to succeed in the marketplace.

1.2 The basic characteristics of multinationals

Beyond all question, international companies are playing the major role in international marketing. However, how to define the international company is a theoretical question. International marketing, like other fields of study, has its own terminology. To assist you in learning the special terminology and understanding the important contents of the book more easily, we have listed the most important terms at the end of each chapter.

Multinational, global, international and transnational

For international companies, as with any new disciplines, definitions of a number of words vary among users. For example, some people use the words "world" and "global" interchangeable with "multinational" to describe a business with widespread international operations; but others define a global firm as one that attempts to standardize operations in all functional areas but that responds to national market differences when necessary. According to this definition, a global firm's management has to meet the following requirements:

(1) Searches for market opportunities in the world, threats from competitors, sources of products, raw materials, and financing, personnel. In other words, it has global vision. For those international managers, the basic qualification is to possess the global vision. If you can not integrate your resources in the world, it is impossible for you to reduce your costs less and take the advantageous position in the world market.

(2) Seeks to maintain a presence in key market. Market exists everywhere, but is different from one place to another, one of the most important for the international managers is to find out the most efficient market for your company, because the market can not only make profits for the company, but also can create the great brand or image for the company.

(3) Looks for similarities, not differences, among markets. This is because all of the marketing operation requires the companies to invest the resources and familiar markets can reduce the expenditures for the company and make the operation easier.

Those who use global in this sense define a multinational company as a kind of holding company with a number of overseas operations, each of which is left to adapt its products and marketing strategy to what local managers perceive to be unique aspects of their individual markets. Some academic writers suggest using terms such as multidomestic and mulitlocal as synonyms for this definition of multinational. You will also find those who consider Multinational Corporation to be synonymous with multinational enterprise and transnational corporation.

The United Nations and the governments of most developing nations have been using transnational instead of multinational to describe a firm doing business in more than one country. Some academic writers have employed the term for a company that combines the characteristics of global and multinational firms.

(1) Trying to achieve economies of scale through global integration of its functional areas.

(2) Being highly responsive to different local environments (a newer name is multicultural multinational).

Businesspeople usually define a transnational as a company formed by a merger (not a joint venture) of two firms of approximately the same size that are from different countries. Example, Unilever (Dutch-English), Shell (Dutch-English), Azko-Enka (Dutch-German), and ABB, a merger of ASEA (Swedish) and Brown-Bovari (Swiss).

Definitions used in this text

In this text, we will employ the definitions listed below, which are generally accepted by businesspeople. Although we primarily use the terms such as "global, multinational, and international firms or companies", at times we may use "multinational enterprise" interchangeable with international company inasmuch as both terms are employed in the literature and in practice. Let's summarize briefly the knowledge about international marketing we have studied.

(1) International marketing is business whose activities involve crossing national borders. This definition includes not only international trade and foreign manufacturing but also the growing service industry in such areas as transportation, tourism, banking, advertising, construction, retailing, wholesaling, and mass communications. In a word, if you take your business from domestic market to a foreign one, you are taking international marketing.

(2) International marketing denotes the domestic operations within a foreign country. This term is sometimes used interchangeably with international business by some writers.

(3) Multinational company is an organization with multicountry affiliates, each of which formulates its own marketing strategy based on perceived market differences.

(4) Global company is an organization that attempts to standardize operations worldwide in all functional areas.

(5) International company refers to both global and multinational companies.

The brief history of international marketing and multinationals

While international marketing as a discipline is relatively new, international marketing as a business practice is not. As a matter of fact, human took international business in early century. For example, the famous "silk road" appeared in Han Dynasty. Of course, the past international business was very different from the present.

According to the foreign history, before the time of Christ, Phoenician and Greek merchants were sending representatives abroad to sell their goods. In 1600s, the British East India Company, a newly formed trading firm, established foreign branches throughout Asia. At the same time, a number of Dutch companies, which had organized in 1509 to open shipping routes to the East, the Dutch East India company also opened branch offices in Asia. American colonial traders began operating in a similar fashion in the 1700s.

Early examples of American foreign direct investment were the English plants set up by Colt Fire Arms and Ford, which were established before the Civil War. However, most academic writers don't think they are the birth of multinationals, because both operations failed after only a few years.

The first successful company that went into foreign market was built by Singer Sewing Machine in 1868 and most scholars admit that it is the signal of the multinational companies. By 1880, Singer had become a worldwide corporation with an outstanding foreign sales organization and several overseas manufacturing plants. Other firms soon followed, and by 1914, at least 37 American companies had production facilities in two or more overseas locations.

Among those firms already established overseas were National Cash Register, with manufacturing plants in Europe; Parke-Davis, with a plant near London; and Ford motor company, which had assembly plants or distribution outlets in 14 countries. General motors and Chrysler soon followed afterward, so that by the 1920s, all three companies had sizable foreign operations. Another early overseas investor was General Electric, which, by 1919, had plants in Europe, Latin America, and Asia. Other investors included American Tobacco, Armour, Coca-Cola, Eastman Kodak, Gillette, Quaker Oats, Western Electric, and Westinghouse.

Although American firms were by far the largest foreign investors, European companies were also moving overseas. Friedrich Bayer purchased an interest in a New York plant in 1865, two years after setting up his plant in Germany. Then, because of high import duties in his oversea markets, he proceeded to establish plants in Russia, France, and Belgium. Bayer, now one of the three largest chemical companies in the world, has operations in more than 100 countries. Its annual sales in 2014 are over €42 billion.

From 2005, lots of Chinese companies like PetroChina, Sinopec, Huawei and Haier began to invest in foreign countries. Just in the first half of 2016, China's total foreign investment has been over $130 billion. And it is influencing the world investment structure greatly, with the fast economic development, the trend will be stronger and stronger. By now, foreign direct investment (FDI) has become the most important mean for multinationals to take international marketing.

Although international firms existed before World War Ⅰ, they have only become the subject of much discussion and investigation after 1970s, especially concerning the increasing globalization of their production and markets. In another word, globalization promoted the development of FDI vastly.

1.3 Reasons for globalization

With economic development, globalization has become one of the most important forms for the world economy. Particularly, after December 11th, 2001, China became a member of WTO, relying on its tremendous production ability. China has become the most important producer in the world and large sums of the products (made in China) not only change the life of people around the world, but also change the rules of the world trade and investment direction. More and more foreign money entered China and utilized cheap labor and other resources to provide the cheap merchandises for the world.

And the situation influenced the world economic structure enormously and promoted the development of the globalization.

At the same time, more and more governments realized that they have to adapt to the globalization trend and take more international cooperation if they want to improve their people's life and get more benefits from international trade and international investment.

Four forces to promote globalization

Four interrelated forces are leading international firms to the globalization of their production and international marketing:

(1) The development of the modern science and technology, especially advances in computer and communications technology permit an increasing flow of ideas and information across borders, enabling customers to learn about foreign goods. Cable systems in Europe and Asia, for example, allow an advertiser to reach numerous countries simultaneously, thus creating a regional and sometimes global demand. Global communications networks enable manufacturing personnel to coordinate production and design functions worldwide so that plants in many parts of the world may be working on the same product. Not only does the situation make management get the cheaper raw materials, but it also, more important, makes the cost less.

(2) The progressive reduction of barriers to investment and trade by most governments is hastening the opening of new markets by international firms that are both exporting to them and building production facilities for local manufacture. Lots of governments realized they had to take the globalization because it is the only way for the country to develop its comparative advantages.

(3) There is a trend toward the unification and socialization of the global communities. Preferential trading arrangements, such as the north American free trade agreement and the European Union, which group several nations into a single market have presented firms with significant marketing opportunities. Many have moved swiftly to enter, either through exporting or producing in the area. At the same time, lots of countries signed bilateral or multilateral FTA (free trade agreement, for example, FTA between China and ASEAN began to carry out in January 1st, 2010). Not only have these agreements promoted the development of world trade, but also accelerated the integration of the world resources. That is to say, more multinational companies can establish their plants in foreign countries.

(4) More and more governments realize the most important mission for them is to promote the economic development and improve the domestic living standard and if they want to reach the goal they have to use foreign resources. Cooperation is the only way to achieve the target.

In general, lots of forces promoted the development of the globalization and all of the factors not only influence various national polices, but they also influence the marketing strategies of international companies. Today, it is very impossible for any company to establish their brand name or become world-famous company if they ignore the effect of the globalization and it is the only way for them to take the global competition if they want to win the markets. Another word, the globalization influences and changes the rules of the world business and the regulations of the international companies.

1.4 Explosive growth

Since China became a member of WTO in 2001, the world trade achieved an explosive growth. One variable commonly used to measure where and how fast internationalization is taking place is the increase of total foreign direct investment.

For example, although influenced by the financial crisis in 2008, Chinese FDI grew 27.3% compared with that in 2007, and the foreign investment in actual use reached $92.4 billion. In the first half of 2016, no-financial FDI is over $80 billion and the volume increased 58.7% than the same period last year. By now, America is the largest country to invest in foreign markets and the international firms in Japan and Europe have, since the beginning of the 1980s, increased their share of the total foreign investment. At the same time, China, as an emerging market country, invested foreign countries over $118 billion in 2015, its total export-import volume exceeded $4,000 billion and became the largest trade country in the world in 2013. Additional, since 2009, China has become the largest exporting country in the world.

By now, America is the most important market for foreign investors and it can take in $200 billion foreign money every year and international firms coming from the United Kingdom, Japan, Germany, China, and other countries seem to have focused more on the U.S. domestic market, mainly because the expansion of Japanese, Chinese and European firms in the United States increased their international competition.

We also have estimated the importance of global and multinationals in the world economy. The division on transnational corporations and investment, a specialized agency of the United Nations, estimated that there are at least 80,000 international firms in the world. They control over 650,000 foreign affiliates and according to statistics published by *fortune*, the total revenue of fortune 500 surpasses $27 trillion in 2015. Moreover, the 600 largest multinational or global firms account for one-fifth to one-fourth of the value added in the production of all the goods in the world's market economies. In Japan, just nine general trading companies account for 34.2 and 55.6

percent of all the exports and imports, respectively.

As a result of this expansion, foreign companies' subsidiaries have become more and more important for developed and developing countries. This situation is in sharp contrast to the one that existed when the dominant economic interests were in the hands of local citizens.

The expanding importance of foreign-owned firms in local economies came to be viewed by a number of governments as a threat to their autonomy. However, beginning in the 1980s, there has been a marked liberalization of government policies and attitudes toward foreign investment in both developed and developing nations. Leaders of these governments know that local firms must obtain more commercial technology in the form of direct investment, purchase of capital goods, and the right to use international companies' expertise if they are to be competitive in world markets.

Despite this change in attitude, there are still critics of large global firms who cite such statistics as the following to "prove" that host governments are powerless before them (Table 1-1, Table 1-2):

Table 1-1 The top 20 multinationals of the world in 2011

Rank in 2011	Rank in 2010	Company name	Operating revenue	Profits	Country
1	1	Wal-Mart Stores	421,849	16,389	U. S. A.
2	2	Royal Dutch Shell	378,152	20,127	Holland
3	3	Exxon Mobil	354,674	30,460	U. S. A.
4	4	BP	308,928	-3,719	England
5	7	Sinopec Group	273,421.9	7,628.7	China
6	10	China Petroleum	240,192.4	14,366.9	China
7	8	State Grid	226,294	4,556.1	China
8	5	Toyota Motor	221,760.2	4,765.7	Japan
9	6	Japan Post Holdings	203,958.1	4,891.2	Japan
10	11	Chevron	196,337	19,024	U. S. A.
11	14	Total	186,055	14,000.9	France
12	17	Conocophillips	184,966	11,358	U. S. A.
13	16	Volkswagen	168,041	9,052.7	Germany
14	9	AXA	162,235.9	3,640.9	France
15	27	Fannie Mae	153,825	-14,014	U. S. A.
16	13	General Electric	151,628	11,644	U. S. A.
17	12	Ing Group	147,052.2	3,678	Holland

continued

Rank in 2011	Rank in 2010	Company name	Operating revenue	Profits	Country
18	54	Glencore International	144,978	1,291	Switzerland
19	28	Berkshire Hathaway	136,185	12,967	U. S. A.
20	38	General Motors	135,592	6,172	U. S. A.

Table 1-2 The top 20 GDP countries in 2011

Rank	Country	GDP ($ million)	Rank	Country	GDP ($ million)
1	U. S. A.	15,064,816	11	Canada	1,758,680
2	China	6,988,470	12	Spain	1,536,479
3	Japan	5,855,383	13	Australia	1,507,402
4	Germany	3,628,623	14	Mexico	1,185,215
5	France	2,808,265	15	Korea	1,163,847
6	Brazil	2,517,927	16	Holland	858,282
7	England	2,480,978	17	Indonesia	834,335
8	Italia	2,245,706	18	Turkey	763,096
9	Russia	1,884,903	19	Switzerland	665,898
10	India	1,843,382	20	Sweden	571,567

The above two tables tell us:

(1) Only 26 nations (No. 27, the GDP of Thailand is $0.412 billion in 2015) have gross national products greater than the total annual sales of Wal-Mart Corporation, the world's largest international company.

(2) Wal-Mart's total sales surpass the sum of the gross national products of 70 nations.

These statements are certainly true. In fact, GDP of most nations is smaller than lots of world-famous multinationals sale. Also, regardless of the parent firm's scale, each subsidiary is a local company that must comply with the laws in the country where it is located. If not, it can be subject to legal action or even government seizure. From 1970 to 1975, there were 336 acts of seizure, but a decade later, this number had dropped to just 15. Now most differences are settled by arbitration. And it indicates the power of the multinationals becomes stronger and stronger; on the other hand, more and more governments realized the benefits of the internationalization and take more favorable polices to attract foreign investors. Of course, giant companies, just like Wal-Mart and Sinopec, can make great achievement depending on the global market.

1.5 Recent developments

Declining of American dominance

Until the 1960s, American internationals clearly dominated world business, but then the situation began to change. European and Japanese firms started challenging American multinationals, first in their home countries and then in third-countries markets dominated by U.S. companies. By the 1970s, large European and Japanese businesses were expanding their overseas production facilities faster than the American multinationals. Particularly, as the strongest economy of the emerging markets, China is changing the world investment layout and it is more and more important for world investment market. It is helpful to compare *Fortune's* lists of the top 20 firms in the world ranked according to sales for 2011 (Table 1-1 and Table 1-2) and to realize the change in the relative importance of American, European, Chinese and Japanese multinationals. As a matter of fact, there are over 110 Chinese companies that appeared on the list of fortune 500 in 2015.

The lists show that although the United States is still the world's preeminent economic power; it has lost some of its superiority. As a matter of fact, firms from developing nations such as Mexico, Brazil, and India are among the world's top 100 industrial concerns; especially, Chinese companies have occupied very important positions in Fortune 500. We can also compare lists over time of the largest firms in a number of industries to see if there has been a change of leadership in sales volume.

Characteristics of the international companies

By now, more and more companies are entering the world markets, not just by exporting as many small firms do, but by opening factories, research facilities, and sale offices overseas. *Business Week* analyzed hundreds of internationally active firms and identified 50 that it considered to be the best. Each is a U.S. manufacturing company that has a minimum of $200 million in sales. At least 20 percent of their sales are international, including both exports from the United States and goods manufactured overseas. The average total annual sales for such firms are $600 million, growing at an average of 22.9 percent annually. International sales amount to 44 percent of total sale. *Business Week* surveyed these companies and found that they had the following characteristics:

(1) Products are often unique because of their technology, design, or cost.

(2) Sharply focused. Their goal is to be first or second globally in technology niche.

(3) Lean operations to save money and speed decision making. Because of relatively open trading regions and newer technologies, they are able to serve the global market with a small number of manufacturing locations, resulting in a smaller bureaucracy.

(4) Open to ideas and technologies from around the world. Many establish research laboratories in other countries.

(5) Using foreigners to head operations and also fill senior positions at headquarters.

These younger, more agile large firms are remaking the global corporation for the new century and beyond. As Christopher Bartlett, an expert on multinational enterprises, says, "The newcomers have the huge advantage of starting fresh. They can develop much more flexible structures."

1.6 Domestic marketing and international marketing

International marketing differs from domestic marketing in that a firm operating across borders must deal with the forces of three kinds of environments—domestic, foreign, and international. In contrast, a firm whose business activities are carried out within the borders of one country needs to be concerned essentially with only the domestic environment. However, no domestic firm is entirely free from foreign or international environmental forces because of the possibility of having to face competition from foreign imports or from foreign competitors that set up operations in its own market. Let us first examine these forces and then see how they operate in these three environments.

Domestic marketing and international marketing both belong to the marketing and both take the consumers to be the center. Enterprises have to analyze market environment and find out market opportunities to select the target market and use marketing strategies to defeat their competitors and achieve the business goal of their companies.

Of course, they are different, it is more complex and difficult for companies to take international marketing than to take domestic marketing, because international marketing has to face different environments including different political rules, different consumers, different laws, different culture and different economic systems, etc. The following table is the brief analysis about the question (Table 1-3).

Table 1-3 Differences between domestic marketing and international marketing

Domestic marketing	International marketing
1. Research data is available in a single language and is easily accessed	1. Research data generally in foreign languages may be extremely difficult to obtain and interpret
2. Business is transacted in a single currency	2. Many currencies involved, with wide exchange rate fluctuations
3. Head office employees will normally possess detailed knowledge of the home market	3. Head office employees might only possess and outline knowledge of the characteristics of foreign markets
4. Promotional messages need to consider just a single national culture	4. Numerous cultural differences must be taken into account
5. Market segmentation occurs within a single country	5. Market segments might be defined across the consumers of the same type in many different countries
6. Communication and control are immediate and direct	6. International communication and control may be difficult
7. Business laws and regulations are clearly understood	7. Foreign laws and regulations might not be clear
8. Business is conducted in a single language	8. Multinational communication is required
9. Business risk can usually be identified and assessed	9. Environments may be so unstable that it is extremely difficult to identify and assess risks
10. Planning and organizational control systems can be simple and direct	10. The complexity of international trade often necessitates the adoption of complex and sophisticated planning, organization and control systems
11. Functional specialization within a marketing department is possible	11. International marketing managers require a wide range of marketing skills
12. Distribution and credit control are straightforward	12. Distribution and credit control may be extremely complex
13. Selling and delivery documentation is routine and easy to understand	13. Documentation is often diverse and complicated due to meeting different border regulations
14. Distribution channels are easy to monitor and controlled	14. Distribution is often carried out by intermediaries, so is much harder to monitor
15. Competitor's behavior is easily predicted	15. Competitor's behavior is harder to observe, therefore less predictable
16. New product development can be geared to the needs of the home market	16. New product development must take account of all the markets in which the product will be sold

Environments are different

As a matter of fact, the difference between domestic and international marketing is that the firms have to face different environments. As the manager of a multinational company, you have to study the environment first if you want to enter the foreign markets.

As used here, environment is the sum of all the forces surrounding and influencing the life and development of the firm. The forces themselves can be classified as external or internal. Furthermore, management has no direct control over them, though it can exert influences such as lobbying for a change in a law, heavily promoting a new product that requires a change in a cultural attitude, and so on. The external forces are commonly called uncontrollable forces and consist of the following.

(1) Competitive—kinds and numbers of competitors, their locations, and their activities.

(2) Distributive—national and international agencies available for distributing goods and services.

(3) Economic—variables (such as GNP, unit labor cost, and personal consumption expenditure) that influence a firm's ability to do business.

(4) Socioeconomic—characteristics and distribution of human population.

(5) Financial—variables such as interest rates, inflation rates, and taxation.

(6) Legal—the many kinds of foreign and domestic laws by which international firms must face.

(7) Physical—elements of nature such as topography, climate, natural resources.

(8) Political—elements of nation's political climates such as nationalism, forms of government, and international organizations.

(9) Sociocultural—elements of culture (such as attitudes, beliefs, and opinions) important to international businesspeople.

(10) Labor—composition, skills, and attitudes.

(11) Technological—the technical skill and equipment that affect how resources are converted to products.

The elements which management can control are the internal forces, such as the factors of production (capital, raw material, and people) and the activities of the organization (personnel, finance, production, and marketing). These are the controllable forces management must administer in order to adapt to changes in the uncontrollable environmental variables. Look at how one change in the political force—the passage of the north American free trade agreement—affected all of the controllable nations, the United States, Mexico and Canada. Suddenly these companies must examine their business practices and change those affected by this new law. And lots of European and Asian companies set up their production bases in these countries which supply this giant free trade region. By doing this, they will avoid paying import duties on products coming from their home countries.

The domestic environment

The domestic environment is composed of all the uncontrollable forces originating in the home country that surround and influence the life and development of the firm. Obviously, these are the forces with which managers are most familiar. Being domestic forces does not preclude their affecting foreign operations, however. For example, if the home country is suffering from a shortage of foreign currency, the government may place restrictions on overseas investment to reduce its outflow. As a result, managements of multinationals find that they cannot expand overseas facilities as they would like to do. In another instance from real life, a labor union striking the home-based plants learned that management was supplying parts from its foreign subsidiaries. The strikers might contact to the foreign unions and demand not to work overtime unless they achieve their targets.

Foreign environment

The forces in the foreign environment are the same as those in the domestic environment except that they occur in foreign nations. However they operate differently for several reasons, including the following contents.

1. Different values

Even though the kinds of forces in the two environments are identical, their values often differ widely, and at times they are completely opposed to each other. A good example is the case to make money or have a rest in China and Europe, lots of Europeans prefer getting more time to enjoy their vocation to working for making money, while most Chinese always make the oppose decision. People have different realization for money, for example, Americans like to overdraw their credit card and Chinese like to save money.

2. Changes difficult to evaluate

Another problem with the foreign forces is that they are frequently difficult to evaluate, especially the legal and political elements. A highly nationalistic law may be passed to appear a section of the population. To all outward appearance, a government may appear to be against foreign investment, yet pragmatic leaders may actually encourage it. A good example is Mexico, which until 1988 had a law prohibiting foreigners from owning a majority interest in a Mexican company. However, a clause permitted exceptions "if the investment contributes to the welfare of the nation." IBM, Eaton, and others were successful in obtaining permissions to establish a wholly owned subsidiary under this clause.

3. Forces interrelated

In the chapters that follow, we'll see it will be evident that the forces are often interrelated. This is no novelty, because the market conditions in various countries are very different and multinational management has to make their decisions according to the specific situations. For instance, the combination of high-cost capital and an abundance of unskilled labor in many developing countries may lead to the use of a lower level of technology that would be employed in more industrialized nations. In other words, given a choice between installing costly, specialized machinery needing fewer workers and less expensive general-purpose machinery requiring a larger labor force, management will frequently choose the latter when faced with high interest rates and a large pool of available workers. Another example is the interaction between physical and sociocultural forces. Barriers to the free movement of a nation's people, such as mountain ranges or deserts, help maintain pockets of distinct cultures within a country.

The international environment

The international environment is the interactions: ① between the domestic environmental forces and the foreign environmental forces; ② between the foreign environmental forces of two countries when an affiliate in one country does business with customers in another, which agrees with the definition of international business—business that involves the crossing of national borders.

For example, personnel at the headquarters of a multinational or global company work in the international environment if they are involved in any way with another nation, whereas those in a foreign subsidiary do not unless they are also engaged in international business through exporting or management of other foreign affiliates. In other words, the sales manager of Goodyear-Chile does not work in the international environment if he or she sells tires only in Chile. Should Goodyear-Chile export tires to Bolivia, then the sales manager would be affected by forces of both the domestic environment of Chile and the foreign environment of Bolivia and therefore is working in the international environment. International organizations whose actions affect the international environment are also properly part of it.

These organizations include ① worldwide bodies (e. g. World Bank), ② regional economic groupings of nations (e. g. North American Free Trade Agreement), and ③ organizations bound by industry agreements (e. g. Organization of Petroleum Exporting Countries).

More complex decision making

Those who work in the international environment find that decision making is more complex than it is in a purely domestic environment. Consider managers in the home office who must make decision affecting subsidiaries in just 10 different countries (many multinationals or global are in 20 or more countries). They must not only take into account the domestic forces, but they must also evaluate the influence of 10 foreign national environments. Instead of having to consider the effects of a single set of 10 forces, as their domestic counterparts do, they have to contend with 10 sets of 10 forces, both individually and collectively, because there may be some interaction.

For example, if management agrees to labor's demands at one foreign subsidiary, chances are that it will have to offer a similar settlement at another subsidiary because of the tendency of unions to exchange information across borders. Furthermore, as we shall observe throughout the text, not only are there many sets of forces, but there are also extreme differences among them.

Another common cause of the added complexity of foreign environments is manager's unfamiliarity with other cultures. To make matters worse, they will impose on others their own preferences and reactions. Thus, the foreign production manager, facing a backlog of orders, offers the workers extra pay for overtime. When they do not show up, the manager is perplexed. "Back home, they always want to earn more money." This manager has failed to understand that the workers preferred time off to more money. This unconscious reference to the manager's own cultural values, called self-reference criterion, is probably the biggest cause of international business blunders. Successful administrators are careful to examine a problem in terms of the local cultural traits as well as their own.

A solid understanding of the business concepts and techniques employed in the United States and other advanced industrial nations is a requisite for success in international business. However, because transactions take place across national borders, three environments—domestic, foreign, and international—may be involved other than just one; thus in international marketing, the international manager has three choices of what to do with a concept or a technique employed in domestic operations: ① transfer it intact, ② adapt it to local conditions, or ③ not use it overseas. International managers who have discovered that there are differences in the environmental forces are better prepared to decide which option to follow.

To be sure, no one can be an expert on all these forces for all nations, but just knowing that differences may exist will cause people to "work with their antennas extended." In other words, when they enter international market, they will know they must look out for important variations in many of the forces that they take for granted in the domestic environment. It is to the study of the three environments that this text is directed.

Summary

1. Appreciate the dramatic internationalization of markets. Global competition is mounting. The huge increase in import penetration, plus the massive amounts of

overseas investment, means that firms of all sizes face competitors from everywhere in the world. This increasing internationalization of marketing is requiring managers to have a global marketing perspective gained through experience, education, or both.

2. Understand the various names given to firms that have substantial operations in more than one country. Although the definitions vary among users, a global company is an organization that attempts to standardize operations worldwide in all functional areas. A multinational firm, on the other hand, is an organization with multicountry affiliates, each of which formulates its own business strategy based on perceived market difference. The term international company is often used to refer to both global and multinational firms.

3. What is market? The "market" is anywhere that goods or services may be sold or traded. Nowadays, it can range in scope from a simple open-air exchange of farm products to a description of an entire economy, like the European Market, or a nebulous commercial function like the stock market.

4. Comprehend why international marketing differs from domestic marketing. International marketing differs from its domestic counterpart in that it involves three environments—domestic, foreign, and international—instead of one. Although the kinds of forces are the same in the domestic and foreign environments, their values of foreign forces are at times more difficult to assess. The international environment is defined as the interactions ① between the domestic environmental forces and the foreign environmental forces and ② between the foreign environmental forces of two countries when an affiliate in one country does business with customers in another. An international marketing model helps to explain this relationship.

5. Describe the three environments—domestic, foreign, international—in which an international company operates. While international businesspeople must understand business concepts and techniques employed in industrialized nations, they must also know enough about the differences in the environmental forces of the markets in which they operate to be able to decide if a concept or a technique ① can be transferred to another country, ② must be adapted to local conditions, or ③ cannot be used elsewhere.

Questions

1. What are the differences among international, global, and multinational companies?

2. Give examples to show how an international marketing manager might manipulate one of the controllable forces in answer to a change in the uncontrollable forces.

3. As a global firm, it has to change its operating means completely when it tries to

open a foreign market. True or false? Why?

4. Discuss the forces that are leading international firms to the globalization of their production and marketing.

5. How do you understand the characteristics of the world famous companies? Why?

6. What do you believe makes foreign business activities more complex than purely domestic ones?

7. Discuss some possible conflicts between host governments and foreign-owned companies.

8. Why, in your opinion, do the authors regard the use of the self-reference criterion as "probably the biggest cause of international marketing blunders?" Can you think of an example?

9. You have decided to take a job after graduation in your hometown. Why should you study international marketing?

10. Although forces in the foreign environment are the same as those in the domestic environment, they operate differently. Why?

Chapter 2 Why and How to Enter Foreign Markets

Concept preview

After reading this chapter, you should be able to

1. Appreciate: why do companies participate in international trade?

2. Understand: the reasons for the international companies to invest in the foreign market directly.

3. Distinguish: the characteristics of foreign trade and foreign direct investment.

4. Comprehend: why do governments limit foreigners to enter their markets.

5. Describe: the different ways for companies to enter the foreign markets.

International firms invest overseas, but they also export

Just like the media mentioned, China has been in an export boom for a long time. Since 1980, total exports have been growing over two times as fast as the gross domestic product percent annually when adjusted for inflation. Are small firms, large firms, or both responsible for this growth?

As a matter of fact, for lots of the developed countries, their foreign trade and foreign investment grow fast too. For example, since 1980, American's total exports grew about four times as fast as the annual GDP growth rate when adjusted for inflation. Many believe that small and medium-sized firms created the economic miracle, because they lack financial and human resources, their foreign markets mainly depend on exporting rather than manufacturing in them and that large international companies do just the opposite. However, the latest annual study by *Fortune* shows that there are at least 50 Fortune 500 whose annual exports range from \$ 14. 9 billion to a minimum of \$ 750 million. In fact, not only most of fortune 500 invest abroad, but they also export their products to lots of foreign countries because of various reasons.

Many large international corporations are marketing in as many as 100 different countries, but none can manufacture in all these markets. The foreign investment is too great and many markets are too small to support local manufacturing. They must be served by exports.

The opening section of this chapter illustrates that both means of supplying overseas markets—exporting and producing in those markets—are essential to most major multinationals. Moreover, these two international business activities are not confined to manufacturing concerns. Of the *Forbes* 100 largest multinationals, 24 are service companies in banking, finance, construction, insurance, entertainment, transportation, and retailing.

But smaller firms also have operations overseas. According to the *World Investment Report* 2015, small and medium-sized international firms comprised 15. 6% of the total 18,000 Chinese international corporations.

In this chapter, we shall examine two topics directly related to exporting and production in foreign countries: ① international trade, which includes exports and imports, and for most of the multinationals, this is the major method when they first enter the foreign markets, and ② foreign direct investment, which multinationals must make to establish and expand their overseas operation. Later, in the chapters on production and importing, we shall discuss the third activity of international marketing—foreign sourcing, the overseas procurement of raw materials, components, and products.

Internationalization is used to describe the relative situation that the countries and companies take the international activities. In the real world, it is very impossible for any company to make great business achievement if it does not take any international activities. This is because:

(1) The companies have to comply with the development trend of the world economy. Based on the theory of mutual complementary, the only way for the company to make more benefits in the real economy is to take the international division and comply with the great trend of international division and cooperation. For any companies, they can not get more profits if they do not use other countries' resources including market, technology, management and nature resources, etc. In particular, for the Chinese companies, it is more significant, because on the one hand, they have to use the foreign technologies and managements skills to improve the company quality; on the other hand, the nature resources are fewer in China with the rapid development.

(2) The international market will provide important production and marketing

factors for the companies, This is because:

Firstly, no country can provides all of the nature resources for its economic development. For example, China has to import about 200 million tons oil every year. This is why the Sinopec invests large sums of money to set up its oversea oil production bases.

Secondly, the companies may lack enough capital and advanced technologies. To take international marketing not only makes the companies get the larger market and make more money, but it is also very important for them to get the capital and advanced technologies. Because in the process of international marketing, they can cooperate with foreign companies and the foreign companies will transfer their capital and technology to the local companies for their own benefits.

And thirdly, the companies can get more business information. Information has become the very important resource for the companies to operate in today's economy, and the international competition is called the information competition. If you do not take international marketing, it is impossible for you to get the latest information and the result is that you will be loss in the real world.

(3) To take the international marketing makes the companies break the trade barriers and expand the export. In lots of countries, the governments take more trade limit polices to protect their own markets, and at the same time, they welcome the foreign direct investment, because FDI not only can improve their employment, but it also can increase their financial revenue. This is the chance for multinationals to develop foreign markets.

In general, the companies can get more benefits if they take international marketing; of course, it is very difficult for the companies to take international marketing compared with domestic marketing. They have to study various situations about the target markets before they take action. And the first step for them is to understand the situation about the world trade and international investments.

2.1 Volume of trade

In 1990, a milestone was reached when the volume of international trade in goods and services measured in current dollars surpassed $4 trillion. Yet, only three years later, it was approaching $5 trillion, and in 2008, the total world trade volume reached over $30 trillion. In 2010, China's export-import volume was $2,972.76 billion and the number accounted for about 9% of the total world trade volume. Of this, exports were $1.5779 trillion, imports were $1.3948 trillion, 5.36 times and 4.65 times what they were just 8 years earlier. In 2013, export and import of China reached

$4.16 trillion, and from that year, its volume of trade surpass the U. S. and became No. 1 of the world.

In fact, inflation was responsible for a large part of this trade increase, but using a quantum index that eliminates the effects of inflation from the data, we see that the volume of world trade in 2003 was 10 times what it was in 1970 (4.9 percent annual increase). Compared the increase in exports measured in current dollars, including the effects of inflation, with volume increases measured by quantum indexes that eliminate the effects of inflation.

How even has this growth been? Have some nations done better than others? Although there are some differences, the exports of most of the major exporting nations have increased at about the same rate as the world average. However, Japan, the European Union (EU), and the developing nations as a whole, especially China, did surpass the world average growth rate (Table 2-1).

Table 2-1 The world trade volume in 2010

Rank	Country/area	Export	Import	Total volume
1	U. S.A.	12,781	19,681	32,462
2	China	15,778	13,951	29,729
3	Germany	12,681	10,664	23,345
4	Japan	7,698	6,926	14,625
5	France	5,204	6,057	11,261
6	Holland	5,720	5,166	10,887
7	England	4,043	5,571	9,614
8	Italy	4,474	4,838	9,313
9	Korea	4,664	4,252	8,916
10	Hong Kong (China)	3,904	4,335	8,239
11	Belgium	4,113	3,902	8,015
12	Canada	3,872	3,912	7,783
13	Singapore	3,519	3,108	6,627
14	Russia	4,000	2,484	6,484
15	Mexico	2,984	3,106	6,090
16	Spain	2,445	3,121	5,566
17	India	2,162	3,227	5,389
18	Taiwan (China)	2,746	2,514	5,260
19	Australia	2,123	2,016	4,140
20	Brazil	2,019	1,915	3,934
	World	150,820	153,050	303,870

Significance to business

The tripling of world exports indicates that export opportunities continue to grow, but the export growth of individual nations also signifies increasing competition from imports in domestic markets. For example, American exports of computers and peripherals increased by $21 billion from 2003 to 2004, but imports increased by $39 billion. In other words, even though the export volume of these products increased from 2003 to 2004, so did the deficit in this account. Nevertheless, for the volume of trade of the U. S. A, the aerospace and aircraft industries continue to export far more than import because of the very strong competitiveness in these fields. And China became the largest car market of the world in 2011, by now, its auto production and consumption volume has been over 10 million. This is why almost all of the famous world automakers established their production bases in China. In general, with the development of the world economy, the situation and trade position of the countries are changing, and not only the bigger world market provides more opportunities for the multinationals but it also brings the huge pressures to the multinationals.

Direction of trade

What are the destinations of these over $15 trillion in exports? If you have never examined trade flows, you may think that international trade consists mainly of manufactured goods exported by the industrialized nations to developing nations in return for raw materials. And this is consistent with the comparative advantage theory established by David Ricardo. However, more than half of the exports from developing nations do go to developed countries; especially China had exceeded Germany to become the largest export country in 2009, but nearly three-fourths of the latter's exports, with two exceptions, go to other industrialized nations, not to developing countries.

The two exceptions—Japan and the United States

Although influenced by the international crisis broken out in 2008, Japan and America are the third and first largest economic entities in the world. One reason why Japan sells more to developing nations than most developed nations do is that it has had an extensive distribution system in these markets since the early 1980s; particularly, Japanese began to set up their production bases and marketing channels in China since Chinese government began to take opening and reform policies in 1980s, and China has been the largest trading partner of Japan by now. Because the country has no local sources of raw materials, it has used general trading companies to import many of the raw materials and components necessary for Japanese industry. The trading companies' offices in developing nations where these materials are obtained also market Japanese manufactured products to those nations. Moreover, when other industrialized nations have imposed import restrictions on Japanese exports to protect their home industries, the Japanese trading companies have made their efforts to sell them to developing nations.

The United States also exported a smaller proportion to other developed countries and more to the developing nations than others developed countries generally did, but for somewhat different reasons from Japan. American firms have significantly more subsidiaries in developing nations than Japanese companies do; these subsidiaries are captive customers for their American owners. In addition, some buyers in Southeast Asian countries, remembering that Japan was an aggressor, prefer to buy from American firms. The volume of the United States exports to Latin America is 2.3 times that of what all the Latin American nations export to each other.

The changing direction of trade

The percentage of total exports of all the categories of developed nations to other developed nations is declining with the exception of Canada, because America is the most important and the largest trading partner for Canada.

Another interesting observation is that the developing nations as a group are selling a smaller percentage of their exports to developed countries (the United States is an exception), but more to each other. This is due in part to their increasing ability to export manufactured goods and the growing intercompany trade among multinationals' subsidiaries. Of course, the most important reason is that China's export structure has been changed very much in these years and the mechanical and electrical products are playing the most important roles in China's export. Note too that members of the Latin American Integration Association are selling more to each other.

It also appears that the percentages of Japan and the United States are converging. An example is the narrowing over the years of the percentage differences between both nations' exports to the developed countries. The change from 11.2 to 18.5 percent of Japan's exports to the European Union is evidence of its efforts to penetrate this important market. In contrast, the American percentages of total exports to the EU have been dropping and are approaching the Japanese values.

2.2 Major trading partners

An analysis of the major trading partners in the firm's home country and those in the nations where it has affiliates that export can provide valuable insights to management.

Who should be your major trading partners?

There are a number of advantages in focusing attention on a nation that has been already a sizable purchaser of goods coming from the would-be exporter's country:

(1) Business climate in importing nation is relatively favorable.

(2) Export and import regulations are not insurmountable.

(3) There should be no strong cultural objections to buying that nation's goods.

(4) Satisfactory transportation facilities have already been established.

(5) Import channel members (merchants, banks, and customs brokers) are experienced in handling import shipments from the exporter's area.

(6) Foreign exchange to pay for the exports is available.

(7) The government of a trading partner may force importers to buy from countries that are good customers for that nation's exports. We have seen the efforts of the Japanese and Korean governments to persuade their citizens to buy more American goods. They have also sent purchase missions to the United States. Of course, most of the multinationals may not enjoy the last condition, in fact, multinationals of the U. S. may be the unique group that can enjoy the benefits in the real world. However, the front 6 conditions should be qualified when you choose your major trading partners and this is the precondition of successful international marketing.

Utility of the data

The analysis of foreign trade that we have described would be helpful to anyone just starting to search outside the home market for new business opportunities. The preliminary steps of ① studying the general growth and direction of trade and ② analyzing major trading partners would provide an idea of where the trading activity is. What kinds of products do these countries import from your country? And in the real world, you have more channels to get the data and information. Another Department of Commerce publication, the Financial Times 925, details the quantities, dollar values, and destinations of specific products.

The topic we have been examining, international trade, exists because firms export. As you know, however, exporting is only one aspect of international marketing. On the other hand, overseas production requires foreign investment, the topic of the next section.

Foreign investment can be divided into two components: portfolio investment, which is the purchase of stocks and bonds solely for obtaining a return on the funds invested, and direct investment, by which the investors participate in the management of the firm in addition to receiving a return on their money. In this book, we will discuss the direct investment and how to improve the business achievement of multinationals, because the portfolio investment is part of the international financial field.

Portfolio investment

Although portfolio investors are not directly concerned with control of a firm, they invest immense amounts in stocks and bonds from other countries. Data from the U. S. Department of Commerce show that people residing outside the United States hold American stocks and bonds valued at $733 billion ($340 billion in stocks). Of this, 57 percent is owned by European residents, 13 percent by Japanese residents, and 10 percent by Canadian residents. American residents, on the other hand, own $518 billion in foreign securities, of which $298 billion is in corporate stocks. As you can see, foreign portfolio investment is sizable and will continue to grow as more international firms list their bonds and equities on foreign exchanges.

2.3 Trade barriers analysis

Beyond all question, as a part of international marketing, international trade promoted the development of the world economy and improved the benefits of relevant countries. But lots of the governments take various countermeasures to limit the world trade, because:

(1) They want to protect their markets.

(2) They want to protect their employment.

(3) They want to protect their national industries.

(4) They want to limit the competitiveness of the foreign companies.

(5) They want to improve their financial revenue.

(6) They want to protect their environment and nature resources, etc.

All of the above reasons may lead the governments to take policies to limit the world trade volume and block the world economic development. Before you enter a new market, you have to study the foreign trade and foreign investment policies of the host and home governments first and avoid the loss because of the policies. It is necessary for you, although by no means an easy job. Some host and home government barriers are listed below and you should pay more attention to them, especially if you are participating in international trade.

Host government trade barriers

The host government of your target market can throw up a vast number of roadblocks to your success—some of them quite arbitrary in appearance. Here are some government-formulated obstructions to look out for when researching a new foreign market.

1. Tariffs

Import tariffs are the means by which a government, in the form of a customs office, controls the in-flow of foreign goods across its borders. It's a form of taxation and a source of revenue for the state. Rather than banning a certain product outright or letting it outcompete local producers, a nation makes its import prohibitively expensive, thus eliminating widespread acceptance. All nations have a sliding scale of tariffs for various categories of products and trading partners with its "normal" rates often being referred to as Most-Favored-Nation status. Imports from foreign countries held in disfavor pay in multiples of MFN rates proportional to that disfavor. Many emerging markets have rather arbitrary tariff rates, which they blame on the fluid nature of their economic development. Tariffs are subject to much political influence and favoritism. This aspect must be calculated into the total pricing portion of a marketing plan.

2. Inspections

No one disputes a government's right to protect its citizen's health and welfare. This is certainly the case with foodstuffs, medical equipment, and farm animals. However, some inspections are performed with intention of delaying your product to reach the marketplace. This can be a very important factor when it comes to perishable goods or those that are particularly time sensitive (e. g, publications). By slowing down the import process, governments protect their home producers without actually having a formal trade restriction. This tactic, like other nontariff barriers, is usually put into practice by economies seeking to diminish domestic consumption levels of foreign products until homegrown producers feel the playing field is level.

3. Import licensing

Like inspections, import licensing is a legitimatized function of government, whereby the product must be formally licensed by the importer's government and a fee paid by the importer. While inspections control the product quality, licensing is used to control those involved on both sides of the transaction. It's a process subject to arbitrary rulings, and licenses are withheld (or "reconsidered") at the first sign of disgruntlement by local producers or bureaucrats. When used as a barrier, the granting of licenses is such an expensive and potentially corrupt practice that some goods in great demand end up being smuggled.

4. Distribution

Distribution will be considered at length in Chapter 12 but warrants some consideration here. In a larger sense, distribution is every aspect of the network that exists between the original seller and the end-user. Many marketers have found that all of their plans came to naught simply because local governments placed inordinate restrictions on distribution or because local distributors are inefficient. Often, the distribution layers are so thick that consumers can't afford the product once it has passed through the sundry middlemen and their add-on charges. Many international marketers have found it common in Asia, especially in highly developed Japan.

5. Environmental controls

Increasingly, governments are protecting the environment within their borders, and much of that control takes place at those borders. Restrictions on packaging pollution controls can be placed on foreign exporters before licensing is granted. While every country has environmental standards, strictness is in direct proportion to wealth. Advanced economies (US, Germany) are famous for their concern, as much of their environments were polluted by their former industries. Their environmental "impact studies" and "green" product packaging requirements can drive a product from market easily to bad pricing. Research and preparation are the keys to avoiding this problem, which often occurs after a product is in the marketplace, when lawsuits are filed by environmental activists. Emerging economies, eager to attract investment, are far more lax, but "environmental colonialism" is fast becoming a rallying cry in the developing world.

6. Customs delays

Even once a product is licensed it can be held at customs without a stated cause for extended periods. Software, music CDs, and videos are usually a target of this practice, and you can rest assured that illegal copying is rampant. Customs may also hold perishables for the purpose of bribery or to protect local markets. The only way to combat it is to solicit the involvement of embassy personnel in advance of the importation.

7. Quarantine

This process applies mostly to goods (such as live animals or foodstuffs) that are suspected of carrying disease or infestation. The goods are held at a controlled location until inspectors can determine whether they pose a health threat. Although the word quarantine means "40 days", there is no set time limit for the holding process on an international level. Some countries may use the quarantine process to hold materials they believe have deleterious cultural ramification. Books, movies, tapes, periodicals, and CDs are some notable targets.

8. Quotas

An import quota is a non-tariff barrier imposed by a government to restrict the quantity of imports it will take from certain national markets or exporters. It is also a means of keeping all of its trading partners happy. For instance, government A will allot 20 percent of its entire importation of a product to each of five trading partners. This process can also be used to protect local producers from foreign trading practices (lower the quota of the most competitive exporter) or as a punishment for political problems between rival powers (lower or eliminate an entire nation's quota). Even the best marketers can expect to suffer if their home government conflicts with the host officials.

Note: Marketers must realize that the quotas set by their home governments can be used as a countermeasure to pry open a target foreign market. Having good political connections at home is as important as having them abroad.

9. Antidumping laws

These laws were instituted to prevent foreigners from selling products at extremely low prices into a market to drive out competition. This is called "dumping". Local competitors are the first to cry "foul", hoping to tie up a foreign firm in court, and the tactic usually works quite effectively. Only countries with sophisticated commercial law can use this type of legislation.

Warning: It's surprisingly easy to prove "dumping", due to the widespread access to trade information. Your overseas competitors are well aware of what it costs you to produce and distribute a product. Selling "under cost" is a dangerous tactic in an information society.

Home government intervention

It's rare for a country to attempt to stop its local companies from exporting. Even when they permit a steady outflow, governments maintain oversight and taxing rights. Marketers, however, may have just as difficult a time handling their own government as they will deal with the overseas variety. As is true of import laws, not all export requirements are written down in all countries and are therefore subject to "negotiation" and arbitrary enforcement. Research and good governmental relations are keys to keep your product in the export pipeline. And the major home government interrentions include:

1. Embargo

While there's much debate as to whether embargoes accomplish their political goals, there's little doubt that they have a disastrous effect on exporters. Blockade running is rarely part of anyone's marketing plan and long-term risk is high. However, enforcements are different in the real world. Some (like the US embargo of Vietnam) are ignored after several years while others (the UN embargo of Iraq) are stringently enforced for a long time.

Note: Marketers must be aware of the political environment they work in and be prepared to calculate, as well as manage risk.

2. National security issues

Some goods are considered too strategic militarily and economically to be freely marketed to other nations, regardless of the profitable potential. These may include nuclear materials, strategic minerals, chemicals, computer chips, technical manuals, or military surplus. Countries that have these restrictions delineate them quite clearly, and violation is a criminal offense.

3. Export tariffs

Government tax exports primarily as source of revenue and use the process as a means of promoting or punishing particular industries. For example, China surcharged on exported rare-earth in 2009, and the purpose was to limit the unordered development of the rare-earth industry. These tariffs are, like import duties, a means of controlling flow and controlling businesses. Export duties can be highly negotiable in some countries and should be thoroughly investigated during the market planning stage. Some countries have set up export processing zones for foreign manufactures, so that goods produced domestically for export will not be tariffed. These zones promote investment and job creation while protecting domestic manufacturers from direct competition.

4. Export licensing

Like export tariffs, licensing is a flow control. It's often used as a means of denying a rival economy access to both raw and finished products without instituting a full embargo. In many cases, exporting licensing comes from the political reasons. So keep your eyes open and avoid political crossfire.

5. Anti-rerouting measures

When embargoes and quotas are in place, exporters often try to reroute their products through less controversial areas and have the "country of origin" changed in the paperwork. However, it is dangerous in common situation, because this tactic can get an exporter in serious trouble with his home government.

6. Job protection sentiments

Governments will often clamp down on their exporters when they detect that the products being exported will result in job losses for the domestic market. Heavy machinery and high-tech manufacturing equipment can be targeted. If export tariffs on your products don't exceed the gain from taxes derived form the potentially lost jobs, watch out for government intervention.

Informal restrictions

All of the materials we discussed above are the very formal and, for the most part, straightforward means by which governments control the marketing of their domestic producers, as well as that of foreign companies. Beyond these codified restrictions, there are a host of constraints, neither codified nor necessarily government enforced, that can affect the marketing of your product in foreign lands. These informal barriers (listed below) are more difficult to detect and, in many cases, harder to overcome than their more official counterparts.

1. Public relations

In a sense, public relations can decide the success or failure of a company, especially when you are taking the internation marketing. From poorly translated brand names to the lack of locally hired management personnel, bad public relations (and even worse, press relations) can sidetrack the best of products. Often these public relations disasters are engineered (or at least exacerbated) by market competitors.

2. Nationalistic

Competitors, host government officials, and political activists are not beyond raising the cry that your marketing efforts are "bad for the nation," and try their best to drive your products out of the their markets. This barrier was used to restrict Australian wines in France, British movies in Argentina, and virtually any major Japanese product in the United States during the 1980s. It is a very powerful force and a difficult one to control.

3. Religious

Religion plays a greater role in business every year, with much of it centering on Islamic beliefs regarding profit taking and interest rates. However, may Christian fundamentalist groups have flexed their muscles as of late (e. g., the Disney boycott), with marked results. Because religion has such an emotional impact, pure reasoning and factual presentation will do little to get your product back on track.

4. Ethnic

Sometimes, your products may be reduced by foreign consumers because of the ethnic question. This is very complex, and sometimes is very difficult to define. For example, in Bosnia or Burundi, ethnic conflicts has never stopped after several centuries. Assumption that our product is ethnically dangerous or inferior can stymie your marketing efforts whether the accusations are true or not. Nestle faced cries of racism over its sales of baby formula in Africa while many of the marketing problems faced with the makers of the Yugo were based on the fact that few people believed the former Yugoslavia were capable of building a proper automobile. Overcoming ethnic stereotypes takes years of work and enormous amounts of money.

5. Societal

Some societies have a structure that simply will not accept certain products, at least not right away. It may be a matter of taste (light beer in Germany) or social restriction ("adult" movies in Iran). Marketers must often approach a market several times before they are permitted entry. Some industries are bound by edict not to promote foreign products. Canada's radio broadcasters, for example, are required by law to limit the playing of foreign-produced music as a means to promote Canadian culture.

6. Scientific

Product lines that are radically innovative have a difficult time overcoming the skepticism of the target market. Medicines, therapies, business software, securities, and other sensitive services are always the major victims when entering foreign markets. It's best to assemble your proof beforehand and tailor its delivery to the target market.

7. Environmental

Water pollution, endangered species, and alleged man-made global warming are typical emotional concerns of very vocal groups, who often look for international companies to pillory. They are well organized and zealous. If your product has any potential ill effect on the environment, you can foresee major market resistance once such effects are brought to light, even if no restrictive legislation. Environmental action groups enlist anyone can devote themselves and are unyielding when it comes to emotionalizing issue.

Note: nine-year-olds wearing "save the dolphins" buttons did as much to reform tuna fisheries (and affect buying habits) as any law. Beware of self-righteous consumers. They carry their wallets next to their hearts.

8. Educational

Sometimes the greatest informal barrier is the educational level of majority of the target market's population. A large proportion of population around the globe are still illiterate and may more are innumerate. It's not unusual for a controlling government to wish the situation to remain in stasis. Even when educational levels aren't such low, many products, from car to computers, have their own particular "learning curve". Training must be part of your marketing plan when educational level is key to a product's acceptance.

Decision making concern

All of above we have discussed may ruin the efforts of a company to enter a foreign market. The experienced marketers always assess the target markets before they enter, and in common situation, the below contents should be noticed.

(1) Have I researched the target market for potential competitors?

(2) Has the target market exhibited interest in our product?

(3) Has the potential size of the target market been quantified?

(4) Will the foreign government permit import of our product?

(5) Will my government permit the export of our product?

(6) Will I be able to get my price?

(7) If exporting, can letters of credit be secured?

(8) Can proper insurance be obtained in the target market?

(9) Is the target market's infrastructure capable of handling my product?

(10) Will the foreign government give us fair treatment?

(11) Can I control distribution?

(12) If I have to use local distributors, are they trustworthy?

(13) Can I maintain the quality of our product overseas?

(14) Can we maintain control our business (rather than give it up to a local partner or agent)?

(15) Does the local government promote imports?

(16) Does the foreign government have a convertible currency?

(17) Will we be permitted to travel freely in the target market?

(18) Has our legal status in the foreign country been researched?

(19) Does the foreign tariff code treat us fairly?

(20) Does the domestic tariff code treat us fairly?

(21) Does the foreign market allow us to promote and advertise our imported products?

While a "no" answer to any of the above questions doesn't automatically eliminate the potential for success. A marketer should reflect on all these question beforehand.

2.4 Foreign direct investment

Volume

In 2007, the book value of all foreign investments is almost $2 trillion and it is the largest volume of world FDI in recent years. The United States has almost double the foreign direct investment of the second largest, China (its FDI was over $123 billion) which in turn has invested 43 percent more than Japan, is the third largest in 2014.

One factor that has contributed to the increase of foreign investment in the United States has been the U.S. dollar's loss of value in terms of other currencies. For example, in dollar terms, Japan's American investment in 2003 was 43.02 times as large as it was in 1980. However, this investment cost Japanese investors only 32.85 times as many yen because by 2003, the yen was worth nearly twice as much in U.S. dollars as it had been in 1980 (Chart 2-1).

According to the Chart above, we can understand that FDI of the world declined in 2008 because of the financial crisis. Not only did the scale of the FDI for developed countries suffer a lot, but also the FDI of developing countries declined too. In the first half of 2009, the foreign investment in actual use of China is 43 billion dollars and compared with 2008, it declined 17.8%, Brazil declined 60%, Russia declined 45% and India declined 56.5%. Although the world economy is reviving, for example, the foreign investment in actual use of China reached $126.27 billion in 2015, it is very difficult for all of the countries to achieve comprehensive economic growth.

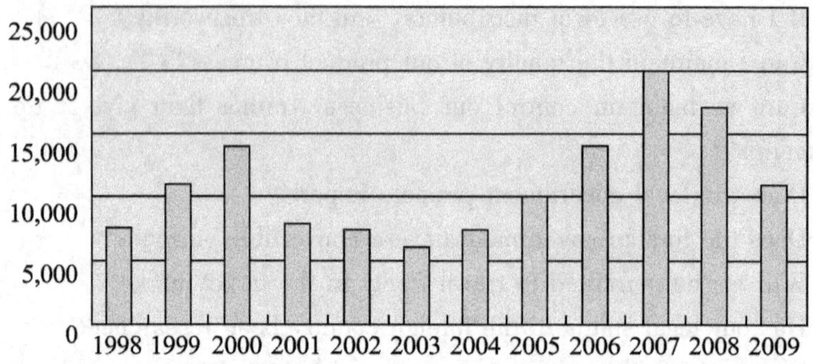

Chart 2-1 Situation of FDI

In general, the FDI began to decrease from 2007 after it reached the peak. And developing countries, especially China, Brazil, India and other emerging market countries are the major acceptance countries of FDI. The following table is the situation about the major investment countries in 2007 and 2008 (Table 2-2).

Table 2-2 Situation of FDI for major OECD countries (unit: billion)

Countries	Flow into			Outflow		
	2007	2008	Change	2007	2008	Change
Australia	44	47	7	17	36	113
Canada	108	45	-59	60	78	30
France	104	97	-7	169	200	18
Germany	56	25	-25	180	156	-13
Italy	40	17	-58	91	44	-58
Japan	23	24	4	74	128	74
Luxembourg	186	80	-57	251	104	-59
Holland	118	-6	-100	29	53	83
Spain	69	65	-5	139	77	-44
England	183	96	-48	276	110	-60
America	276	320	16	399	332	-17
Total	1,583	1,021	-35	2,024	1,631	-19

Direction

Even though it is impossible to make an accurate calculation of the present value of foreign investments, we can get an idea of the rate and amounts of such investments and the places in which they are being made. This is the kind of information that interests managers and government leaders. It is analogous to what is sought in the analysis of international trade. If a nation is continuing to receive appreciable amounts of foreign investment, its investment climate must be favorable. This means that the political forces of the foreign environment are relatively attractive and that the opportunity to earn a profit is greater there than that elsewhere. Other reasons for investing exist, to be sure, but if the above are absent, foreign investment is not likely to occur.

Actually, foreign investment follows foreign trade. Managements observe that the kinds of products they manufacture are being imported in sizable quantities by a country, and they begin to study the feasibility of setting up production facilities there. They are spurred to action because it is common knowledge that competitors are making similar analyses and may arrive at the same conclusion. Often the local market is not large enough to support local production of all the firms exporting to it, and the situation becomes one of competition who can become established first. Experienced managers know, too, that governments often limit the number of local firms producing a given product so that those who do set up operations will be assured of having a profitable and continuing business.

Rapid increase

Foreign direct investment in the United States has risen rapidly from about $6.9 billion in 1960 to $144.5 billion in 2003. Of this, companies in industrial European nations of Europe account for 60.8 percent of the total foreign investment and firms in the United Kingdom and the Netherlands comprise 21.4 and 15.4 percent, respectively. Observe how concentrated foreign direct investment is in the United States. Firms from just five nations: the United Kingdom, Japan, the Netherlands, Germany, and Canada account for over 75 percent of the total.

Notice too that Japanese firms now have a slightly higher stock of direct investments in the United States than the British do. The nationwide distribution and the growth in the number of their manufacturing sites are impressive. And the other force to promote the increase is that China has been one of the most important investors of the world market. In 2010, its foreign investment reached over $60 billion and the volume will increase constantly with its fast economic development.

When the members of congress and government officials talked down the value of the dollar in 2014, they criticized China's government for manipulating the exchange rate, in order to lower the prices stated in other currencies and promote American exports, they may not have realized that they were talking down the prices of American assets as well. Foreign investors, however, did notice the difference and responded by spending twice as much to acquire American firms in 2013 as they did in 2009 because the dollar declined. Observe how the rankings have changed in only three years. Although a few firms, such as Shell, Nestlé, and Unilever have been in the U. S. for years, many of these investments are recently made. You can tell from the names of the American affiliates that their major investment strategy has been to acquire existing firms rather than to start from the ground up. In the first half of 2015, foreign investors spent $282. 26 billion on acquisitions and only $53. 1 billion to establish new companies in America. International firms enter foreign markets for a number of reasons, all of which are linked to the desire to either increase profits or sales or protect them from being eroded by competition.

The U. S. and Europe's foreign direct investment

The United States is by far the largest investor abroad; American firms have invested much more in developed than in developing countries. (Also, as with international trade, the relative importance of regions and countries has been changing.) In a period of 30 years, the percentage of American foreign investment in developed nations has risen from 61 percent to 77 percent. Europe's share has more than doubled, and of the European countries, Great Britain and Germany have become the most important investors for America. Note that although the developing nations as a group have suffered a large decrease, the percentage of investment in other Asia and Pacific region which includes fast growing countries such as China and Singapore has more than doubled.

China's foreign direct investment

According to the China direct investment statistics bulletin in 2010, China has become the fifth largest country to invest overseas in the world, and its characteristics include:

(1) The investment flow shoots to a record and leap into NO. 5 of the world in the field. In 2010, China's outward foreign direct investment reached $68. 81 billion, increased 21. 7% over last year and exceeded Japan ($56. 26 billion) and Great Britain ($11. 02 billion).

(2) The investment stock breaks through $300 billion. By now, the outward investment of China is $317. 2 billion, of which, Australa and Europe are the largest stock areas.

(3) Investment covers lots of industries. By the end of 2010, about 16 thousand Chinese companies invested to 178 countries (areas) and the rate of coverage is 72. 7% of the world, of which, Asia is 90%, Africa is 85% and the investments cover lots of very important industries industries, most investment flow to business service, finance, wholesale, retail, mining, transportation and manufacture industries. The

above industries investment stock is over ＄280 billion and is about 88.3% of the total investment stock.

(4) The proportion of merger is over 40%. In 2010, ＄29.7 billion outward investment is acquisition and increases 54.7% than last year. The merger fields cover mining, manufacture, power production, professional technologies and financial industries. The profit of the overseas investment is ＄24 billion and increases 48.9% than last year.

(5) The rate of increase for the major economic entities is bigger and the investment in Europe is doubled. In 2010, the direct investment in Europe is ＄5.96 billion, the increase rate 101%; ＄4.4 billion is in ASEAN; ＄1.308 billion is in America; ＄568 thousand is in Russia and ＄338 thousand is in Japan (Chart 2-2).

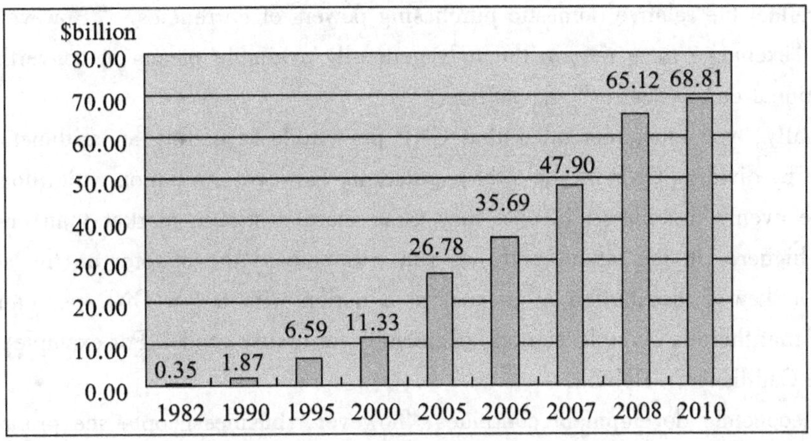

Chart 2-2 China's foreign direct investment

2.5 Reasons for investing overseas

Enter new markets

Managers are always under pressure to increase the sales and profits of their firms, and when they face a mature, saturated market at home, they begin to search for new markets outside. They find that ① a rising GNP per capita and population growth appear to be creating markets that are reaching the critical mass necessary to become viable candidates for their operations and ② the economies of some nations where they are not doing business are growing at a considerably faster rate than the economy of their own market. In fact, for most of developed countries, their companies are deeply in love with the emerging markets because of above two reasons.

New market creation

Although nearly everyone looks to GNP per capita as a basis for making comparisons of nations' economies, extreme care must be exercised to avoid drawing unwarranted conclusions. In the first place, because the statistical systems in many developing nations are deficient, the reliability of the data provided by such nations is questionable.

Second, the World Bank and other international agencies convert local currencies to dollars. The Bank uses an average of the exchange rate for that year and the previous two years, after adjusting for differences in relative inflation between the particular country and the United States. World Bank economists admit that official exchange rates do not reflect the relative domestic purchasing powers of currencies. "However," they said, "exchange rates remain the only generally available means of converting GNP from national currencies to U. S. dollars."

Finally, you must remember that GNP per capita is merely an arithmetic means obtained by dividing GNP by the total population. However, a nation with a lower GNP but more evenly distributed income may be a more desirable market than one whose GNP is higher. On the other hand, as you will note in the chapter on the economic forces, a skewed distribution of income in a nation with a low GNP per capita may indicate that there is a viable market, especially for luxury goods. For example, people do drive Cadillac's in Bolivia.

As economic development continues, however, businesspeople see profit-making opportunities in ① producing locally the kinds of consumer goods that require simple technology or ② assembling the imported parts, and in common situation, the latter demands more advanced technology. Given the tendency of governments to protect local industry, the importation of goods being produced in that country will normally be prohibited. Thus, the exporters of the easy-to-manufacture consumer goods, such as paint, adhesives, toilet articles, clothing, and almost anything made of plastic, will begin to lose this market, which now becomes a new market to producers of the inputs to these "infant industries."

Preferential trading arrangements

The fact that most nations have experienced population and GNP per capita growth does not necessarily mean they have attained sufficient size to warrant investment by an international firm in either ① an organization for marketing exports from the home country or ② in a local manufacturing plant. For many products, a number of these nations still lack sufficient market potential.

However, when such nations have made some kind of a preferential trading arrangement (for example, the European Union and the European Free Trade Association), the resultant market has been so much larger that firms frequently have bypassed what is often the initial step of exporting to make their initial market entry with local manufacturing facilities.

Faster-growing markets

Not only are new foreign markets appearing, but many of them are growing at a faster rate than the home market. One typical example has been the growth of China's GNP per capita from $145.8 in 1980 to $7,750 in 2015. At the same time, according to statistics, Japan's real annual growth rate for that period averaged 3.6 percent compared to Switzerland's 1.4 percent or Sweden's 1.5 percent. Note the annual growth rates of the Asian nations: Singapore, 5.3 percent; and Korea, 8.5 percent, the highest growth rate listed by the World Bank. China and Thailand, with growth rates of 9.6 and 6.0 percent respectively, are other Asian markets attracting the attention of multinationals. The faster-growing markets provide a very great market future for international businesspeople and this is why lots of multinational companies invest in Asia, especially in China.

Improved communications

This might be considered a supportive reason for opening up new markets overseas, because certainly the ability to communicate with subordinates and customers by telex and telephone has given managers confidence in their ability to control foreign operations if they should undertake them, especially on the Internet that makes the multinational managers contact their staff and consumers easily and cheaply. In addition, improved transportation enables managers to either send home-office personnel to deal with local problems or be there themselves within a few hours if necessary.

Good, relatively inexpensive international communication enables large insurance, banking, and software firms to establish their overseas "body shop", and transmit computer-oriented tasks worldwide to a cheap but skilled labor force. New York Life, for example, employs 50 people in Ireland to process insurance claims in a computer linked to the firm's computer in New Jersey. American employees coming to work in the morning find that the claims processed during the night in Ireland have been transmitted to their computer in the United States. Some computer consultants in the United States are earning $75 an hour while their Indian counterparts are working for the same firms via an overseas telecommunications link for $5 an hour.

Shorter travel time has also opened up numerous business opportunities because foreign businesspeople have come to the home country to look for new products to import or new technology to buy. The Department of Commerce, in Business America, regularly publishes a list of arrivals who desire to contact suppliers.

Faster growth in the markets of developing nations frequently occurs for another reason. When a firm that has supplied the market by exports builds a factory for local production, the host government generally prohibits imports. The firm, which may have had to share the market with 10 or 20 competitors during its exporting days, now has the local market all to itself or shares it with only a small number of other local producers. For example, before General Tire (an American company) began manufacturing tires in Chile, probably a dozen exporters, including General Tire, were competing in the market. However, once local production got under way, there was only one supplier for the entire market—General Tire, because the import tariff and strong competiveness of the company stopped other competitors entering the market.

Higher overseas profits as an investment motive

As you know, greater profits may be obtained by either increasing total revenue or decreasing the cost of goods sold, and often conditions are such that a firm can do both with international marketing.

1. Greater revenue

Rarely will all of a firm's domestic competitors be in every foreign market in which it is located. Where there is less competition, the firm may be able to obtain a better price for its goods or services. For example, General Tire had only three competitors in Spain for its V-belt line when dozens of brands were available in the United States and Sony may not meet Samsung in Thailand.

Increasingly, firms are obtaining greater revenue by introducing products into overseas markets and their domestic markets simultaneously. This results in greater sales volume while lowering the cost of goods sold and this is one of the most important reasons for lots of the multinationals to develop foreign markets.

2. Lower the cost of goods sold

Going abroad, whether by exporting or by producing overseas, can usually lower the cost of goods sold. Increasing total sales by exporting will not only reduce R&D costs per unit, but will also make other economies of scale possible. The president of a Westinghouse division stated: "The people who can spread their R&D and engineering and manufacturing development costs across those three markets (Europe, Japan, and North America) have a substantial advantage." Westinghouse, like many companies, obtains lower unit costs through long production runs made possible by having one factory supply one product internationally.

The management of Warner-Lambert, a global health care and consumer products manufacturer, evidently agrees as it states, "Warner-Lambert is addressing each new product as a global opportunity, particularly pharmaceuticals. Only in the context of a worldwide marketplace can Warner-Lambert hope to recapture the escalating costs of bringing new drugs to market. Estimates conservatively place development costs at more than $230 million for a single drug."

The president of Bristol-Myers Squibb, the second-largest pharmaceuticals manufacturer in the United States, claims that "only 1 in 5,000 compounds synthesized in the laboratory makes it to the marketplace. It costs an average of $359 million to develop a new drug and can take up to 12 years to reach the marketplace."

Another factor that can significantly reduce the cost of goods sold is the inducements that some governments offer to attract new investment. For example, Greece offers the following to new investors: ① investment grants of up to 50 percent of the investment, ② interest subsidies to cover up to 50 percent of the interest cost of bank loans, and ③ reduction of up to 90 percent of a firm's taxes on profits. Incentives such as these are designed to attract prospective investors and generally are not a sufficient motive for foreign investment. Nevertheless, they do have a influence on the cost of goods sold.

There is no question that greater profits from overseas investments were a strong motive for going abroad. Business International reported that 90 percent of 140 *Fortune* 500 companies surveyed had achieved higher profits on foreign assets in 2010, for example. The survey showed that in the period from 2003 to 2010 the average growth in foreign earnings outpaced foreign sales growth (5.9 percent versus 4.1 percent), whereas domestic earnings were down by an average of 27 percent despite a domestic sales growth of 5.2 percent. American firms continue to earn more from their foreign sales. In 2009, of the 100 largest U.S. multinationals, only 18 earned more than 50 percent of their revenue overseas, but 33 earned over 50 percent of their profits from their foreign operations. Look at the statistics of General Motors, the industrial firm with the greatest sales. While only 28 percent of its revenue came from foreign operations, 91 percent of its profit did. By now, China has been the largest and most important market for General Motors.

Sometimes, the reasons for going abroad are more related to the protection of present markets, profits, and sales.

Follow customers overseas

Service companies (accounting, advertising, marketing research, banks, law) will establish foreign operations in markets where their principal customers are, to prevent competitors from gaining access to them. They know that once a competitor is able to demonstrate to top management what it can do by servicing a foreign subsidiary, it may be able to take over the entire company. Similarly, suppliers to original equipment manufacturers (for example, battery manufacturers to automobile producers) often follow their large customers. These suppliers have an added advantage in that they are moving into new markets with a guaranteed customer base.

This is true for the over 250 Japanese auto parts makers that have come to the United States, the world's largest auto parts producer, to supply the eight Japanese auto plants in this country. For example, Tokyo Seat has established a subsidiary to make seats, exhaust systems, and other parts for Honda, which also asked Nippondenso, a Japanese producer of radiators and heaters, to set up an American plant.

Companies from the Mitsubishi group in Japan created a version of the Japanese supplier network in Ohio to supply the plant of the Mitsubishi-Chrysler joint venture, Diamond Star. In addition, there are captive suppliers that are not part of the Mitsubishi group. Just an hour's drive away from the Diamond Star factory, now wholly owned by Mitsubishi, a cooperative of 16 nonaffiliated suppliers to Mitsubishi in Japan built a $37 million plant to produce components such as engine mounts and bumpers. "We had a direct request from Mitsubishi to build this project here in the United States," said the cooperative's president Isamu Kawasaki. According to a study by University of Michigan, a similar situation exists in Honda's plant in Marysville, Ohio. Researchers found that U.S. companies supplied only 16 percent of the parts; the other 84 percent is supplied either by Japanese plants or by Japanese-owned plants in the United States. Among the 63 U.S. parts suppliers to Toyota's American plant, only 32 are American-owned. And it is not only parts suppliers—Mitsubishi bank, the lead bank for Toyota in Japan, opened an office in Columbus, Ohio, to serve Honda's Ohio plant.

Occasionally, a firm will set up an operation in the home country of a major competitor with the idea of keeping it so occupied and defending that it will have less energy to compete in the home country of the first company. Although Kodak claimed that its decision to open a manufacturing plant in Japan had nothing to do with its Japanese competitor (Fuji), its announcement came just 10 days after Fuji began construction of its first manufacturing facility in the United States.

Using foreign production to lower costs

A company may also go abroad to protect its domestic market when it faces competition from lower-priced foreign imports. By moving part or all of its production facilities to the countries from which its competitor is coming, it can enjoy such advantages as less costly labor, raw materials, or energy. Management may decide to produce certain components abroad and assemble them in the home country; or, if the final product requires considerable labor in the final assembly, it may send the components overseas for this final operation.

Zenith Electronics, the last American-owned producer of television sets in the

United States, announced in 1992 that it would move its television assembly operations from Missouri to Mexico. Zenith, which had not brought any profit since 1984, expected to save many millions of dollars in annual labor costs after relocation. A spokesman said the cutbacks in Missouri should help the company remain competitive in areas such as color picture tubes.

Zenith was able to take advantage of the lower-cost Mexican labor because of the in-bond (maquiladora in Mexico) program, a version of the export processing zones that began in the 1960s in Hong Kong and Taiwan of China, as well as Singapore. These all pertain to using foreign production to lower costs.

Many developing nations have established specialized economic zones in which firms, mostly foreign manufacturers, enjoy almost free taxation and regulation of materials brought into the zones for processing and subsequent reexport. In 1980s and 1990s, this was very important countermeasure for China to attract the foreign investment and until today, lots of foreign companies develop their international business in the zones, not only can they enjoy favorable policy, but also the large industry scale will provide enough labor, technology, management and other resources in the zones.

Protect foreign markets

In order to protect foreign markets, it is usually necessary to change the method of going abroad form exporting to overseas production. The management of a firm supplying a profitable overseas market by exports may begin to note some ominous signs that this market is being threatened.

(1) Lack of foreign exchange

One of the signs is a delay in payment by the importers. The importers may have sufficient local currency but may be facing delay in buying foreign exchange (currency) from the government's central bank. The credit manager in the exporting firm, by checking with his bank and other exporters, learns that this condition is becoming endemic—a reliable sign that the country is facing a lack of foreign exchange. When examining the country's balance of payments, the financial manager may find that its export revenue has declined while the import volume remains high. Experienced exporters know that import and foreign exchange controls are in the offering and that there is a good chance of losing the market, especially if they sell consumer products. In times of foreign exchange scarcity, governments will invariably give priority to the importation of raw materials and capital goods.

If the advantages of making the investment outweigh the disadvantages, the company may decide to protect this market by producing locally. Managers know that once the company has a plant in the country, the government will do its utmost to provide foreign exchange for raw materials to keep the plant in operation as a source of employment. Because imports of competing products are prohibited, the only competition, if any, will come from other local manufacturers.

(2) Local production by competitors

Lack of foreign exchange is not the only reason a company might change from exporting to manufacturing in a market. For instance, while a firm might enjoy a growing export business and prompt payments, it may still be forced to set up a plant in the market. It may be that its competitors have also noticed their export volumes will support local production.

Should a competing firm move to put up a factory in the market, management must decide rapidly whether to follow suit or risk losing the market forever. Managers know that many governments, especially those in developing nations, will not only prohibit further imports once the product is produced in the country but will also permit only two or three other companies to enter so as to maintain a sufficient market for these local firms. General Motors tried for years to enter Spain, but the Spanish government, believing there were already enough automobile manufacturers in the country, refused it. Only when Spain joined the European Community was General Motors permitted to enter. This is the best example.

Downstream markets

A number of OPEC nations have invested in refining and marketing outlets, such as filling stations and heating oil distributors, to guarantee a market for their crude oil at more favorable prices. Petroleos de Venezuela, owner of Citgo, is one of the largest foreign investors in the United States. Kuwait bought Gulf Oil's refining and marketing network in three European countries and also owns 20 percent of British Petroleum, which has the third-largest foreign investment in this country. These are just two examples.

Protectionism

When a government sees that local industry is threatened by imports, it may erect import barriers to reduce or stop them. Even threats to do so can be sufficient to induce the exporter to invest in production facilities in the importing country. This and the high-priced yen, which makes it difficult for Japanese exports to compete with American products, are the principal reasons for Japanese investment in the United States.

Guarantee supply of raw materials

Few developed nations possess sufficient domestic supplies of raw materials. Japan and Europe are almost entirely dependent on foreign resources, and even the United

States depends on imports for more than half of its aluminum, chromium, manganese, nickel, tin, and zinc.

To ensure a continuous supply, manufacturers in the industrialized countries are forced to invest primarily in the developing nations, where most new deposits are being discovered. Interestingly, although Japan does this as well, for years it has also looked to the United States as a source of raw materials. A Japanese deputy general consul once stated, the United States offered an abundance of raw materials. Because Japan has long depended on the United States for various materials, such as grain, coking coal, and lumber, it is definitely logical for Japanese firms to establish facilities close to the sources of these essential raw materials.

Some analysts claim that the Japanese-American trade flows approximate those between an industrialized and a developing country: the industrialized nation sends manufactured goods to the developing nation in return for raw materials. This is somewhat exaggerated, but according to the statistic data of recent years, 97.4 percent of Japan's exports to America consisted of manufactured goods, and over 40 percent of American exports to Japan were foodstuffs, raw materials, and mineral fuels.

Acquire technology and management know-how

A reason often cited by foreign firms for investing in this country is the acquisition of technology and management know-how. Nippon Mining, for example, a copper mining company, came to Illinois and paid $1 billion for Gould Inc. to acquire technology leadership and market share in producing the copper foil used in printed circuit boards. In a similar situation, Acer Inc. from Taiwan of China wanted to learn about small business computers so it bought Counterpoint Computers in California for $20 million, saving millions in research.

Geographic diversification

Many managements have chosen geographic diversification as a means of maintaining stable sales and earnings when the domestic economy or their industry goes into a slump. Generally, when one economy or industry (building materials, for example) is in a tough time, it is at its peak elsewhere in the world. In the early 1980s, the foreign operations of American multinationals were outperforming their domestic counterparts. Sunbeam and Ford, for example, reported that their Mexican business was unusually strong, and Twin-Disc, a transmission manufacturer, said that the slowdown in the European market "wasn't nearly as bad as in the United States." In 2007, earnings jumped 32 percent for Hoechst, the German chemical producer, solely because of the earnings of its American subsidiary, Celanese. "Without those earnings, the company would have shown a profit decline." Declared Hoechst's chairman.

Satisfy management's desire for expansion

The faster growth mentioned previously helps fulfill management's desire for expansion. Stockholders and financial analysts also expect firms to continue to grow, and those companies operating only in the domestic market have found it increasingly difficult to sustain that expectation. As a result, many firms have expanded into foreign markets. This, of course, is what companies based in small countries, such as Nestlé (Switzerland), SKF Bearing (Sweden), and Shell (Great Britain and the Netherlands), discovered decades ago.

Another aspect of this reason sometimes motivates the company's top managers to begin searching for overseas markets. Being able to claim that the firm is a "multinational" creates the impression of importance, which can influence its customers. Sun Microsystems, a manufacturer of computer workstations, opened a technical center in Germany and built a factory in Scotland. "To be a major player in the marketplace, you have to be internationally recognized," said head of Sun's European operations. We also know of instances in which a company has examined and then entered a market because its president brought it to the attention of the market planners after enjoying a pleasant vacation there.

How else can you explain the fact that in pre-Castro Cuba, there were three American tire factories in Havana, the "fun capital" of the world, with Miami just 90 miles away? Delivery of tires to Cuba could have been made in hours and at better prices. That was the time of the year when the Cuban subsidiary customarily had financial, marketing, and production problems that required the presence of Akron executives.

Political stability

For most of the western multinationals, they have not been motivated by political stability to go overseas, although it is often the prime factor in their choice of where to go. However, the Third World firms may actually make foreign investments (usually in the United States and other developed countries) for that reason. Because the political stability is the basic condition for the multinationals to make money and if your country is experiencing war or revolution, the best choice for the companies is to invest abroad, although you may have to face an unfamiliar environment.

Saturated markets in the home country

Lots of the multinationals take their international marketing just because the domestic market is too small to develop their business, or their home market is saturated. For example, Sony, Panasonic Toshiba and lots of other Japanese electronic companies are the very famous international electronic brands. However, if they did not develop foreign markets and compete with each other only in Japanese market, the result is that there would not be any famous Japanese electronic companies in the world. The reason is the market is too small and very easy to be saturated.

Other reasons to take international marketing

Another reason for the multinationals to take international marketing is scale economies. Not only can the huge scale reduce the unit cost of the products, but can also expand the effect of the products and companies in the world. But, the scale economies might not be available if consumer's tastes in the foreign markets necessitate numerous product modifications. Likewise, the costs of market entry (advertising, and promotion, establishment of distribution networks and so on) could themselves outweigh production savings. Operating in foreign markets can also facilitate the experience curve effect. After accumulation experience of certain types of activity, function of product, cost can be reduced and efficiency can increase. These effects differ from economies of scale in that they result from longer experience of doing something rather than producing a large output.

Doing business in foreign markets exposes management to fresh and different approaches to solving problems. Individual executives develop their general management skills and personal effectiveness, become innovative and adopt broader horizons. The contacts and experience acquired through selling abroad can give a firm a competitive edge in its home country. Further reasons for firms becoming involved in international marketing include the following.

(1) Today, new product development always requires so much expenditure, and in many cases, firms intending to introduce new products must take an international perspective to satisfy the demands of the world consumers.

(2) The higher turnover resulting from international sales might trigger a firm to initiate new product research and development that in the long term will give it a competitive edge.

(3) Corporate plans can be anchored against a wider range of (international) opportunities.

(4) There might be less competition in some foreign markets.

(5) A sudden collapse in market demand in one country may be offset by expansion in others.

(6) Opportunities may be created by new trade agreements between nations, or the opening-up of new markets in countries that were previously closed to imports. And example of this is the gradual opening-up of trade with China.

(7) Consumers in some foreign markets might be wealthier than those in the firm's

own country.

(8) Firms are often forced to think globally due to the entry of foreign competitors into the home markets. Foreign business accounts for a large proportion of the total cross-national products of all major industrialized countries. As the world becomes "smaller" in business terms, domestic customers are more likely to look abroad for suppliers.

(9) A major reason for the increasing internationalization of business is that cross-border trade is today much easier to organize than in the past. The Internet revolution has actually been the most noticeable and most successful in business-to-business markets. Disappointing results in consumer markets have been widely publicized, but as a business tool the Net has been a resounding success. International telephone and fax facilities to "remote" regions are today vastly better than before. Just a few years ago, facilities for international business travel were more extensive, and business service firms (advertising agencies, market research companies, banks and tourism companies, etc.) now operate internationally. Hence it is simpler to visit and examine foreign markets, to select the best locations for operations and thereafter to control international activities.

Other factors to influence your decision

Lots of multinationals may ultimately choose foreign manufactures to achieve their developing strategy. It is very important for them to consider the following factors before they make the decisions, because these barriers may ruin all of the efforts of the company in the real world.

(1) Local partnerships

It's not unusual for a government to require the use of a local partner to represent your products or to "invest" in your business. At times, the local is declared to be the majority partner, regardless of the size of their investments. Besides, the local governments hope to borrow management knowledge and skills for its population as a form of technology transfer. Part of a solid marketing plan in such an environment requires the studied selection of the right partner. Keep in mind that in some countries (Indonesia, Vietnam), the government will assign a partner for certain industries.

(2) Local content requirements

If your plans include the construction or purchase of manufacturing plants overseas, you will find that most governments require you to use some local companies as parts suppliers. No matter how efficient it may be for your business, you will not be allowed to simply import all the parts from your headquarters. While this requirement can be planned for, little can be done if local suppliers raise prices. This can occur when they are ready to push you out of the market and take over your facility, so vigilance and good government connections are required.

(3) Contract language

Contracts with foreign firms are typically binding in the dialect of the locality in which the contract will be executed. (Although you may have signed a translation as well, it's meaningless and unenforceable.) Before you sign anything, please make sure that your own translators have gone through the document thoroughly and remember local courts will favor local businesses.

(4) Technology transfers

A target company can insist that any joint venture, product importation or manufacture under license with a foreign marketer must ultimately involve a transfer of technology. It's a way to "catch up" with competitors without expensive research or investment. Most developing markets insist on technology transfers if a product is to be sold within their national boundaries. There may be a "grace period" of several years while the transfer takes place. These same markets have the least stringent patent, and copyright piracy or domestication is inevitable.

Note: Coca-Cola's has refused to reveal its recipe to its local partner in India, which kept the beverage giant barred from that gigantic market for many years. As is true of business travel, if you can't afford to lose it, don't bring it with you.

2.6 How to enter a foreign market

Few of multinationals take foreign manufactures to develop the foreign markets directly, especially when they have no any experience in this field. And the various companies may develop the foreign markets based on different market conditions, various market targets or different resources when they enter the foreign markets. That is why we should study the question how to enter the foreign markets.

Exporting

Exporting means the sale in a foreign market of an item produced, stored or processed in the supplying firm's home country, as opposed to the supplier being involved in foreign manufacture or processing of goods.

In practice, however, the distinction between pure "exporting" and wider foreign operations has become increasingly blurred as businesses increasingly internationalize their activities. There is nevertheless a distinct set of commercial practice and techniques with which the would-be exporter has to become familiar. These techniques relate in particular to foreign trade documentation, transport and logistics, and means of payment.

Most firms began their involvement in international marketing by exporting—that is, selling some of their regular production overseas. This method requires little investment and is relatively free of risks. It is an excellent means of getting a feel for international marketing without committing any great amount of human or financial resources. If management does decide to export, it must choose between direct and indirect exporting.

1. Indirect exporting

Indirect exporting, is also called inactive exporting, is simpler than direct exporting because it requires neither special expertise nor large cash outlays. Exporters based in their home country will do the work. Management merely follows instructions. Among the exporters available are ① manufacturer's export agents, who sell for the manufacturer; ② export commission agents, who buy for their overseas customers; ③ export merchants, who purchase and sell for their own account; and ④ international firms, which use the goods overseas (mining, construction, and petroleum companies are examples).

Indirect exporters, however, pay a price for such service: ① they will pay a commission to the first three kinds of exporters; ② foreign business can be lost if exporters decide to change their sources of supply; and ③ firms gain little experience from these transactions. This is why many companies that begin in this manner generally change to direct exporting.

2. Direct exporting

Direct exporting is called active exporting. If the companies engage in direct exporting, managers must assign the job of handling the export business to a specialized ernployee. The simplest arrangement is to give someone, usually the sales manager, the responsibility for developing the export business. Domestic employees may handle the billing, credit, and shipping initially, and if the business expands, a separate export department may be set up. A firm that has been exporting to wholesale importers in an area and servicing them by visits from either home office personnel or foreign-based sales representatives frequently finds that sales have grown to a point that will support a complete marketing organization.

Management may then decide to set up a sales company in the area. The sales company will import in its own name from the parent company and will invoice in local currency. It may use the same channels of distribution, though the new organization may permit the use of a more profitable arrangement. This type of organization can grow quite large, often invoicing several millions of dollars annually. Before building a plant in Mexico, for many years Eastman Kodak imported and resold cameras and photographic supplies while doing a large business in local film developing. Many firms that began with local repair facilities later expanded to produce simple components.

Gradually, they produced more of the product locally until, after a period of time, they were manufacturing all of the components in the country.

A firm's foreign business may evolve sequentially over the path just traced, or a company may move directly to foreign production (nonsequentially) for any of the reasons discussed previously in the section "Why Enter Foreign Markets?"

Before examining foreign manufacturing, we want to describe briefly the turnkey project, which is an export of technology, management expertise, and in some cases, capital equipment. The contractor agrees to design and erect a plant, supply the processing technology, provide the necessary supplies of raw materials and other production inputs, and then train the operating personnel. After a trial run, the facility is turned over to the purchaser.

The exporter may be a contractor that specializes in designing and erecting plants in a particular industry such as petroleum refining or steel production. It may also be a company in the industry that wishes to earn money from its expertise by delivering a plant ready to run rather than merely selling its technology. Chemical companies sold numerous turnkey projects to the developing countries, for example. Another kind of supplier of turnkey projects is the producer of a key input that sells a complete plant in order to obtain a contract to provide its product to the finished factory.

2.7 Foreign manufacturing

When management does decide to become involved in foreign manufacturing, it generally has five distinct alternatives available, though not all of them may be feasible in a particular country. These are:

(1) Wholly owned subsidiary.

(2) Joint venture.

(3) Licensing agreement.

(4) Franchising.

(5) Contract manufacturing.

A sixth arrangement, the management contract, is utilized by both manufacturing and service companies to earn income by providing management expertise.

1. Wholly owned subsidiary

The company that hopes to wholly own a foreign subsidiary may ① start from the ground up by building a new plant, ② acquire a going concern, or ③ purchase its distributor, thus obtaining a distribution network familiar with its products. In this last case, of course, production facilities will have to be built. For the most of the famous world companies, they certainly prefer wholly owned subsidiaries because they do not want other companies to share their advanced technology, management, brand and other resources, and more important is that they can make their marketing decisions themselves and do not have to be influenced by their partners. Obviously, all of the resources can make large sums of profits and the independence decision system can improve the efficiency of the companies.

However, this is not the case for foreign investors in the United States, who prefer to acquire going concerns for the instant access to the market they are in. Moreover, they also have one less competitor after the purchase. Rather than build a U. S. plant, YKK, a leading Japanese zipper manufacturer, paid $50 million for Universal Fasteners, a competitor based in Kentucky. "They bought instant market share with no headaches," said a banker familiar with the transaction.

According to the *Yearbook of World Economy*, nearly 90 percent of the Chinese foreign investments are used to acquire foreign firms. Only about 10 percent was used to establish new companies.

However, sometimes it is not possible to have a wholly owned foreign subsidiary. This is because ① the host government may not permit it; ② the firm may lack either enough capital or expertise to undertake the investment alone, or ③ there may be tax and other advantages that favor a joint venture.

2. Joint venture

A joint venture may be ① a corporate entity formed by an international company and local owners, ② a corporate entity formed by two international companies for the purpose of doing business in a third market, ③ a corporate entity formed by a government agency (usually in the country of investment) and an international firm, or ④ a cooperative undertaking between two or more firms of a limited-duration project. Large construction jobs such as a dam or an airport are frequently managed in this last form.

Although joint ventures can reduce the business risk of the international companies and sometimes the multinationals can use their partner's resources to improve their competitiveness, lots of famous multinationals don't like to establish joint ventures, because few of joint ventures make the huge success in the real world. For example, in 1987, Ford and Volkswagen formed a novel joint venture in which their operations in Argentina and Brazil were merged into a holding company, Autolatina, in an effort to eliminate losses suffered by both. The joint venture, owned 51 percent by Volkswagen and 49 percent by Ford, assembled products based on VW and Ford designs, but both companies marketed the vehicles through their own distribution channels. Although 1993 sales reached $7.58 billion, the companies decided to terminate the operation. One industry expert says that Ford wanted to leave because Autolatina did not fit its new global strategy of having global vehicles. The two companies clashed about sharing models when they were facing increasing pressure from General Motors, which has sold so many of its Corsa subcompacts that it undertook an ad campaign telling consumers not to be in a hurry to buy the car. In 1994, Volkswagen dealers refused to share the company's new subcompact with Ford, prompting Ford to rush its program to produce the small Fiesta. In a news release, the companies said the termination of the joint venture reflected "the necessity of the companies to make better use of the force and resources of their worldwide organizations."

When the CEO of General Mills decided to enter the European market where a very tough rival, Kelloggs, had established itself, he knew it would be very expensive to set up manufacturing facilities and a huge marketing force. However, he knew that another food giant, Nestlé, the world's largest food company, had a famous name in Europe, a number of manufacturing plants, and a strong distribution system. It also lacked strong cereal a brand names, something like that General Mills, the number two American cereal company had. Just three weeks after the initial discussions, General Mills and Nestlé formed a joint venture, Cereal Partners Worldwide. General Mills provided the cereal technology, brand names, and its cereal marketing expertise. Nestlé supplies its name, distribution channels, and production capacity. Cereal Partners Worldwide would distribute worldwide, except in the United States.

When the government of a host country requires companies to have some local participation, foreign firms must engage in a joint venture with local owners to do business in that country. In some situations, however, a foreign firm will seek local partners even when there is no local requirement to do so. This is because the joint venture can bring other benefits for multinationals, and the additional benefits include acquiring expertise, tax incentive, and other benefits.

Other factors that influence managements to enter joint ventures are the ability to acquire an expertise that is lacking, special tax benefits that some governments extend to companies with local partners, or the need for additional capital and experienced personnel.

Merck, the largest U. S. maker of ethical drugs, spent $313 million in acquiring 50. 5 percent of Banyu Pharmaceutical in Japan. Management had been dissatisfied with the performance of Merck's Japanese subsidiary in the world's second-largest ethical drug market. With this acquisition, the 600-person sales force of Merck-Japan was augmented by Banyu's 350 sales representatives. Merck's chairman said, "To bring new products effectively to market in Japan required a larger and more effective marketing organization. With a controlling interest in Banyu, I would hope for a better penetration of the Japanese market."

To take advantage of Israel's lower labor costs and the 1985 U. S. -Israel Trade Agreement, which ① reduced import duties on Israeli-made shirts and ② permitted them quota-free access to the United States, Van Heusen decided to buy the production facilities of an insolvent Israeli clothing manufacturer. When the government refused to sell on Van Heusen's terms, the company formed a joint venture with another Israeli textile-and-apparel conglomerate. Van Heusen would purchase the plant's output for five years, with the option to extend the agreement if satisfied with the local partner's performance, and would have exclusive control over marketing. Although it had trained Israeli engineers and would maintain its own engineers at the operation, the Israeli partner has had to invest all of the capital to expand an existing plant.

In practice, the major reason for some firms to enter joint ventures is to reduce investment risk. Their strategy is to enter into a joint venture with either native partners or another worldwide company. Still others, such as Ford and Volkswagen, have joined together to achieve economies of scale. Incidentally, any division of ownership in a joint venture is possible unless there are specific legal requirements.

Although a joint venture arrangement offers the advantage of less commitment of financial and managerial resources, and thus less risk, there are some disadvantages for the foreign firm. The first, obviously, is that profits must be shared. Furthermore, if the law allows the foreign investors to have no more than a 49 percent participation, they may not have control. This is because the stock markets in some countries are either small or nonexistent, so it is generally impossible to distribute shares widely enough to permit the foreign firm with its 49 percent to be the largest stockholder.

Lack of control over the joint venture is why many managers resist making such arrangements. They feel that they must have tight control of their foreign subsidiaries to obtain an efficient allocation of investments and production and to maintain a coordinated marketing plan worldwidely. For example, local partners might wish to export to markets that the global company serves from its own plants, or they might want to make the complete product locally when the global company's strategy is to produce only certain components there and import the rest from other subsidiaries.

In recent years, with the development of globalization, many governments begin to take more open foreign investment policies and do not limit the foreign companies to set up wholly owned companies, but, numerous governments of developing nations have passed laws requiring local majority ownership for the purpose of giving control of firms within their borders to their own citizens. Despite these laws, control with a minority ownership is still feasible.

Despite of these laws, controlling with a minority ownership is still feasible. There have been occasions when the foreign partner is able to circumvent the spirit of the law and ensure its control by taking 49 percent of the shares and giving 2 percent to its local law firm or some other trusted nationals.

Another method is to take in a local majority partner, such as a government agency, an insurance company, or a financial institution, that is content to invest merely for a return while leaving the venture's management to the foreign partner. If neither arrangement can be made, the foreign company may still control the joint venture, at least in the areas of major concern, by means of a management contract.

3. Management contract

The management contract is an arrangement under which a company provides managerial know-how in some or all functional areas to another party for a fee that ranges from 2 to 5 percent of sales. International companies make such contracts with ① firms in which they have no ownership (examples: Hilton Hotel provides management for non-owned overseas hotels that use the Hilton name, and Delta provides management assistance to foreign airlines), ② joint venture partners, and ③ wholly owned subsidiaries. The last arrangement is made solely for the purpose of allowing the parent to siphon off some of the subsidiary's profits. This becomes extremely important when, as in many nations short of foreign exchange reserve, the amount of profit the parent can repatriate is limited. Moreover, because the fee is an expense, the subsidiary receives a tax benefit.

At the same time, management contracts can enable the global partner to control many aspects of a joint venture even when holding only a minority position; if it supplies key personnel, such as the production and technical managers, the global company can be assured of product quality with which its name may be associated and be able to earn additional income by selling the joint venture inputs manufactured in the home plant, possibly that because the larger global company is more vertically integrated.

A local paint factory, for example, might have to import certain semi-processed pigments and driers that the foreign partner produces in its home country for domestic operations. If these can be purchased elsewhere at a lower price, the local majority could insist on other sources of supply. This rarely happens, because the production and technical managers can argue that only inputs from their employer will produce a satisfactory product. They are experts, and they generally have the final word.

4. Purchasing commission

There is another source of income that a global or multinational company derives not only from firms with which it has a management contract but also from joint ventures and wholly owned subsidiaries. The latter source is a commission for acting as a purchasing agent of imported raw materials and equipment. This relieves the affiliates of having to establish credit lines with foreign suppliers and assures them that they will receive the same materials used by the foreign partner. The commission received for this service averages about 5 percent of invoice value and is in addition to the management contract fee.

5. Licensing

Frequently, worldwide companies are called on to furnish technical assistance to firms that have sufficient capital and management strength. By means of a licensing agreement, one firm (the licensor) will grant to another firm (the licensee) the right to use any kind of expertise, such as manufacturing processes (patented or unpatented), marketing procedures, and trademarks for one or more of the licensor's products.

General Tire, before it was bought by Continental, the German tire manufacturer, was both a licensor and a licensee. It licensed some firms to use its tire technology and others to use its know-how to produce plastic film. At the same time, it made licensing agreements with manufacturers of conveyor belting and V belting to use their technology in General Tire plants overseas.

The licensee generally pays a fixed sum when signing the licensing agreement and then pays a royalty of from 2 to 5 percent of sales over the contact duration (five to seven years, with option for renewal). The exact amount of the royalty will depend on the amount of assistance given and the relative bargaining power of the two parties.

In the past, licensing was not a primary source of income for international firms. This changed in the 1980s, however, especially in the U. S., because ① the courts began upholding patent infringement claims more than they used to, ② patent holders became more vigilant in suing violators, and ③ the federal government pressed foreign governments to enforce their patent laws.

These forced foreign companies to obtain licenses instead of making illegal copies. Texas Instruments, for example, sued nine Japanese electronics manufacturers for using its patented processes without paying licensing fees. The defendants have paid the company over $1 billion. It is estimated that Union Carbide, which has a special division to sell its technology and services, added 5 percent to its pre-tax profit just by licensing its process to make a single product—polystyrene, a plastic. According to the Department of Commerce, American firms received $20.4 billion in payment of royalties and licensing fees from foreign customers in 2005 and paid out only $4.8 billion.

However, more than know-how is licensed. In the fashion industry, a number of designers license the use of their names. Pierre Cardin, the largest licensor, has 840 licenses worldwide on everything from skis to frying pans. These earn the company $75 million annually, including $12 million from 32 American licensees. Even Russia pays the firm three-quarters of a million dollars every year.

Are you giving Coca-Cola free advertising on your T-shirt? The company's manager for merchandise licensing expects the company to make millions from an agreement with the founder of Gloria Vanderbilt. He says the firm agreed to the arrangement because "clothes enhance our image. The money is not important."

Despite the opportunity to obtain a sizable income from licensing, many firms, especially those that produce high-tech products, will not grant licenses. They fear that a licensee will become a competitor after expiration of the agreement or that it will aggressively seek to market the products outside of its territory. At one time, licensors routinely inserted a clause in the licensing agreement that prohibited exports, but most governments will not accept such a prohibition.

6. Franchising

Since the 1980s, American firms have gone overseas with a new kind of licensing—franchising. Franchising permits the franchisee to sell products or services under a highly publicized brand name and a well-proven set of procedures with a carefully developed and controlled marketing strategy. Of the 35,000 overseas outlets operated by 374 American franchising companies, fast-food operations (such as McDonald's, Kentucky Fried Chicken, and Tastee-Freeze) are the most numerous—McDonald's alone has about 2,500 outlets in 40 countries.

Other types of franchisors are hotels (Hilton, Holiday Inn), business services (Muzak, Manpower), soft drinks (Coca-Cola, Orange Crush), home maintenance (Servicemaster, Nationwide Exterminating), and automotive products (Midas).

7. Contract manufacturing

International firms employ contract manufacturing in two ways. One way is as a means of entering a foreign market without investing in plant facilities. The firm contracts with a local manufacturer to make products for it according to its specifications. The firm's sales organization markets the products under its own brand, just as Haier sells washing machines made by India in Germany.

When Gates Rubber licensed its V belt technology to General Tire's Chilean plant, it drew up a novel licensing agreement that included contract manufacturing. General Tire was obliged to produce part of its output with the Gates label. Gates executives knew that in Chile, once General Tire began production, the government would stop the importation of all V belts including theirs. Gates would gain in a number of ways: ① it would earn a royalty on all belts made in Chile, ② it would have belts made in Chile to Gates specifications without making any investment in production facilities, and ③ competition from a dozen importers would be eliminated. There would be only one local competitor, General Tire, which benefited because it increased its product mix and offered another product to its present channels of distribution.

The second way is to subcontract assembly work or the production of parts to independent companies overseas. Although an international firm has no equity in the subcontractor, this practice does resemble foreign direct investment. When the international firm is the largest or exclusive customer of the subcontractors, it has in effect created in another country a new company that generates employment and foreign exchange for the host nation. Frequently, the international firm will lend capital to the foreign contractor in the same way that a global or multinational firm will lend funds to its subsidiary. Because of these similarities, this practice is called foreign direct investment without investment.

8. Strategic alliances

Faced with ① expanding global competition, ② the growing cost of research, product development, and marketing, and ③ the need to move faster in carrying out their global strategies, many firms are forming strategic alliances with competitors (called competitive alliances), suppliers, and customers. Their aim is to achieve faster market entry and start-up; to gain access to new products, technologies, and markets; and to share costs, resources, and risks.

Alliances include various types of partnerships. Companies ready to share technology will cross-license their technology (one will license its technology to the other). If their aim is to pool research and design resources, they will form an R&D partnership. Take Texas Instruments and Hitachi for example, which have had technical information exchange to develop together a common design and manufacturing process for computer memory. Each firm will handle its own mass production and marketing.

(1) Alliances may be joint ventures

Other companies carry the cooperation further by forming joint ventures in manufacturing and marketing. In 1990s, Westinghouse and Toshiba formed an equity joint venture to produce color display tubes for computer terminals and picture tubes for TV sets. Westinghouse, which was making monochrome tubes, formed an alliance to use the technology to produce color tubes. The joint venture gave Toshiba an opportunity to be involved in a manufacturing facility that could supply tubes to its TV plant in Tennessee. The Japanese also expected that another U. S.-based venture would help deflect protectionist pressure from Toshiba. It provided the technology and Westinghouse provided a factory building and helped arrange financing, including $46 million in low-cost public loans. However, within just two years, Westinghouse sold its interest to Toshiba, which then became the sole owner of the facility.

(2) Alliances can be mergers and acquisitions

Swedish ASEA and Swiss Brown Bovari, both energy generation and transmission specialists, merged to form an $18 billion company. The reason, according to the CEO of the new firm, was that the two firms individually were too small to compete with U. S. and Japanese rivals such as Westinghouse, General Electric, Hitachi, and Toshiba.

(3) Future of alliances

There is no question that some alliances have accomplished what they set out to accomplish. CFM International, the alliance between General Electric and France's Snecma, has been producing jet engines for two decades. Airbus, an alliance among British, French, German, and Spanish aircraft manufacturers, is now the world's second-largest commercial aircraft producer.

Nevertheless, many alliances fail or are taken over by one of the partners. The management consulting firm, McKinsey & Co., surveyed 150 companies involved in alliances that had been terminated. It found that three-quarters of the alliances had been taken over by Japanese partners. Professor Chalmers Johnson, an expert on Japan, warns, "I find the idea of joint ventures no longer makes any sense at all. They are a way for the Japanese to acquire technology."

Many large global and multinational firms with numerous manufacturing subsidiaries all over the world began their foreign operations by exporting. Once succeeding at this stage, they established sales companies overseas to market their exports. Where sales companies were able to develop sufficiently large markets, their firms set up plants to assemble imported parts. Finally, complete products were manufactured locally. However, this sequence does not represent the only way firms can enter foreign markets. In some countries, conditions may require a complete initial entry.

Huawei, in its 2015 annual report, stated that "manufacturing operations are conducted at 78 facilities in 38 countries, and products are distributed through wholesalers, retailers, and agents in near 100 countries and territories."

Summary

1. Appreciate the magnitude of international trade and how it has grown. How do the Chinese forces influence the international trade layout?

2. Identify the direction of trade. The percentage of total exports of all the categories of developed nations to other developed nations is declining with the exception of Canada's. And China has been the largest export country of the world since the end of 2009.

3. Recognize the value of analyzing trade statistics. The analysis of trade statistics is useful to anyone searching outside the home market for new trade opportunities. Studying the general growth and direction of trade and analyzing the major trading partners will give a picture of where the trading activity is.

4. Explain the size, growth, and direction of American foreign direct investment. Foreign direct investment (FDI) has also grown rapidly and now totals almost \$2 trillion. The American FDI almost double that of Japan, which is the next largest foreign investor. The direction of foreign direct investment follows the direction of international trade; that is, developed nations invest in each other just as they trade with each other.

5. Understand the reasons for entering foreign markets. Companies enter foreign markets (exporting to and manufacturing in) to increase sales and profits and to protect markets, sales, and profits. Foreign firms often buy American firms to acquire technology and marketing know-how. Foreign investment also enables a company to diversify geographically.

6. Recognize the weaknesses in using GNP per capita as a basis for comparing economies. One must be careful in using GNP as a basis for comparing nations' economies. First, the reliability of the data is questionable. Second, the World Bank and other international agencies convert national currencies to USD. Official exchange rates do not reflect the relative domestic purchasing powers of currencies. To overcome this deficiency, the agencies use exchange rates based on purchasing power parity of the currencies.

7. Understand the international market entry methods. The two basic methods of entering foreign markets are through exporting to or manufacturing in them. Exporting may be done directly or indirectly. A firm may become involved in foreign production through various methods: ① wholly owned subsidiaries, ② joint ventures, ③ licensing, ④ franchising, and ⑤ contract manufacturing.

8. Explain the many forms of strategic alliances. Many firms form strategic alliances with competing companies, suppliers, and customers to gain access to new products, technology, and markets and to share resources, costs, and risks. Strategic alliances take many forms, including licensing, mergers, joint ventures, and joint research and development contracts.

Questions

1. The greater part of international trade consists of exchanges of raw materials from developing nations for the manufactured goods from developed nations. True or false? Explain.

2. The volume of exports has increased, but the ranking of Chinese trading partners in order of importance remains the same year after year. True or false? What is the use of this information for a businessperson?

3. What is the value of analyzing foreign trade data? For example, why should you analyze the trade data of America if you are a manager of an international company?

4. What does it signify for a marketing analyst to know that a nation is a major trading partner of another?

5. How can a firm protect its domestic market by investing overseas?

6. Why might the management decide to bypass indirect exporting and go to direct exporting right from the start?

7. Under what condition might a company prefer a joint venture to a wholly owned

subsidiary when it wants to make a foreign investment?

8. Why would a foreign partner in a joint venture wish to have a management contract with its local partner? Why would a global or multinational require a wholly owned foreign subsidiary to sign a management contract when it already owns the subsidiary?

9. Do you think Chinese government should encourage foreign direct investment? Why?

Chapter 3 Economic and Social Economic Forces

Concept preview

After reading this chapter, you should be able to

1. Appreciate: how economic and social economic forces influence your international marketing decision.

2. Understand: what factors you have to study when you research the economic environment.

3. Distinguish: economic and social economic forces.

4. Comprehend: the importance of the GNP and GNP/capita for international management.

5. Describe: how various data influence the investment environment.

3.1 Different economic development stages

The most striking difference between domestic and international marketing is that managers have to adapt to a different environment. And for managers of international companies, the first task is to study the economic and social economic environment of the host countries before they enter it.

The truth is simple. International marketing is largely influenced by the host countries' economic and social economic factors. So, the precondition for multinationals to develop the foreign markets is to understand the stage of the target markets. According to Walt W. Rostow, a famous American economist, different countries are in different developing stages and every stage possesses distinct characteristics. In other word, different stages may decide the different means of international companies when they want to develop a foreign market.

The stage of traditional society

In this stage, productivity level of the host country is lower and they are not capable of applying modern science and technology to production. Local residents are not well educated. There is no any basic infrastructure. Income of the local residents is very low. The market is very small because of the lower revenue. And the natural economy is put in the first place. By now, lots of less-developed countries are in this stage.

The stage before economy take-off

In this stage, science and technology has been used in agriculture and industry; transportation, communication and power infrastructure has been established; social attention, though not much, begins to be paid to education and health. By now, lots of emerging market countries are in this stage, where local people's income zooms, and they need more foreign capital and other production resource to promote economic development. At the same time, the demand is growing fast too. Because natural economy exists in these countries too, so the scope of the market is limited by the factors.

The stage of economy take-off

In this stage, social facilities and human resources have been enough to maintain the stability of the economy; industry and agriculture are achieving modernization step by step. In general, lots of emerging countries, for example, China, Brazil and Russia, are in this stage—economic take off. There are some very developed industries in these countries, especially in the manufacture fields. The investment grows very fast and the emerging industry departments come forth constantly, and the situation leads to great market opportunities for the industry products. With the faster individual income, the scale of consumption goods market becomes bigger and bigger, and the demand for durable consumer goods begin to grow. The demand level is rising constantly. In common situation, the countries which are in this stage always can attract more international investments because of more market opportunities.

The stage of maturity

In this stage, not only can the countries maintain the great economic progress, but also they want to use more modern science and technology to serve various economic activities. At the same time, they will take more international marketing. Most of the western countries are in this stage. At the same time, the demands for various durable consumer products will increase rapidly because of income growth and more leisure time, and more expenditure on amusement and health. In this stage, the advertising and publicity expenses will be higher, because the image of products and companies will influence the operational achievement directly.

The highly developed stage

In this stage, the society will pay more attention to the production of the durable consumer products. Individual income grows fast, the public facilities and social welfare facilities will be perfect step by step and mass production and mass consumption appear in the whole society. The stage is the representative of highly developed industry society, and the most important characteristic is that the third industry becomes the most important industry for the country. More and more consumers make more disposable income. By now, only few countries reached this stage and in this stage, the social service departments develop very fast, the exchange and settlement of information become more and more important; innovation and development will be the key factors for the companies to make more market opportunities, because the market maturity of products has reached higher level. It is very difficult for multinationals to expand their market share; they must develop the new market, particularly the foreign markets, constantly.

Of course, for different markets, managers of the multinationals can not give very clear definition of these stages. This is because it is very difficult for multinationals to get detailed economic reference of the host country; on the other hand, for the specific host countries, economic level of the various areas is very different. For example, Eastern China is very developed while it is very poor in its western areas. Even so, managers can make their different marketing strategies based on the economic stages.

That means the international managers have to take the different marketing countermeasures to adapt to the characteristics of the various economic stages. For example, they have to choose the correct distribution channels when they want to sell their products; they have to take different products to develop the various markets; they have to make different price decisions in various countries; and they have to take different advertising models to promote their products in various countries.

For example, the relationship between the economic stages and distribution channels includes:

(1) Higher economic development stages need complex and wide range distribution channels, various distribution forms and departments stores are developed. Because only these advanced distribution channels can help multinationals to sell their products and set up their image in the foreign markets. At the same time, higher economic development stages mean higher income and large market, which means it is easier for multinationals to develop the markets. This is why lots of multinationals choose

the developed countries and China as their oversea markets.

(2) In higher economic development stages, the position of import commission house will be improved with the economic development, because lots of multinationals have to use local distributors to sell their products, especially when they just enter a new market or they can not establish their own distribution channels because of the local laws. The key for multinationals is whether or not they can find out the proper local distributor to support their international marketing in most cases.

(3) With the economic development, the functions of manufactures, retailers and wholesalers will be independent and the responsibility of the specific distribution channel will not be undertaken by any single member. At the same time, the internet makes it easy for multinationals to develop new markets. So, higher economic stages mean more distribution channels and more competition.

(4) With the development of economy, the numbers of the small stores is declining, and the large-scale shopkeepers will dominate the markets. This is because the higher stages mean less spare time and hard jobs, people hope to buy all merchandises in one store to save time and the small stores can not satisfy the demand. This is why Wal-Mart and other many retail giants can make more money and these commercial magnates are always the first choice for multinationals to be as their distributors when they want to develop overseas markets.

In a word, managements of multinationals have to study the economic stages before they enter a new market and the most important question for them is whether or not their resources adapt to the new market. In most cases, managers of international companies observe GNP per capita and they think this is the most important for them to make their decisions. Although it is right and this is the first question when we study a new market, it is very important for international managers to notice the following questions.

3.2 The importance of the economic data

As the international marketers, the first task for you is to study the economic data of the target markets before you take the real actions. However, not all data you want are available and sometimes the data even mislead you to make mistakes. For example, GNP/capita is very important for managers to study when they want to enter a new market, but it is not enough for the marketers to assess the markets only based on it. For example, the GNP/capita of India is only about $ 1,610 in 2014; can you say the market is with the economic development no value for international companies? As a matter of fact, the market is very large and attracts more multinationals to invest. This is because GNP/capita is an average number, and lots of people in India must earn more than $1,610 annually. In fact, GNP per capita is only a data and it cannot reflect the real purchasing power of a currency and cannot reflect the real living level of a country. Do people have sufficient income to purchase cars in India? How can the analysts find out?

(1) First, they know that because India's living costs are lower than that of developed countries and India's average income of 1,430 GNP/capita in reality represents more purchasing power than one thinks. To find out the actual purchasing power, one can consult the World Bank's data and find that this amount is equivalent to 4,210 USD. This is the purchasing power parity (PPP).

(2) Next, they want to know the purchasing power of the middle and upper classes. They first obtain the GNP in dollars of equivalent purchasing power by multiplying the dollar equivalent of India's GNP/capita by the population: $4,210 × 1.2 billion = $5.052 trillion.

(3) How much of the gross national product goes to the middle and upper classes? Assume that the upper and middle class occupy the half of GDP, the capacity of the market will be over 2 trillion.

Thus, it is very important for the multinationals to study how the GDP is segmented by specific class (Table 3-1).

Table 3-1 The top 20 countries of GNP/Capita of the world in 2011

Rank	Country/area	GNP/Capita	Rank	Country/area	GNP/Capita
1	Qatar	107,721	11	Switzerland	39,924
2	Liechtenstein	83,717	12	Netherlands	36,402
3	UAE	59,993	13	Andorra	36,095
4	Singapore	52,569	14	Sweden	35,837
5	Luxembourg	50,557	15	Austria	35,719
6	Kuwait	47,926	16	Canada	35,166
7	Norway	47,557	17	Germany	34,854
8	Brunei	45,753	18	Australia	34,431
9	Hong Kong (China)	44,805	19	Denmark	34,347
10	U. S. A.	43,017	20	Belgium	33,357

The table shows that the GNP/Capita of lots of countries or area is very high; however, these markets are very small because the population is very small. Although the GNP/Capita of China is only $7,380 in 2014. The result is that data can not tell us all of information about the target markets, as a matter of fact, you may make a mistake if you only rely on the official economic data to make your international marketing decisions. You have to consider the following questions carefully.

The data may not be correct

For management of multinationals, economic forces of a foreign market are most significant uncontrollable forces. How the scarce resources of land, labor, and capital are being allocated to the production and distribution of goods and services and the manner in which they are consumed are of paramount importance for managers.

Even though the data published by governments and international organizations, such as the World Bank and the IMF, are not as timely or accurate as business economists would like. However, economists do not work solely with government-published data. Private economic consulting specialists—such as Data Resources, Inc., Chase Econometric Associates, Business International, the Economist Intelligence Unit, and Wharton Economic Forecasting Associates-provide economic forecasts (some provide industry forecasts as well) to which many multinationals subscribe. Other sources are various industry associations, which generally provide industry-specific forecasts to their members.

In addition, economists and marketers use certain economic indicators that they have found to predict trends in their industry. Pitney Bowes' Data Documents division, for example, uses changes in the growth of the U. S. GNP to predict the sales of its business forms because its sales have for years generally lagged changes in GNP growth by six months. We shall discuss the use of market indicators in latter chapter, Market Assessment and Analysis.

The above table is published by UN, and we can know the GDP/capita is very different based on the different statistical methods and the range and number changes every year because of different economic growth rate. Especially, the growth rate is very fast in some of the emerging markets like China, if you only make your decision based on the finical data to take international marketing you will lose marketing opportunities. As a matter of fact, the purpose of economic analysis is, to appraise the overall outlook of the economy and then to assess the impact of economic changes on the firm.

Various forces may influence your international marketing decision

In the real world, not only do the managers have to understand the overall situation of the host country's markets, but they also have to notice the interaction of various factors. An examination will illustrate how a change in just one factor of an economy can impact all the major functions of the company.

A forecast of an increase in employment would cause most marketing managers to revise upward their sales forecasts, which, in turn, would require production managers to augment production. This might be accomplished by adding another work shift, but if the plant is already operating 24 hours a day, new machinery will be needed. Either situation will require additional workers and raw materials, which will result in an extra workload for the personnel and purchasing managers. Should both the raw materials and labor markets be tight, the firm will probably have to pay prices and wage rates that are higher than normal. The financial manager may then have to negotiate with the banks for a loan to enable the firm to address the greater cash outflow until additional revenue is received from increased sales.

Note that all of this occurs because of a change in only one factor. Actually, of course, many economic factors are involved, and their relationships are complex. By means of economic analysis, an attempt is made to isolate and assess the impact of those factors believed to affect the firm's operations.

When the firm enters overseas markets, economic analysis becomes more complex because now managers must operate in two new environments: foreign and international. In the foreign environment, not only are there many economies other than one, but they are also highly divergent. Because of these differences, policies designed for the economic conditions in one market may be totally unsuitable for the economic conditions in another market.

For example, headquarters may have a policy requiring its subsidiaries to maintain the lowest inventories possible, and the chief financial officer may decree that they make only foreign currency-denominated loans because of more favorable interest rates. For nations whose annual inflation rates are low (0 to 5 percent), these policies usually work well. But if the inflation rate is very high, for example over 100 percent, the policy will not work. The last thing headquarters wants is for the subsidiaries in these countries to have cash or foreign currency-denominated loans, so the policy for markets with high inflation rates will be just the reverse of what it is for countries with low inflation rates.

Besides monitoring the foreign environments, economists must also keep abreast of the actions taken by components of the international environment, such as regional groupings (EU, NEFTA) and international organizations (UN, IMF, World Bank). American firms are very attentive to the EU's progress in reaching its goals and to the impact it will have on EU-U. S. trade relations. They are also following closely the UN's progress in developing world pollution standards, health standards, and so forth. Any of these actions can seriously affect firms.

International economic analysis should provide economic data on both actual and prospective markets. Also, as part of the competitive forces assessment, many companies monitor the economic conditions of nations where their major competitors are located, because changing conditions may strengthen or weaken their competitors' ability to compete in the world market.

Because of the importance of economic information to the control and planning functions at headquarters, the collection of data and the preparation of reports must be the responsibility of the home office. However, foreign-based personnel (subsidiaries and field representatives) will be expected to contribute hugely to studies concerning their markets. Data from areas where the firm has no local representation can usually be somewhat less detailed and are generally available in publications from national and international agencies. The reports from central or international banks are especially good sources for economic information on each country. Other possible sources are the Chinese chambers of commerce located in most of the world's capitals, the commercial officers in China. Embassies, the United Nations, the World Bank, the International Monetary Fund, and the Organization for Economic Cooperation and Development are also very important information resources for your international marketing.

3.3 Trading environment

International marketing is subject to a set of international laws and local marketing conditions that provide constraints and opportunities with which the global firm must operate. Because the international marketing includes international trade and international investment, we should discuss the trading environment first.

International trade is conducted against a raft of international regulations, treaties, trade agreements, alliances and enmities. Different regions of the world can be grouped in terms of their economic and cultural similarities. In the same way customers can be grouped in segments. This type of grouping enables global marketers to apply similar marketing approaches.

The balance of payments

A country's balance of payments is the total of all the transactions that occur between residents of that country and foreigners over a specific period of time. Receipts resulting from exports or inflows of capital are recorded as credit items, payments for imports and capital outflows appear as debits.

Most countries publish their balance of payments figures monthly, quarterly and annually. The accounts themselves show the structure of a country's external trade, its net position as an international lender or borrower, and trends in the direction of its economic relationships with the rest of the world. Balance of payments accounts attempt to identify the reasons behind various categories of international receipts and payments. Hopefully, therefore, it becomes possible to establish the values of total payments by domestic residents to foreigners for purposes as the purchase of imports, the use of services, short and long term lending, and direct foreign investment.

Balance of payments accounts are constructed on the principle of double-entry bookkeeping, meaning that each receipt and payment is recorded twice, once in each of two columns (debit and credit), so that the two columns should add up to the same amount. In practice, it may be affected by measurement errors and delays in the reporting of transactions, so that a balancing item has to be inserted in order to reconcile the two sides of the account. A country's balance of payments accounts can be presented in several ways. There is a standard United Nation recommended layout that apply to all countries in order to make international comparisons possible. Additionally, each country typically drafts its accounts in a number of other formats so as to highlight particular features of its international trading situation. Distinctions that have the most analytical significance are those between:

(1) Transactions involving goods, services and movements in financial capital.

(2) Long-term and short-term financial transactions.

(3) Transactions initiated by national monetary authorities and all other monetary movements.

(4) Unilateral transfers (such as gifts or wages sent by workers in one country to their relatives in others) and payments for goods, services or financial assets.

Since the balance of payments always balances in consequence of how the accounts are prepared, how is it possible to speak of "deficit" or "surpluses" in a country's balance of payments? In practice, particular groups of transactions of the accounts are selected to examine surplus or deficit.

The most widely reported group is perhaps the "current account" of the balance of payments, which records physical imports and exports plus "invisible" international transactions, including non-physical items such as residents receipts of pensions, interest and royalties from abroad (and payments of such items to foreign countries), domestic firms' fees for arranging transportation of goods belonging to firms in other countries, private gifts (foreign workers sending part of their wages to families in other countries for example), and so on. The balance of trade within the current account is the balance on visible imports and exports.

A country's capital account shows the balance on its transactions in financial assets, including portfolio investments in foreign shares and debentures (and foreigner's purchases of these assets within the country concerned), movements in short-term financial assets such as Treasury Bills and other short-dated stock, intergovernmental loans, and changes in the country's official gold and foreign exchange reserves. The last will decline if, for example, there is a current account deficit but no offsetting inflow of capital account funds. This is because residents' demand for foreign exchange to pay for imports will exceed foreigners' demand for the deficit country's currency, so that a deficit country's currency exchange rate will fall via the forces of supply and demand for foreign exchange.

To prevent the exchange rate dropping too much, deficit countries' governments used to sell part of their stock of foreign exchange reserves in the open market in order to satisfy the excess demand for foreign currency. The growth of international trade in the last 10 years or so, however, has become so large that very few governments carry sufficient reserves to adopt this solution except China and Japan. The typical countermeasure now is to adjust interest rates. This affects the flow of short-term capital deposits by multinationals, which in turn affects the value of the currency.

For example, a firm such as IBM has huge cash reserves on hand: the payroll bill alone runs to billions of dollars a month. This cash could be deposited in any countries where IBM does business, and firms of that size find it worthwhile to employ analysts who move the money to where it will earn the most interest. Even an extra thousandth of a per cent interest of the money more than covers the salaries of the analysts. The "hot money" is sufficient to affect the value of the currency in which it is deposited, because it increases demand for the currency in the short term. For example, Japanese Yen faced very strong appreciation pressure in 2016 after United Kingdom voted to leave EU. One of the very important reasons is that hot money enters Japanese market. At the same time, the inflation will be expected if a large sum of hot money enter a market.

Why global marketers care about the balance of payments

Global marketers take an interest in the balance of payments accounts of the countries in which they do business because they indicate the following for each country:

(1) Its overall economic health.

(2) The extent of competition likely to be encountered from other imported products.

(3) The likelihood of internal deflationary government policies and/or imposition of trade and exchange controls.

Equally, analysts need to beware of the extent of difficulties associated with the interpretation of balance of payments statements, which include the following:

(1) Groups of transactions within the accounts are to some extent arbitrary. A "deficit" becomes a surplus if certain items are removed and others inserted in a particular category.

(2) Current account deficits only become a problem if there is no corresponding inflow of private capital. Indeed, a number of countries almost operate in perpetual current account deficit, which is offset by capital account transactions.

(3) The magnitude of the balancing item can be enormous compared to other elements of the accounts. Sometimes the balancing item exceeds the total value of a

country's current account deficit or surplus.

(4) Accounts for the same period can change radically over time as more data becomes available. For example, the current account for the first quarter of a certain year might show a deficit, but it may be a surplus when subsequently revised in about 12 months' time. Yet media attention (and stock exchange reaction) focuses on the preliminary figures as they appear.

(5) Not all transactions are included. In some countries, smuggling is a significant activity, but not a single transaction is recorded in the country's balance of payments. Also there might be innocent non-recording or under-recording of some consignments of imported or exported items. Agents might conduct business on behalf of foreigners but not be aware that this should be included in the statement, and companies might engage in transfer pricing (selling products to their own overseas subsidiary in order to avoid tax) and so forth.

(6) A country's balance of payments accounts represent a statement of its external trade position over a particular period. They do not indicate the cause of the underlying forces that led to the results.

Barriers to international marketing

Trade is generally regarded as a way of increasing welfare for the country. Wherever an exchange takes place, both parties are better off as result: if this were not true, trade would be impossible since one or he other party would not agree to the terms. Therefore governments seek to free up trade.

The world wide liberalization of international trade practices and procedures has been an outstanding feature after World War Ⅱ. Overall, tariffs have tumbled since 1945, and begin fall in the developing countries. Governments increasingly recognize the benefits of free trade: more jobs, more choices of goods for consumers, wider markets for business, economic growth and improved living standards, closer political links, etc. Yet despite their notional support for free trade, many countries continue to use restrictive measures in order to improve their balance of payments. All countries have import tariffs that, apart from their impact on the level of imports, it is also a valuable source of state revenue. Some have exchange controls and non-tariff restrictions (import quotas, for example), and others impose a variety of hidden import barriers.

The reasons for this are very complex. Some countries seek to protect fledgling industries from cheap imports from established firms in other countries: others try to protect their balance of payments position by restricting imports and encouraging exports. Still others impose barriers for political reasons. For example, America always takes the trade embargoes to punish the so-called rogue administrations. Whatever the reasons, restricting trade damages welfare.

3.4 Dimensions of the economy

To estimate market potential as well as to provide input to other functional areas of their firms, managers require data on the size and the change rates of a number of economic and socioeconomic factors. For a place to be a potential market, it must have sufficient people with purchasing power to buy a firm's products. Socioeconomic data provide information about population, and the economic factors tell us if they have purchasing power.

Among the most important economic dimensions are GNP, distribution of income, personal consumption expenditures, personal ownership of goods, private investment, unit labor costs, exchange rates, inflation rates, and interest rates.

GNP

Gross national product means the total of all final goods and services produced, and gross domestic products means GNP less net foreign factor incomes, they are all the very important statistic data for marketers used to measure an economy's size. GNPs range from \$16.19 trillion for the United States to \$23 million for Principe (in the Gulf of Guinea off the coast) in 2015. What is the significance of GNP for the international businessperson? Is India, with a GNP of \$1.7175 trillion, a more attractive market than Denmark, with \$316.2 billion? They will want to examine the data of individual countries in the area and compare growths with their subsidiaries' growths. The data might indicate that some markets where they have no operations need to be investigated. Of course, this is only the initial step. To compare the purchasing power of nations, managers also need to know among how many people this increase in GNP or GDP is divided. Otherwise, when you examine the data, you have to understand GNP based on PPP (price power parity) (Table 3-2).

Table 3-2 20 top GNP countries of the world in 2010

Rank	Country	GNP	GNP based on PPP
1	the United States	145,616.98	145,616.98
2	China	59,063.27	101,322.80
3	Japan	56,241.83	44,321.23
4	Germany	33,579.87	31,161.20
5	France	26,067.80	22,342.10
6	England	22,920.90	22,768.54

continued

Rank	Country	GNP	GNP based on PPP
7	Brazil	20,491.72	21,289.56
8	Italy	20,239.16	18,829.87
9	India	17,175.80	41,708.54
10	Russia	14,314.59	27,204.75
11	Spain	13,887.44	14,582.45
12	Mexico	10,251.99	16,291.84
13	Korea	10,147.60	14,179.36
14	Netherland	7,859.88	7,079.20
15	Turkey	7,274.45	11,041.26
16	Indonesia	6,866.33	10,007.49
17	Switzerland	5,548.53	3,831.03
18	Belgium	4,718.65	4,112.32
19	Sweden	4,664.33	3,720.09
20	Poland	4,512.03	7,261.24

GNP/Capita

It is not a satisfactory method of using GNP/Capita to compare purchasing power directly. For example, Denmark is far ahead of India, with $61,310 versus $1,741. In other words, although India's pie is twice as big as Denmark's, there are 19 times as many people to eat it. What can we learn from GNP/Capita? As we saw in Chapter 2, we can generally assume that the higher its value, the more advanced the economy. Generally, however, growth rate is more important to marketers because a high growth rate indicates a fast-growing market—for which they are always searching. Frequently, given the choice between investing in a nation with a higher GNP/Capita but a low growth rate and a nation in which the conditions are reversed, management will choose the latter (Table 3-3).

Table 3-3 Comparison the GDP/Capita with the different calculate methods

GDP/capita in 2010			GDP/capita in 2010 based on PPP		
Rank	Country/area	GDP/capita	Rank	Country/area	GDP/capita
1	Luxembourg	104,390	1	Qatar	88,232
2	Norway	84,543	2	Luxembourg	80,304

continued

GDP/capita in 2010			GDP/capita in 2010 based on PPP		
Rank	Country/area	GDP/capita	Rank	Country/area	GDP/capita
3	Qatar	74,422	3	Singapore	57,238
4	Switzerland	67,074	4	Norway	52,238
5	Denmark	55,113	5	Brunei	47,200
6	Australia	54,869	6	the United States	47,123
7	Sweden	47,667	7	Hong Kong (China)	45,277
8	United Arab	47,406	8	Switzerland	41,765
9	the United States	47,132	9	Netherlands	40,777
10	Netherlands	46,418	10	Australia	39,692
95	China	4,283	75	China	7,518

Although differences in GNP/capita do tell us something about the relative wealth of a nation's inhabitants, the information is somewhat misleading because few of them have the equal share indicated by what is an arithmetic means. This first crude estimate of purchasing power must be refined by incorporating data on how the national income is actually distributed.

Income distribution

Data on income distribution are gathered by the World Bank from a number of sources and published yearly in the World Development Report. This distinction is important to market analysts because households with low per capita income are frequently large households with a high total income, while households with a lower total income are often smaller households with higher per capita income. Unfortunately, only a few countries gather data on the distribution of per capita income.

Despite the difficulties associated with income distribution studies, such as inconsistent measuring practices and wide variations in the representativeness of samples, the data provide some useful insights for businesspeople:

(1) They confirm the belief that, generally, income is more evenly distributed in the advanced nations, although there are important variations among both developed and developing nations.

(2) From comparisons over time, it appears that income redistribution proceeds very slowly, so that older data are still useful.

(3) These same comparisons indicate that income inequality increases in the early stages of development, with a reversal of this tendency in the later stages. This is true

for developed, developing, and emerging nations. Especially, it is very important for international businesspeople to study how much the middle class share the GNP when they want to enter a new market, because it is the market foundation for lots of products.

Contingent on the type of product and the total population, either situation (relatively even or uneven income distribution) may represent a viable market segment. For example, although Costa Rica's GNP is $6.2 billion, the fact that just 20 percent of the population receives over 50 percent of that income (10 percent gets 34.1 group of people who are potential percent) indicates that there is a sizable customers for low-volume, high-priced luxury products. On the other hand, the market is rather small (2.9 million population) for low-priced goods requiring a high sales volume.

This simple calculation based on GNP, total population, and income distribution may be enough to determine whether or not a particular country is a good market; however, if the results look promising, the analyst will proceed to gather data on personal consumption.

Personal consumption

One area of interest to marketers is the manner in which consumers allocate their disposable income (after-tax personal income) between purchases of essential and nonessential goods. Manufacturers of a certain class of essentials (household durables, for instance) will want to know the amounts spent in that category, whereas producers of nonessentials will be interested in the magnitude of discretionary income (disposable income less essential purchases), for this is the money available to be spent on their products. Fortunately, disposable incomes and the amounts spent on essential purchases are available from the UN Statistical Yearbook, and discretionary income may be obtained by subtracting the total of these items from disposable income. Although it is impossible for businesspeople to get all of the data in every country, more detailed expenditure patterns can frequently be found in economic publications.

Note how the consumption patterns have changed in only 20 years. With the exception of Ecuador, consumers in all countries have decreased the percentage spent on food as their total consumption expenditures have increased. This follows Engle's law (19th century German statistician) that says, holding demographic factors constant, as income increases, the percentage of income spent on food decreases.

As you would expect, a significantly higher percentage goes for food in the poorer nations, and less is spent on durable goods. Interestingly, the clothing percentages do not vary much among nations. Will you expect the percentage spent on clothing in Italy to be over 50 percent more than in France?

Don't underestimate the importance of the small percentage differences among nations because each percentage point is equal to a large sum of money. For example, if every Chinese spend more \$1 on clothing, it means over \$1.3 billion sale will be added to the industry. And one percent market share for P&G or Unilever mean over \$60 million revenue.

Other indicators that add to our knowledge of personal consumption are those concerned with the ownership of goods. In addition, the per capita values for the consumption and production of strategic materials, such as steel and energy, serve as measures of a nation's affluence and level of development.

Private investment

The amount of private investment (the part of national income allocated to increasing a nation's productive capacity) is another factor that contributes to the analysis of market size and growth. New investment brings about increases in GNP and the level of employment, which are signals of a growing market. A history of continual investment growth signifies, furthermore, that a propitious investment climate exists; that is, there are numerous profitable investment opportunities, and the government boasts the confidence of the business community.

Because of the financial crisis of the world, only few countries got smaller increase in private investment during the 2008—2009 periods. However, the increase was not evenly distributed over all nations—57 percent of the high-income nations experienced an increase during the 2005—2015 periods, but only 39 percent of the middle and low income nations did. Consumer spending also suffered from the recession, and only 47 nations had increases in private consumption in the 2005—2015 periods. The high-income nations in this group were Switzerland, Finland, the United Kingdom, Singapore, and New Zealand. But, the emerging markets got very fast growth from 2001 until today. Especially, China is the fastest growing economic entity of the major economic entities of the world.

Similarly, the third area of expenditure, government spending, experienced global reduction because of the financial crisis, especially the Europe's expenditure declined very fast because of its debt crisis. Lots of countries including the United States, Switzerland, Japan, Pakistan, and some developing nations of Africa have been suffering the economic recession since 2008. In this environment, few investors are willing to put money in plants and inventories.

Unit labor costs

One factor that contributes to a favorable investment opportunity is the ability to obtain unit labor costs (total direct labor costs/units produced) lower than those currently available to the firm. Foreign trends in these costs are closely monitored because each country experiences a different growth rate.

Countries with slower-rising unit labor costs attract management's attention for two reasons. First, they are investment prospects for companies striving to lower production costs, as discussed in Chapter 2; second, they may become sources of new competition in the world markets if other firms in the same industry are already located there.

Changes in wage rates may also cause the multinational firm that obtains products or components from a number of subsidiaries to change its sources of supply.

Zenith, the American TV and computer manufacturer, moved the production of its monochrome computer monitors from China Taiwan to Mexico in 1992 because of the lower Mexican wage rates.

What are the reasons for the relative changes in labor costs? Three factors are responsible: ① compensation, ② productivity, and ③ exchange rates. Hourly compensation tends to vary more widely than wages because of the appreciable differences in the size of fringe benefits. Unit labor costs will not rise in unison with compensation rates if the gains in productivity outstrip the increases in hourly compensation. In fact, if productivity increases fast enough, the unit labor costs will decrease even though the firm is required to pay more to the workers.

The United States had the highest hourly rate from 1982 to 1986, when it was surpassed by Switzerland, Germany, and Norway. By 1989, it had dropped to the 10th place behind Italy. In 2010, the United States was in the 8th place, but after Sweden. Italy had dropped to 29th in the rankings of international labor costs measured in U. S. dollars.

For a long time, the unit labor of China has been very low and this is why lots of international companies invested in China in the late 1980s and this is one of the biggest advantages for China to attract foreign capital. With the economic development, its unit labor costs increase very fast too and the reality obliged lots of Korean companies to transfer their production foundation to Vietnam and India. By now, China has lost the advantage in using the lower labor cost to attract the foreign investors, especially in eastern China and south China.

Besides, if you were to calculate the percentage changes in the hourly rates expressed in dollars and in the local currency, they would usually different. The reason is that the change stated in dollars is the result of the real change in local currency plus that currency's appreciation or depreciation with respect to the dollar from one year to another. This is why China is losing its advantage in the field of lower unit labor with the RMB appreciation step by step since 2000.

Other economic dimensions

We have mentioned only a few of many economic indicators that economists study and you learned about the importance to businesspeople of interest rate, balance of payment, and inflation rate. The economic measures the analyst applies to study will depend on the industry and the purpose of the study. Executives of an automobile manufacturer, for example, will want the economist's opinion as to where interest rates are headed and what is the growth rate of a nation's GNP which as you saw earlier, is important to other producers of industrial products.

The large international debts of a number of middle and low income nations are causing multiple problems not only for their governments but also for multinational firms. As a matter of fact, even the giant companies of the world can suffer the debt crisis. For example, GMC would have gone bankrupt in 2009 if the U. S. government would not support it with over $18 billion.

Is this a problem for international bankers only, or should it concern multinational managements as well? Is it significant to global and multinational firms with subsidiaries in these countries that a high percentage of the countries' export earnings must go to service their foreign debts? Many analysts believe that annual interest payments greater than 10 percent of a nation's export revenue are a cause for concern. If the management agrees, then it will expect periodic reports on this situation from its economist(s).

If a large part of the foreign exchange a nation earns cannot be used to import components used in local products, then either local industries must manufacture them or the companies that import them must stop production. Either alternative can cause the multinational to lose sales if it has been selling the parts made in one of its home country plants to its subsidiary, a common occurrence because the home plant is usually more vertically integrated than its subsidiaries.

A scarcity of foreign exchange can also make it difficult for the subsidiary to import raw materials and spare parts for its production equipment. If headquarters want its affiliate to continue production, it may have to lend the foreign exchange and wait for repayment. For example, the America companies such as Campbell Soup, Revlon, and Gerber closed their operations in Brazil because of this problem. Other multinationals have resorted to barter or have begun to export their subsidiaries' products even though these actions have reduced exports or even local sales of their domestic plants.

Governments may impose price controls (which make it difficult for a subsidiary to earn a profit), cut government spending (which reduces company sales), and impose wage controls (which limit consumer purchasing power). The economic turmoil that follows can turn into a political crisis, such as what occurred in Greece and other

Europe countries in 2011 when rioting arose after the presidents tried to impose austerity measures.

An aspect of debt reduction that has interested some countries is debt-for-equity swaps. Argentina is among this league. Foreigners are able to buy Argentine dollar debt at a discount and convert it into Argentine currency at a rate closer to face value. They then invest the money in local firms. Campbell Soup took advantage of this situation to build a new meatpacking plant. The company purchased $60 million worth of Argentine foreign-debt paper in the world market at 17 percent of the par value. Argentina's central bank agreed to redeem the paper in Argentine currency at the equivalent of 30 cents on the dollar if the company used the money to build the plant. The debt-for-equity swap saved Campbell $8 million. Grupo Visa, a Mexican conglomerate, reduced its foreign debt from $1.7 billion to $400 million with a private debt-for-equity swap. The company gave its foreign creditors a 40 percent share in the company in return for debt cancellation.

Scarcity of foreign exchange can affect even those firms that merely export to nations with high foreign debt because the governments will surely impose import restrictions. When Latin American debt increased rapidly from 1981 to 1983, that region's share of U. S. exports dropped by one-third. To protect these export markets, firms had to extend long-term credit. From this you can see that management will expect to receive information on the status of the foreign debt of heavily indebted nations in addition to other economic data we have been examining. This is especially important now when the same American banks involved in the Third World debt crisis in the 1980s are once again lending huge sums to developing nations. However, the more serious problem is that the developed countries, such as lots of Europe countries and including America and Japan are puzzled by their government-debts and the situation is hurting the world economic growth today.

Exchange controls

These restrict importer's abilities to obtain the foreign currency needed to pay for imports, either via direct prohibition or through the government artificially increasing the exchange rate prices of certain foreign currencies (for example, by limiting the supply of these currencies available for importers to purchases). Administration of exchange controls is problematic for the authorities of the country and may involve any or all of the following:

(1) Legal requirements that firms hand over to the national central bank for all the foreign exchange they acquire.

(2) Government rules that different exchange rates apply to different types of transaction (although this is extremely rare, following a long-standing international

agreement that prohibits the use of multiple exchange rates for normal import/export activity).

(3) Restriction of foreign exchange availability to the import of specified products.

(4) Selection of particular firms that may obtain foreign exchange.

(5) Issue of foreign exchange licenses and quotas.

(6) Only allowing foreign exchange to importers who enter into joint of venture domestic manufacturing arrangements with exporting companies.

Exchange controls are becoming rarer as governments are better able to use the interest rate mechanism to maintain the value of their currencies. They are still common in developing countries, however, and they can cause problems for global firms who wish to repatriate profits from those countries.

3.5 Socioeconomic dimensions

A complete definition of market potential must also include detailed information about the population's physical attributes as measured by the socioeconomic dimensions. Just as we began with GNP in the study of purchasing power, we shall begin this section with an analysis of the total population.

Total population

Total population, the most general indicator of potential market size, is the first characteristic of the population that analysts will examine. They readily discover that there are immense differences in population sizes. The fact that many developed nations have less than 10 million inhabitants make it apparent that population size alone is a poor indicator of economic strength and market potential. Switzerland, for example, with only 6.9 million people, is far more economically important than Bangladesh, with 114 million. Clearly, more information is needed; only for a few low-priced, mass-consumed products, such as soft drinks, cigarettes, and soap, population size alone does provide a basis for estimating consumption.

For products not in this category, populations that are increasing rapidly may not signify an immediate enlargement of the market; but if incomes grow over time, eventually at least a part of the population will become customers. Insight into the rapidity with which this is occurring may be obtained by comparing population and GNP growth rates. Where GNP increases faster than the population, there is probably an expanding market, whereas the converse situation not only indicates possible market contraction but may even point out a country as a potential area of political unrest. The former possibility is strengthened if an analysis of the educational system discloses an accruement of technical and university graduates. These workforce army expect to be employed as and receive the wages of professionals, and when more jobs are not created to absorb them, the government can be in serious trouble. Various developing nations already face the difficulty: Egypt and India are two notable examples. In 2011, rioting occurred in Egypt and not only destroyed the economy of Egypt, especially its tourism industry, but it also triggered "the spring of Arab" and the result is that lots of the multinationals had to withdraw from the area. The second largest population country of the world, India, is puzzled by the same question, because the large population not only can provide the cheaper labor, but it also dilutes the average income, the economic growth will decline if government or multinationals can not create enough jobs, unemployment is always the basic reason for breaking out the political crisis.

Age distribution

Because few products are purchased by everyone, marketers must identify the segments of the population that are more apt to buy their goods. For some firms, age is a salient determinant of market size; but unfortunately, the distribution of age groups within populations varies widely.

Generally, because of higher birth and fertility rates, developing countries have more youthful populations than industrial countries. It is the tremendous difference in age distribution between developed and developing countries, which is the result of much higher birthrates in the developing nations. Of course, the situation is changing. In particular Chinese birth rate is declining. According to the estimation by UN, the world population would increase by about 500 million if Chinese government did not take the family planning policy over the past 30 years. And with the fast growth of the education cost and other social expenditures, more and more Chinese youth would not like to give birth to more than one child. It lead China to a aging society rapidly. According to the estimation by the Chinese economists that the demographic bonus of China will disappear before 2030 and the old people market will be developed at that time. Under the circumstance, Chinese government adjusted its population policies and allowed the family to give birth to the second child in 2015.

In a word, age distribution is the basic question for international managers to study when they want to enter a new market, because the structure of the population determines the market structure to a great degree. By now, the total population of the world is over 7 billion, whether or not it is a benefit for the human is a subject to study. As multinational managers, focusing on the change of the question will influence their marketing decision.

Significance for businesspeople

What does this signify for businesspeople? In the developed nations, there will be a decrease in the demand for products used in schools and for products bought by and for children, a smaller market for furniture and clothing, but an increased demand for medical care and related products, tourism, and financial services. Firms confronted with a decreasing demand for their products will have to look for sales increases in developing economies, where the age distribution is reversed. The high growth rates in developing nations will provide markets for transportation systems, higher-yield food grains, fertilizers, agricultural tools, appliances, and so forth.

Whirlpool, concerned about the decline in the number of householders aged 25 or less in the United States while noting the opportunities in overseas markets, acquired 53 percent of the Dutch electronics giant Philips' domestic appliance business in 1988. The acquisition enabled Whirlpool to become the world's largest major home appliance company, although it has to compete with the Chinese manufacturer—Haier (the largest white home appliance manufacturer of the world), with manufacturing facilities in 11 countries and a distribution network covering 45 countries. In August 1991, Whirlpool bought the remaining 47 percent of the business from Philips.

Many forces are responsible for reductions in birthrates. Governments are supporting family planning programs, to be sure, but there is ample evidence that improved levels in health and education along with an enhanced status for women, a more even distribution of income, and a greater degree of urbanization are all forces to reduce traditional family size. In Mexico, for example, 71 percent of the women with seven or more years' education practice contraception, but only 40 percent of those with no formal education do. In the Philippines, the percentages were 45 percent to 22 percent. Experts claim that the combined effect of an effective family planning program and female education beyond the primary level is extremely powerful in reducing family size.

While this is welcomed by governments in developing nations, declining birthrates are causing concern in the governments of industrialized nations. According to the World Bank's World Development Report, the birthrates in developed nations have been considerably below the replacement number of 2.1 children. Of these countries, Australia's birthrate is the highest (1.4 percent). An increasing number of young Europeans are not getting married, and those who do are marrying later and having fewer children. By the year 2020, near 9 percent unemployment rate in the European Union will be replaced by a shortage of workers. European governments will have to provide medical care and pensions for 25 percent of their population that will be over 65 years old, and there will be fewer working taxpayers. This is why former French president Sarkozy wanted to extend the retirement age and Chinese goverment will publish the similar plan in 2016.

Japan's situation appears to be even more serious. Its fertility rate is only 1.57 per woman, well below the 2.1 population replacement value, and in the year 2025, Japan's population aged 65 and older will make up 25.7 percent of its population, whereas the same age group in the United States will amount to only 19.1 percent of the total population. The labor shortage has inflated wages to the point where the average manufacturing pay in Japan is $20.42 an hour as compared to $17.30 in the United States.

To counteract the shortage of workers, Japanese companies invested heavily in robots and raised their mandatory retirement ages from 60 to 65. To attract younger employees, they reduced the large difference between the wages paid to the newly hired and the older workers and began to promote younger employees faster. They also were hiring more women.

Early retirement and the fact that retirees are living longer are straining the social security system of Japan and many other countries. In industrialized nations, not only are social security system costs rising because of the growing number of retirees, but there are also fewer people working and funding the system. However, in most developing nations, just the opposite is occurring. The higher birthrate result in a younger population, which reduces the dependency ratios and the burden to workers supporting the system.

Population density and distribution

Other aspects of population that concern management are population density and population distribution. Densely populated countries tend to make product distribution and communications simpler and less costly than those with low population density; thus you might expect Pakistan, with 149 inhabitants per square kilometer, to be an easier market to serve than Canada (2.8 inhabitants/square kilometer) or Brazil (18.1 inhabitants/square kilometer). The expectation, though, is another statistic based on an arithmetic mean. We must know how these population are distributed.

One needs only to compare the urban percentages of total population to learn that Canada and Brazil possess population concentrations that facilitate the marketing process. While only 33 percent of Pakistan's population is urban, the percentages for Brazil and Canada are 77 and 88 percent, respectively. Physical forces contribute heavily to the formation of these concentrations.

An important phenomenon that is changing the population distribution is the rural-to-urban shift, which is occurring everywhere, especially in developing countries. For example, about over 500 million Chinese farmers will enter cities to live in the future 20 years, as people move to cities in search of higher wages and more conveniences. By now, China's urban population has been over rural population. This shift is significant to marketers because city dwellers, being less self-sufficient than people living in rural areas, must enter the market economy. City governments also become customers for equipment that will expand municipal services to handle the population influx.

An indicator of the extent of this movement is the change in the percentages of urban population. According to statistics, the greatest urban shifts are occurring in the low and middle income countries. In no country anywhere is there a net flow in the other direction.

Other socioeconomic dimensions

Other socioeconomic dimensions can provide useful information to management. The increase in the number of working women, for example, is highly significant to marketers because it may result in larger family incomes, a greater market for convenience goods, and a need to alter the promotional mix. Personnel managers are interested in this increase because it results in a larger labor supply. It also signifies that changes may be required in production processes, employee facilities, and personnel management policies.

Data of the country's divorce rate, when available, will alert the marketer to the formation of single-parent families and single-person households, whose needs for product and buying habits differ in many respects from those of a two-parent family. In many countries, important ethnic groups require special consideration by both marketing and personnel managers.

National economic plans

One other source of economic data that may prove useful to a firm, especially for its marketers, is the national economic plans that many countries publish. These range from the annual and five-year plans (in reality, budgets) used as production control instruments by the remaining communist nations, such as Cuba, Vietnam, and China, to the indicative plans of some free market economies. Instead of production targets, the five-year indicative plans contain the basic targets set by the government and some general policy statements on how the goals will be achieved. The government then attempts by means of the usual monetary and fiscal tools to create favorable conditions for business so that the targets may be attained. This favoritism may be manifested in many ways, among which are special tax concessions to investors and foreign exchange allocations (when foreign exchange is controlled) to purchase imported capital equipment and raw materials. As the second largest entity of the world, Chinese five-year plan is the most important information for all of multinationals, because it is one of the most important markets for them. It is the precondition for the international companies to study the government policies before entering a new market, and the five-year plans will give you the direction to develop the market.

Information about national development plans and budgets is regularly reported in such publications as *Business International* and *Business America* and if you want to study the subject, the government report is the most important source. In China, you have to study not only the central government report but also the local government reports if you want to enter the market. Notice, the most accurate information comes from the government. Of course, commercial attaches in every country's embassies and the overseas chambers of commerce are additional sources of information.

Industry dimensions

Every firm is concerned about the general economic news because of its impact on consumer purchases, prices of raw materials, and investment decisions, but certain factors are more significant than others to a given industry or to a specific functional area of a firm. The size and growth trend of the automobile industry is of paramount importance to a tire manufacturer, for example, but is of no interest to an appliance manufacturer. Nor would the quantity of machine operators graduated from technical schools be useful to financial officers, although these data are of vital interest to human resources managers of manufacturing plants. Managers want data not only about the firm's industry but also about industries that supply and purchase from the company.

As a matter of fact, some industries influence other relative industries very much. For example, as the foundational industry, the real estate will influence the development of steel, building materials, cement industries and so forth. According to relative information, it can cover about 63 industries in China. This is why the Chinese government, especially the local governments, encourages the development of real estate, not only can it incent the economic growth, but it also can create many job opportunities.

Industry studies are generally made by the firm's economists or its trade association, but they can also be purchased from independent research organizations, such as Fantus (New York) and The Economist Intelligence Unit (London). Government agencies, chambers of commerce, and trade publications such as *Advertising Age* publish them as well. Many international banks publish free newsletters containing useful economic data.

In general, economic and socioeconomic environments are the most important for international companies to study, because they will influence your international marketing directly and all of the information is the foundation for multinationals to make their international marketing strategies.

Summary

1. Understand the purpose analysis. To keep abreast of economic developments and also for the future, firms regularly assess and forecast economic conditions at the local, state, and national levels. When they enter international operations, the complexity of economic analysis increases because managers are operating in two new environments: foreign and international. There are more economies to study, and these economies are frequently highly divergent.

2. Recognize the economic and socioeconomic dimensions of an economy. The various functional areas of a firm require data on the size and change rates of a number of economic and socioeconomic factors. Among the most important economic dimensions are GNP, GNP/capita, distribution of income, personal consumption expenditures, private investment, unit labor costs, and financial data, such as exchange rates, inflation rates, interest rates, and the amount of a nation's foreign debt. The principal socioeconomic dimensions are total population, growth rates, age distribution, population density, and population distribution.

3. Observe how a nation's consumption patterns change over time. Marketers must know how consumers allocate their discretionary incomes since this is the money being spent on their products. Because consumers' spending patterns change over time as their incomes increase, businesspeople must study their consumption patterns.

4. Identify what factors cause changes in hourly wage rates expressed in dollars. Hourly labor rates, especially when stated in U. S. dollars, change rather rapidly. There are three factors responsible: ① real changes in compensation, ② changes in productivity, and ③ changes in exchange rates.

5. Understand the significance for businesspeople of large foreign debts of some nations. Large foreign debts may indicate that the government will impose exchange controls on its country's businesses. If a large part of the country's export earnings go to service its external debt, there will be little remaining for use by firms in the country to pay for imports of raw materials, components used in their products, and production machinery. The government could impose price and wage controls. There is also the possibility that firms can buy some of the discounted debt to obtain local currency at a favorable exchange rate.

6. Ascertain the reasons for the worldwide downward trend in birthrates and its implications for businesspeople. Birthrates are declining in nearly all nations because ① governments are providing family planning programs, ② women are continuing their education and marrying later, and ③ a greater degree of urbanization is enabling women to become employed and self supporting, which contributes to a delay of marriage.

7. Understand indicative plans and their importance for businesspeople. National economic plans, for which no American counterpart exists, provide an insight into government expectations. In lots of emerging countries, especially China, national plans are often the equivalent of market studies. Many developed and developing nations use indicative plans to set out their goals and provide some general policy statements about how they will be achieved.

Questions

1. The management learns from the economic analysis of Country A that wage rates are expected to increase by 10 percent next year. Which functional areas of the firm will be concerned? Why are they concerned?

2. Check the World Development Report in the library to learn which country in each income group (low-, medium-, and high-income economies) is the leader in the growth rate of GNP per capita over the last 15 to 20 years. In each case, is the growth rate greater than the population growth rate? What can you deduce from that?

3. What are the common problems of the use of GNP per capita and population density values?

4. What is the relationship between population and income? How can you use this information?

5. If the clothing industry association to which your firm's Swiss subsidiary belongs could mount a successful promotional program to lead the Swiss to increase their clothing expenditures by 1 percent annually, what would be the total increase in sales for the clothing industry?

6. In 2015, Switzerland had the second-highest average hourly compensation rate. True or false? Please explain.

7. Why do international managers have to study the exchange rates?

8. What was the growth rate of the labor cost stated in RMB?

9. Describe China's population situation and give your own opinions about the question.

10. Do you think which index (GNP and GNP/Captita) is more important for you to study a foreign market? Why?

11. What problems do the reduction of birthrates cause to European governments?

12. Choose a country and a product, and estimate the market potential of the product based on economic and socioeconomic dimensions. What other environmental forces should you investigate?

Chapter 4 Social Cultural Forces

Concept preview

After reading this chapter, you should be able to

1. Appreciate: why the international business people have to study social culture forces.

2. Understand: the difference between various countries in regard to culture.

3. Comprehend: the social cultural structures of various countries.

4. Describe: how languages influence your international marketing decision.

4.1 Social cultural forces overview

Whether you aim to sell computers in London or soft drinks in Kuala Lumpur, it is as important to know your customers anywhere in the world as it is at home. Each culture has its logic, and the logic will influence the manners in which its people treat the foreigners. If a salesperson can figure out the basic pattern of the culture, he or she will be more effective interacting with foreign clients and colleagues. As a matter of fact, barriers coming from culture forces may be the biggest when you take international marketing, because it is very difficult for a foreigner to understand the local culture completely in the real world, the following six rules of thumb are helpful.

1. Be prepared

Whether traveling abroad or selling at home, no one should approach a foreign market without doing his or her homework. A mentor is most desirable, complemented with sufficient reading on social and business etiquette, history and folklore, current affairs (including current relations between two countries), the culture's values, geography, sources of pride (artists, musicians, sports), religion, political structure, and practical matters such as currency and hours of business. Mimi Murphy, an exporter who trades primarily in Indonesia, said, "Whenever I travel, the first thing I do in any town is read the newspaper. Then when I meet my customer, I can talk about the sports or the news of the day. He knows that I am interested in the things he is interested in, and he will want to do business with me."

2. Slow down

German is a clock-watcher. Time is money. In many countries, they are seen to be in a rush, in other words, unfriendly, arrogant, and untrustworthy. Almost everywhere, they have to learn to wait patiently. For example, you may have to wait more than two years to get your driver license in India.

3. Establish trust

The foundation of international marketing is trusting each other, especially when you are doing your business with the foreigners. Product quality, pricing, and clear contracts are not as important as the personal relationship and trust that are developed carefully and sincerely over time. Marketers must be established as simpatico, worthy of the business and dependable in the long run.

4. Understand importance of language

Obviously, copy must be translated by a professional who speaks both languages fluently, with a vocabulary sensitive to nuance and connotation, as well as talent with idiom and imagery in each culture. An interpreter is often critical and may be helpful even where one of the parties speaks the other's language.

5. Respect the culture

Manners are important. The traveling sales representative is a guest in the country and must respect the rules of the host. Remember, you are a foreigner when you take the international marketing in other countries and you have to obey the law of the host and cultural habits if you want to make money, so to study and respect the culture of the host is the basic precondition.

6. Understand components of culture

A region is a sort of cultural iceberg with two components: surface culture (fads, styles, food, etc.) and deep culture (attitudes, beliefs, values). Less than 15 percent of a region's culture is visible, and strangers must look beneath the surface. Consider the British habit of automatically lining up on the sidewalk when waiting for a bus. This surface cultural trait results from the deep cultural desire to lead neat and controlled lives.

Please remember that the national characteristics in this chapter and elsewhere in this book are generalizations. They are broadly true, but there are always exceptions. Furthermore, characteristics change over time. Before we examine the significance of culture for international businesspeople, let us first define culture.

Although there are almost as many definitions of culture as anthropologists, most anthropologists view culture as the sum total of the beliefs, rules, techniques, institutions, and artifacts that characterize human population. In other words, culture consists of the learned patterns of, behavior common to members of a given society—the unique lifestyle of a particular group of people. Most anthropologists also agree that:

(1) Culture is learned, not innate.

(2) The various aspects of culture are interrelated.

(3) Culture is shared.

(4) Culture defines the boundaries of different groups.

Because society is composed of people and their culture, it is virtually impossible to speak of one without relating to the other. Anthropologists often use the terms interchangeably or combine them into one word—sociocultural. This is the term we shall use, because the variables in which businesspeople are interested are both social and cultural. When people work in societies and cultures that differ from their own, the problems they encounter in dealing with a single set of cultures are multiplied by the number of cultural sets they find in each of their foreign markets.

All too often, unfortunately, people who are familiar with only one cultural pattern may believe they have an awareness of cultural differences elsewhere, but in reality they do not. Unless they have had occasions to make comparisons with other cultures, they are even probably not aware of the important features of their own. They are probably also oblivious to the fact that many societies consider their own culture superior to all others (ethnocentricity) and that their attempts to introduce the "German way" or the "American way" may be met with stubborn resistance.

How do international businesspeople learn to live with other cultures? The first step is to realize that there are cultures different from their own. Then they must go on to learn the characteristics of those cultures so that they may adapt to them. E. T. Hall, a famous anthropologist, claims this can be accomplished in only two ways: ① spend a lifetime in a country or ② undergo an extensive, highly sophisticated training program that covers the main characteristics of cultures, including languages. The program he mentions must be more than a briefing on a country's customs. It should be a study of what culture is and how it works, imparting some knowledge of the various ways in which human behavior has been institutionalized in a country.

4.2 Culture affects all business functions

Marketing model

In marketing, for example, the wide variation in attitudes and values prevents many firms from using the same marketing mix in all markets.

In Japan, Procter & Gamble (P&G) used an advertisement for Camay soap in which a man meeting a woman for the first time compared her skin to that of a fine porcelain doll. Although the ad had worked well in South America and Europe, it insulted the Japanese. "For a Japanese man to say something like that to a Japanese woman means he is either unsophisticated or rude." Said an advertising man who worked on the account. Interestingly, P&G used the ad despite the warning from the advertising agency.

Another Camay ad that failed in Japan was one showing a Japanese woman bathing when her husband walks into the bathroom. She begins to tell him about her new beauty soap, but the husband, stroking her shoulder, hints that suds are not what is on his mind. Although it was well received in Europe, it failed badly in Japan where it is considered bad manners for a husband to intrude on his wife.

P&G also erred in Chinese market because it lacked knowledge of the business culture. The company introduced Cheer detergent by discounting its price, but this lowered the soap's reputation. Said a competitor, "Unlike in Europe and the United States, once you discount your product here, it's hard to raise the price again." Wholesalers were alienated because they made less money due to lower margins. Moreover, apparently P&G didn't realize that Chinese housewives do not have a family car to carry groceries, so they shop in the neighborhood morn-and-pop stores close to home. These small retailers sell at a profit margin of 30%.

Unlike P&G, Disney seemed to have an ideal global product and global promotion. According to the Tokyo Disneyland Guidebook, the Tokyo theme park is the same as those in California and Florida. Euro Disney, now called Disneyland Paris, is also similar, although, because of the French insistence on protecting their language and culture, Mickey and Donald developed French accents and the Sleeping Beauty castle is called Le Chateau de la Belle au Bois Dormant. The Worldview illustrates the problems a global firm can have if its management errs when making culturally sensitive decisions.

Human resource management

National culture is also a key determinant for the evaluation of managers. In the

United States, results are generally the criteria for the selection and promotion of executives; but in Great Britain, an American general manager complained that people were promoted because of the school they attended and their family background but not for their accomplishments. School ties are important in France, too. IBM would hire an Italian who fits within the IBM way of doing things, but Olivetti, whose corporate culture is informal and nonstructured with little discipline, looks for strong personalities and not "too good grades." You can get Olivetti's address from the nearest AT&T office.

Production and finance

Personnel problems can result from differences in attitudes toward authority, another sociocultural variable. Latin Americans have traditionally regarded the manager as the patron (master), an authoritarian figure responsible for their welfare. When American managers accustomed to a participative leadership style are transferred to Latin America, they must become more authoritarian, or their employees will consider them weak and incompetent and they will encounter serious difficulties in having their orders carried out.

A production manager who had been sent to Peru from the United States was convinced that he could motivate the workers to higher productivity by instituting a more democratic decision-making style. He brought in trainers from the home office to teach the supervisors how to solicit suggestions and feedback from the workers.

Shortly after the new management style was introduced, the workers began quitting their jobs. When asked why, they replied that the new production manager and his supervisors apparently didn't know what to do and were therefore asking the workers for advice. The workers thought the company wouldn't last long with that kind of management, and they wanted to quit before the collapse, because then everyone would be busy hunting for a job at the same time.

Production managers have found that attitudes toward change can seriously influence the acceptance of new production methods; even treasurers come to realize the strength of the sociocultural forces when, armed with excellent balance sheets, they approach local banks, only to find that the banks attach far more importance to who they are than to how strong their companies are. One reason for Disney's financial problems in Paris has been the arrogant and insensitive attitude of Disney executives to European business culture. A top French banker involved in the negotiations to restructure the park's debt claimed, "The Walt Disney group is making a major error in thinking it can impose its will once more." These are just a few examples to show sociocultural differences do affect all of the business functions. As we examine the components of the sociocultural forces, we shall mention others.

From the foregoing, it should be apparent that to be successful in their relationships with people in other countries, international businesspeople must be students of culture. They must have factual knowledge, which is relatively easy to obtain, but they must also become sensitive to cultural differences, and this is more difficult. Hall, as we saw, recommended spending a lifetime in a country or, in lieu of this, undergoing an extensive program to study what the culture is and what it does. But most newcomers to international marketing do not even have the opportunity for area orientation. They can, however, take the important first step of realizing that there are other cultures. In this short chapter, we cannot do more than point out some of the important sociocultural differences as they concern businesspeople, in the hope that you will become more aware of the need to be culturally sensitive—to know that there are cultural differences for which you must look. Remember that the more you know about other's culture, the better your predictions of that person's behavior will be.

The concept of culture is so broad that even the ethnologists (cultural anthropologists) have to break it down into topics to facilitate its study. A listing of such topics will give us a better understanding of what culture is and may also serve as a guide to international managers when they are analyzing a particular problem from the sociocultural viewpoint.

As you can imagine, experts vary considerably specifying the components of culture, but the following list is representative of their thinking.

(1) Aesthetics.
(2) Attitudes and beliefs.
(3) Religion.
(4) Material culture.
(5) Education.
(6) Language.
(7) Societal organization.
(8) Legal characteristics.
(9) Political structures.

We shall examine the first seven components in this chapter and leave the legal characteristics and political structures for later chapters.

Aesthetics

Aesthetics pertains to a culture's sense of beauty and good taste and is expressed in its art, drama, music, folklore, and dances.

Art

Of particular interest to international businesspeople are the formal aspects of art: color, and form, because of the symbolic meanings they convey. Colors, especially, can be deceptive because they mean different things to different cultures. The color of mourning is black in the United States and Mexico, black and white in the Far East, and purple in Brazil. Because green is a propitious color in the Islamic world, any ad or package featuring green is considered favorable there. However, it is repugnant in parts of Asia, where it connotes illness and death of the jungle. While in the United States mints are packaged in blue or green paper, in Africa the wrapper is red. These examples illustrate that marketers must be careful to check if colors have any special meanings before using them for products, packages, or advertisements.

Be careful of symbols too. Seven signifies good luck in the United States but just the opposite in Singapore, Ghana, and Kenya. In Japan and China, the number four is unlucky. If you are giving your Japanese or Chinese client golf balls, make sure there are more or less than four in the package. Also, in general, avoid using a nation's flag or any symbols connected with religion.

For example, in the last century, the Yokohama Rubber Company (very famous tire company of the world) had to recall tires with a tread pattern that Moslems claim resembles the Arabic word for Allah. A representative said the company had stopped producing the tires and was replacing them with new ones free of charge. He also said that the treads were designed by a computer and were not meant to blaspheme Allah.

It is also important to learn whether there are local aesthetic preferences for form that could affect the design of the product, the package, or even the building in which the firm is located. The American style of steel and glass in the midst of oriental architecture will be a constant reminder to the local population of the outsider's presence.

Music and folklore

Musical commercials are generally popular worldwide, but the marketer must know what kind of music each market prefers, because tastes vary. Thus, a commercial that used a ballad in the United States might be better received to the tune of a bolero in Mexico or a samba in Brazil. However, if the advertiser is looking to the youth market with a product patently American, then American music will help reinforce its image.

Those who wish to steep themselves in a culture find it useful to study its folklore, which can disclose much about a society's lifestyle. Although this is usually not in foreign business people's schedule, the incorrect use of folklore can sometimes cost the firm a loss of market share. For example, associating a product with the cowboy would not obtain the same results in Chile or Argentina as it does in the United States, because in these countries the cowboy is a far less romantic figure—it's just a job.

For another instance, a U. S. company may pay handsome royalties to use American cartoon characters in its promotion, only to find they are considerably less important in foreign markets. In Mexico, songs of the "Singing Cricket" are known to all youngsters and their mothers, and a commercial tie-in with that character would be as advantageous to the firm as its use of Peanuts or Mickey Mouse. In many areas, especially where nationalistic feeling is strong, local firms have been able to compete successfully with foreign affiliates by making use of indigenous folklore in the form of slogans and proverbs. Tales of folklore are valuable in maintaining a sense of group unity. Familiarity with them is an indication that one belongs to the group, which recognizes that outsiders is unfamiliar with its folklore.

Attitudes and beliefs

Every culture has a set of attitudes and beliefs that influence nearly all aspects of human behavior and help bring order to a society and its individuals. The more managers can learn about certain key attitudes, the better prepared they will be to understand why people behave as they do, especially when their reactions differ from those that managers have learned to expect in dealing with their own people.

Among the wide variety of subjects covered by attitudes and beliefs, some are of prime importance to businessperson. These include attitudes toward time, toward achievement and work, and toward change.

Attitudes toward time

This cultural characteristic probably presents more adaptation problems for Americans overseas than any other. Time is important in lots of countries, especially in the United States and China, and much emphasis is placed on it. If they must wait past the appointed hour to see an individual, they feel insulted. This person is not giving the meeting the importance it deserves. Yet the wait could mean just the opposite elsewhere. Latin American or Middle Eastern executives may be taking care of the minor details of their business so that they can attend their important visitor without interruption.

An American who has worked in the Middle East for 20 years explains the Middle Eastern concept of time this way: "A lot of the misunderstandings between Middle Easterners and foreigners are due to their different concepts of time and space. At worst, there is no concept at all of time in the Middle East. At best, there is a sort of open-ended concept." The head of Egypt's Industrial Design Center, an Egyptian, stated: "The simple wristwatch is, in some respects, much too sophisticated an instrument for the Middle East." One of the first things a foreigner should learn in Egypt is to ignore the second hand. The minute hand can also be an obstacle if he expects Egyptians to be conscious as his time ticks away.

Probably even more critical than short-term patience is long-term patience. American preoccupation with monthly profit and loss statements is a formidable barrier to the establishment of successful business relationships with Asian and Middle Eastern executives, especially during the development of joint ventures and other business relationships that have good potential in the long run—precisely the factors in which these people are most interested.

Chinese, be prompt

Few cultures give the same importance to time that the Chinese and the Germans do. If any appointment is made with a group of Chinese or Germans to see them at 12:00, we can be sure they will be there; but to get the same response from a Brazilian, we must say noon English hour. If not, the Brazilian may show up anytime between noon and 2 o'clock. Compare this with Japan, where a description of an apartment in the rental contract includes the time in minutes required to walk to the nearest train station.

Should Americans follow the local custom or be prompt? It depends. In Spain, a general rule is never to be punctual. If you are, you will be considered early. However, in the Middle East, the American penchant for punctuality is well known, and lateness from Americans is considered impolite. The Arabian executives, nonetheless, will usually not arrive at the appointed hour; why should they change their lifetime habits just for a stranger?

Mahana

Probably one of the most vexing problems for newcomers to Latin America is the mahana attitude. Ask the maintenance man when the machine will be ready, and he responds "mahana". The American assumes this means "tomorrow", the literal translation, but the maintenance man means "sometime in the near future," and if he is reprimanded for not having the machine ready the next day, he will be angry and bewildered. He reasons that everyone knows mahana means "in the next few days".

This example illustrates that the ability to speak the local language is only the half task of communicating. A manager of an American subsidiary in Saudi Arabia says, "You can be talking the same language with someone, but are you talking on the same wavelength?" He states that he has met few Japanese or Koreans fluent in Arabic, yet they are able to understand and adapt to local conditions much better than Westerners can because they seem to be more sensitive to the Middle Easterner's psychology.

Directness and drive

The American pride in directness and drive is interpreted by many foreigners as being brash and rude. Although they believe it expedient to get to the point in a discussion, this attitude often irritates others. Time-honored formalities are a vital part of doing business and help to establish amicable relations, considered by people in many countries to be a necessary prerequisite to business discussions. Any attempt to move the negotiations along by ignoring some of the accepted courtesies invites disaster.

Deadlines

Our emphasis on speed and deadline is often used against us in business dealings abroad. In Far Eastern countries such as Japan, an American may be asked how long he or she plans to stay at the first meeting. Then negotiations are purposely not finalized until a few hours before the American's departure, when the Japanese know they can wring extra concessions from the foreigner because of his or her haste to finish and return home on schedule.

Three Americans, none of whom had ever been to Japan, went to sell tractors to Japanese buyers. They thought the discussions had gone well and prepared to wrap up the deal. However, there was no reaction from the Japanese. The silence became disquieting, and so the Americans lowered the price. Because there was still no reaction, they again lowered the price. This went on until their price was far lower than they had planned. What they didn't know was that the Japanese had become silent not to indicate rejection of the proposition, but merely to think it over, a customary Japanese negotiating practice.

Attitudes toward achievement and work

"Greeks put leisure first and work second," says a Greece-born woman now living in the United States. "In America, it's the other way around." Angela Clark was born in Greece but now works for J. C. Penney as merchandising manager in Washington, DC. Andreas Drauschke has a comparable job for comparable pay in Athens. There is no comparison, however, between the working hours. Drauschke works a 37-hour week, with a six-week annual vacation. The store closes at 2:00 P.M. on Saturdays and opens again on Monday. It is open one night a week. Clark works a minimum of hours a week, including evenings and often on Saturdays and Sundays. She brings work home and never takes more than one week's vacation at a time. "If I took any more, I'd feel like I was losing control," she says.

In the United States, Germans are known for their industriousness, but a comparison of workloads shows that there is little basis now for that stereotype. The average workweek in U. S. manufacturing plants is 37. 7 hours and is increasing, whereas, in Germany, it is 30 hours and has been falling over recent years. All German workers are guaranteed by law a minimum of five weeks' annual vacation.

Like the Greeks, the Mexicans say "Americans live to work, but we work to live." This is an example of the extreme contrasts among cultural attitudes toward work. Where work is considered necessary to obtain the essentials for survival, once they are obtained, people may stop working. They do not make the accomplishment of a task an end in itself. This attitude is in sharp contrast to the belief in many industrial societies that work is a moral, and even a religious, virtue.

To the consternation of a production manager with a huge back order, the promise of overtime often fails to keep the workers on the job. In fact, raising employees' salaries frequently results in their working less (economists call this effect the backward-bending labor supply curve).

It is important, however, to note that an additional change has occurred repeatedly in many developing countries as more consumer goods have become available. The demonstration effect (seeing others with these goods) and improvements in infrastructure cause workers to realize they can have greater prestige and pleasure by owning more goods. Thus, their attitude toward work changes, not because of any alteration of their moral or religious values, but because they now want what only money can buy.

In industrialized nations, the opposite trend is being observed. As noted, in Germany there is a tendency toward shorter workweeks and longer vacations. Even in Japan the 48-hour week has been reduced to 40 hours. The Japanese still take far fewer paid vacation days annually (9) than workers in the United States (19), Great Britain (24), France (26), and Germany (29).

Prestigious jobs

Another aspect of the attitude toward work is the prestige associated with certain kinds of employment. In some countries, some types of work are considered more prestigious than others, but there is nowhere near the disdain for physical labor here as in many other developing countries. The result is an overabundance of attorneys and economists and a lack of toolmakers and welders even when the wages are higher for the latter. The distinction between blue-collar workers and office employees is especially great, as typified by the use of two words in Spanish for the worker—obrero (one who labors) signifies a blue-collar worker, whereas empleado (employee) signifies an office worker.

4.3 Significance to businesspeople

The lesson to be learned from this discussion is that it is highly possible that managers will encounter sharp differences in the attitudes toward work and achievement in other cultures compared to their own when they go overseas. However, they must recruit subordinates with a need to progress, whatever the underlying motive. One good source for such people is among relatively well-educated members of the lower social class who view work as a route to the prestige and social acceptance that have been denied to them because of their birth.

Attitudes toward change

American firms, accustomed to the rapid acceptance by Americans of something new, are frequently surprised to find that lots of other countries reflect very slowly when they face the new products, advanced technologies or new international marketing methods. Europeans are fond of reminding Americans that they are a young nation lacking traditions. And in the real world, it is more difficult for an European production manager to install a new process, a marketer to introduce a new product, or a treasurer to change an accounting system, because they think that they should respect their traditional methods.

New ideas

Yet, undeniably, international firms are agents of change, and their personnel must be able to counter resistance to it. A new idea will be more readily acceptable more closely it can be related to the traditional one while at the same time being made to show its relative advantage. In other words, the more consistent a new idea is with a society's attitudes and experiences, the more quickly it will be adopted.

Economic motivation

In these times of rising expectations, economic motives can be a strong influence for accepting change. Thus, if factory workers can be shown that their income will increase with a new machine or housewives can be convinced that a new frozen food will enable them to work and still provide satisfactory meals for their families, they can be persuaded by the gain in their economic welfare to accept ideas that they might otherwise oppose.

Religion

Religion, an important component of culture, is responsible for many of the attitudes and beliefs affecting human behavior. A good knowledge about the popular religions will contribute to a better understanding of why people's attitudes vary so greatly from country to country.

Work Ethics

We have already mentioned the marked differences in the attitudes toward work and achievement. Chinese, Europeans and Americans generally view work as a moral virtue and look down on the idle. This view stems in part from the Protestant work ethic as expressed by Luther and Calvin, who believed it was the duty of Christians to glorify

God by hard work and the practice of thrift.

In Asian countries where Confucianism prevails, this same attitude toward work is called the Confucian work ethic, and in Japan, it's called the Shinto work ethic after the principal religion of that nation. Interestingly, because of other factors—such as a growing feeling of prosperity and a shift to a five-day workweek (with two days off, workers develop new interests) —Japanese employers finds that younger workers no longer have the same dedication to their jobs that their predecessors had. Workers rarely show up early to warm the oil in their machines before their shifts start, and some management trainees are actually taking all of their 15 days' vacation time. A representative of the Employers Association states: "Our universities are leisure centers." A recent college graduate claims: "Students ski in the winter and play tennis in the summer. What the companies sometimes find out is that some new employees like skiing better than working."

The importance of religion to management

You have seen that religions have a pervasive influence on business. How effective can offers to pay time and a half for overtime and bonuses based on productivity be in a company whose workers are mainly Buddhists or Hindus? Strict adherents to these religions attempt to rid themselves of desires, and thus they have little need for an income beyond the amount necessary to sustain their lives. When their incomes begin to rise, they have a tendency to reduce their efforts so that personal incomes remain unchanged.

Religious holidays and rituals can affect employee performance and work scheduling. When members of different religious groups work together, there may even be strife, division, and instability within the work force. Managers must respect the religious beliefs of others and adapt business practices to the religious constraints present in other cultures. Of course, to be able to do this, they must first know what those beliefs and constraints are.

4.4 Material Culture

Material culture refers to all man-made objects and is concerned with how people make things (technology) and who makes what and why (economics).

Technology

The technology of a society is the mix of the usable knowledge that the society applies and directs toward the attainment of cultural and economic objectives; it exists in some form in every cultural organization. It is significant in the efforts of developing nations to improve their living standard and a vital factor in the competitive strategies of multinational firms.

Technological superiority is the goal of most companies, but it is especially important to international companies because:

(1) It enables a firm to be competitive or even attain leadership in world markets. At one time, Procter & Gamble and Unilever were competing worldwide for the laundry detergent market, but then P&G introduced Tide, a synthetic detergent with superior cleaning power. Its sales took off and left Unilever far behind. Finally, Unilever introduced its own synthetic detergent, but P&G had taken the lead.

(2) It can be sold (licensing or management contract), or it can be embodied in the company's products.

(3) It can give a firm confidence to enter a foreign market even when other companies are already established there.

(4) It can enable a firm to obtain better-than-usual conditions for a foreign market investment because the host government wants the technology that only the firm has (for example, permission for a wholly owned subsidiary in a country where the government normally insists on joint ventures with a local majority). For example, IBM, confident of its superior technology, insisted on and obtained permission from the Mexican government to set up a wholly owned subsidiary when other computer manufacturers were forced to accept local partners.

(5) It can enable a company with only a minority equity position to control a joint venture and preserve it as a captive market for semiprocessed inputs that it produces other than the joint venture.

(6) It can change the international division of labor. Some firms that had moved production overseas where labor was cheaper have now returned to their home countries because production methods based on new technology have reduced the direct labor content of their products, and because the labor costs are as low as 5 percent of the total cost in automated production systems. Numerous electronics manufacturers such as Tandy, Compaq, and Xerox have brought production back to these countries.

(7) It is causing major firms to form competitive alliances in which each partner shares technology and the high costs of research and development. When IBM realized that it needed liquid-crystal displays for portable computers, it formed a joint venture with Toshiba. IBM supplied the expertise in materials and Toshiba furnished superior manufacturing processes.

Cultural aspects of technology

Technology includes not only the application of science to production, but also skill in marketing, finance, and management. Its cultural aspects concern governments because their people may not be ready to accept the cultural changes a new technology may bring.

Technology's cultural aspects are certainly important to international managers, because new production methods and new products often require people to change their beliefs and ways of living. Self-employed farmer frequently finds the discipline of a factory worker excessively demanding. If workers have been accustomed to the production conditions of cottage industries in which each individual performs all of the production operations, they find it difficult to adjust to the monotony of tightening a single bolt.

The "throw away instead of repair" philosophy behind the design of so many new products necessitates a change in the habits of people who have been accustomed to repairing something to keep it operating until it is thoroughly worn out. Generally, the greater the difference between the old and new method or product, the more difficult it is for the firm to institute a change.

High GNP—high level of technology

The differences in levels of technology among nations are used as a basis for judging whether nations are developed or developing. Generally, a nation with a higher GNP per capita utilizes a higher level of technology than one whose per capita income is smaller. Because of technological dualism, however, analysts must not assume that since the general technological level in a market is low, the particular industry they are examining is employing a simple technology.

Technological dualism

Technological dualism is a prominent feature of many developing nations. In the same country, one industry sector may be technologically advanced, with high productivity, while that of another may be old and labor intensive. This condition may be the result of the host government's insistence that foreign investors import only the most modern machinery rather than used-but-serviceable equipment that would be less costly and could create more employment.

Sometimes, the preferences are reversed. The host government, beset by high unemployment, may argue for labor-intensive processes, while the foreign firm prefers automated production, because it is the kind the home office is most familiar with and because its use lessens the need for skilled labor, which is usually in short supply. To understand which policy the host government is following, management must study its laws and regulations and talk with host country officials.

Appropriate technology

Rather than choosing between labor-intensive and capital-intensive processes, many experts in economic development recommend appropriate technology, which can be labor-intensive, intermediate or capital-intensive. The guiding principle is to match technology with specific society. For example, in Africa, bricks are usually made in large-city factories using modern technology or locally in hand-poured, individual molds. In Botswana, an American group, designed an inexpensive small press with which four people can produce 1500 bricks a day. This is not only an intermediate technology but also an appropriate technology.

In India, a small manufacturer, Patel, has taken three-fourths of the detergent market from Lever, a giant multinational, by using labor-intensive technology. Lever's Surf brand dominated the market until Patel, realizing that a high-quality, high-priced product was not appropriate for a poor country, set up a chain of shops in which people mixed the ingredients by hand. This primitive method is tailored to Indian conditions and now enables the company to outsell Lever on the basis of price.

Boomerang effect

One reason firms sometimes fear to sell their technology abroad is the boomerang effect. For example, Japanese firms have become less willing to sell their technology to new industry economies, such as Korea and China. They fear that by giving Korea and China their technology today, they make the countries a tougher competitor tomorrow. As a result, Korea and China are turning more to the United States for technical assistance. This suggests why Korean-American ties of all kinds are strengthening. As an official from the Korean Ministry of Science and Technology said on a visit to the United States: "If America and Korea join together, we can overcome Japan." Interestingly, fear of the boomerang effect has caused some American firms to restrict the sale of their technology to the Japanese.

Government controls

The level of technology used by a foreign investor in a new manufacturing facility has a widespread impact. It affects the size of the investment, the quality and a number of workers employed, the kinds and quality of production inputs, what the facility can produce, and even what the host country can export. If the product cannot compete in the world market because its production costs are excessive, quality is inferior, or the design is obsolete, the host government will not obtain the foreign exchange.

For these reasons, plus what many governments consider abuses in the sale of technology, many developing countries enacted strong laws that control the purchase of technical assistance by, for example, limiting both royalties paid to and the requirements made by multinationals. The latter could include requiring licensees to transfer to licensors any improvements they make in the technology, prohibiting licensees from exporting, and obliging licensees to purchase raw materials from the licensor. Recently, however, host governments have recognized that technology is probably the most powerful stimulus to economic growth, so many are loosening controls as they pursue policies to attract foreign investment.

Economics

The decision global or multinational headquarters make as to the kind of technology to be used by a subsidiary will, within any constraints imposed by the host government, depend on various measurements of the material culture. Economic yardsticks such as power generated per capita and the number of high school graduates can pose possible problems in the distribution and promotion of the product, help determine market size, and provide information on the availability of resources such as raw materials, skilled and unskilled labor, capital equipment, economic infrastructure (communications, financial system), and management talent.

Education

Although education in its widest sense can be thought of as any part of the learning process that equips an individual to find his or her place in the adult society, nearly everyone in the Euramerican culture equates education with formal schooling.

Education yardsticks

The firm contemplating foreign investment has no indicators of the educational level of a country's inhabitants except the usual yardsticks of formal education: literacy rate, types of schools, quantity of schools and their enrollments, and possibly the amount per capita spent on education. Such data underestimate the size of the vocationally trained group in many developing countries where people learn to trade through apprenticeships starting at a very early age (12 to 13 years).

Like other international statistics, the published literacy rate must be suspected. One definition of adult literacy used by UNESCO is "the proportions of the population over the age of 15 who can, with understanding, read and write a short, simple statement on their everyday life." In some countries, the literacy census consists of asking respondents whether they can read and write, and the signing of their names is taken as proof of their literacy. Nevertheless, these data do provide some assistance. Marketers are interested in the literacy rate because it helps them decide what type of media to employ and at what level they should prepare advertisements, labels, point-of-purchase displays, and owner's manuals. Personnel manager will use the literacy rate as a guide in estimating what kinds of people will be available for staffing the operation.

As with most kinds of data, the trends in education should be studied. It is important to realize that the general level of education is rising throughout the world.

Note that in a little over 10 years, the percentage of adults aged 20 to 24 in post-high school education tripled in the low-income nations, increased by 11 times in the oil-exporting countries, and more than doubled in the high-income nations. The implication for international businesspeople is that they must prepare to meet the needs of more sophisticated and better-educated consumers. They also can expect a better-educated work force.

Although these data are indicative of the general level of education, unfortunately they tell us nothing about the quality of education, nor do they indicate how well the supply of graduates meets the demand.

Educational mix

Until the 1970s, management education in Europe lagged far behind what was available in the United States. There was a feeling that "managers were born, not made, and that they could be trained only on the job." Thus, there was little demand for formal business education.

However, a combination of factors has caused a proliferation of European business schools patterned on the American model:

(1) Increased competition in the European Union, resulting in a demand for better-trained managers.

(2) The return to Europe of American business school graduates.

(3) The establishment of American-type schools with American faculty and frequently with the assistance of American universities.

This trend has been much slower in developing countries except China, where, historically, higher education emphasized the study of the humanities, law, and medicine. Engineering was not popular because, with the exception of architecture and civil engineering, there were few engineering job opportunities in these preindustrial societies. Business education has been less popular than other fields because a business career lacked prestige. But, China's education has made great progress in recent years and over 6 million university students graduate from various universities every year, not only improving the quality of the nation but it also attracting more multinationals to invest, because they do not have to train their staff with large sums of money in China.

As developing nations industrialize, there is a greater competition in the marketplace and the job opportunities for engineers and business school graduates increase. Not only do the multinationals recruit such personnel, but local firms do so as well when they find that the new competition forces them to improve the efficiency of their operations.

4.5 Brain drain

Most developing nations are convinced that economic development is impossible without the development of human resources, and for the last two decades especially, governments have probably overinvested in higher education in relation to the demand for students. The result is raising unemployment among the educated, which has led to a brain drain, the emigration of professionals to industrialized nations. A study done by UNCTAD estimated that about 800,000 professionals had left Third World countries since World War II. However, the incidence of brain drain varied enormously because most come from a limited number of countries in Asia, such as India, Pakistan, Egypt, and Korea.

Brain drain facts

(1) Each year, 6,000 Taiwanese come to study in the United States, but only 20 percent return home.

(2) There are 8,000 Israeli engineers in the United States, which has created a severe bottleneck in its own development of sophisticated industry.

(3) About one-half of the 1,000 students who graduate annually from the 27 Philippine medical schools go abroad.

(4) The United States alone has 4,000 Greek research scientists, compared with just 5,000 living in Greece. There are also 1,200 Greek business professors working in the United States, but there is no MBA program in Greece and there is an acute shortage of skilled managers.

(5) In U.S. graduate schools of engineering, half of the assistant professors under age 35 are foreigners.

(6) At IBM's research headquarters, 27 percent of the researchers are foreigners.

Government authorities are deeply concerned about the loss of skills and have come to realize that there must be faster new job creation, not only to stop the costly loss but also to avoid serious political repercussions. To provide more jobs, they are adopting developmental plans that encourage labor-intensive exports and discourage the introduction of labor-saving processes. The pressure of the unemployed educated is also forcing officials in many areas to soften the terms for foreign investment.

Reverse brain drain

A reverse brain drain is preoccupying American educators and businesspeople. After suffering a severe brain drain for over 30 years, Korea and China are luring home those Korean and China's engineers and scientists with American doctorates and 10 or more years' experience in American high-tech firms. The attractions are higher salary and opportunities to start businesses in these industrializing countries. The returnees are having a visible effect on their countries' competitiveness. The director of the science office at Sun Microsystems says: "Half the engineering vice presidents in Taiwan electronics companies went to school in the United States, worked at Sun, worked at Hewlett-Packard, and brought back cash to Taiwan to start companies."

By now, more than 48 percent of those who obtained engineering doctorates at American universities were citizens of other countries. Because, after graduation, many stay to work in Silicon Valley and top R&D centers such as AT&T Bell Laboratories, they provide a vast talent pool to meet the needs of American industry. The director of the Commission on Professionals in Science and Technology said: "We've been counting on foreign graduates to stay here and fill our needs because we haven't been filling our own needs for a long time. There's nobody to replace them." Of course, with the development of Asia, especially the fast development of China, the situation is changing. Lots of engineers and scientists are coming back, because they think they can get better R&D conditions and returns in China. This is why lots of giant companies established their R&D centers in China.

Women's education

Another important trend is the fall of women's illiteracy rate. The literacy differences between older and younger female age groups are striking. In Africa, which has the world's highest illiteracy rate, the percentage of women who could read and write grew from 18 percent in 1970 to 50 percent by the end of last century.

Nearly every government now has a goal, if not an actual policy, of providing free and compulsory education for both genders. Many more women are enrolling in universities worldwide. The percentage of women attending universities in Africa and the Arab states has tripled in just 30 years.

These statistics are significant to businesspeople because in almost any country, educated women have fewer, healthier, and better-educated children than uneducated women do. They achieve higher labor force participation rates and higher earnings. Undoubtedly, this is leading to an increased role for women in the family's decision-making, which will require marketers to redo their promotional programs to take advantage of this consequential trend.

4.6 Language

Probably the most apparent cultural distinction that newcomers to international marketing perceive is in the means of communication. Differences in the spoken language are readily discernible, and after a short period in the new culture it becomes apparent that there are variations in the unspoken language (manners and customs) as well.

Spoken language

Language is the key to culture, and without it, people find themselves locked out of all but a culture's perimeter. At the same time, in learning a language, people can't understand nuances, double meanings of words, and slang unless they also learn the other aspects of the culture. Fortunately, the learning of both goes hand in hand; a certain overview a people and their attitudes naturally develops with a growing mastery of their language.

Languages delineate cultures

Spoken languages demarcate cultures, just as physical barriers do. In fact, nothing equals the spoken language for distinguishing one culture from another. If two languages are spoken in a country, there will be two separate cultures (Belgium); if four languages are spoken, there will be four cultures (Switzerland); and so forth.

A poll taken of the German-speaking and French-speaking cultures in Switzerland illustrates how deeply opinions on crucial issues diverge even in a small country. For example, 83.3 percent of the German Swiss regard environmental protection as one of Switzerland's five major problems, compared to 45.1 percent of the French Swiss.

Each linguistic region attaches different importance to particular problems. In German-speaking Switzerland, drugs head the list of worries. In French-speaking Switzerland and the Ticino (Italian-speaking), where jobless figures are higher, unemployment is seen as the No. 1 problem by far, ahead even of drugs. The energy tax that receives only guarded support of the German-speaking Swiss is opposed by the majority of the French-speaking area and totally rejected in Ticino.

What is occurring in Canada because of the sharp divisions between the English- and French-speaking regions is ample evidence of the force of languages in delineating cultures. The differences among the Basques, Catalans, and Spaniards and the differences between the French and Flemish of Belgium are other notable examples of the sharp cultural and often political differences between language groups. However, it does not follow from this generalization that cultures are the same wherever the same language is spoken. As a result of Spain's colonization, Spanish is the principal language of 21 Latin American nations, but no one should believe that Chile and Mexico are culturally similar. Moreover, generally because of cultural differences, many words in both written and spoken languages of these countries are completely different. Even within a country, words vary from one region to another, also due in part to cultural differences.

Foreign language

Where many spoken languages exist in a single country (India and many African nations), one foreign language usually serves as the principal vehicle for communication across cultures. Nations that were formerly colonies generally use the language of their ex-rulers; thus French is the lingua franca, or "link" language, of the former French and Belgian colonies in Africa, English in India, and Portuguese in Angola. Although they serve as a national language, these foreign substitutes are not the first language of all and, consequently, are less effective than the native tongues for reaching mass markets or for day-to-day conversations between managers and workers. Even in countries with only one principal language, such as Germany and France, there are problems of communication because of the large numbers of Greeks, Turks, Spaniards, and others who were recruited to ease labor shortages.

A German supervisor may have workers from three or four countries and be unable to speak directly with any of them. To ameliorate this situation, managements try to separate the work force according to origin; for instance, all Turks are placed in the paint shop, all Greeks on the assembly line, and so on. But the preferred solution is to teach managers the language of their workers. Invariably, such training results in an increase in production, fewer product defects, and higher worker morale.

General Tire-Chile sponsored a reverse language training program in which every employee could take free English courses given on the premises after work. Not only managers but also supervisors and even workers attended classes. The program was an excellent morale builder.

English, the link language of marketing

When a Swedish businessperson talks with a Japanese businessperson, the conversation generally will be in English. The use of English as a business lingua franca is spreading in Europe so rapidly that it is replacing French and German as the most widely spoken language among Europeans. Satellite television is credited for bringing it to millions of homes where English was previously not spoken. Already 10 million homes receive English news broadcasts from the Super Channel in England, and this number is growing today. Especially, with the fast development of China, more and more Chinese speak English and learning English is one of the most important tasks for lots of staff serving foreign companies.

In Norway, for example, learning English is compulsory; but even where it is not, young Europeans choose to study it as their second language. English is now spoken by 42 percent of the 15-to-25-year olds. This doubles the number of people who have learned French and is over four times as many who know German. A number of European multinationals such as Philips, the Dutch electronics manufacturer ($32 billion annual sales), and Olivetti, the Italian computer manufacturer ($6 billion annual sales) —have adopted English as their official language. Similarly, some major Japanese firms, such as Panisonic and Sony, use English as their international marketing language.

The local language

Even though more and more businesspeople are speaking English, when they are buyers, they insist on doing business in their own language. Sellers who speak it has a competitive edge. Moreover, knowing the language of a region indicates respect for its culture and its people.

In many countries, it is a social blunder to begin a business conversation by talking business. Most foreigners expect to establish a social relationship first, and the casual, exploratory conversation that precedes business talks may take from 15 minutes to several meetings, depending on the importance of the meetings. Obviously, people can establish a better rapport in a one-on-one conversation than through an interpreter. Look at the trouble this person would have avoided if he had spoken Spanish.

A German engineer, in Colombia to work on a pipeline, arrived at a hotel in the interior, where he tried to explain to the desk clerk that he had a suitcase full of cash that he wanted the hotel to keep. Because he knew no Spanish, he was having difficulty making himself understood. During the conversation, the desk clerk opened the suitcase in front of everyone in the lobby. A week later, the engineer was kidnapped by a guerrilla group and held for a month.

Translation

The ability to speak a language well does not eliminate the need for translators. Even the smallest of markets requires technical manuals, catalogs, and good advertising ideas, and a lack of local talent to do the work mean it is very difficult for organizations to achieve their marketing aims. The solution, even when the parent firm does not insist on international standardization, is to obtain this material from headquarters and have it translated if the costs are not prohibitive and suitable reproduction facilities are available locally. If the catalog or manual cannot be reproduced locally, the translation can be made and sent to the home office for reproduction. The home office already has the artwork, so the only additional cost is setting the type for the translation. Remember, though, French or Spanish translation will be up to 25 percent longer.

Resorting to headquarters to translate can be extremely risky because words from the same language frequently vary in meaning from one country to another or even from one region to another, as was mentioned earlier. A famous example that illustrated how only a single incorrectly translated word can ruin an otherwise good translation occurred in Mexico. The American headquarters of a deodorant manufacturer sent a Spanish translation of the manufacturer's international theme, "If you use our deodorant, you won't be embarrassed in public." Unfortunately, the translator used the word embarazada for embarrassed, which in Mexican Spanish means pregnant. Imagine the time that the Mexican subsidiary had with that one.

Use two translations

To avoid translation errors, experienced marketers will prefer what are really two translations. The first will be made by a bilingual native, whose work will then be translated back to a bilingual foreigner to see how it compares with the original. This work should preferably be done in the market where the material is to be used. No method is foolproof, but the double-translation approach is the safest way devised so far.

Some problems with translations

(1) Information about the air conditioner in a Japanese hotel— "Cooles and heates. If you want just condition of warm in your room, please control yourself."

(2) A Hong Kong dentist advertises— "Teeth extracted by the latest Methodists."

(3) The person that wrote this menu for a restaurant in Hong Kong got nothing right— "Rainbow troat, fillet streak, popotoes, chocolate mouse."

(4) A sign at a German campsite— "It is strictly forbidden on our camp site that people of different sex, for instance men and women, live together in one tent, unless they are married with each other for that purpose."

(5) A car rental agency in Tokyo suggests this to its customers— "When passenger of foot heave into sight, tootle the horn. Trumpet him melodiously at first but if he still obstacles your passage, then tootle him with vigor."

Technical words

Typically, translators have a problem with technical terms that do not exist in a language and with common words that have a special meaning for a certain industry. Portuguese, for example, is rich in fishing and marine terms, a reflection of Portugal material culture; but unlike English, it is exceedingly limited with respect to technical terms for the newer industries. The only solution is to employ English words or fabricate a new word in Portuguese. Unless translators have a special knowledge of a certain industry, they will go to dictionarys for a literal translation that frequently makes no sense or is erroneous.

Resolving such problems by using English words may not be a satisfactory solution even if the public understand them, especially in France or Spain, which have national academies to keep the language "pure". The French, in their continuous effort to keep their language free from English words, passed a bill in 1994 prohibiting the use of foreign words and phrases in all business and government communications, radio and TV broadcasts, and advertising when there are suitable French equivalents. This was the second victory for the Cultural Ministry that is in charge of "protecting the language from corruption." Earlier in 1994, the National Assembly adopted a law requiring the minimum 40 percent of the songs broadcast on radio to be in French.

International businesspeople need to know that other governments have similar programs to keep the local culture pure. For example, Canada has a heritage minister whose job is to "safeguard Canadian culture," and Mexico, as Wal-Mart learned, has tough laws about measurements on imported goods requiring labels in Spanish and in metric.

Wal-Mart has had language problems with the governments of both of America's NAFTA partners. Its New York stores broke the laws of Ontario by mailing circulars in English to residents of that French-speaking province; then the company was criticized for sending memos in English ordering Canadian employees to work extra hours without extra pay. Two months later, Mexican trade inspectors closed Wal-Mart's first supercenter store in Mexico City, charging the company with violating import regulations by not putting Spanish-language labels on its merchandise.

More than pride is involved here. The president of the Association of French-Speaking Computer Specialists, a former air force general, says foreign jargon makes work more difficult for French computer specialists who are not fluent in English and worse, it creates the impression among consumers that computing is a uniquely American science and that French computers are imitations that French buyers should avoid. The French culture minister says the time has come to head off an aggressive expansion of English in culture and trade: "A foreign language often becomes a tool of domination, uniformization, a factor of social exclusion, and, when used snobbishly, a language of contempt."

Note the economic reason for keeping the language pure and separate it from other languages. Those learning a foreign language are not only potential tourists but are likely to be empathetic toward anything that comes from that country. An Argentine engineer who reads French and not English will turn to French technical manuals and catalogs before specifying the machinery for the new power plant he is designing. However, if he constantly finds English technical terms in the French text, which forces him to consult his Spanish-English dictionary, he may decide to learn English and read American manuals and catalogs. Moreover, as the French general stated, if the French language didn't have the technical terms and American English did, this indicated that the discovery and development of the industry were occurring in the United States and China, not France, and that the Americans were the experts.

In Japan, the reverse situation exists, probably because for decades the country coveted foreign products while it struggled to overtake the more advanced West. Even now, most Japanese cars sold in the domestic market have almost nothing but English on them. A Nissan official explains that English is thought to be more attractive to the eye. Perhaps this is why people quench their thirst with a best-selling soft drink called "Pocari Sweat" and order from menus announcing "sand witches" and "Miss Gorilla" (mixed grill). They also puff away on a cigarette called Hopes.

No unpleasantness

One last aspect of the spoken language worthy of mention is the reluctance in many areas to say anything disagreeable to the listener. The politeness of Japanese and their consideration for others make "no" a little-used word even when there are disagreements. An American executive, pleased that her Japanese counterpart is nodding and saying yes to all of her proposals, may be shaken later to learn that all the time the listener was saying "yes" (I hear you) and "not yes" (I agree). Western managers who ask their Brazilian assistants whether something can be done may receive the answer rneio deficil (somewhat difficult). If managers take this answer literally, they will probably tell the assistants to do it anyway. The assistants will then elaborate on the difficulties until, hopefully, it will finally dawn on the executives that what they ask is impossible, but the Brazilians just don't want to give them the bad news.

Unspoken language

Nonverbal communication, or the unspoken language, can often tell businesspeople something that the spoken language does not—if they understand it. Unfortunately, the differences in customs among cultures may cause misinterpretations of communication.

Gestures

Although gestures are a common form of cross-cultural communication, the language of gestures varies from one region to another. For instance, Americans and most Europeans understand the thumbs-up gesture meaning "all right", but in southern Italy and Greece, it transmits the message for which we reserve the middle finger. Making a circle with the thumb and the forefinger is friendly in the United States, but it means "you're worth zero" in France and Belgium and is a vulgar sexual invitation in Greece and Turkey. The best advice for the foreign traveler is to leave gestures at home.

Closed doors

Americans know that one of the perquisites of an important executive is a large office with a door that can be closed. Normally, the door is open as a signal that the occupant is ready to receive others, but when it is closed, something of importance is going on. Contrary to the American open-door policy, Germans regularly keep their doors closed. Hall, the noted anthropologist mentioned at the beginning of this chapter, says that the closed door does not mean that the person behind it wants no visitors but only that he or she considers open doors sloppy and disorderly.

Office size

Although office size is an indicator of a person's importance, it means different things to different cultures. In the United States and China, the higher the status of the executive, the larger and more secluded the office; but in the Arab world, the president may be in what for us is a small, crowded office. In Japan, the top floor of a department store is reserved for the "bargain basement" (bargain penthouse) and not for top management. The French people prefer to locate important department heads in the center of activities, with their assistants located outward on radii from this center. To be safe, never gauge people's importance by the size and location of their offices.

Conversational distance

Anthropologists report that conversational distances are smaller in the Middle East and Latin America, though our personal experience in Latin America has not shown this to be the case. Whether this generality is true or false, we must remember that generalities are like arithmetic means; perhaps more people don't act in a certain way based on their own cultural traditions, but business people will be dealing with just a few nationals at a time. Luck may have it that he or she will meet exceptions to the stereotype.

The language of gift giving

Gift giving is an important aspect of every businessperson's life in both China and overseas. Entertainment outside office hours and the exchange of gifts are part of the process of getting better acquainted. However, the etiquette or language of gift giving varies among cultures, just as the spoken language does, and although foreigners will usually be forgiven for not knowing the language, certainly they and their gifts will be better received if they follow local customs.

Acceptable gifts

In Japan, for example, one never gives an unwrapped gift or visits a Japanese home empty-handed. A gift is presented with the comment that it is only a trifle, which implies that the humble social position of the giver does not permit giving a gift in keeping with the high status of the recipient. He in turn will not open the gift in front of the giver because he knows better than to embarrass him by exposing the trifle in the giver's presence.

The Japanese use gift giving to convey one's thoughtfulness and consideration for the receiver, who overtime builds up trust and confidence in the giver. Japanese never give four of anything or an item with four in the name because the word sounds like the one for death, White and yellow flowers are not good choices for gifts because in many areas they connote death. In Germany, red roses to a woman indicate strong feelings for her, and if you give cutlery, always ask for a coin in payment so that the gift will not cut your friendship. Cutlery is a friendship cutter for the Russians and French also.

Traditions vary greatly throughout the world, but generally safe gifts everywhere are chocolates, red roses, and a good Scotch whiskey (not in the Arab world, however—instead, bring a good book or something useful for the office).

Gifts or bribes?

The questionable payments scandals (called bribery scandals by the press) exposed the practice of giving very expensive gifts and money to well-placed government officials in return for special favors, large orders, and protection. Some payments were bribes; that is, payments were made to induce the payee to do something for the payer that is illegal. But others were extortion made to keep the payee from harming the payer in some way. Still others were tips to induce government officials to do their jobs.

All three are payments for services, and usually they are combinations of two or possibly all three types. To distinguish among them, look at this example. If you tip the headwaiter to get a good table, that is a bribe; but if you tip him because you know that without it, he'll put you near the kitchen, that's extortion. If you tip him for good service after eating, that is a tip. Part of the problem of adhering to American laws is the difficulty in making this distinction.

Although the media exposure about questionable payments is fairly recent, for a long time it has been common knowledge in the international marketing community that gifts or money payments are necessary to obtain favorable action from government officials, whether to obtain a large order, avoid having a plant shut down, or receive faster service from customs agents.

Their pervasiveness worldwide is illustrated by the variety of names for bribes—mordida (bite in Latin America), dash (West Africa), pot de vin (jug of wine—France), la bustarella (envelope left on Italian bureaucrat's desk), or grease (United States). Even Russians were not exempt according to a Business International study of multinational managers, who declared that representatives of the Russian state trading organization permitted gifts to be deposited in their Swiss bank accounts.

Questionable payments

These come in all forms and sizes, from the petty "expediting" payments that were necessary to get poorly paid government officials to do their normal duties to huge sums to win large orders.

Included by the Securities and Exchange Commission (SEC) as questionable payments are contributions to foreign political parties and the payment of agents' commissions, even when these actions are not illegal in the country where they are made. By means of the Foreign Corrupt Practices Act, the United States is, in effect, requiring American firms to operate elsewhere according to this country's laws, which frequently places these firms at a competitive disadvantage. Many managers have responded by issuing strict orders not to make any questionable payments, legal or illegal, and some have been surprised to find that their business has not fallen off as they expected. Their action has been reinforced by a number of governments that have either passed stricter laws or begun to enforce those they already have. Given the combination of low salaries of foreign officials and the intense competition for business, one should not be too sanguine about the prospects for completely eliminating this practice.

One of the first acts is to require the chairmen or presidents of foreign firms that do business with Ecuador and government buyers to sign statements promising there will be no bribes. One early task is to enforce tight rules when awarding contracts for a hydroelectric project costing several hundred million dollars. Some American firms are supportive, but Japanese companies have rebuffed the group as they are not eager to halt bribery. EU companies, for whom bribe payments are legitimate business deductions, also show little interest.

4.7 Societal organization

Every society has a structure or an organization that is the patterned arrangement of relationships defining and regulating the manner by which its members interface with one another. Anthropologists generally study this important aspect of culture by breaking down its parts into two classes of institutions: those based on kinship and those based on the free association of individuals.

Kinship

Family is the basic unit of institutions based on kinship. Unlike the American family, which is generally composed of parents and their children, families in many nations—especially in developing ones—are extended to include all relatives by blood and by marriage. In common situation, families in developed countries are smaller than those in developing countries and it will influence international marketing very much.

Extended family

For the foreign firm, the extended family is a source of employees and business connections. The trust that people place in their relatives, however distant, may motivate them to buy from a supplier owned by their cousin's cousin, even though the price is higher. Local personnel managers are prone to fill the best jobs with family members, regardless of their qualifications. In China, the situation is very popular in some areas although it has changed with the development of economy. And family firms occupy the very important position in economy, especially in the private sector.

Member's responsibility

Although an extended family is large, each member's feeling of responsibility is strong. An individual's initiative to work is discouraged when he or she may be asked to share personal earnings with unemployed extended family members, no matter what the kinship is. Responsibility to the family is frequently a cause of high absenteeism in developing countries where the workers are called home to help with harvesting. Management has spent large sums to provide comfortable housing for workers and their immediate families, only to find them living in crowded conditions when members of the extended family have moved in.

For example, in Latin America, the extended family form is common. Individuals use the maternal surname (Marin) as well as the paternal (Diaz) to indicate both branches of the family. It is a common sight to find two businesspeople or a businessperson and a government official, when meeting for the first time, exploring each other's family tree to see whether they have common relatives. If they find any kinship at all, the meeting goes much more smoothly. After all, they're relatives.

Associations

Social units not based on kinship, known as associations by anthropologists, may be formed by age, gender, or common interest.

Age

Manufacturers of consumer goods are well aware of the importance of segmenting a market by age groups, which often cut across cultures. This fact has enabled marketers to succeed in selling such products as clothing and records to the youth market in both developed and developing nations. However, international marketers may go too far if they assume young people everywhere exert the same buying influence on their parents as they do in this field.

For example, Kellogg's attempt to sell cereals in Great Britain through children was not successful because English mothers are less influenced by their children with respect to product choice than Chinese mothers. Senior citizens form an important segment in the United States, where older people live away from their children; but where the extended family concept is prevalent, older people continue to live with and exert a powerful influence on younger members of the family.

Gender

Generally, the less developed the country, the less equal are the genders with respect to job opportunities and education. Even in the US, the salary of male is higher than the female although they are doing the same job.

But the situation is changing with the development of economy and society. As nations industrialize, more women enter the job market and thus assume greater importance in the economy. This trend is receiving further impetus as women's movement for equality of the sexes spreads to the traditionally male-dominated societies of less developed countries. Among the industrialized nations, the United States has the greatest percentage of women in upper management. Although women in Germany, Great Britain, Denmark, and France make up 40 percent of the work force, only 4 percent are in executive positions. According to a United Nations report, women do two-thirds of the world's work, receive a tenth of its income, and own a hundredth of its property.

A word of caution, however, must be given to those who, noting the apparently sequestered life of women in some areas, conclude that they have little voice in what the family buys or how it acts. Despite the outward appearance of male domination, women exert a far more powerful influence behind closed doors than the unknowing outsider might suspect.

Common interest

Common interest groups are composed of people joined together by a common bond, which can be political, occupational, recreational, or religious. Even before entering a country, management should identify such groups and assess their political and economic power. As we will see in later chapters, consumer organizations have forced firms to change their product, promotion, and prices, and investments have been supported or opposed by labor unions, which are often a powerful political force.

Class mobility

In most countries, the ease of moving from one social class to another lies in a continuum. For example, from the rigid caste system of India to the relatively flexible social structure of western countries. Less developed countries tend to be located nearer the position of India, whereas industrial nations are closer to the U. S. position. As industrialization progresses, barriers to mobility weaken. Management must assess mobility between classes because interclass rigidity, especially when accompanied by low social status for business, can make it extremely difficult for a firm to obtain good management personnel locally.

To help managers of IBM understand many national cultures in which the company operates, Geert Hofstede, a Danish psychologist, interviewed thousands of employees in 67 countries. He found that the differences in their answers to 32 statements could be based on four value dimensions: ① individualism versus collectivism, ② large versus small power distance, ③ strong versus weak uncertainty avoidance, and ④ masculinity versus femininity.

Individualism versus collectivism

According to Hofstede, the Danish psychologist, people in collectivistic cultures belong to groups that are supposed to look after them in exchange for loyalty, whereas people in individualistic cultures are only supposed to look after themselves and their immediate family. Therefore, organizations operating in collectivistic cultures are more likely to rely on group decision making than those in individualistic cultures where the emphasis is on individual decision making.

Large versus small power distance

Power distance is the extent to which members of a society accept the unequal distribution of power among individuals. In large power distance societies, employees believe their supervisors are right even when they are wrong, thus employees do not take any initiative in making nonroutine decisions. On the other hand, a participative management style of leadership is likely to be productive for an organization in a low power distance country.

Strong versus weak uncertainty avoidance

This is the degree to which members of a society feel threatened by ambiguity and are reluctant to take risks. Employees in high risk-avoidance cultures such as Japan, Greece, and Portugal tend to stay with their organizations for a long time. Those from low risk-avoidance nations such as the United States, Singapore, and Denmark, however, are much more mobile. It should be apparent that organizational change in high uncertainty-avoidance nations is likely to receive strong resistance from employees, which makes the implementation of change difficult to administer.

Masculinity versus femininity

This is the degree to which the dominant values in a society emphasize assertiveness, acquisition of money and status, and achievement of visible and symbolic organizational rewards (masculinity) as compared to the degree to which they emphasize people relationships, concern for others, and the overall quality of life (femininity).

In a word, culture will influence your international marketing in various layers and the managers of international companies have to study the differences between their own culture and that of the target markets if they want to be successful in international marketing. Compared with the famous international companies, Chinese companies lost more in the world market, and one of the most important reasons is that they don't understand foreign culture, especially the western culture.

Summary

1. Understand the significance of culture for international marketing. To be successful in their relationships overseas, international businesspeople must be students of culture. They must not only have factual knowledge, but also become culturally sensitive. Culture affects all functional areas of the firm.

2. Understand the sociocultural components of culture. Although experts differ as to the components of culture, the following is representative of what numerous anthropologists believe to exist: ① aesthetics, ② attitudes and beliefs, ③ religion, ④ material culture, ⑤ education, ⑥ language, ⑦ societal organization, ⑧ legal characteristics, and ⑨ political structures.

3. Appreciate the significance of religion to businesspeople. Knowing the basic contents of other religions will contribute to a better understanding of their follower's attitudes. This may be a major factor in a given market.

4. Comprehend the cultural aspects of technology. Material culture, especially technology, is important to management contemplating overseas investment. Foreign governments have become increasingly involved in the sale and control of technical assistance. Technology may enable a firm to enter a new market successfully even where competitors are already established. It often enables the firm to obtain superior conditions for an overseas investment because the host government needs technology.

5. Discuss the impact of the "brain drain" and the "reverse brain drain" on developed and developing nations. Developed nations have received thousands of scientists and highly-trained professionals from developing nations without contributing any part of the cost of their education. They also have lost hundreds of scientists who obtained industrial experience in developed countries because of the reverse brain drain.

6. Appreciate the importance of the ability to speak a local language. Language is the key to culture. An understanding a people and their attitudes naturally develops with a growing mastery of their language.

7. Recognize the importance of the unspoken language in international business. Because the unspoken language can often tell businesspeople something that the spoken language does not, they should know something about this form of cross-cultural communication.

8. Discuss the two classes of relationships within a society. A knowledge of how a society is organized is useful because the arrangement of relationships within it defines and regulates the manner in which its members interface with one another. Anthropologists have broken down societal relationships into two classes: those based on kinship and those based on free association of individuals.

9. Discuss Hofstede's four cultural value dimensions. Geert Hofstede, a Danish psychologist, interviewed IBM employees in 67 countries and found that the differences in their answers to 32 statements could be based on four value dimensions: ① individualism versus collectivism, ② large versus small power distance, ③ strong versus weak uncertainty, ④ masculinity versus femininity. These dimensions assist managers to understand how cultural differences affect organizations and management methods.

Questions

1. Why is it helpful for international businesspeople to know that a national culture has two components?

2. The knowledge of culture has been responsible for Disney's success in Tokyo, and ignorance of culture has been responsible for the company's large losses in Paris. Discuss.

3. Why do international businesspersons need to consider aesthetics when making marketing decision?

4. Give an example to demonstrate how to use the culture factors to improve productivity and sales.

5. Some societies view change differently from Americans. What impact does this have on the way American marketers operate in those markets?

6. Why must international businesspeople be acquainted with the beliefs of the major religions in the areas in which they work?

7. What questions do you have to care when you want to develop your business in a Buddhist belief country?

8. Why is technological superiority especially significant for international firms?

9. What is the significance of the extended family for international managers?

10. Use Hofstede's four dimensions to analyze this situation: John Adams, with

20 years' experience as general foreman in the United States, is sent as production superintendent to his firm's new plant in Colombia. He was chosen because of his outstanding success in handling workers. Adams has never been to Colombia and he does not understand the local management style. Can you foresee him having any problems on this new job?

Minicase

Be Attuned to Business Etiquette

The proverb "When in Rome, do as the Romans do" applies to business representatives as well as tourists. Being attuned to a country's business etiquette can make or break a sale, particularly in countries where 1,000-year-old traditions can dictate the rules for proper behavior. Anyone interested in being a successful marketer should be aware of the following considerations:

(1) Local customer, etiquette, and protocol. An exporter's behavior in a foreign country can reflect favorably or unfavorably on the exporter, the company, and even the sales potential for the product.

(2) Body language and facial expressions. Often, actions do speak louder than words.

(3) Expressions of appreciation. Giving and receiving gifts can be a touchy subject in many countries. Doing it badly may be worse than not doing it at all.

(4) Choices of words. Knowing when and whether to use slang, tell a joke, or just keep silent is important.

The following informal test will help exporters rate their business etiquette. See how many of the following you can answer correctly.

1. You are in a business meeting in an Arabian Gulf country. You are offered a small cup of bitter cardamom coffee. After your cup has been refilled several times, you decide you don't feel like any more. How do you decline the next cup offered to you?

A. Place your palm over the top of the cup when the coffee pot is passed.

B. Turn your empty cup upside down on the table.

C. Hold the cup and twist your wrist from side to side.

2. In which of the following countries are you expected to be punctual for business meetings?

A. Peru

B. America

C. Japan

D. China

E. Morocco

3. Gift giving is prevalent in Japanese society. A business acquaintance presents you with a small wrapped package. You should:

A. open the present immediately and thank the giver.

B. thank the giver and open the present later.

C. suggest that the giver open the present for you.

4. In which of the following countries is tipping considered an insult?

A. Great Britain

B. Iceland

C. Canada

5. What is the normal workweek in Saudi Arabia?

A. Monday through Friday

B. Friday through Tuesday

C. Saturday through Wednesday

6. You are in a business meeting in Seoul. Your Korean business associate hands you his business card, which states his name in the traditional Korean order: Park Chul Su. How do you address him?

A. Mr. Park

B. Mr. Chul

C. Mr. Su

7. In general, which of the following would be good topics of conversation in Latin American countries?

A. Sports

B. Religion

C. Local politics

D. The weather

E. Travel

8. In many countries, visitors are often entertained in clients' homes. Taking flowers as a gift to the hostess is usually a safe way to express thanks for the hospitality. However, both the type and color of the flower can have amorous, negative, or even ominous implications. Match the country with the flower which, if presented is regarded as a social faux pas.

Brazil	Red roses
France	Purple flowers
Switzerland	Chrysanthemums

9. In Middle Eastern countries, which hand does one use to accept or pass food?

A. Right hand

B. Left hand

C. Either hand

10. Body language is just as important as spoken language in many countries. For example, in most countries, the thumbs-up sign means "OK." But in which of the following countries is the sign considered a rude gesture?

A. Germany

B. Italy

C. Australia

Chapter 5 Political Forces

Concept preview

After reading this chapter, you should be able to

1. Appreciate: how political forces influence your international marketing decisions.

2. Understand: an oppressive government is to be more feared than a tiger.

3. Distinguish: the different effects of the domestic, foreign and international political forces.

4. Comprehend: the importance of the political climate.

5. Describe: the difference between the conservative and liberal trade policies.

Among all of the environmental factors, political forces are decisive to influence the business results of the multinationals. In order to gain international renown, multinationals must appease the political environment of host countries. After all, the political environment plays a very important role in business success. Because every country has its own independent political system and regulations, the governments have the power to permit or prohibit foreign companies to do business in their own countries. When facing the various regulations coming from the host governments, the multinational companies should understand that they always can do nothing, except accepting. They are guests and the regulations are made by the hosts.

At the same time, politics is the concentrated reflection of the economy and influences the economy very much. In the real world, no economic activities can be independent out of the politic. In this chapter, we will discuss some questions about how to overcome the political barriers and how to avoid the political risk as a multinational company.

5.1 The international political relationship

All of the international marketing activities of multinationals will be influenced by the political factors in the practice and the effect will be great and far-reaching. This is why the managements of multinationals have to study and care international relationships in the real world.

International political relationship is the relationship between separate countries, for example, Sino-U. S. relations, Sino-Japan relations and Sino-EU relations, etc. Sometimes it is the relationship between international political groups, for example the western-eastern relation and south-north relation. International political relationship is a very complicated question and in this book we will discuss some questions that influence international marketing directly.

Bilateral ties

For international companies, if they want to develop a new market, the first question that they have to consider is the bilateral ties between the home and host countries. Bilateral ties may not only include the economic relationship, but also includes the political, culture, law and military relationships. For example, it is very impossible for an America company to develop Iran's market today and an India company will have to face lots of insurmountable difficulties if it wants to establish a plant in Pakistan.

Every country has a special relationship with other countries and their political relationship changes with the social and economic development of the world. All of the relationships will influence your international marketing, sometimes it may be favorable for you and sometimes it may be unfavorable for you. As the multinational manager, you have to focus on the change and use it as leverage for your business in the real world. For example, in the 1970s, the relationship between China and America began to take a turn for the better and the situation created very huge business opportunity for American companies. Furthermore, the better relationship between China and America influenced other countries, especially Japan and the European countries. Today, China is the largest export country of the world and this would've been unimaginable if China had bad political relationships with other countries.

Sometimes, the political relationship will influence international marketing dramatically. For example, Israel does not accept any investments coming from the Arab countries, its trade partners are only the countries that support its polices and the most important factors influencing the international market for Israel are political forces, not the economic forces. Before 1960, Cuba was one of the most important oversea markets for lots of American companies, the situation changed after Castro came into power. The same case happened in Iran, most of the American companies had to draw out from Iran's market after Ruhollah Khomeini controlled the government.

In a word, political relationships between two countries always can decide your trade partners and it can decide which country you should choose to invest in the practice. For a multinational manager, you have to notice the following questions when you want to study how the political force influences your international marketing:

The government's attitude to the foreign investment

For different countries, they take different policies to achieve their countries' goals in the real world. Because of this, they will have a different attitude towards foreign investments. Some of them welcome the foreign investment to support their economic development, some of them are against foreign investments and some of them welcome foreign investments under some preconditions, etc. In general, the various countries will take different policies for foreign trade and foreign investment; specific policies include:

1. Encourage

Most countries, especially the developing countries encourage foreign investment, because not only can the investment create more employment for the country, but it also can help the local companies improve their technology and management. As a matter of fact, the Chinese economy has made great progress in the past 30 years, one of the most important reasons is that foreign companies have, not only, brought capital for China, but they have also created large sums of output value, and improved the technology of production and management.

At the same time, the foreign investors develop oversea markets for the local companies. Although the foreign companies seized lots of the profits in the Chinese market, the advantages far outweigh the disadvantages. This is why the Chinese government encourages the local governments to take more favorable policies such as establishing the free trade areas and free trade ports to spur multinational companies to invest in China, besides, the Chinese government offered the tax favorable policies to attract the foreign investments.

2. Limitation

As some governments want to protect the national industries, they take strict restrictions to prevent foreign companies from entering their markets. Particularly, if the multinational companies want to enter ares in telecommunication, electric equipment, oil, chemical and financial industries, they must face the strict restrictions. And sometimes, the government will only permit the foreign companies to take joint ventures with the local companies. The wholly owned subsidiaries are stopped. For example, the Indian government asked the foreign exporters to obey the import quota, paid the inconvertible currency to the exporters and asked that the Indian should take enough management positions in joint ventures, even in the wholly owned subsidiaries. IBM had to withdraw from India in the late 1990s because they could not accept these rules.

Even the developed countries may take restrictions to limit foreign companies to enter their markets, for example, the European countries offered the strict computer chip price to limit Asia's chip to enter their markets and Korea took higher tariffs for the car to support the local car production.

The major countermeasures for the governments to limit the multinational companies include: tariff control, price control, labor, import quota, exchange control and administration intervention, etc. Almost all host countries may control the profit and credit; control the impact on the local companies; and control the foreign equity to protect their national industries. In the real world, the government always take the multi-polices to limit the foreign companies to take the advantageous market position, especially if you want to enter some of the important industries, like telecommunication and finance industries of China, you can expect the strict restrictions from the government.

3. Prohibition

Few countries use prohibition policies to stop foreign companies to enter their markets. However, some governments may take secluding policies to protect their industries and markets. The reason for the countries to enact these policies is that they are afraid of international investment and international trade. More specifically:

(1) They are afraid that giant international companies may acquire the local companies.

(2) They are afraid that giant multinational companies may hurt the benefits of the host countries and weaken their economy.

(3) They think that the multinational companies may not promote the development of the country because of some special reasons.

(4) They think the multinational companies will bring the negative effect on the host country's society and culture.

Of course, whether or not these policies are enacted to stop the foreign companies from entering the market depends on the political atmosphere and political sensitivity of the country, this so called political sensitivity is how much effect the imported products or foreign investment may influence the local politics. If the political sensitivity is very strong, it indicates the products or foreign investment will influence the local living and the government very much and the government will keep close watch on it or the government may think the products or foreign investment are a threat for the political system and they do not welcome the foreigners to enter their markets. Even the world's largest economic equity, America, doubts some of the foreign investments. For example, Huawei failed when it wanted to acquire an America company in 2010, because the American government thought the merger would harm the local or even the country's benefit. So the multinational companies have to balance the relationship between acquiring profits and promoting the local economic development.

The famous professor, Richard Robinson, offered a method to assess the political sensitivity. The specific procedure asked managers of multinational companies to answer the following 12 questions first, then he would give each question specific amount of points, "yes" is 10 points, "no" is 1 point, and other answers you can give 2～9 points based on your specific situations. The higher point represents the higher political sensitivity. The questions are:

(1) Whether or not you have to get the permission from the host government or relative legislative assembly body if you want to take your international marketing in the host market.

(2) Whether or not the other industries rely on your products or your products are the materials for the other industries? For example, cement, steel, or electricity, etc.

(3) Whether or not your products are socially or politically sensitive? For example, medicine, food, or financial, etc.

(4) Whether or not your products will influence the host country's national defense? For example, the transportation and telecommunication products, etc.

(5) Whether or not your products will influence the host country's agriculture? For example, chemical fertilizer and agricultural machinery, etc.

(6) Whether or not your products have to rely on the local resources to produce or sell? For example, local labor and local materials, etc.

(7) Whether or not the competitive industries will occupy your market in a short time? Example, if the various small scale investments will influence your market share, etc.

(8) Whether or not your products contact to the mess communication? For example, print and TV, etc.

(9) Whether or not your products are service products? Example, financial and security, etc.

(10) Whether or not your products rely on the demand of the law.

(11) Whether or not your products may hurt the consumers.

(12) Whether or not your products will reduce the host country's foreign exchange because of your international marketing.

5.2 The stability of the government's policy

The stability of the host government's policies will influence the international marketing result directly. For example, after 1992, foreign investment began to grow very fast in China, because Mr. Deng Xiaoping said that reform and opening-up policy of China would continue 100 years in Shenzhen. For the international managers, they have to pay close attention to the factors that may change the policies of host countries and whether or not the policies made by host governments are stability. In a common situation, the instability comes from the change of government structure or head of government, and the result is that they may change the foreign investment and trade policies.

It is impossible for any government to make no changes in foreign policies, but the long-term stability is very important for any multinational company to develop the foreign markets, because the stability means more profits for the multinational companies in the real world. This is because they have to operate a long time in a market if they want to make enough investment return. We cannot image that the international companies can make more money in a country that the government or its foreign policies often change. As a matter of fact, the Liberal Democratic Party of Japan controlled the government for over 50 years, and in that period, the Japanese economy grew very fast. However, the economic development of Japan is facing various problems, the very important reason is that the multiparty political system makes the government unstable and its foreign policies can not last for a long time. This is why Japan lost its advantages in lots of economic fields.

In a number of ways, the political climate of the country in which a business operates is as important as the country's topography, its natural resources, and its meteorological climate. Indeed, we shall see examples in which a hospitable and stable government can encourage business investment and growth despite geographic or weather obstacles and scarcity of natural resources. The opposite is equally true. Some areas of the world that are relatively blessed with natural resources and manageable topography and weather have developed very slowly because of government instability. Occasionally, a country's government is hostile to investment in its territory by foreign companies even though they might provide capital, technology, and training for the development of the country's resources and people.

Many of the political forces with which business must cope have ideological sources, but there are a large number of other sources. These include nationalism, terrorism, traditional hostilities, unstable governments, international organizations, and government-owned business.

It should be pointed out that the international company itself can be a political force. Some firms have budgets or sales larger than the GNP of some of the countries with which they negotiate. Although budgets and GNPs do not translate directly or necessarily into power, it should be clear that companies with bigger budgets and countries with bigger GNPs possess more assets and facilities with which to negotiate.

This chapter will provide an indication of the types of risks to private business posed by political forces. As we shall see, some of the risks can stem from more than one political force. Such names as communism, socialism, capitalism, liberal, conservative, left wing, and right wing are used to describe governments, political parties, and people. These names indicate ideological beliefs.

5.3 The different political system

Capitalism

Capitalism, the free enterprise idea is that all the factors of production should be privately owned. Under ideal capitalism, government would be restricted to those functions that the private sector cannot perform: national defense, police, fire, and other public services and government-to-government international relations. In fact, no such government exists.

The reality in so-called capitalist countries is quite complex. The governments of such countries typically regulate privately owned businesses quite closely, however, the private companies always can occupy the dominant position in the economic field, and the foreign policies of these countries are influenced or even decided by some of the private consortium in such countries. The U. S. is the typical example of capitalism.

Socialism

Socialism advocates government ownership or control of the basic means of production, distribution, and exchange. Profit is not an aim. In practice, the so-called socialist governments have frequently performed in ways which are not consistent with the doctrine. One of the most startling examples of this is Singapore, which professes to be a socialist state but in reality is aggressively capitalistic.

European socialism

In Europe, socialist parties have been in power in several countries, including Great Britain, France, Spain, Greece, and Germany. In Britain, the Labor party has nationalized some basic industries, such as steel, shipbuilding, coal mining, and the railroads, but has not gone much further in that direction. A vocal left wing of the Labor party advocates nationalizing all major British businesses, banks, and insurance companies.

Social Democrat is the name the Germans use for their socialist political party. During the several years that this party was in power before it lost to the Christian Democrats in 1982, it nationalized nothing and, in action and word, seemed more capitalist than socialist. The socialist governments of France and Spain have embarked on programs to privatize government-owned businesses; such programs do not conform to pure socialist doctrine.

LDC socialism

The less developed countries (LDCs) often profess and practice some degrees of socialism. The government typically owns and controls most of the factors of production. Shortages of capital, technology, and skilled management and labor are characteristic of an LDC, and DCs (developed countries) or international organizations often provide aid through the LDC government. Also, many of the educated citizens of an LDC tend to be in or connected with the government. It follows that the government would own or control major factories and farms.

Most socialist LDCs make occasional exceptions and permit capital investment. This happens when the LDC perceives advantages that would not be possible without the private capital, such as more jobs for its people, new technology, skilled managers or technicians, and export opportunities.

Risks for businesses dealing with socialist countries

The practices of the countries that profess socialism range widely. In Singapore, for example, businesspeople must be careful to comply with all the applicable laws and regulations, as in any capitalist country. At the other extreme, such as in an LDC, most or all of the major production factors are government-owned, that is to say, your international marketing must rely on the local officials in most cases. Because the stock equity belongs to the country, you have to use more no-market countermeasures to achieve your business targets.

Conservative or liberal

We should not leave the subject of ideology without mentioning of these words as they have come to be used today. Politically, in the United States, the word conservative connotes a person, group, or party that wishes to minimize government activity and maximize the activities of private businesses and individuals. Conservative used to mean something similar to right wing, but in the United States and the United Kingdom, the latter is more extreme. For instance, the Conservative party, one of the major political parties in the United Kingdom, is said to have a right-wing minority.

Politically, in the United States in the 20th century, the word liberal has come to mean the opposite of what it meant in the 19th century. It now means a person, group, or party that urges greater government participation in the economy and regulation or ownership of business. Liberal and left wing are similar, but the latter generally indicates more extreme positions closer to socialism.

We do not want to overemphasize the importance of the labels conservative, liberal, right wing, and left wing. For one thing, individuals and organizations may change over time or may change as they perceive shifts in the moods of voters. Some feel that these labels are too simplistic or even na? ve and that reality is more complex. Nevertheless, we wanted to bring them to your attention because they are frequently used in discussions of international events and because different political forces flow from, for example, a right-wing government than from a left-wing one. Businesspeople must do their best to influence those political forces and then forecast and react to them.

One might reasonably assume that government ownership of the factors of production is found only in socialist countries, but that assumption is not correct. Large segments of business are owned by the governments of numerous countries that do not consider themselves as either capitalist or socialist. From country to country, there are wide differences in the industries that are government owned.

Regulations and red tape

All businesses are subject to countless government laws, regulations, and red tape in their activities in the United States and all other capitalist countries. Special government approval is required to practice profession such as law or medicine. Tailored sets of laws and regulations govern banking, insurance, transportation, and utilities. States and local governments require business licenses and impose use restrictions on buildings and areas. Complying with all the laws and regulations and coping with the red tape require expertise, time, and of course, expense. A business found in noncompliance may incur fines or even the imprisonment of its management.

5.4 Reasons for nationalization

There are a number of reasons, sometimes overlapping, why governments collectivize firms. Some of them are:

(1) To extract more money from the firms, the government suspects that the firms

are concealing profits.

(2) An extension of the first reason, the government believes it could run the firms more efficiently and make more money.

(3) Ideological, when left-wing governments are elected, they sometimes nationalize industries, as has occurred in Britain, France, and Canada.

(4) To catch votes as politicians save jobs by putting dying industries on life-support systems, which can be disconnected after the election.

(5) Because the government has pumped money into a firm or an industry, and control usually follows money.

(6) Happenstance, as with the nationalization after World War II of German-owned firms in Europe.

All governments are in business to some degree, but outside the LDCs, none is so far into business as Italy or France.

Unfair competition?

Where government-owned companies compete with privately owned companies, the private companies sometimes complain that the government companies have unfair advantages. Some of the complaints are:

(1) Government-owned companies can cut prices unfairly because they do not have to make profits.

(2) They get cheaper financing.

(3) They get government contracts.

(4) They get export assistance.

(5) They can hold down wages with government assistance.

Another huge advantage of state-owned companies have over privately owned business comes in the form of direct subsidies, payments by the government to their companies. The EU Commission is trying to discourage such subsidy payments. In 1991, it began requiring annual financial reports from state-controlled companies as part of a crackdown on the subsidies that can distort competition.

Government-private collaboration difficult

The objectives of private firms and those of government agencies and operations usually differ. And this is the most important reason for government – private collaboration difficulty. Britain's former Prime Minister, Margaret Thatcher, was the acknowledged leader of the privatization movement. During her 11 years in office, Thatcher decreased state-owned companies from 10 percent of Britain's GNP to 3.9 percent. She sold over 30 companies, raising some $65 billion. Thatcher pioneered in what has become a worldwide movement to privatize all sorts of government activities.

Airports, garbage, postal services

The American Lockheed Company, after quietly and profitably running Burbank Airport in California for decades, is expanding abroad. As owner or manager, Lockheed is operating or bidding to operate airports in Canada, Russia, Turkmenistan, Australia, Turkey, Hungary, Argentina, and Venezuela. Hughes Aircraft Company is in the business with Trinidad and Tobago and has completed studies for the Ukraine on ways to upgrade that country's airports.

Several countries are privatizing their postal services; the British are studying such a move and the Germans are moving. In Germany, the three operating divisions of the Federal Bundespost (postal services, telecommunications, and the postal bank) are being converted into three public companies, the stock of which can be sold to nongovernment owners.

Private buyers do well, but an American needs a passport

Privatization is the political trend all over the world that is everywhere except in the United States. In the new century, over $1350 billion worth of public assets were privatized. Since 1980, the People's Republic of China has gone from nearly 80 percent to less than 30 percent state ownership. Chile has privatized 75 percent of its state-owned enterprises, and Mexico, about 33 percent. Now France, Germany, Italy, and other European countries are selling, especially, when European debt crisis is more and more serious, the privatization will show in 10 years.

A study by Alliance Capital discovered that over the past five years, stocks of privatized companies have climbed by 174 percent versus an 85 percent rise in 1990s. But the privatization trend has not begun in the United States, by either the national or state governments. However, American investors can partake in the trend by buying mutual funds that do hold shares of the world's newly privatized companies.

Privatization anywhere and any way

As you can see privatization is worldwide. It is an advertisement by a Japanese investment bank, Daiwa, bragging about its senior role in privatizations in Australia, Britain, Italy, Malaysia, Scotland, and Singapore.

It should be noted, however, that privatization does not always involve ownership transfer from government to private entities. Activities previously conducted by the state may be contracted out, as Indonesia has contracted a Swiss firm to run its customs administration, and Thailand has contracted private companies that operate some of the passenger trains of its state-owned railroad.

Governments may lease state-owned plants to private entities, as Togo has done.

They may combine a joint venture with a management contract with a private group to run a previously government-operated business. Rwanda did this with its match factory.

The percentages in the figure total 100 without including the United States, which illustrates the previously made point that neither the U. S. government nor the individual state governments are participating in the privatization trend.

Nationalism has been called the "secular religion of our time." In most of the older countries, loyalty to one's country and national pride were based on such shared common features as race, language, religion, or ideology. Many of the newer countries, notably in Africa, have accidental boundaries resulting from their colonial past, and within these countries, there are several tribes and languages. This has resulted in civil wars, as in Rwanda, Nigeria, and Angola, but it has not prevented these new countries from developing instant and fierce nationalism.

Nationalism is an emotion that can cloud or even prevent rational dealings with foreigners. For example, the chief of the joint staff of the Peruvian military, when taking charge in Peru, blamed the ills of its society on foreign companies.

Some of the effects of nationalism on international companies

(1) Requirements for minimum local ownership or local product assembly or manufacture.

(2) Reservation of certain industries for local companies.

(3) Preference of local suppliers for government contracts.

(4) Limitations on the number and types of foreign employees.

(5) Protectionism, using tariffs, quotas, or other devices.

(6) Seeking a "French solution" instead of a foreign takeover of a local firm.

(7) In the most extreme cases, expropriation or confiscation.

A historical function of government, whatever its ideology, has been the protection of the economic activities such as farming, mining, manufacturing, and so forth within its geographic area of control. These must be protected from attacks and destruction or robbery by terrorists, bandits, revolutionaries, and foreign invaders.

Since the 1970s, the world has been plagued by terrorism. Various groups have hijacked airplanes, shot and kidnapped people, and bombed people and objects. A common denominator of these terrorist groups has been hatred of the social, economic, and political orders they find in the world. Another characteristic is their confusion as to what sort of order they would substitute if they had the chance.

By 2013, European countries, especially France, were particularly hard hit by terrorist violence directed against businesses and politicians. Between 2013 and 2016, terrorist groups made lots of bomb and shooting events in Paris, Nice and other big cities of France.

Kidnapping is another weapon used by terrorists. The victims are held for ransom, frequently, the ransom is a very large amount, which provides an important source of funds for the terrorists. For example, industry in Argentina has paid ransom of several hundred million dollars for the release of kidnapped business executives. In 2009, lots of countries send their naval forces to Somalia to fight against pirates and protect the merchant ships.

By 1986, Colombia and Peru had become the most dangerous places for American executives, and a long stay by a high-ranking American executive in either country is risky. Brief visits are usually fairly safe because kidnappings take a while to plan, so top executives from the United States practice what is called commando management. They arrive in Bogota or Lima as secretly as possible, meet for a few days with local employees, and fly off before kidnappers learn of their presence.

Countermeasures by industry

Insurance to cover ransom payments, antiterrorist schools, and companies to handle negotiations with kidnappers have come into being. As kidnapping and extortion directed against businesses and governments have become common fund-raising and political techniques for terrorists, it promoted the development of an industry, insurance against such acts has grown into a multimillion-dollar business. The world's largest kidnapping and extortion underwriting firm is located in London. The firm, Cassidy and Davis, underwriter for Lloyd's of London, says that it covers some 9,000 companies. Cassidy and Davis do not sit back and wait for claims to be filed. It runs antiterrorism training courses for executives, with subjects ranging from defensive driving techniques—escape tactics and battering through blockades—to crisis management. Country-by-country risk analyses are instantly available on international computer hookups.

Cassidy and Davis work closely with Control Risk, Ltd., a London-based security service company that advises firms or families in negotiations with kidnappers. Cassidy and Davis encourages its clients to use Control Risk services. The premiums for the insurance underwritten by Cassidy and Davis range from some $3,000 a year for $1.5 million of coverage in low-risk England to $60,000 a year for the same coverage in high-risk Peru.

5.5 Some famous political organizations of the world

United Nations (UN)

The UN is highly politicized. The member-countries vote as blocs formed because of ideology or perceived similar objectives.

UN personnel advise member-countries on such matters as tax, monetary, and fiscal policies. The UN is active in the harmonization of laws affecting international trade. It had a hand in drafting an international commercial arbitration convention. The UN has drafted a code of conduct for multinational business. Any of the political ideologies we have discussed can be reflected in the content and spirit of tax, trade, and arbitration laws, conduct codes, and fiscal or monetary policies.

The Transnational Corporations Division of the UN has had a change of attitude resulting from a change of political orientation. During the early UN years, the division tended to be hostile to private international companies, saying they cheated and victimized LDCs that needed UN protection. The new, changed attitude is that LDCs should encourage investment by those companies to obtain such things as capital, technology, and management skills.

UNCTAD is credited with having influenced the IMF to ease its restrictions on loans to LDCs. This is important to banks lending to and suppliers selling to LDCs.

Virtually all of the specialized UN agencies are now actively advising LDCs about what to buy for their agriculture, industry, airlines, health programs, weather stations, and so forth. These are huge markets for business.

EU

Slowly, the member-nations of the EU are surrendering parts of their sovereign powers to the Brussels headquarters. Mention of only a few areas will illustrate the extent of the EU's influence on international marketing. Among other things, the EU is working to harmonize laws dealing with taxes, patents, labor conditions, competition, insurance, banking, and capital markets.

Harmonization of differing national laws is one matter, but the EU has finished its very important job—lawmaking in 1990s. This related to such fields as company law, antitrust, and consumer and environmental protection. The objective of some Europeans is to create a political, as well as an economic power to rival America and China. However, European Union is changing with the economic development of the world. In June 2016, England people voted to leave European Union, and it is the subject for businesspeople to study how the situation may influence the international marketing.

Organization for Economic Cooperation and Development (OECD)

This 30-member organization of industrialized countries has issued "Guidelines for Multinational Enterprises." Although it has been said that OECD guidelines merely create a voluntary set of principles upon which to build sound international relations, they can have significant impact. For example, when Badger, Raytheon's subsidiary in

Belgium, closed shop, it did not have enough money to meet its labor termination obligations under Belgian law. The Belgian government and labor unions used the pressure of the OECD "voluntary" guidelines to convince Raytheon to pay Badger's obligations.

Workers and labor unions sometimes influence the political environment too. The European labor unions are ideologically oriented, usually toward the left. The American unions are said to be more pragmatic, but in practice they are extremely politically active. They supply large amounts of money and workers to support the political candidates they favor.

In Europe, the United States, and, increasingly, China and Japan, political force are felt not only at the polls but also in the legislatures, because of labor. Unions lobby for or against laws as these are perceived to be for or against the interests of labor. International business is not merely a passive victim of political forces. It can be a powerful force in the world political arena. Otherwise, some of the giant companies take very important role in world politics, because the large financial size carries power, and an international company's power need not rest solely on size. The company's power can come from the possession of scarce capital, technology, and management, plus the capability to deploy those resources around the world. An international company may have the processing, productive, distributive, and marketing abilities necessary for the successful exploitation of raw materials or for the manufacture, distribution, and marketing of certain products. Those abilities are frequently not available in less developed countries. Recognition of the desirability of multinationals investments is growing.

5.6 The political risk

It is arbitrary to place this subject in a chapter on political forces because country risk assessment (CRA) involves many risks other than political risks. It is probably important enough to warrant a separate chapter, but one of our objectives was to avoid an overlong book. We shall introduce our readers to CRA here; there is a growing literature about it, and those who are interested can find much material.

The political events of recent years have caused firms to concentrate much more on the CRA. Firms that had already done CRA updated and strengthened the function, and many other companies began the practice.

Types of country risks

Country risks are increasingly political in nature. There are wars, revolutions, and coups. Less dramatic, but nevertheless important for businesses, are government changes by election of a socialist or nationalist government, which may be hostile to private business and particularly to foreign-owned business.

The risks may be economic or financial. There may be persistent balance-of-payments deficits or high inflation rates. Repayment of loans may be questionable. Labor conditions may cause investors to pause. Labor productivity may be low, or labor unions may be militant. Laws may be changed about taxes, currency convertibility, tariffs, quotas, or labor permits. The chances for a fair trial in local courts must be assessed. Terrorism may be present. If it is, can the company protect its personnel and property?

The types of information a firm will need to judge country risks will vary according to the nature of its business and the length of time required for the investment, loan, or other involvement to yield a satisfactory return.

Nature of business

Consider, for example, the needs of a hotel company compared with those of heavy-equipment manufacturers or manufacturers of personal hygiene products or mining companies. Banks have their own sets of problems and information needs. Sometimes there are variations between firms in the same industry or on a project-to-project basis. The nationality of the company may be a factor; does the host country bear a particular animus, or friendly attitude, toward the home country?

Length of time required

Export financing usually involves the shortest period of risk exposure. Typically, payments are made within 180 days (usually less) and exporters can meet insurance or bank protection.

Bank loans can be short, medium, or long term. However, when the business includes host country assembly, mixing, manufacture, or extraction (oil or minerals), long-term commitments are necessary.

With long-term investment or loan commitments, there are inherent problems with risk analysis that cannot be resolved. Most such investment opportunities require 5, 10, or more years to pay off. But the utility of risk analyses of social, political, and economic factors decreases precipitously over longer time spans.

Who does country risk assessing?

General or specific analyses, macro or micro analyses, and political, social, and economic analyses have been conducted (perhaps under different names) for years. The Conference Board located bits and pieces of CRA being performed in various company departments. For example, the international division and public affairs, finance, legal, economics, planning, and product- producing departments. Sometimes the efforts were duplicative, and the people in one department were unaware that others in the company were similarly involved.

Efforts are now being made to concentrate CRA and to maximize its effectiveness for the company. These efforts include guidelines about the participation of top management.

Outside consulting and publishing firms is another source of country risk analysis. As CRA has mushroomed in perceived importance, a number of such firms have been formed or have expanded.

Instead of or in addition to the outside consultants, a number of firms have buttressed their internal risk analysis staff by hiring such experts as international business or political science professors or retired State Department, or military people.

5.7 CRA procedures

The Economist Intelligence Unit breaks its assessments down into three categories. First is medium-term lending risk, covering such factors as external debt and trends in the current account. Second is political and policy risk, including factors such as the consistency of government policy and the quality of economic management. Third is short-term trade risk, including foreign exchange reserves.

The International Country Risk Guide (ICRG), put out by a U. S. division of International Business Communications Ltd. of London, takes a somewhat different approach. It offers individual ratings for political, financial, and economic risk, plus a composite rating. The political variable includes factors such as government corruption and how economic expectations diverge from reality. The financial rating looks at such things as the likelihood of losses from exchange controls and loan defaults. Economic ratings take into account such factors as inflation and debt service costs. The ICRG, Credit Suisse, and other organizations publish country risk rankings periodically. Another highly regarded publisher of rankings is Euro money.

But, if you just want to enter the international market, the managers should take the following procedures when they want to assess the political forces:

Assessment about the political environments external of the company

(1) Bilateral relations—if the other market conditions are same or familiar, the better bilateral relations between home and host country will make more and better international marketing opportunities for your company.

(2) Industry and product—the politically sensitive for the various industry and

product is different, and the government will take the various protection levels. If your industry or product is very politically sensitive, expect the government intervention.

(3) Scale and address—if your subsidiary is very large and addressed in the major cities of the host countries, it is very easy for you to face the political risk.

(4) Awareness of the company—in common situation, the more famous the company in the world, the more political risk the company has to take.

(5) The political situation of the host country—in common situation, the more instable political situation will make more political risk for the companies.

Assessment about the political environments inner of the company

(1) Activity of the company—the better image of the company in the host country will reduce the political risk.

(2) Contribution of the company for the host country—the larger the contribution of the company for the host country, the fewer the political risk.

(3) Localization degree—if you can use the local materials or parts and employ more local people to serve your business in host country, you can reduce your political risk in the real world.

Otherwise, for avoiding the political risk as possible as you can, the multinational managers should insist on the following principles:

(1) Respect and match up the development target of the host country and define your host position to make the better relation with the local government, local enterprises and local media.

(2) Take the proper profits with the fair price; if you take large sums of profits through harming the local benefits, you are taking the political risk.

(3) Do in Rome as Rome does, it is the precondition for you to respect the local habits if you want to take international marketing in a foreign country.

(4) To be as the sponsor of the local culture activities and local charitable institution.

(5) To train the local managements and technicists.

(6) Send your relative information about your company culture to the local governments and let them understand you.

(7) The staff and their family members should take the proper action when they work and live in the host country.

(8) To employ more local people to take the higher position of the company.

Lessons of the international debt crisis

There are at least five lessons that CRA analysts should have learned. First, many developing countries are vulnerable to external shocks. One thing that has become apparent is the importance of a country's export and import structure in weathering an external economic shock. For example, the newly industrialized countries of Asia with their diversified export structures have been in a much better position to deal with the collapse of commodity prices and the erection of protectionist barriers than have been other countries with a comparable level of development but lopsided export structures (such as Indonesia and Mexico).

Second, the development of the debt crisis has shown clearly that the economic policies of debtor countries have a decisive impact on default risk. The countries that have become most deeply mired in the crisis are the ones that adopted expansionary fiscal and monetary policies. The results were inflation, current account deficits, loss of international competitiveness, and capital flight. Such has been the fate of the Philippines and the high-debt countries of Latin America.

By contrast, those countries that allowed the altered world market prices and demand conditions to take effect on their economies and adapted their economic policies to accommodate changed conditions have fared much better. Restrictive fiscal and monetary policies damped inflation, while occasional devaluations of their currencies kept trade balances under control.

Third, sustained economic growth is a major requirement for high-debt countries to service their debt and reduce its burden. Austerity alone cannot be a solution, economically, politically, or socially.

Fourth, the social and potential political costs of over indebtedness combined with austerity are proved high. Social and political tensions have risen sharply and threaten the survival of several democratically elected governments. That, in turn, greatly increases the danger of a debt moratorium.

The fifth lesson from the debt crisis for CRA analysts is the global ripple effect of seemingly independent risks or economic shocks. For example, the oil price collapse at the beginning of 1986 jacked up oil-exporting countries' default risk while lessening that risk for oil importers, thus affecting international interest and exchange rates and triggering a whole series of fiscal and monetary policy responses. The tequila effect was the phrase applied to the global ripples caused by the financial crises in the Mexican economy at the end of 1994 and into 1995.

The 1987 stock market crash caused worldwide economic reverberations. Other events that would have global effects if they were to occur include sustained changes in world interest rates, recession in major market countries, creation of debtor-country cartels, or the banking system's loss of confidence in an entire region.

So much worse is that the debt crisis occurred in Europe and America by now, because the economic equity are very large, the debt crisis occurred in the developed countries will be a burden on the development of the world economy, although we cannot estimate its order of severity. Otherwise, it will bring the negative effect for the political and social systems. The better evidence is that multi shooting incident were made in Europe and the international companies have to pay more attention to the change and result.

Summary

1. Identify the ideological forces that affect business and understand the terminology used in discussing them. We discussed capitalism, socialism, conservative, liberal, right wing, and left wing.

2. Understand that although most governments own businesses, they are privatizing them in growing numbers. Even governments that consider themselves capitalist and conservative own some businesses. But almost all governments are privatizing and getting out of businesses.

3. Country risks are increasingly political in nature. There are wars, revolutions, and coups. Less dramatic, but nevertheless important for businesses, are government changes by election of a socialist or nationalist government, which may be hostile to private business and particularly to foreign-owned business.

4. Explain steps that traveling international business executives should take to protect themselves from terrorists. Before international business executives travel abroad and after they arrive in the host country, they should take steps to protect themselves from terrorists.

5. Understand the importance to business of government stability and policy continuity. Business can rarely thrive in a country with an unstable government or rapid, drastic policy changes.

6. Discuss the power sources of international organizations, labor unions, and international companies. Large international businesses have political power, as do labor unions and international organizations such as the UN and the EU.

7. Understand country risk assessment by international business. Country risk assessment is now considered a necessity by most international businesses before they commit people, money, or technology to a foreign country. CRA involves evaluating a country's economic situation and policies as well as its politics.

Questions

1. What is political system? Why is it important to international business?

2. Give an example to describe how political forces may influence your international marketing decisions.

3. What impact can terrorism have on business?

4. Why do enterprises fear sudden changes in government policies?

5. How can traditional hostilities affect business?

6. How can multinationals use their strengths to influence government policies?

7. Is country risk assessment (CRA) an exact science? Explain.

8. In terms of exposure to political risk (for example, expropriation), which of the following businesses would you consider the most and least vulnerable? Banks; mines; oil fields; oil refineries; heavy-equipment; manufacturers; cosmetics; manufacturers of personal hygiene; products; hotels; automobile manufacturers.

9. Are the most vulnerable businesses high profile or low profile? What are some ways to change the profile of a company in a foreign country?

Minicase

Company Privatization

You are the chief executive officer of a company that the government has just denationalized by selling the company's stock to the company's employees. In the past, any major decision about company policy required approval by a government agency, which was time consuming. Wages and salaries had been established by reference to civil service "equivalents" and incentive payments were unheard of. Maintenance of the plant and equipment was lax, break-downs were frequent and expensive, and utility expenses were high.

You want the newly privatized company to be a success. Suggest some programs that you would institute to improve its chances of success.

Chapter 6 Legal Forces

Concept preview

After reading this chapter, you should be able to

1. Appreciate: the importance to study foreign legal forces for international managements.

2. Understand: the various legal structures in different target markets.

3. Distinguish: the difference between the legal forces and the political factors.

4. Comprehend: how to understand the difference between the code law and the common law.

5. Describe: the type of the legal system.

The multinationals are operating out of the motherland and they have to face the different law environments in different countries, especially all of the laws may be very different from the domestic laws. Because of the different history, every country has its own law system and the characteristics are different. Although the countries are narrowing their law differences and try to replace the domestic laws with international laws or regional laws, there is a long way for us to standardize the international business activities with the global or the regional laws. As the international company, it has to study the host legal system and contrast the differences with the domestic legal system, try its best to take the legal weapon to reach the goal to draw on advantages and avoid disadvantages.

6.1 The types of the legal system

In general, the law in the world can be divided into two systems, code law and common law. The code law is also called Roma law, civil law, or Roma-Germanic law, and it's generic terms of law based on the Roma law and its represents are France and Germany. Most of the European countries, total Latin America, part of Africa, near east countries and Japan are taking this law system.

The code law emphasizes the function of statute law and in the field of organizations, it emphasizes systematization, methodization, codifications and logicality. The basic method to form the law is to conclude various laws and rules and classify with several great law categories. At the same time, the countries that carry out the code law divides the law into public law and private law. The public law includes constitution, administrative law, penal code, procedural law and international public law, etc. The private law includes civil law, commercial law, etc. All of the countries that take the code law are same in the fields of legal system and legal concepts, although they are different when they come to the specific legal clauses and code edit systems.

The common law is also called England law system, common law system or case law system. It is a special legal system based on England law from Middle Age to today, especially, the common law is its foundation. The represent countries include the Great Britain and United States. By now, some countries and areas that were colonized by England, for example, Canada, Australia, New Zealand, Malaysia and Singapore belong to the common law except England and US. Some other countries like South Africa, Sri Lanka and the Philippines carried out the code law in the past but now get influenced by the common law in the deep way, they are the mixture of code law and common law.

The differences between the code law and the common law

(1) In the field of law reasons, the code law was inherited and developed from Roma law and the statue law is its major reason; however, the common law was inherited and developed from Teutonic customary law and case law is its major law sources.

(2) In the field of legal reasoning, the code law carries out the deduction from common rules to individual judgment. And it is the typical form of syllogism: the laws and regulations are the major premise, and the fact is the minor premise, then the result is based on the major and minor premise. The legal consciousness is generalized and abstracted. The common law carries out the induction from case to case, and gets the general rules and the inference methods among the similar legal cases. Its legal consciousness is specific and practical. In the countries that take the common law, the judges always give their judgments based on the legal cases, because every case should be recorded in detail and the records form the general regulations gradually.

(3) About the codifications, the code law takes the codifications traditionally, that is to make their functional laws of their countries become system codification.

However, the common law countries do not take the code format. But it is not universally applicative: some common law countries take the code format meanwhile, some law departments (for example, administrative law and labor law) in the code law countries take the single but more flexible statues or administrative regulations, instead of the code format, which happened especially after the world war Ⅱ.

(4) About the law structure, according to the tradition, the code law is divided into public and private law and the common law is divided into common law and equity. With more governmental intervention among social and economical issues, the laws which the code countries based on with both public and private quality become more and more. Meanwhile in the common law countries, the trend to divide the public and private law are growing. In another word, the two law systems are mixing together.

(5) About the legal action system, traditionally, the code law takes the officiousness system and the judges mainly rely on the substantive law. They emphasize more on the substantive law than the procedural law. The common law takes the adversary system and the judges mainly rely on the legal action to try a case. Obviously, they emphasize more legal action procedural.

(6) In the field of administration of justice, the countries which traditionally take code law divide the courts into common courts and administrative courts. The common law system is common court-based, which means even if they have the administrative courts, the appealers can appeal to the common court if they refuse to obey the judgment.

(7) About the function of legal administration, in the code law system countries, the legislative bodies always have the vantage ground and the judicial offices belong to the subordinate status. The judicial offices must take judicial activities based on the statute law clauses, but the judicial offices have the vantage ground, because legal cases are the major reasons and the legal cases are found and created by the judges of high courts in common situation. Even the legislative bodies make the statute law, the clauses or regulations play a part after the judges tried the relative cases, formed the legal cases and gave explanations and affirmation. This is why the judicial offices in the common law countries always have the advantageous position in common situation.

6.2 How does the law of host countries influence your international marketing mix?

As an international company, not only does it have to pay more attention to the differences of various countries' legal systems, but it also has to be careful of the different countries' domestic amendments to the same international laws, because the four basic factors of the international marketing, product, pricing, promotion and place all will be influenced by the host country's law and regulations, and in various countries, the effect is very different.

The impact on products

Most countries make laws to regulate products, and a large portion of the laws directly pertain to physical and chemical properties for them. All of these laws require products to reach defined safe standards; for example, America draws up the strict anti-pollution standards for imported cars, ordering that imported cars must be installed with the environmental control system and must reach the automobile exhaust gas control standards of America. According to Engand laws, milk must be sold by the pint. Because French milk is sold by kilograms, it could not be sold in the English market. Domestic product standards always become trade barriers in the real world. Especially if the domestic market is impacted by foreign products, it is very important for Chinese companies to pay more attention to the question when they want to develop foreign markets.

In addition to regulating the product itself, every country's product laws limit the foreign products to enter their markets with logos, packaging, product guarantees and trademarks, etc. For example, according to Japanese law, food and medicine products that are sold in the Japanese market must be illustrated in Japanese. In general, countries with code laws draw up stricter laws for the imported products than do countries with common laws. This is because of culture and tradition.

Besides, many countries have formulated or are beginning to formulate green marketing laws and regulations for products. For example, Germany has gotten through strict green marketing laws that regulated how to treat packaging rubbish and recovery. With the development of society and economy, laws for products become stricter. It is very impossible for a marketer to occupy the foreign market if one does not study foreign product laws.

The impact on price

Many countries' governments draw up price policies to control their markets; commonly, developing countries formulate stricter pricing policies than developed countries. Food and medicine are two important products controlled by governments. Some of governments control all product prices, and some governments only control individual product prices. For example, apart from a few public products, the American government does not control other product prices, and the Japanese government does not control any product prices, except the price of rice.

Some governments control the price by setting up a standard for marginal profits.

For example, the Ghanaian government regulates that the profit rate of the manufactures is between 25%~40%; the Argentina government permits the profit rate to be 11%; the Belgian government limits the profit rate for medicine wholesalers to be 12.5% and for medicine retailers to be 30%; and although the German government does not make regulations about profits, it requires enterprises to report in detail about their price and profits.

The impact on distribution

In general, there is small limitation on distribution. Depending on different market conditions, manufacturers can choose their own various distribution channels to develop their markets. Of course, manufacturers cannot choose channels that are inapplicable to the markets; for instance, the French government prohibits door to door marketing. In Muslim countries, small street retailers are prohibited from seeing women in houses.

As a matter of fact, the strictest legal regulations cannot influence the distribution of international company products fundamentally in host countries. But companies that export their products and sell their products using local distributors or agencies will be limited by these legal regulations. On the one hand, it is very important for multinationals to choose local distributors and agencies carefully; only higher-quality distributors can help multinationals reach success in the world market; at the same time, it is either very difficult for international managers to abolish the distribution contracts or the price is very high. So, international managers must be familiar with the relevant legal clauses concerning distribution to avoid losses.

The impact on promotion

Promotion includes advertising, personal selling, sales promotion, and public relations, etc. Of these, advertising is the easiest link to trigger the conflict, so, most governments make very strict legal regulations to control the activities of companies. Otherwise, many advertising agencies make common rules regarding advertising based on the law.

In general, various countries make stricter laws to limit business activities in the following aspects:

(1) Concerning the contents and the truth of the advertising: in Germany, the "comparative degree" is prohibited; for example, the usage of words like "better" and "the best" are prohibited in advertising. These words in advertising are accepted in the U.S., but they may be judged as false advertising in Canada. In Argentina, enterprises have to get the permission of the public health authorities before using such words in their advertising.

(2) To control the range of advertising: for some sensitive products, the

government limits their promotional material; for example, cigarette and wine advertisements are prohibited on TV in the U. S. and Britain. In Finland, the government is even stricter as it does not allow political groups, regulation groups, wine products, diet pills, and illegal literature to advertise on the TV or in newspapers. Other governments limit advertising by levying a heavy duty. For example, the Peruvian government levies an 8% advertising duty for outdoor advertisements, and the Spanish government levies a special duty for advertising via movies.

(3) To control promotion skills: some governments restrict any companies from publishing their revenues in advance, and many governments limit the scale of commission and types of commissions, even including to the specific methods to promote products, the commission is only a small part of the revenue, and the commission must be related to the special products. For example, the commission of a watch is prohibited to promote soap, etc.

Apart from advertising, many governments limit other promotional methods. For example, according to the discount law of Austria, enterprises are prohibited from providing the various consumers with differentiated discounts when they take the prize-giving sales. According to Finland's laws, the companies can promote their products in a large range, but the precondition is that they cannot use the word "free" and cannot force consumers to buy their products in the promotional sales. The French government prohibits the enterprises from promoting their products with the price under the cost or give as a present or monetary award based on whether or not the consumers buy some special products. As a matter of fact, the French government prohibits any business person from selling goods with a prize. In Germany, the government prohibits companies from providing any type of promotional activities to attract the customers and the enterprises prohibit over 3% discount for their consumers.

In a word, the different legal restrictions will influence your international marketing mix and you have to study the laws seriously before you enter your target markets; particularly, you have to study the following questions first, because they are closely related to your international markets.

6.3 Taxation

Purposes

The primary purpose of certain taxes is not necessarily to raise revenue for the government, which may surprise those who have not studied taxation. As a matter of fact, the purposes of the state taxes may include: to redistribute income, to discourage consumption of some products such as alcohol or tobacco, to encourage consumption of domestic rather than imported goods, to discourage investment abroad, to achieve equality of the tax amounts paid by taxpayers earning comparable amounts, and to grant reciprocity to resident foreigners under a tax treaty.

Even this short list of purposes illustrates the economic and political pressures on government officials responsible for tax legislation and collection. Powerful groups in every country push for tax policies that favor their interests. These groups and interests differ from country to country and frequently conflict with each other, which accounts in part for the complexity of the tax practices that affect multinationals.

Tax levels

For one thing, tax levels range from relatively high in some Western European countries to zero in tax havens. Some countries have capital gains taxes, and some do not. Those that have the capital gains tax have it at different levels. Incidentally, the United States levels, one of the highest long-term capital, has capital gains taxes.

The tax levels rely on the different situation of the countries, and in the real world, they are very different. For example, the total tax is about 24% of GDP in the U. S., and the number in China and EU is about 35% and 41%, respectively. Of course, the different tax levels provide different profit spaces for the multinationals. Actually, the tax level reflects the different benefits of the social groups and the question is always the conflict focus for the different political groups.

For instance, in the United States, the capital gains tax is controversial. Those defined in the previous chapter as "liberal" argue the tax rate should remain high because any reduction would reward the rich, the group having the most assets that have increased in price. The "conservatives" argue that the capital gains tax locks in money that would be better invested elsewhere to create jobs and increase productivity. Some maintain that the United States should levy no capital gains tax, following the example of many countries.

Tax types

There are different types of taxes. We have just introduced one, the capital gains tax. Although the United States levies a relatively high capital gains tax, it relies on income tax for most of its revenue. As indicated by the name, this tax is levied on the income of individuals and businesses. To generalize (subject to exceptions, of course): the higher the income, the higher the income tax. In the 1970s and 1980s, much discontent developed among Americans over the impact of income tax and other taxes. Possibly as a result, there has been growing support for a value-added tax (VAT) in the U. S..

Many suggest that the United States ought to instead income tax with the VAT which is used in all European Union countries, where VATs are main sources of revenue. VATs function in this way (for the purposes of this example, we shall assume a VAT of 10 percent): A wheat farmer sells to a miller the part of the wheat that eventually becomes the loaf for 30 cents. So far, the farmer has added 30 cents of value by planting, growing, and harvesting the wheat. The farmer sets aside 3 cents (10 percent of 30 cents) to pay the VAT. The miller makes loaves of bread out of the wheat and sells them to a wholesaler for 50 cents each. Thus, the miller has added 20 cents of value (50 percent of 30 cents) and must pay a VAT of 2 cents (10 percent of 20 cents). The wholesaler now advertises and distributes the loaves, selling them to retailers for 70 cents. The wholesaler has added 20 cents of value and owes 2 cents VAT. Finally, the retailer adds 40 cents by its display, advertising, and sales efforts and owes 4 cents of VAT. The loaf of bread is sold for $1.10 retail and has borne a cumulative VAT of 11 cents, 10 percent of $1.10.

The VAT has proponents and opponents. In general, their arguments are as follows: The proponents say the VAT is relatively simple and can be raised or lowered easily to balance desired income with tax burden. The opponents argue that it is a consumption-type tax that burdens the poor the most.

In addition, some U. S. VAT proponents argue that the present situation, in which the major European countries rely heavily on the value-added tax, is unfair to the United States because of WTO regulations. The WTO permits the rebate of VAT when a product is exported from a country but does not permit the rebate of income taxes. The rebates enable exporting countries to offer lower-priced, more competitive goods, and VAT proponents want the United States to inaugurate the VAT and lower income taxes to take advantage of those WTO rules.

Another form of tax on industrial countries has been a bone of contention for at least two decades: the unitary tax system that several U. S. states had imposed. Most have since repealed those tax laws under threats of retaliation by foreign governments.

International tax treaties are almost always built on the "arm's length" or "water's edge" principle: taxable profits for a subsidiary in a country will be assessed as though it were conducting its business independently. The unitary system, by contrast, calculates the worldwide income of the industrial country and then assesses the tax due in proportion to the percentage of the group's property, payroll, and sales in the state.

California was the last state to move away from the unitary principle. The 1986 and 1988 changes in California's tax laws did not completely eliminate the unitary approach, but instead now permit industrial companies to choose either water's edge or unitary system. A company's circumstances (for instance, the sources or types of income involved) would determine which would be more advantageous.

6.4 Complexity of tax laws and regulations

From country to country, the complexity of tax systems differs from each other. Many consider that of the United States to be the most complex; the Internal Revenue Code runs over 5,000 pages long and official interpretations add more than 10,000 to that number. In addition to the code and Treasury interpretations, there are many thousands of pages of judicial notations.

Who obeys the law?

Compliance with tax laws and their enforcement vary widely. Some countries, such as Germany and the United States, are strict. Others, such as Italy and Spain, are relatively lax. The Italian practice allows the taxpayer to declare a very low taxable income, which the government counters with a very high amount. They then negotiate a compromise figure.

Other differences

There are many other differences, too numerous to list all here; but a few are tax incentives to invest in certain areas, exemptions, costs, depreciation allowances, foreign tax credits, timing, and double corporate taxation—that is, taxation of the profits of a corporation and then of dividends paid to its stockholders.

Tax conventions, or treaties

Because of the innumerable differences in nations' tax practices, many of them have signed tax treaties with each other. Typically, tax treaties define such points of interest as income, source, residency, and what constitutes taxable activities in each country. They address how much each country can tax the income earned by a national of one country living or working in the other. All of these treaties contain provisions for the exchange of information between the tax authorities of the two countries.

The presence or absence of a tax treaty is often a factor in both international business and investment location decisions. It is now fully accepted that treaties facilitate international flows of goods, capital, services, and technology.

However, countries sign treaties for different reasons. Most OECD countries regard treaties as providing a standard framework for all countries in allocating taxing jurisdiction. In countries with emerging markets, treaties are viewed as a key tool in giving foreign investors confidence in their stability.

In the tax area, it is the taxpayers (here, international companies) who are against the tax collectors (the governments). Antitrust actions also involve business versus government, and occasionally, government versus government.

The differences in U. S. laws and attitudes

The U. S. antitrust laws are stricter and more vigorously enforced than those of any other country. However, other countries, as well as the EU, are becoming more active in the antitrust field. In the EU, these laws are referred to as restrictive trade practices laws.

German antitrust laws are the toughest after those of the United States, and, during 1986, the German Federal Cartel Office tightened its grip literally, in some cases. Wolfgang Kartte, president of the Cartel Office, tells a story about a raid his investigators made on the office of a heating equipment supplier. One of the suppliers' managers stuffed a memo in his mouth and tried to swallow it, but a quick-thinking investigator grabbed the man by the throat and forced him to spit out the memo. Half-chewed but still legible, it provided valuable evidence of illegal price-fixing.

In 1991, the European Court of Justice gave a major boost to EU efforts to inject competition into economic sectors still largely dominated by powerful state monopolies. The Court confirmed that the EU Commission can force EU member-governments to dismantle state monopolies that block progress toward an open, community-wide market.

Article 85 of the Treaty of Rome outlaws any agreement or action to rig markets or distort competition. Under the authority of that article, the Commission fined the Dutch chemicals group, Akzo, ECU 7.5 million in 1991. Later in 1991, empowered by Article 86, which bans abuse of dominant positions, the Commission imposed a record ECU 75 million fine on Tetra Pak, a Swiss-based liquid packaging group, for eliminating competitors in the European market. That record was broken in 1994 as the EU Commission levied fines totaling $158.58 million on 19 carton-board producers. They had formed what the Commission described as Europe's "most pernicious" price-fixing cartel.

In 1991, for the first time, the Commission used its authority under a 1990 law to veto a major business transaction. Using its greater power, it blocked the acquisition of Boeing's de Haviland subsidiary by a French-Italian consortium, Avions de Transport Regional (ATR). The Commission said the acquisition would have given ATR an unfair advantage that would allow it to crowd out competition.

A number of important differences in antitrust laws, regulations, and practices exist between the United States, other nations, and the EU. One difference is the effort of the United States to apply its laws extraterritorially. We deal with that later in this chapter. Another difference: under U. S. law, certain activities, such as price-fixing, are illegal per se (even though no injury or damage results from them).

The Treaty of Rome articles dealing with restrictive trade practices do not contain the per se illegality concept of U. S. antitrust laws. For example, a cartel that allows consumers a fair share of the benefits is legally acceptable in the EU. Also, the treaty is not violated by market dominance—only by misuse of that dominance to damage competitors or consumers.

The EU versus Hoffman-La Roche

The EU Court of Justice upheld the Commission's decision that the giant Swiss drug company Hoffman-La Roche was guilty of abusing its dominant position. Hoffman was fined $732,000. There was at least one bizarre element in the Hoffman case. Stanley Adams, a British subject, was an employee at the company's head office in Basel, Switzerland. He took some confidential documents about Hoffman's pricing and marketing practices and made them available to the EU antitrust regulators, who were already investigating the company. The company and the Swiss government reacted furiously, and when Adams, who was in Italy when the loss of the documents was discovered, returned to Switzerland, he was arrested and convicted under Swiss laws against industrial espionage. He was sent to prison, and his wife committed suicide on being told that he would be there at least 20 years. At last, the EU bailed him out of the Swiss prison and he left the country.

Although Adams had his freedom, his troubles were not over. He was unable to get credit or employment, and he lost a farm he tried to operate in Italy. He then moved to England and sued the EU Commission for $500,000 damages for revealing his identity to Hoffman and for not warning him of the danger he faced if he returned to Switzerland. At last, Adams won his case in the European Court of Justice.

The U. S. government versus other governments

More common examples of government-versus-government conflict occur when the U. S. government attempts to enforce its antitrust laws outside the U. S. borders. These are referred to as extraterritorial application of laws. In 1979, a grand jury in Washington, DC, indicted three foreign-owned ocean-shipping groups on charges of fixing prices without getting approval from the U. S. Federal Maritime Commission. The European and Japanese governments protested bitterly, arguing ① that shipping is international by definition, so the United States has no right to act unilaterally and ② that the alleged offenses were both legal and ethical practices outside the United States.

Sir Freddie Laker's airline, a low-price transatlantic service, ceased operations last century. Shortly thereafter, its liquidators commenced a private antitrust suit in an American court, alleging that the British Airways (BA) had conspired to put Laker out of business. They asked for over $1 billion in damages. Sir Freddie settled his personal suit for $ 10 million and retired to the Bahamas.

Other governments versus the U. S. government

In the 20th century, the United States tried to force seven executives of the British company Rio Tinto-Zinc to testify in connection with an antitrust action in the United States. In that instance, Britain's highest court, the House of Lords, turned down U. S. demands on the grounds that they infringed on British jurisdiction and sovereignty and that the United States was trying to investigate the activities of companies not subject to U. S. jurisdiction.

A number of countries have passed statutes to prevent persons within their territories from cooperating with the United States and have established criminal sanctions for those who comply with U. S. law in violation of those statutes. Among these countries are Australia, Canada, Britain, the Netherlands, and Germany. Under these sanctions, persons or companies can find themselves in the position of being forced to break the law of either the United States or of a country with this type of statute.

In January 1991, Sir Leon Brittan, the EU Commission's vice president of competition policy, met with U. S. attorney general Dick Thoruburgh in Washington, DC, to begin coordinating U. S. and European antitrust policy. Brittan's goal was some variety of formal agreements that would prevent Europe and the United States from colliding over mergers involving both countries.

However, a change of U. S. policy in 1992 may cause collusions. The new policy is to enforce antitrust laws against foreign companies suspected of colluding to hurt U. S. exporters. Prior to the policy change, the Justice Department challenged anticompetitive activity by foreign companies only if direct harm to U. S. consumers resulted from the activity. Some 15 countries, including Canada, Japan, and some in Europe, urged the United States to be cautious in implementing the new policy.

Japan's toothless tiger

Japan's Fair Trade Commission (FTC), which is supposed to enforce antitrust laws, has been nicknamed the toothless tiger. It is viewed as one of the weakest bodies in government, easily bullied by the powerful ministries of finance and international trade and industry, both of which have vested interests in ensuring that Japan's cozy ways of doing business prevail. Most of FTC's victims are small and weak; when it has investigated powerful industries such as automobiles, construction, glass, and paper, it punished them at worst with raps on the knuckles and "recommendations". These are all businesses from which foreigners complain they are excluded.

A major difference between American and Japanese trust-busting is that around 90 percent of the U. S. complaints are initiated by private parties, while in Japan a private antitrust action can be brought only if the FTC has investigated the case first. Because of Japan's arcane discovery laws, the only way the FTC can obtain information on a firm is to raid it. As a result, the FTC won't make a move unless it is sure the laws are being broken. Of course, it is almost impossible to be sure of that without information. Given all this, it is easy to understand why the FTC is considered to be a toothless tiger.

6.5 Tariffs, quotas, and other trade obstacles

Although we introduced these subjects in Chapter 2, they are legal forces, for that reason, we mention them again here.

Every country has laws on one or more of these subjects. The purposes of tariffs are to raise revenue for the government and to protect domestic producers. Quotas, which limit the number or amount of imports, are for protection too.

In national laws, there are many other forms of protection or obstacles to trade. Some are health or packaging requirements. Others deal with language, such as the mandatory use of French on labels and in advertising, manuals, warranties, and so forth for goods sold in France.

As a matter of fact, these governments not only limit imports, but also some products that are exported to other countries. For example, for reasons political or economically competitive, the U. S. enforces very strict regulations for its high-tech products, and these regulations relate to the export products, export destinations, and the trade barriers encountered at the destinations. In other countries, U. S. exports may encounter weak patent or trademark protection, very high tariffs, zero quotas, quarantine periods, or a variety of other obstacles.

Of course, the United States imposes barriers against the import of a number of products. It sometimes uses tariffs, sometimes quotas, and often a more modern form of quota called by some "voluntary" restrain agreements (VRAs) and by others "voluntary" export restraints (VERs). "Voluntary" is in quotes because these barriers are imposed by the U. S. government on the exporting countries. The inevitable result is higher costs to American consumers as exporters send only the higher-priced, top of the line products, and importers charge more for scarcer products.

One justification for protectionism is that it saves domestic jobs. The cost for the American consumer to save one job in the U. S. car industry was estimated to be $250,000.

The United States is not the only country that imposes VRAs and VERs on its trading partners—far from it. Japan, Canada, the EU countries, and many others require countries exporting to them to "voluntarily" limit the number or value of goods exported.

In 1982, the French came up with a novel protectionist device. Japanese videotape recorders were one of the French imports causing a large balance-of-payments deficit with Japan. The recorders normally entered France through the major port of Le Havre, which had a large detachment of customs officers to process imports. Then the French government issued a decree requiring all of the recorders to enter France through Poitiers, which had a tiny customs post. The result was long delays that reduced the number of recorders entering France. Japan then "voluntarily" agreed to limit the number of recorders it exported to France.

6.6 Product liability civil and criminal

Beginning in the 1960s and continuing into the 21 century, manufacturers' liability for faulty or dangerous products was a boom growth area for the American legal profession. Liability insurance premiums have soared, and there are concerns that smaller, weaker manufacturing companies cannot survive.

Now that boom may spread to Europe, where directives of the EU Commission are pushing new product liability laws that would standardize and toughen existing ones. There are several reasons to believe that the impact of strict liability upon product designers and manufacturers in Europe and Japan will not be as heavy or severe as it is in the United States. In Europe, the directive permits the EU member-countries to allow "state-of-the-art" or "developmental risks" defenses, which allow the designer/manufacturer to prove that, at the time of design or manufacture, the most modern, latest-known technology was used. The countries are also permitted to cap damages at amounts no less than 70 million Euros. Damages awarded by American juries have been in the hundreds of millions of dollars.

Major differences in legal procedures in the United States as compared with those in Europe and Japan will limit or prevent product liability awards by European and Japanese courts. In the United States but not elsewhere, lawyers take many cases on a contingency fee basis whereby the lawyer charges the plaintiff for free to begin representation and action in a product liability case. The lawyer is paid only when the defendant settles or loses in a trial; but then the fee is relatively large, running between one-third and one-half of the settlement or award. In addition, outside the United States, when the defendant wins a lawsuit, the plaintiff is called upon to pay all defendants' legal fees and other costs caused by the plaintiff's action.

In the United States, product liability cases are heard by juries that can award plaintiffs actual damages plus punitive damages. As the name indicates, punitive damages have the purpose of punishing the defendant, and if the plaintiff has been grievously injured or the jury's sympathy can be otherwise aroused, it may award millions of dollars to "teach the defendant a lesson." Outside the United States, product liability cases are heard by judges, not juries. Judges are less prone to emotional reactions than juries, and even if the judge were sympathetic with a plaintiff, punitive damages are not awarded by non-U. S. courts.

As indicated at the beginning of this discussion of product liability, the EU (then, the EC) adopted a directive in 1985, imposing a system of strict liability, which was to be effective beginning in 1988. But, because the concept of strict liability is abhorrent to some cultures, the directive had not been implemented by France, Ireland, or Spain as late as 1994. In order to encourage them to pass implementing laws, the EU permits "state-of-the-art" defenses and caps on damage awards, both mentioned above.

Buyer beware in Japan

The Japanese law on product liability is similar to that in the United States prior to 1963. The plaintiff must prove design or manufacturing negligence, which, particularly with complex, high-tech devices, is virtually impossible. The plaintiffs' difficulties are exacerbated by the failure of Japanese legal procedures to provide discovery, the process by which plaintiffs can seek defendants' documents relevant to their cases. Discovery is available to plaintiffs in U. S. courts but not in Europe.

In a survey of more than 500 chief executives by the Conference Board, more than one-fifth believe strict American product liability laws have caused their companies to lose business to foreign competitors. But, as foreign firms buy or build U. S. plants, they are being hit by the same liability and insurance problems long faced by American companies.

Price and wage controls

Although some countries call their price and wage controls "voluntary," governments can apply pressure to companies or labor unions that raise prices or demand wage increases above established percentages. The U. S. government, for example, has withheld government business from companies that violate its guidelines. This has resulted in union lawsuits challenging the legality of such punishment.

With the development of economy, Chinese government ruled the lowest wage, although the lowest wage is different in various areas. Of course, there are no completely free markets and no effective labor unions that are not government agencies. Most countries also have some price and wage control laws. As inflation spreads and grows in the world, price and wage controls can be expected to become more widespread and more restrictive.

Labor laws

Virtually every country has laws governing working conditions and wages for its labor force. Even though hourly wages may be low in a country, employers must beware, because fringe benefits can greatly increase labor costs. Fringe benefits can include profit sharing, health or dental benefits, retirement funds, and more. Some labor laws make the firing of a worker almost impossible or at least very expensive.

Currency exchange controls

Almost every country has currency exchange controls-laws dealing with the purchase and sale of foreign currencies. Most countries, including less developed countries and developing countries, have too little hard foreign currency. There is the rare country, such as Switzerland and China, that sometimes feels they have too much.

Exchange control generalities

The law of each country must be examined, but some generalizations can be made. In countries where hard foreign currency is scarce, a government agency allocates it. Typically, an importer of productive capital equipment gets priority over an importer of luxury goods. People entering such a country must declare how much currency of any kind they are bringing in. On departure, they must declare how much they are taking out. The intent is twofold: ① to discourage travelers from bringing in the host country's national currency bought abroad at a better exchange rate than inside the country, and ② to encourage them to bring in hard foreign currency.

Switzerland—a special case

Switzerland is a special case because its government has imposed controls to keep foreign currencies out rather than in. Switzerland enjoyed relatively low inflation during the 1970s and in the 21 century, and its Swiss franc has remained one of the hardest of the hard currencies. As a result, people from all over the world have wanted to get their money into Switzerland, and the Swiss have felt the need to defend against being inundated with too much currency, which would escalate their inflation. They have used several devices to discourage the inflow of foreign money. Among these devices are low interest rates and even a negative interest rate on some kinds of deposits. Limitations have been placed on the sale to foreigners of bonds denominated in Swiss francs.

6.7 Miscellaneous laws

Individuals working abroad must be alert in order to avoid falling afoul of local laws and of corrupt police, army, or government officials. Followings are good examples.

A Plassey (small town of India) employee, a British subject, is serving a life sentence in Libya for "jeopardizing the revolution by giving information to a foreign company." In the summer of 1986, two Australians were executed in Malaysia for possession of 15 grams or more of hard drugs. Saudi Arabia and other Muslim countries strictly enforce sanctions against importing or drinking alcohol or wearing revealing clothing. Foreigners in Japan who walk out of their homes without their alien registration cards can be arrested, as happened to one man while he was carrying out the garbage. In Thailand, people can be jailed for mutilating paper money or for damaging coins that bear the picture or image of the royal prince, as was one foreigner who stopped a rolling coin with his foot.

Travelers and vacationers can also run afoul of unexpected laws in different countries. In Greece, travelers who exceed their credit card limits may be sentenced to prison for as long as 12 years.

A Philadelphia law firm, International Legal Defense Counsel (ILDC), has made a reputation dealing with countries where American embassies and consulates are of little legal help and where prison conditions are so squalid that survival is the first concern. One of their cases involved a Virginia photographer named Conan Owen. He was duped into transporting a package of cocaine from Colombia to Spain, where he was arrested and slapped with a stiff prison sentence. The U. S. attorney general personally interceded with no success, and Owen languished in prison for nearly two years. Then ILDC sprang him by use of a bilateral prisoner transfer treaty that permits American inmates in foreign jails to do their time in a facility back home. Once in the United States, Owen was quickly freed.

Among ILDC publications that give travelers legal advice are The Hassle of Your Life: A Handbook for Families of Americans Jailed Abroad and Know the Law: A Handbook for Hispanics Imprisoned in the United States.

Business contracts

When contracting parties are residents of a single country, the laws of that country govern contract performance and any disputes that arise between the parties. That country's courts have jurisdiction over the parties, and the court's judgments are enforced in accordance with the country's procedures. When residents of two or more countries sign a contract, those relatively easy solutions to disputes are not available.

United Nations solutions

When contract disputes arise between parties from two or more countries, which country's law is applicable? Many countries, including the United States, have ratified the UN Convention on Contracts for the International Sale of Goods (CISG) to solve such problems.

The CISG established uniform legal rules to govern the formation of international sales contracts and the rights and obligations of the buyer and seller. The CISG applies automatically to all contracts for the sale of goods between traders from different countries that have ratified the CISG. This automatic application will take place unless the parties to the contract expressly opt out of the CISG.

European Union solutions

The law applicable to contracts between EU residents is determined by a 1991 amendment to Rome Convention. It established two principles. First, if the parties agree at the outset which country's law should apply, then that choice will be upheld. Second, if no such choice is made, the law of the country most closely connected with the contract will apply. A set of rules has been established to make this work in practice.

Private solutions, arbitration

Many parties either cannot or do not wish to accept UN or EU solutions. Instead of going to court in any country, they choose for arbitration. At least 30 organizations now administer international arbitrations, the best known of which is the International Court of Arbitration of the International Chamber of Commerce in Paris. More than 450 disputes were filed with that body during 1993, and the number is expected to increase 15 to 20 percent annually over the next several years. People and businesses may prefer arbitration for several reasons. They may be suspicious of foreign courts, but regardless of that, arbitration is always faster than law courts, where cases are usually backlogged and procedures are formal. Arbitration procedures are informal. They can also be confidential, avoiding the perhaps unwelcome publicity accompanying an open court case.

Although London, New York, and Paris are traditional arbitration centers, Hong Kong is growing as one. This follows from the explosive growth of business and trade in the Pacific Rim countries and a 1991 cooperation agreement between the Hong Kong International Arbitration Center and its counterpart in the People's Republic of China.

Enforcement of foreign arbitration awards

Enforcement can pose problems. One solution is the UN Convention on the Recognition and Enforcement of Foreign Arbitral Awards. The United States and most UN member-countries of industrial importance have ratified this convention. It binds ratifying countries to compel arbitration when the parties have so agreed in their contract and to enforce resulting awards.

For instance, when the contract in dispute involves investment in a country from abroad, another arbitration tribunal is available. This is the International Center for Settlement of Investment Disputes, sponsored by the World Bank. Investors were encouraged in 1986 when Indonesia proved willing to abide by a decision of the center even though an adverse opinion could have cost the country several million dollars.

Other organizations are working toward a worldwide business law. The Incoterms of the International Chamber of Commerce and its Uniform Rules and Practice on Documentary Credits now enjoy almost universal acceptance. The UN Commission on International Trade Law and the International Institute for the Unification of Private Law are doing much useful work. The Hague-Vishay Rules on Bills of Lading sponsored by the International Law Association have been adopted by a number of countries.

Despite legal uncertainties, trade grows

It is to the credit of international business that, with the exception of the recession years between 1990 and 2008, world trade has grown each year. That is evidence that despite legal uncertainties, most international contracts are performed fairly satisfactorily.

In 2009, China became the world's largest merchandise exporter by selling over 1500 billion of its products to foreigners. Germany was second at about 1300 billion, followed closely by the U. S. at about 1000 billion. Historically, trade contracts dealt mostly with merchandise trade, but in recent years, service trade has grown rapidly and of course, it is the subject of international contracts. Although the United States runs a persistent deficit in its merchandise trade, it enjoys a smaller but growing surplus in its services trade.

6.8 Patents, trademarks, trade names, copyrights, and trade secrets—intellectual properties

A patent is a government grant giving the inventor of a product or process the exclusive right to manufacture, exploit, use, and sell that invention or process.

Trademarks and trade names are designs and names, often officially registered, by which merchants or manufacturers designate and differentiate their products. Copyrights are exclusive legal rights of authors, composers, play- wrights, artists, and publishers to publish and dispose of their works. Trade secrets are any information that a business wishes to hold confidential. All are referred to as intellectual properties.

Trade secrets can be of great value, but each country deals with and protects them in its own fashion. The duration of protection differs, as do the products that may or may not be protected. Some countries permit the production process to be protected but not the product. Therefore, international companies must study and comply with the laws of each country where they might want to manufacture, create, or sell products.

Patents

In the field of patents, some degree of standardization is provided by the International Convention for the Protection of Industrial Property, sometimes referred to as Paris Union. About 90 countries, including the major industrial nations, have adhered to this convention.

Most Latin American nations and the United States are members of the Inter-American Convention. The protection it provides is similar to that afforded by the Paris Union.

A major step toward the harmonization of patent treatment is the European Patent Organization (EPO). Members are the EU countries and Switzerland. Through EPO, an applicant for a patent need file only one application in English, French, or German to be granted patent protection in all member-countries. Prior to EPO, an applicant had to file in each country in the language of that country.

The World Intellectual Property Organization (WIPO) is a UN agency that administers 16 international intellectual property treaties. It is an open question whether WIPO will work with or compete with a new organization created in the Uruguay GATT negotiations, which is called TRIPS for "trade-related aspects of intellectual property." TRIPS will operate under the aegis of the World Trade Organization.

WIPO's activities are increasing, as nearly 29,000 international patent applications were filed in 1993 under the Patent Cooperation Treaty, which enables investors to apply for registration in several countries with a single application. This is five times the number in the mid-1980s, and the average number of designated countries per application has jumped from 10 to 31. In addition, WIPO advises developing countries on such matters as running patent offices or drafting intellectual property legislation. Interest in LDCs about intellectual property matters has been growing.

At the UN, representatives of the developing nations have been mounting attacks on the exclusivity and length of patent protection. They want to shorten the protection periods from the current 15 to 20 years down to 5 years or even 30 months. But companies in industrialized countries that are responsible for the new technology eligible for patents are resisting the changes. They point out that the only incentives they have to spend the huge amounts required to develop the technology are periods of patent protection long enough to recoup their costs and make profits.

Trademarks

Trademark protection varies from country to country, as does its duration, which may last from 10 to 20 years. Such protection is covered by the Madrid Agreement of 1891 for most of the world, though there is also the General American Convention for Trademark and Commercial Protection for the Western Hemisphere. In addition, protection may be provided on a bilateral basis in friendship, commerce, and navigation treaties.

An important step in harmonizing the rules on trademarks was taken in 1988 when regulations for a European Union trademark were drafted. A single European Trademark Office will be responsible for the recognition and protection of proprietary marks in all EU countries, including trademarks belonging to companies based in non-EU member-countries.

Trade names

Trade names are protected in all countries adhering to the Industrial Property Convention, which was mentioned above in connection with patents. Goods bearing illegal trademarks or trade names or false statements on their origin are subject to seizure at importation into these countries.

Copyrights

Copyrights get protection under the Berne Convention of 1886, which is adhered to by 55 countries, and the Universal Copyright Convention of 1954, which has been adopted by some 50 countries. The United States did not ratify the Berne Convention until the need for greater protection arose in 1988, by which time it was driven to do so against pirating of computer software.

Trade secrets

Trade secrets are protected by laws in most nations. Employers everywhere use employee secrecy agreements, which in some countries are rigorously enforced.

Industrial espionage

Industrial espionage among companies that develop and use high technology is not unusual, but 1983 saw the end of an extraordinary example of corporate warfare between two of the world's mightiest and most technologically advanced corporations. Hitachi tried to obtain trade secrets of IBM, and in June 1982, two Hitachi employees were arrested by the FBI. IBM and the FBI had cooperated in what Fortune called a "superbly executed sting." In February 1983, Hitachi and two of its employees pleaded guilty to an indictment of conspiring to transport stolen IBM property from the United States to Japan.

Malaysia and Thailand have accused other Japanese companies, including Mitsubishi, of being too slow to transfer intellectual properties and technology to them. But a Japanese diplomat in Bangkok says that is a myth. More telling is the Japanese businessman's perspective: "The Thais think they can sit behind their desks and the technology will fall on them from the sky. If they want the technology, they should have the guts to do what we did, which is to go out and steal it."

Costly intellectual property rip-offs

The U. S. International Trade Commission says unauthorized use abroad of American-owned intellectual property costs the United States more than $61 billion a year. That is the amount of lost exports, domestic sales, and royalties. But total extended losses are actually much higher since the $61 billion does not reflect related losses such as increased unemployment that stems from intellectual property piracy.

U. S. industry and the government are trying to combat this. Among other means, several companies have gathered evidence of pirating in countries that have laws against such activities but whose police are unwilling or unable to actively enforce them. On being presented with evidence of illegal practices, they have no excuse not to do their duty.

The U. S. government is using bilateral aid and trade pressures to push other countries, including Japan, Korea, Thailand, and Indonesia to pass and enforce intellectual property protection laws.

Antitrust

Earlier in this chapter, we mentioned the hostility aroused among foreign governments by the aggressive enforcement abroad of U. S. antitrust laws. The laws impede U. S. exports. The U. S. antitrust rules prevent American companies from teaming up to bid on major products abroad impede U. S. exports. For example, General Electric and Westinghouse had to compete against each other for pieces of the $450 million Brazilian Itaipu Dam generator and turbine contracts. The contracts went to a huge European group led by Siemens of Germany and Brown Boveri of Switzerland. The European governments actively supported their companies. The U. S. government, however, would not let GE and Westinghouse cooperate and did nothing to support their efforts.

Such restrictions on cooperation abroad were cited as the worst obstacle to exports caused by the U. S. antitrust regulations and enforcement procedures in a study by the National Association of Manufacturers (NAM). About 70 percent of the over 100 companies that responded to the NAM questionnaire said U. S. antitrust laws and practices caused a decline in their international competitiveness.

Taxing Americans who work abroad

Observing a so-called national tax jurisdiction, rather than a territorial tax jurisdiction, the United States is almost alone among countries in taxing its people according to nationality rather than on the basis of where they live and work. As a result, Americans living or working in another country must pay taxes there and to the United States. In addition to higher tax payments, this requires the time and expense of completing two sets of complicated tax returns. In 1981, the sections of the IRC dealing with this subject were again amended. Although the burden of completing two tax returns was not lifted, the new law gave relief, starting in 1982, in the amount of American taxes to be paid by exempting the first $ 85,000 of earned income. Form 1986, this exemption was lowered to $ 70,000.

When American taxes are anti-American

Suppose an American multinational wants to open a new factory, store, warehouse, or office building in the United States. That would create new jobs for Americans, along with all the benefits that flow from new jobs.

But when the company's executives look at the new U. S. tax law, they hesitate because of the section dealing with allocation of interest expense. When an American company with subsidiaries in many countries borrows money to finance a U. S. business, the interest is treated as if it were paid in part to finance foreign operations. That results in a partial loss of the tax deduction and thus higher after-tax interest cost.

Foreign companies, including foreign-based multinationals, have no such requirement and can deduct 100 percent of interest on borrowings to finance a U. S. operation. Therefore, they have lower after-tax interest costs and, to that extent, can be more competitive in the United States than many U. S. companies.

There is much more to be said about how America's tax system burdens the competitiveness of U. S. business throughout the world. We lack space in this book for a comprehensive discussion but refer you to the endnotes cited in this section for more on the subject.

Uncertainties

There were a number of uncertainties about terms used in the FCPA (Foreign Corrupt Practice Act). An interesting one involves grease: according to the FCPA drafters, the act does not outlaw grease, or facilitating payments made solely to expedite nondiscretionary official actions. Such actions as customs clearance or telephone calls have been cited. There is no clear distinction between supposedly legal grease payments and illegal bribes. To confuse matters further, U. S. Justice Department officials have suggested that they may prosecute some grease payments anyway under earlier anti-bribery laws written to get at corruption in the United States.

Other doubts raised by the FCPA concerned the accounting standards it requires for compliance. That matter is connected to questions about how far management must go to learn whether any employees, subsidiaries, or agents may have violated the act; even if management were unaware of an illegal payment, it could be in violation if it "had reason to know" that some portion of a payment abroad might be used as a bribe.

Other countries' reactions to bribes

Attitudes of business and government officials in Europe toward the FCPA range from amusement to incredulity, and no other government has taken a position similar to that represented by the FCPA—quite the opposite. German tax collectors, for example, permit resident companies to deduct foreign bribes, which are called special expenses. In Britain, corrupt payments, even to British government officials, qualify for tax deductions.

Leading industrial nations such as Britain, France, Germany, and Japan cite many reasons for not adopting FCPA-type laws. They claim such laws might be seen as meddling in other countries' affairs, and unlike the Americans, they aren't eager to regulate their own citizens overseas, especially in business and tax matters. In response to suggestions that Japan enact an FCPA-type law, a foreign ministry official in Tokyo said, "We cannot accept the idea of foreign recommendation somehow obliging Japan to change its criminal law system."

Of course, greed and distrust play their parts. Recessions at home have driven European and Japanese companies to compete much more vigorously for exports. Add to that the prevalence of bribery, and companies will not trust their competitors to play fair or obey an FCPA law if it existed.

Just how pervasive these practices are was disclosed by Lloyd N. Cutler, a Washington attorney who did a study of the subject for the Northrop Corporation. Cutler said, "Almost all European and Japanese export sales of the type that generate corrupt payments are arranged with government export financing or other government support." So far, no other industrialized nation has a law resembling the FCPA, and an anti-commercial bribery treaty proposed by the United States is languishing in an inactive committee of the United Nations.

In 2005, Dancare Corporation, a Danish company, got in trouble because of $ 730,000 in bribes it had paid to get a contract in Saudi Arabia. The trouble was not that it had paid the bribes, but that the bribes were not clearly indicated as such in the company's tax records. The Danish tax chief now advises Danish firms to book illicit payments openly under "bribes." Whether the bribes are in the form of cash, sexual favors, or luxury goods doesn't matter, as long as their value is noted on the tax records. Receipts are desirable but not essential.

Bribes paid in Denmark are illegal; bribes paid abroad to secure export business are both legal and tax-deductible expenses. In the contest for the Saudi Arabian business, the Dancare Corporation bid was more than $ 730, 000 above potential American competitors. Of course, they would have been in violation of the FCPA if they paid a bribe to get the contract and certainly would have been unable to deduct the payment from American taxes.

Billions lost overseas

There are estimates of losses in the billions of dollars. Critics have cited the ambiguities in the FCPA as one of the possible causes of U. S. business foregoing legitimate overseas opportunities. It cannot operate comfortably in an environment where management is unsure of the FCPA's interpretation and application.

In response to the negative feedback about the FCPKs effect, the General Accounting Office completed a survey in 1981. It randomly selected 250 companies from Fortune's list of the 1,000 largest industrial firms. About one-third of the respondents stated they had lost overseas business as a result of the FCPA. Over 60 percent were of the opinion that, all things being equal, U. S. multinationals could not profitably compete against foreign companies that could legally bribe to make sales.

Are export contracts being lost?

Is the anti-boycott law causing American exporters to lose business? Yes, according to Chase Manhattan Bank, especially in the relatively hard-line Arab countries, such as Iraq, Libya, and Syria. Even in Arab countries friendlier to the United States, the law causes difficulties and burdens not faced or borne by most non-American competitors. Commenting on the law and the government's tough enforcement of it, Philip Hinson, Middle East affairs director of the U. S. Chamber of Commerce, says "They've had a randomly harmful effect on U. S. exports."

Another complaint by American companies about the law is the cost of compliance. Joseph Komalick, editor of the Boycott Law Bulletin, says that some U. S. multinationals have as many as 20 lawyers check the legality of Middle East contracts to make sure they don't violate the law.

One argument against the boycott legislation is that it hurts American business but does no harm to the Arab countries. They can buy whatever they want or adequate substitutes from Europe or Japan.

Some laws and agencies aid U. S. exports and investment

We do not mean to give the impression that all U. S. laws and government agencies pose obstacles to the international business of U. S. companies. The U. S. Department of Commerce actively encourages exports by American companies. U. S. embassies and consular offices can be helpful with information and connections for Americans who wish to export to or invest in foreign countries. The FSC provides some tax incentives for U. S. exporters.

Historically, there has been a clear distinction between common law, which developed in England and spread to the English colonies, and civil law, which originated on the continent of Europe. Courts made common law as they decided individual cases; civil law was made by kings, princes, or legislatures issuing decrees or passing bills.

As time has passed, legislatures and government agencies in the United States have made more and more laws and regulations. The courts, in turn, have interpreted these laws and regulations as parties have argued about what they mean. That is the sort of procedure one finds in Europe, but vast differences in practices have developed that have less to do with the traditional common-civil law approaches than with historical government-citizen (or subject) relationships and attitudes.

European practice

Europe has a history of thousands of years of tyranny, which recently has been covered with a veneer of democracy. People have greater reason to fear their governments in Europe than in the United States, and government service is more prestigious. Before a new law is presented to the legislature (which, unlike legislatures in the United States, is always controlled by the same political party that controls the executive branch), consensus is achieved among most of the people, businesses, and government agencies that will be affected.

In contrast to American practices, European legislation is rarely amended, and regulations are rarely revised. Courts are not as often asked to give their interpretations, and if they are, the decisions are rarely appealed. Once a consensus has been reached, it is considered very bad form to open the subject again, and those who do may find themselves left out of the consultations the next time around.

American practice

In contrast to European custom, Americans have a weaker tradition of obeying their governments and have had very little fear of them. Americans are much more likely than Europeans to challenge laws in the courts, in the streets, or by disobedience. Legislation in America is a product of an ongoing adversarial proceeding, not of consensus; law is written by one independent branch of government for implementation by a second and for interpretation by yet a third. Different political parties or people with conflicting philosophies frequently control the three different branches of government.

Laws and regulations are constantly being amended or revised by legislatures and agencies. Courts interpret laws in ways that are sometimes surprising, the courts may strike laws down as being unconstitutional.

In the United States, the legislative body is now called Congress, and it convened as representatives of the several English colonies even before the United States become a country. In Europe, the legislative body of the European Union is called the European Parliament. It was brought into being by the Treaty of Rome, signed in 1957. Bear in mind that the European Parliament is gradually gaining power and can be expected to be a growing force in the EU.

Summary

1. Appreciate the complexity of the legal forces that confront international business. International business is affected by many thousands of laws and regulations issued by states, nations, and international organizations. Some are at cross-purposes, and some diminish the ability of firms to compete with foreign companies.

2. Understand that many taxes have purposes other than to raise revenue. Certain taxes have purposes other than to raise revenues. For example, some aim to redistribute income, discourage consumption of certain products, encourage use of domestic goods, or discourage investment abroad. In addition, taxes differ from country to country. Tax treaties, or conventions, between countries can affect decisions on investment and location.

3. Discuss enforcement of antitrust laws. The United States, which has the toughest antitrust laws, tries to enforce them outside as well as inside the country, or extraterritorially. Although the EU does not attempt extraterritorial enforcement of its

antitrust laws, they can have serious effects. In 1994, the EU levied a $158.58 million fine on a carton-board cartel. Japan's enforcement of its antitrust laws is weak to nonexistent.

4. Recognize the importance of tariffs, quotas, and other trade obstacles to international business. Tariffs are taxes on imports. Quotas limit the number or amount of a product that may be imported. Quotas are frequently called "voluntary" export restraints or "voluntary" restraint agreements.

5. Appreciate the risk of product liability legal actions, which can result in imprisonment for employees or fines for them and the company. Product liability refers to the civil or criminal liability of the designer or manufacturer of a product for injury or damages it causes. In several ways, product liability is treated differently in the U. S. legal system than in other countries. For example, only in the United States does one find lawyers' contingency fees, jury trials of these cases, and punitive damages. Though the principle of strict liability has been adopted in Europe, defendants are permitted to use state-of-the-art defenses and countries can put a cap on damages. Product liability is virtually unknown in Japan.

6. Appreciate the effects of price and wage controls, labor laws, and currency exchange. Price and wage controls, labor laws, and currency exchange controls must be observed in each country where you do business.

7. Recognize the importance of being aware of peculiarities of local law. Miscellaneous laws in host countries can trip up foreign businesspeople or tourists. Charges can range from simply not carrying an alien registration card to narcotics possession.

8. Understand contract devices and institutions that assist in interpreting or enforcing international contracts. International contracts should specify which country's law and courts should apply when disputes arise. The UN's CISG and the EU's Rome Convention have established rules for solving contract disputes. Arbitration is an increasingly popular solution.

9. Anticipate the need and methods to protect your intellectual properties. Patents, trademarks, trade names, copyrights, and trade secrets are referred to as intellectual properties. Pirating of those properties is common and is expensive for their owners. The UN's World Intellectual Property Organization (WIPO) was created to administer international property treaties. But it is an open question whether the WIPO will cooperate or compete with TRIPS, a WTO agency with a similar purpose.

10. Recognize how industrial espionage affects international business. Industrial espionage, a crime punishable in some countries by fines or imprisonment, is one company's attempt to steal another company's trade secrets.

11. Understand the numerous difficulties and burdens placed by U. S. laws and practices on American ICs, which other countries do not impose on their ICs. The FCPA and Arab boycott legislation are unique to the U. S. and are costly obstacles to U. S. ICs. Although the common law and the civil law have different roots, the differences between them are gradually eroding.

Questions

1. Explain some purposes of taxes other than to raise revenues.

2. Why do some people feel that a VAT should replace some or all of the U. S. income tax?

3. Why does a national tax system put citizens of that country at a disadvantage?

4. What objections do other countries have to extraterritorial application by the United States of its antitrust laws?

5. When a Chinese citizen runs afoul of the criminal traveling abroad laws of a foreign country, are the China embassies or the China consulates likely to be of much help? Where else can the traveler look for aid?

6. As opposed to using the courts, what are some advantages that arbitrating contract disputes may have?

7. Are tariffs the only type of obstacle to international trade? If not, name some others.

8. Can product liability be criminal? If so, in what sorts of situations?

9. Does the Foreign Corrupt Practices Act forbid all bribes? Explain.

10. Does the anti-boycott law permit U. S. exporters to go to Arab countries to certify that the products are not of Israeli origin?

11. What are the differences in practices in making, amending, and interpreting laws between the United States and Western Europe? What are the reasons for those differences?

Minicase

Italian Law

A California-based company is expanding very well and has just made its export. All of its sales and procurement contracts up to now have contained a clause providing that if any disputes should arise under the contract, they would be settled under California law and that any litigation would be in California courts.

The new foreign Italian customer objects to these all-Californian solutions. The company says it is buying and paying for the products, so the Californian company should compromise and allow Italian law and courts to govern and handle any disputes.

You are CEO of the Californian company, and you hope to get this order. You are pleased with the service your law firm has given, but you know it has no international experience. What sorts of solutions would you suggest that your lawyers research as possible compromises between your usual all-Californian clause and the customer's wish to go all-Italian?

Chapter 7 International Marketing Strategy

Concept preview

After reading this chapter, you should be able to

1. Appreciate: the importance for international companies to establish their international marketing strategies.

2. Understand: why multinationals take different marketing strategies in various countries.

3. Distinguish: standardization strategy and adaptation strategy.

4. Comprehend: the advantages and disadvantages of various international marketing strategies.

5. Describe: how to analyze the foreign environments when you want to make your international marketing strategy.

The international marketing strategy of Disney's international group

In 1975, Disney established the first theme park in California in the U. S., and in 1983, it established the Tokyo Disneyland to transfer its brand and technology. In 1992, it established another Disneyland in Paris, and the total investment reached $5 billion. But both theme parks had extremely different fortune. The Tokyo Disneyland made huge benefits for the company because of the attendees from Asian countries, at he same time, the Paris Park lost over $900 million in the first year, and it was called "the hapless land of Europe for Disney".

Many of scholars' research results suggest that the reason for Disney's success in Asia is that its international marketing strategy was effective; by taking the methods of joint operation with the Japanese companies and transferring its intellectual property, Disney used local resources for the greatest efficiency. The most important reason for the loss in Paris was that Disney took direct investment to operate the project, but the local markets of Asia and Europe are very different.

According to a theory of Dunning, a famous English economist, if a company wants to take FDI, it has to possess the ownership advantage, location advantage and internalization advantage simultaneously. But Disney possessed none of these advantages when it established its theme park in Paris, which is why it lost money in Paris. Based on the foundation of summing up experience, Disney targeted China's market. Thinking China's market as the biggest potential market of the world, in 2005 it established a theme park in Hong Kong, and the investment proved to be a huge success. Because not only the citizens of China's Hong Kong and Macau bring an enormous profit to Disney, but many mainland Chinese citizens take their families to play in Disneyland, and these mainland citizens have become the most important income source for the company with the fast economic development of China. In addition, the Disneyland of Hong Kong attracted the tourists of South-East Asia.

Obviously, the marketing strategy is the vital for a good marketing result. Particularly if you want to develop foreign markets, you have to face more complex and more difficult environments. In the real world, it is not very easy for the multinationals to finish the job, because it needs more international marketing professionals to study various resources of the companies and complicated external environments. In this chapter, we will discuss some questions about how to make international marketing strategies for the multinationals.

7.1 The nature of strategy

The word "strategy" derives from a Greek word meaning "general", and the concept was used to indicate how to direct the army with someone's wisdom. The concept is used in various fields like economics, politics and education, and it generally refers to far-reaching, significant and decisive plans for the organizations.

Marketing strategy may be similarly described. It means choosing a general direction for the firm, together with organizational designs, policies, systems and a style of management best suited for beating the competitors in the markets. The optimal marketing strategy enables the firm to carry the right products to the right markets at the right time with right price, right promotional policies and the right channels.

Strategy differs from "tactics", in that strategy involves the formulation of general and wide-ranging policies while tactics concern practical methods for implementing strategic decisions. Examples of tactical management in the international marketing field include: concerning the choice of an advertising agent, selection of distributors, or the determination of advertising budgets for particular international markets. Tactical objectives within each national market are likely to include target sales by product and market sector, timescales for entry to a certain number of new distribution systems, attaining brand awareness among a specified proportion of consumers, and the completion of ad hoc projects involving the introduction of new models, analyzing the results of research exercises and so on. However, strategies define the major overall goals of the organization, and plans state how these goals are to be accomplished. Strategy concerns ideas, creativity, and grand conceptions; plans involve instrumental measures for the efficient allocation of resources.

In general, strategy is a very important method for a company to remain invincible in the market, and it is a basic policy for companies' development.

Why do the companies establish their strategies?

Some businesses do not bother to formulate strategies; they prefer to respond to situations as they arise. There are several reasons for this line of approach: inaccuracy of forecasts, sudden and unforeseeable changes in laws, regulations, technical and market environments, the costs and inconveniences of long-range planning, and so on. There are nevertheless many real and significant advantages of having coherent and well prepared strategies. Diverse activities can be better coordinated, resources allocated more effectively, and activities monitored and controlled. Special benefits include the following:

(1) The firm is compelled to recognize its strengths and weaknesses and to assess critically the feasibility of its goals.

(2) Reactions to changes in its competitor's behavior can be decided in advance.

(3) Results may be compared against a logically predetermined target.

(4) Foreseeable pitfalls can be avoided. Indeed, the systematic consideration of likely environments could even lead to the discovery of fresh opportunities.

(5) The administrative processes of strategy formulation themselves require people and departments to meet, discuss issues, exchange ideas and cooperate; this should motivate employees (since the staff who participate in devising a strategy will want it to succeed), encourage initiative avoid the duplication of effort and help eliminate unnecessary waste.

(6) The existence of a strategy provides a focal point towards which all the company's promotional efforts may be directed.

The clearer the strategy, the more obvious the objective, in terms of target market share, revenues and net profits, establishment of market position, that needs to be attained for its successful implementation. It is particularly important not to neglect strategic matters until forced to do so by an unexpected catastrophe, such as loss of major customers, failure to penetrate a lucrative new market, and collapse of an expensive campaign, that indicates that the firm's current activities and approaches are inadequate. Otherwise the firm will be forced to take important decisions in chaotic situations without proper information or the time necessary to consider all relevant factors. A firm without a strategy is ill-prepared to adapt its activities to meet the demands of rapid environmental change.

7.2 How to understand the traits of the strategy

What is the strategy of enterprise? There is not a uniform or normative definition. Although scholars and businesspeople accept the importance of strategy for companies, they always explain strategy according to their own views. Mechael Porter, a professor of Harvard University, said: "Strategy is the combination of the company's targets and the ways which the companies try their best to get their goals." And this definition summarizes popular viewpoints about the strategy of scholars, because it emphasizes the traits of the strategy—planning, uniform outlook and globality. Andrews, a famous economist, thought that strategy encompasses targets, purposes, or goals, and it is the major direction and plan to achieve these targets. Philip Kotler thought when an organization clearly defines its targets and goals, it will understand where it will go; the question is how to get there, and under the circumstances, the company needs a general plan—strategy.

In general, it is very important for a company, using strategy, to take and direct the international managers to make their specific countermeasures to capture clients and beat the competition according to internal and external conditions and to define the mission of the company, future development targets, business scope, and resources distribution. And it is important for the company to remain invincible in the process of the market competition. The purpose of strategizing is tó satisfy consumers' demands and achieve better business performance. Because the company needs to maintain, consolidate, and improve its competitive position in the market with strategy, the company should try to maintain the advantage position in the process of the conflict and improve its scale and strength to maintain constant and healthy development.

Although different scholars give the different definitions about strategy, all of them think that the strategy should possess the following characteristics.

Globality

The objective of company strategy is take into account the entirety of the enterprise, and it is made based on the overall development of the company. At the same time, it directs the total activities of the company. Although the strategy includes the local activity of the company, the local activity should be only an important ingredient of total activity. Specifically, the strategy does not emphasize the importance of the specific business unit or functional department, but the function of the strategy is to coordinate the activities of the various departments of the enterprise based on achieving the mission and target of the company. And in the process of assessment and control, the strategy does not emphasize the self performance of the various departments; it pays more attention to their contribution to achieving the mission and target of the company. This is called the globality of the strategy.

A long-term master plan

The strategy answers the question about how the company will survive and develop in a long term, at least 3 to 5 years. In other words, strategy is the overall direction and plan of the company in the long term. Some enterprises consider planning strategies over even longer timelines, for example, a 10 to 20 years plan. The external environment and the internal resources are the foundation for management to make its strategy, and the strategy should direct and limit the present activities of the company. The company strategy serves for the longer development of the company, and it is the start from the ground of the longer development.

Resist your competitors

The purpose of making company strategy is to become stronger in extreme market competition and to make a company get relative advantages in the process of striving for market shares and resources with competitors. The strategy is the long-term action scheme to face the various impacts, pressures, threat and difficulties coming from the marketing environment and competitors. It is different from action schemes that only improve the enterprise situation, increase economic benefits, or raise the management level but do not consider the competition and challenges. All company work may not become part of the content of the company strategy unless all of the efforts connect to the mission to strengthen the competitiveness of the company This is why the companies have to make their strategy possess the competitive nature and skill to defeat their competitors and guarantee their survival and development.

Programmatic

Programmatic strategy serves the long-term target of the company, is the development direction and the key emphasis in work of the company, and is the regulation of principle and recapitulative. In practice, strategy is the broad-brush design for the company's future. It should not be caught up in minor details; strategy does not emphasize the meticulous, and it emphasizes to have an insight into the direction. This is why programmatic strategy points out the future development direction of company. It is the total program for the staff. So, if you want strategy to be significant, you must introduce, resolve and practice your strategy, and apply a strategy in specific company-action contexts.

Relative stability

Strategy must be relative stable in a certain timeframe so that it can be goal-oriented for business operation practices. If you make frequent changes in policies, the business operation will be in confusion, and the company will most likely lose revenue. At the same time, strategy is subject to dynamic change. Companies must update their strategies based on the changes of the environment and make their strategies more reasonable and protected against their competitors.

7.3 The hierarchy of company strategy

Multinationals may use different strategies to develop foreign markets. However, in general, all of these strategies can be divided into three different levels: corporate strategy, business strategy and functional strategy.

Corporate strategy

Corporate strategy is also called company strategy and it is the highest level strategy for multinationals. That strategy is to choose a market where the company possesses enough resources to beat its competitors, integrate these resources reasonably, and facilitate coordination between the company's branches within the market. It is a globality scheme for a company's management to direct the specific operations of a company.

The major mission of corporate strategy is to answer the question of which fields the enterprise should cover, and the most important factors in this field are how to integrate the company's resources and how to choose and define the business scope. Of this, we should emphasize two questions: to make clear the company's mission and target system and define the scale and important points of the enterprise, and to answer the question of how to develop the business. The most important question is how to distribute resources. Because resources are limited and companies must use these limited resource to generate more value for society and themselves. At the same time, various departments of the company will strive for these limited resources, so company executives must distribute the resources reasonably in a company and try their best to make all of the resources produce more benefits for a company. The important points of any corporate strategy should be following:

(1) To define the mission of the enterprise, especially in choosing the fields of business, consumers, and the orientation of development that fits the resources of the company.

(2) To select the strategic business units, create a developing plan for each of the units, and define different positions for these various business units.

(3) To utilize the strategy for key business units and make the targets of the key business units adapt to the corporate strategy.

Business strategy

Business strategy, also called business unit strategy or competition strategy, is the second level strategy for companies. If your company is a diversification company, you should create a business strategy for your company; otherwise, business strategy is a global criterion strategy. For example, GE (General Electric) should utilize a business unit strategy, because its business fields relate to medical apparatuses, aircraft engines, financial services, and home appliances. Because different fields possess different characteristics, and market situations are very different, GE should use different strategies for its various units. In the case of the company Microsoft, it may only need one strategy to direct its business, because its major business is software development. To ensure a company's competitive advantage, business unit strategies should aim at different external environments and use the company's resources reasonably to defeat their competitors in various business fields.

Notice: only diversification companies need to distinguish between total strategy and operation strategy; for single business companies, operation strategy and total strategy are the same.

The mission of a business strategy is to decide which products a company should develop and how to provide these products to appropriate markets; to decide the degree to which it will satisfy the demand of the consumers versus reaching the objective of a company. Objectives of a company can include long-term profitability, increasing speed of market growth, and improving the efficiency of the company to increase profit.

Based on overall company marketing goals, business strategy should pay more attention to two questions: ① how to enable a company to achieve better business performance and to make great efforts to set up competitive advantage in various operation fields, and ② how to make effective plans to utilize the market forces that will reasonably influence the success and failure of the company in various industries. To achieve these goals, business strategy should emphasize the following:

(1) How to implement the enterprise's mission.

(2) How to understand the opportunities and threat of business units.

(3) How to analyze the internal micro-conditions of business units.

(4) How to define the total target and specific requirements of business units.

(5) How to define the strategic focus, period, and implementation scheme for business units.

Functional strategy

Functional strategy, also called functional level strategy, is short term strategy. Functional strategy relates to the various departments of a company, such as finance, production, marketing, human resources, and information technology. Because of the different missions of each department, various departments carry out different functions. It is very difficult to summarize the core elements and characteristics of functional strategy. But concertedness is an important core element for various functional strategies. This is because: firstly, the effect of concertedness reflects in a single department's activity; secondly, the various functional strategies must maintain consistency for guaranteeing the success of a company's total strategy.

The mission of functional strategy is to improve the use ratio of the company resources and to make the company get the best business achievement with the least cost. Under the condition of certain total strategy, the various departments should collect the resources to take action based on the functional strategy, and they should coordinate with each other to support the implementation of company strategy and guarantee the company to achieve its strategy targets. The emphasis points of the functional strategy include:

(1) How to carry out operation strategy and how to refine the functional targets, such as scale, productive power, leading product and variety, quality, technology, market share and sale growth rate, quality of labor forces, and benefit and efficiency.

(2) How to define a strategy's emphasis, period, and major tactics.

(3) How to design a proper system to meet various real-world risks.

Compared with corporate strategy and business strategy, functional strategy is more detailed, specific, and possesses operability. It is composed by a series of detailed schemes and plans. It relates to all of the management areas of the company, including financial, production, sales, research and development, public relations, purchase, storage, transportation, and human resources. Functional strategy can be divided into marketing strategy, human resource strategy, financial strategy, production strategy, research and development strategy, and public relations strategy.

We can understand corporate strategy, business strategy and functional strategy as very important parts of a company's strategy, and the difference is that their emphasis and effects are different in a company.

7.4 Marketing strategy

Concept of marketing strategy

Marketing strategy is the long-term overall idea, policy, and scheme for marketing actions based on the resources of the company. The purpose of a marketing strategy is to adapt to various market environments, to satisfy customer demand, to achieve the long-term survival and development of the company under the direction of total strategy.

Based on the corporate strategy hierarchy, marketing strategy is a part of corporate strategy and is one type of functional strategy. On the one hand, marketing strategy is subject to corporate strategy, Its starting point and targets are to achieve the corporate strategy goal. Marketing strategy is the principle line for a company to operate its marketing, and it is the total policy in directing all the marketing works of a company.

Contents of marketing strategy

Marketing strategy is established by the marketing department, and it is a functional strategy. The most important contents of the marketing strategy include: how to choose the target market, how to position your company or your products in the market, and how to develop and expand your market share, and so on.

1. How to select your market

You must define your market specifically if you want to carry out your marketing strategy. You should know where your consumers are, because for any enterprises, products or services are all limited, and the enterprise only can satisfy one or two demands of their consumers. This is why the marketing strategy should define the market first and find out who are company's consumers.

2. How to finish the market position

When you establish your marketing strategy, you should understand your present market position and what higher market position you wish to achieve. To do this, you have to define your competitive advantage in present market, and you must decide which tactics you will take to reach your market position goal. You should understand what kind of image you should set up in your consumers' mind.

3. How to define whether or not business structure can satisfy demand to finish market position

You should understand whether or not your business structure is reasonable in the present market, if you have enough cash flow, if you will survive financial crisis, if you have the clear business prospects. All of these factors are very important for your marketing strategy and they are the basic guarantee for you to achieve your corporate strategy.

4. How to establish the marketing mix tactics to bring about its marketing strategy targets

If a company wants to achieve its marketing goals, the first job is to segment the market and to occupy enough market shares in specific markets to make more profit. However, the precondition for you to carry out your business scheme is that you have to establish detailed plans to finish lots of specific work, and all of the plans should be included in your marketing strategy. "The details will decide your success or failure."

5. How to distribute your limited resources in various departments of the company reasonably

There is no any company to possess unlimited resources, and excellent managers can always distribute the company's resources reasonably. Marketing strategy should not only illustrate the priority of how the different departments use various resources of the company, but it should also help the managers to make decisions on how to distribute limited resources in various markets during different strategic periods.

7.5 Characteristics of the marketing strategy

Marketing strategy is the strategy for the marketing department. Contrasted with overall strategy and business strategy, its characteristics include:

Technicality

While corporate strategy directs the long-term orientation of a company and overall works of a company, and business strategy directs the various works of specific business units, marketing strategy only directs the various activities of the marketing department. That means the marketing strategy should be designed according to a company's mission and resources, based on specific market environments. A company's marketing strategy designers should utilize basic marketing skills to develop marketing strategy, including market research skills, market analysis skills, market forecast skills, and so forth.

Submissiveness

Marketing strategy is subject to the overall strategy of a company. That means it is the strategic plan established by a company to guarantee the achievements of the company's corporate and business strategies. The direction and content of the marketing strategy should be made according to the corporate strategy and business strategy, and should be made in favor of carrying out the total and business strategies. The implementation of a marketing strategy should serve to reach the target of the overall strategy of the company. Marketing strategy will influence other departments and company very much, because for any enterprises, all of a company's efforts will come into naught if the marketing department does not sell the company's products. Therefore, managers should pay more attention to marketing strategy, because it is a very important part of the overall strategy, a part that interacts dynamically with all other strategies of a company.

Relative independence

A marketing department is different from other departments in a company, and it has to face both external environments and internal environments of a company, and all the environments often change every day, so a marketing department possesses its own rules. As opposed to other departments of a company, marketing is a very independent function. This is why we must establish and implement a marketing strategy based on "the rule of the market". A marketing strategy should not be limited too much by company resources; that is to say, the leaders of a company should support their marketing department more and make its strategy a better fit for the market situation.

Relative mutability

A marketing strategy established based on relative laws and market situation is very important for company managers; however, the regulations and environments often change, because of various factors, both external and internal. The managers must supervise any change of the market closely when they want to update and carry out their marketing strategy, and, if the occasion arises, they should make adjustments to their marketing strategy according to local resources and the market change. There are no marketing strategies that do not make any adjustments.

Mutual integration

A marketing strategy directs the various jobs of the marketing department; it does not only limit the marketing department. Marketing strategy relates to corporate strategy, business strategy and other functional departments' strategy. In practice, if you want to finish a marketing job, you have to rely on the coordination and support from other departments. Marketing strategy should be integrated with other departments' strategies. For example, if the marketing department needs special talent, it has to rely on the human resources department; its new product strategy relates to the production department; if it wants to create a better market position it has to rely on the purchasing department to provide higher price but better quality raw materials or parts. In a word, the basic demand for a marketing strategy is to integrate with other departments' strategies if you want to achieve the overall strategy objectives of the company.

7.6 International marketing strategy

International marketing strategy

International marketing strategy is the strategy that companies establish for developing the international market and achieving their international business targets. International marketing strategy is a part of the overall strategy of a company and it is subject to the overall strategy of the company. As with common marketing strategy, international marketing strategy is the preferred plan for companies to survive and develop in foreign markets and it is established by the marketers based on the company resources and external environments.

However, compared with common strategies, you have to face more complex external economic environments when you want to establish international marketing strategy, and managers have to consider more characteristics and demands of foreign markets. International marketing strategy possesses variability, externality, and diversity; as such, the emphasis of international marketing strategy is different from domestic marketing strategy.

By now, many companies have realized the importance and particularity of international marketing, and so they strive to establish specialized international marketing strategy to direct their international marketing actions. In a way, the international marketing strategy can decide the success or failure of a company that goes international. Of course, it is not very easy for companies to establish their international marketing strategies, and they should pay more attention to the following questions when designing their international marketing strategies:

1. How to select your international markets

International marketing has to face different economic, political, and cultural environments, and consumers of various countries are very different; a company cannot satisfy all of the demands of the consumers, regardless of how large the company is. It is impossible for companies to try to make great achievements in all economic fields. So, the company can only enter one or several proper international markets. These international markets must meet the following conditions: ① the market condition fits to the resources of the company; ②in these markets, the advantages of the company can be developed furthest; ③ the company can seize a better opportunity to occupy enough market shares and make more profit in the markets.

Companies always classify markets as first, second and third target markets. The standard of the distinction is how large of a degree the company's resources can fit the foreign market environments. If you want to achieve your international marketing target, you have to integrate your resources and optimally allocate your company's resources in relation to external environments. For example, IBM divided its oversea markets into 3 areas. The first target market was the European market. Here, the connection degree was highest between its resources and the market environments. The second target market included China, Japan, and other Asia and Pacific countries. Other countries and areas were its third target markets. In general, the first step that multinationals take in crafting their strategies is to determine how to select their foreign markets. This is also called international market segmentation.

2. Entry strategies for international target markets

After finishing market segmentation, companies have to decide how to enter a foreign market. That means determining how to integrate your products, equipments, technologies, trade marks, and management resources to enter a new market.

In a large part, the mode of entry decides the eventual international marketing mode. In practice, the entry mode is divided into 3 types: ① export, including indirect and direct export; ② foreign investment, including taking money and other resources to enter a foreign market to set up a manufacturing plant, or signing a long-term contract with the local company with your patent and trade mark, to collect royalties from the local company; ③ portfolio, also called indirect investment; it means you can purchase the foreign stocks or bonds to get a return.

Before entering a new foreign market, the first question for a company is to define the entry mode, because every mode has different forms, requiring different conditions and resources, and each form possesses different advantages and disadvantages. Excellent managers can always use the correct entry mode to achieve their international marketing goals. For example, McDonald's always takes the trade mark transfer mode to enter a new market, IBM always takes direct investment (and wholly-owned subsidiary is the primary form) to enter foreign markets, and GMC took a joint venture deal with China's auto companies to enter Chinese market, and the biggest reason Disney failed in the European market was that it took the wrong entry mode. In general, the different entry mode will influence your future international marketing result very much and the key to solving the problem is to correctly assess the internal resources and external environment.

3. International marketing competition strategy

With the development of globalization, international competition has become more complex and intense; the actions of competitors will influence your business directly. Marketers have to realize the characteristics of the competitors and analyze their strategy, target, advantage and disadvantage to establish their own pertinent competition strategy to adapt to different environments.

In many cases, competitors are same-industry rivals or potential rivals, but in today's international market, any producer or merchant who does business in the same product line as you may occupy your market. This is why Poter (a very famous American economists) said that marketers have to face 5 real-world competition forces: consumers, suppliers, present rivals, new rivals, and substitute goods. International marketers have to study all of the complex situations and establish their market position; this is the foundation for them to craft their competition strategy.

Of course, the decisions of competitors are not only a threat, they are very important references for international companies to make their own strategies. Based on different market environments and resources, marketers can establish different competition strategies, including market leader strategy, market challenge strategy, market follower strategy, and market niche strategy. Because of market difference, every company should make different competition strategies in various markets based on present market situation, marketing targets, and company resources. In general, it is more difficult for you to make international competition strategies in the real world, and the first step for you to finish the job is to understand the various situation of your target markets.

4. International marketing organizational design strategy

With the expanding of the internationalization scale and increasing of international actions, an efficiency international marketing organization can always play a very important role. As a matter of fact, the most important reason that GE has become one of the most famous multinationals of the world is that it has the highest efficiency management organization of the world. Additionally, the flat management (established by GE) has become the classic management mode, one from which many contemporary international companies draw from in designing their own organization strategy.

International organization may be an export department, an international business department, or a department which manages all of the global business of the company. No matter what organizational modes you are using, the most important factor for you to notice is that your international marketing organization must be efficient enough to control the international marketing actions. You have to design an organization to satisfy the demands of internationalization and international market development for your company.

The contents for international marketing strategy plan

1. The difference between strategy and plan

The strategy and plan are both related to and distinguished from each other. In the broad sense, both strategy and plan are the matter of the whole scheme for the company's future, and they can all be called "plan." In narrower terms, though, the strategy is the core of the plan and the plan includes the content of the strategy; the plan, in contrast to the strategy, is the specific method for the company to achieve its strategy. First, we should establish the strategy, and then specify the plan; this way, the plan links specifically and directly to the broader strategy of the company.

In implementation, the company strategy is the overarching theme, while company plan may be overarching or partial. In the time of implementation, the company strategy is long-term, while the company plan may be long-term, medium-term or short-term. In implementation content, the company strategy is the principle, while the company plan is the detail. In implementation methods, the company strategy gives priority to the qualitative aspects of business, and the company plan gives priority to the quantitative aspects. In general, upper management's major job is to establish the strategy and direct the development direction of the company, while the specific departments of the company set up their own business plan to achieve the strategy goal of the company.

2. The details of international marketing strategy plan book

The international strategy plan contains methods and countermeasures that a company can use to fit different foreign environments and achieve its international marketing targets. This plan is based on the assessment of the company's resources, basic mission and marketing targets.

For modern companies, especially large-scale international enterprises, if they want to make their business work regularly and high efficiently, they have to establish their international marketing strategies to fit the demand of the various markets. The international marketing strategies are indispensable for international companies to guarantee their international marketing targets to be achieved. As a matter of fact, famous international companies have their own international marketing strategies, and their occupation of superior market positions is directly correlated to the care and attention they pay to their international marketing strategies.

Different international companies have their own various international marketing strategies, and even within the same company, it may take many different international marketing strategies in various markets or in different periods. However, most of international marketing strategies include the following content.

1) Summary

Summary is the interpretation for specific targets and countermeasures, and the purpose of writing a summary is to allow managers to understand the core details of a strategy. If managers want to study a plan carefully, they can check the relative materials of the plan, so a strategy book should include the catalogue and relative pages of the total plan. The strategy book should make the roles of every staff member clear by defining their missions.

2) Current situation analysis

In this part, strategies should provide background materials related to domestic and foreign markets, products, competition, distribution, information media, and macro environments. Of this, the following contents should be included:

(1) Current market situations: the market size and growth situation in the past several years or during certain periods; most times, the most important indicator is the revenue.

(2) Current product situations: the revenue, price, and profit situation of major products in the past several years or during certain periods.

(3) Distribution situations: the efficiency, performance, and change of distribution channels in the past several years or during certain periods.

(4) Competitive situations: our competitors, their targets, scale, market share, marketing strategies and other characteristics; situations about their marketing purpose and actions.

(5) Current environmental situations: the change trends of the global economy, political, cultural, legal, and social environments, and situations related to the target countries, and how the change trends influence international marketing strategies.

3) Opportunities and threats analysis

Based on the past, current and future marketing situations, managers should analyze their resources and related products to find major opportunities for and threats to the company. They have to define strengths and weaknesses in their product's market, as well as major problems they have to face. In this field, we can utilize the following analyses:

(1) Opportunity analysis: analysis of external forces that an international company has to face. Because these forces may heavily influence marketing policies, managers should understand which opportunities they can take and which threats they have to try their best to avoid.

(2) Advantages and disadvantages analysis: analysis of factors which lead to the success or failure of a company.

(3) Problem analysis: analysis of how to clear the risks and disadvantages of a company and consider how to solve problems.

Opportunity and threat analysis are the foundation for marketers to craft international marketing strategies.

4) Marketing targets

These are the core of a marketing strategy plan and they are defined based on opportunity and threat analysis and also future market assessment. Marketing targets typically include: revenue, market share, distribution cover degree, profit ratio, and the rate of profit on investment. All of these indicators should be quantified and coordinated. In general, market targets are the objectives for a company to achieve in a specific market or a certain time period.

5) Marketing strategy

This is the method used to achieve a company's marketing targets. It includes how to get the information of the target markets, how to select the target markets, how to enter the foreign markets, how to finish the market position, how to allocate the marketing expenditures, and how to take the international marketing mix. In regards to its marketing strategy, a company should pay most attention to the following:

(1) Target market definition: screening what kinds of markets the company should enter, and which is the first, second and third markets for the company to enter. The company has to define whether or not the market conditions fit its resources, especially for the first target market. Many managers think the large markets like America or China are the key markets in the world, and that their companies should enter these markets; however, the markets may not fit their companies because of the intense competition, political climate, cultural problems, or other issues, even if their companies market the best products in the world.

(2) Product position: product is always the core of marketing. For example, in a domestic market, you have to establish the market position for your products first before you enter a new foreign market, and you may lose money in foreign markets if you cannot get your product to stand out to consumers in the market.

(3) Product line: includes confirming the length and width of the product line, because more length and width means more resources that a company has to invest. A company should consider its marketing targets before making decisions regarding its product line.

(4) Pricing: for any company, pricing policies not only confirm unit profit of a product, but also reflect the company's operation intention. You must establish your price decision system before you enter a new market, especially if you want to develop a foreign market; you have to face lots many unfamiliar competitors and strange operation environments.

(5) Distributors: focus on how you plan to carry your products to your end-users; most products rely on the distributors to sell them. Because of the distribution system, policies are very different in various countries; you have to study what kinds of distribution mode to take and how to establish your standards to screen your channel members.

(6) Service: not only do you have to confirm your service mode, but you also have to establish the service standard for your staff based on different market conditions before you enter a foreign market. This is always very important for any company, even if the company sells tangible products. For example, the company Haier is very famous

for its five-star service system. With the economy's development, consumers need first-rate service, and this is a very important tactic to establish and confirm your brand in a new market.

(7) Promotion: beyond question, foreigners don't understand your company and your products, so you must advertise and promote in foreign markets. You have to solve problems like the following: how to select the proper media to help you, how to organize promotional activities, and how much money you want to invest. All this should be in your strategy book.

(8) Research and development: in the new market, decide whether or not you want to develop new products. Decide whether or not there is enough technical ability and equipment in local markets and how you will utilize these resources. Based on analysis result, you will make a research and development budget. This will allow all of your staff, especially your technicians, to understand your new product development strategy.

(9) Marketing research: this includes research content, methods, budget, time, and your implementation plan.

Although the strategy book cannot include everything about international marketing, it is very important for international managers to plan well. As marketers, it is impossible follow every detail of a plan; however, you should understand the procedures and contents of the plan at least, and this is a basic quality requirement for international managers.

6) Action plan

An action plan is when international companies establish specific active plans to achieve previously mentioned goals. They must make marketing tactics materialize and make their plan as a specific action. And in this field, you should answer the following questions in your strategy book.

(1) What is your specific business?

(2) When do you start and when do you finish?

(3) Who is responsible for the job?

(4) How much does it cost?

You should list detailed procedures for every action in order to implement and assess your plan. An action plan defines which actions can promote a company to achieve its marketing targets and to keep a lookout on actions that depart from goals based on the action time, space, human resources, procedures and founds. The purpose is to avoid confusion and waste when a company carries out its marketing strategy in a new market. In general, an action plan is a major mean for a company to achieve its business targets. Managers should pay more attention to details in this field, and it is very important to select the proper staff for the right jobs.

7) Budget

A budget is a report about specific activities, the quantization of the income and expense, and at the same time, a very important control means for managers to supervise an operation.

The business units usually draw up budgets first, and then budgets should be examined and approved by top managers. If these budgets are authorized, they allow various business units to arrange production, labor, personal, and marketing jobs.

Remember, budgeting is not just a financial concept; in fact, every business unit of an international company should work out its own budget. It is a very important reason for managers to punish and reward their staff, because many budgets include the detail indicators for the staff.

8) Control

Control means how managers supervise the plan process and schedule; superior managers will often decide the how to execute a plan depending on the month or season, and they would find out problems and their causes in the process. Experienced managers always can provide better methods for solving problems and can supervise and urge weaker departments to improve their work efficiency. The purpose is to guarantee that a company would achieve its marketing targets.

The classification of an international marketing strategy plan

Marketing plans are very different in various companies. In common situation, an international marketing strategy should make the following kinds of plans:

1. Short-term plan

A short-term plan is also called an annual plan, which includes annual marketing indicators, area business indicators, product marketing targets and methods, and various marketing means to achieve the aforementioned goals. A short-term plan is made by superior managers, middle management, and the planning department. A short-term plan is a very important part and foundation of marketing strategy.

2. Long-term plan

A long-term plan can be a 5-year plan, 7-year plan, 10-year plan, 20-year plan, or more. A long-term plan includes a long-term marketing target, growing plan, competition plan, and methods and means to achieve the marketing targets. The long-term plan is established by upper management or a planning department. In addition, a company should establish its product marketing plan to confirm its product targets, product tactics, and product budgets. A company should also establish its investment plan to confirm its new product research and development plan. Finally, a company should specify tactics with regards to establishing a new company branch or subsidiary in a new market and/or acquiring a foreign company. Another integral part of a company's long-term plan is the action program plan. It should include a detailed action schedule and specific methods and means targeted towards a company's various goals.

In general, the short-term plan defines the specific marketing tactics and the long-term plan defines the total marketing targets of the company, and combining both the short-term and long-term plans successfully results in great achievements for the company, assuming that the various resources of the company continue to work in tandem from short-term to long-term.

How to establish your marketing strategy plan

Various companies take different ways to make marketing strategies because of the companies' different natures, different leadership structures, and different resources. In general, you can choose the following methods:

1. Transmit to lower level style

Upper management establishes the target plan for all of lower level management. Managers who use this method think that their staff prefer taking orders from other people and taking responsibility. In centralization companies, the whole plan is established by upper management and lower level departments are in charge of specific implementation. In contrast, in the divided decentralized companies, the CEO may transmit the plan direction summary and asks the lower level managements to create the plan specifics and then submit the specific action plan to upper management.

2. Aggregation style

Various departments of a company draw up their own marketing targets and plans independently, then submit the plans to upper management and get permission from upper management to carry them out. The managers who use aggregation style to make their strategies believe that the staff likes to take responsibility, and that upper-level managers will enhance their creativeness and responsibility if they participate in implementing their company's plan. The contents of the plan made by various departments includes the analysis of opportunity and threats, major targets, methods to achieve the targets, turnover, profit, market share, and allocation of capital and human resources.

3. Cooperation style

The headquarters of international companies direct their subordinates and/or subsidiaries in drawing up their company's marketing plan, and the subordinates and subsidiaries establish the marketing plan drafts and submit them to the headquarters. If the headquarters agree the plans, the plans become the formal marketing plans of the companies and the headquarters are responsible to supervise the implementation.

4. Teamwork style

Typically, in small-and medium-centralization companies, upper management have department managers act as plan team members to assist them in establishing the formal plan. Some of the larger companies also utilize teamwork style. The advantage of teamwork style is that the companies can finalize the company plan in one process, since all levels of management take part in the work to establish the marketing plan.

The significance of establishing and implementing an international marketing plan

For any company, strategy management demands constant attention. For international companies, the success or failure of their international marketing strategies directly influence their international marketing situation. Put simply, strategies give direction to the development of a company, ergo, a company's international marketing strategies are vital for that company's success in the international market. Action of international marketing strategy include:

1. Guaranteeing management to have a clear direction

Corporate strategy identifies a company's broad-scope job emphasis and development direction, while marketing strategy specifically stresses work emphasis and development direction of the marketing department. It can ensure that the marketing department's work proceeds steadily, so that, even in the event that the company encounters a violent shift in its business environment, the corporate strategy can stabilize the company's development. Better strategies generally offer better means to navigate various changes in business environment. A superior marketing plan can help a company to face more complex environments and guarantee that the company can maintain a superior marketing position over its competitions.

2. To enhance adaptability to increasingly complex environments

In the international market, the market situation of different countries varies greatly, and there are many competitors fighting for market dominance in each country. The marketing strategy plan is a company's systemic scheme for both current and future market competition. An excellent marketing strategy can guarantee that the company has enough preparation to navigate market change.

3. To enhance stability of marketing action

All of a company's marketing departments should be directed by the company's marketing strategy, and the stability of this strategy decides the stability of the company's marketing action. A stable, yet dynamic, marketing strategy can aid a company's marketers in adhering to their company's fundamental marketing goals while coping with shifting market events, improving the chances of success of the company.

4. To enhance the successful possibility of a company

Companies with stable yet dynamic international marketing strategies are almost always more successful than companies without established strategies. Marketing strategy informs a company's overall plan based on analysis of a company's competitors and the market environment; these factors are carefully considered before a company launches its marketing strategy. Once a marketing strategy is launched, it strives to maximize the effectiveness of all of a company's various resources. A company that correctly and effectively assesses the company's competitors, market environment, and available resources greatly increases the chances of getting the best benefits with the lowest cost in the market. This is why famous companies have their own detailed international marketing strategies and thrive for a long time.

7.7 Formulating procedures for an international marketing strategy

To analyze international marketing environments

Environment analysis is the foundation and starting point for international companies to make their international marketing strategies. International marketing environments are very complex, and sometimes companies have to face market environments with different characteristics and tendencies. Companies have to analyze and understand the current situation and future developmental trends of the market before they enter foreign markets. In general, there are both internal and external environments, and international managers should analyze all factors before making international marketing strategies.

1. External environments analysis

To a certain extent, the survival and development of a company depends on external environments, and the change of external environments may bring new opportunities and threats to the companies. The purpose of analyzing environments is to discover potential opportunities and threats for companies in international markets. If you want to analyze external environments, pay more attention to the following points:

(1) The development trends of international trade, such as growth or decline; the situation concerning multinationals and whether or not they invest in international markets zealously; whether or not there is serious protectionism in the major countries; whether or not the multinationals can earn more money very easily, and so on.

(2) The situation concerning international relations, especially whether or not your government maintains good political relations with your host government, because if the conflict between the governments breaks out, you might suffer from political

crossfire.

(3) Technology and technology development trends related to the company's products, because it is impossible for a company to occupy foreign markets for a long time or make more profits if it cannot utilize more advanced technologies to produce new products.

(4) The situation and development trends concerning law, politics, economy, and society of a host country, because the environmental changes will influence international marketing very directly.

(5) The situation concerning your competitors; many situations concerning your competitors will influence your international marketing tactics; studying carefully, so that you can handle the competition, the market positions, market share, marketing tactics, product technology, management style, and so forth.

2. Internal environments analysis

A company must develop its strategy plan to analyze strengths, weaknesses, and limitations of a company's business development. The major content in this field includes:

(1) Talents and management, which means that the quality, skill level, and decision-making ability of top management will influence the result of a company's international marketing. International managers not only have to improve their own management skills but also should establish a proper training system in their company to improve their staff's business ability. Management is one of the most important factors for international marketing.

(2) Products, which means that the managers should choose the best or most proper products to enter a new market and meet the demand of foreigners, especially when the products enter a new market for the first time. The managers should analyze their production ability, raw material supply, R&D, and so on.

(3) Finances, the current and future capital source, the ability of capital transfer, the profit target, cost control, and various budgets for marketing mix are very important factors for managers to study. Of course, the purpose is to make the various resources of the company develop the highest efficiency.

(4) Marketing, the current product markets, the situation of product sale, distribution of oversea markets, promotion tactics, and competitive countermeasures are all important points for international managers to study.

Environment analysis is the foundation for companies to enter a foreign market, and managers have to utilize opportunities and avoid threats made by the environments adequately if they want to achieve their business goals in international markets.

Determining corporate mission

After analyzing international marketing environments, a company should confirm another very important aspect of its strategy: formulation of the company mission. A company mission is a company's reasons to enter a specific market. The company mission reflects its market position and desired public image. The mission of the company confirms the basic guiding ideology, principle, direction, and operation philosophy. The mission is not a specific objective, nor is it an abstract concept; however, it influences the thought process and subsequent decisions of a company's management.

If you want to understand what the company mission is, you have to answer the following questions:

(1) What are our businesses?

(2) Who are our consumers?

(3) What values can we provide to our consumers?

(4) What are our future businesses?

(5) What businesses should we take?

Companies should consider the following basic factors when they want to establish their company missions:

1. Company history

Generally speaking, the history of a company can influence the company in establishing its mission in aspects such as production, technology, management, market reputation, and connections in marketing channels.

2. The preference of managers

To some extent, the individual psychological situation of any given manager may influence their assessments about various market opportunities, and thus influence a company's mission. For example, managers who dream to make great sucess in marketing tend to select high-risk, high-reward missions, while overcautious managers prefer to choose smaller-risk, smaller-reward missions.

3. Market environments

Changes in market environments can lead to variations in market opportunities. Various political, economic, social, and natural factors all influence the demand quantity and structure. The result is that some demands grow fast, while others decline. These dynamic situations alter the benefits and risks for a company. Companies have to adjust their production and business according to changes in the market environment.

4. Resource conditions

Companies have to consider the availability of their resources when they decide on their production or operation mission. These companies' managers have to consider whether or not their human resources, capital, technology, material resources, and even their ability to gather raw data can fit the demand of the mission, because they may loss if they lack these resources.

5. The core competence

Selection of a company's mission should be established based on the core competence of the company itself, since this is the only way for the companies to develop their own unique characteristics and market advantages. Although the available resources and company's raw ability may alter the company's implementation of its production or marketing mission, they will succumb to powerful competitive pressure in the market if they inaccurately assess their core competence. That is why a company must strive for a core competence that is best to their competitors', or at least to their major competitors'. For example, in the fields of capital, technology, cost, environments, resources, and even the government or public relations, if a company possesses unique advantages, it can adopt a rival company's good points and avoid its shortcomings and beat that company in market competition.

7.8 Making strategic objectives

After establishing the mission of a company, the company should transform the company's mission into specific objectives. Companies need to take correct company strategies, utilize external and internal environments and optimize management to achieve the strategic objectives. A company must execute well-planned strategies related to this vision, and utilize external environments, internal environments and optimal management to achieve these strategic objectives.

Strategic objectives

The company objective is a goal that a company wants to achieve, but at the same time, it is a performance dimension assessment for the company. In the process of forming the strategy, the strategy objective should be based on an objective system. The strategy should always include various objectives directed at different actions based on the different environments and it should also include objectives directed at various departments and personnel. Total objectives always include profit rate, sales volume, market share, brand awareness and quality and so forth. The following table is the objective system offered by management guru named Peter Drucker, a famous economist, to guarantee the company that a company will be able to achieve its mission (Table 7-1).

Table 7-1 Objective system and objective contents

Objective system	Objective contents
Objectives about the market	Describe the company's expected market share and its competitive position in the market
Objectives about improving and developing technology	Describe content and countermeasures about improving and developing new products or new services
Objectives about improving productivity	Describe how to measure the usage of raw materials and how to improve the output and quality of the products
Objectives about materials and financial resources	Describe how to get materials and financial channels and how to use them efficiently
Objectives about profits	Illustrate the expected profit rate with one or several economic indicators
Objectives about human resources	Describe how to acquire, train and develop human resources and how to train management and develop individual talents
Objectives about how to develop the enthusiasm of personnel	Describe how to develop personnel enthusiasm and create system for rewarding desired behavior and correcting undesired behavior
Objectives about social responsibility	Describe specific social responsibility of the company and list specific countermeasures to implement

Objective requirements

The purpose for creating an objective is to enhance the strength of the company and establish competitive advantage in the markets. This is why a company has to obey the following requirements when it formulates its marketing objectives.

1. Advancement

The various objectives should be forecasted and calculated carefully, which means that every indicator must be based on scientific and reasonable situation. The target goals should be ambitious but feasible. And proper objectives should be able to be achieved by the company if personnel make a great effort.

2. Hierarchy

A company has a lot of target goals when it wants to develop international markets. Some of these goals are major objectives and some of them are derived objectives, and a company should divide various objectives into the different priorities and clear the essential objectives. The purpose for this is to maximize the use of company resources and achieve the overall strategic objectives of the company.

3. Quantification

It is impossible for managers to objectively examine the achievements of the staff if the indicators are not quantified. Not only are quantifiable objectives a precondition for managers to control the process and make a reasonable reward and correction system, but they are also a very important resource for the managers when they make their marketing plans. In addition, the quantification indicators enable the managers to survey and adjust their plans in a timely manner.

4. Feasibility

The adaptation between company resources and market environments is a basic precondition for a company which wants to develop any markets. If the company breaks away from this precondition when it makes its marketing strategy, it is impossible for the company to win in the markets. Unrealistic plans not only can't create value for companies but they also waste the resources of a company. However, external environments and internal resources are changing every day and marketers need to adjust their tactics according to new situations constantly. So, feasibility is another necessary consideration for a company when it makes its international marketing strategy.

5. Harmony

To achieve the company's objectives, the various targets should be coordinated and not conflicted. Thus, various resources like money, materials, and human resources can be integrated and allocated efficiently. Of course, it is not easy for the managers to coordinate objectives in the real world, because various objectives reflect the different benefits and different resource allocation in various departments of a company.

6. Time-based

All of the company strategic objectives should limited by time. Not only can clear time limits spur staff to finish their jobs by a certain period, but it also enables the leaders to control the process efficiently. In addition, any strategies made by a company based on market forecasts and should be adjusted according to the change of the market environments.

7.9 Analysis about current business portfolio

To achieve strategy targets, companies should allocate their resources to specific businesses. Usually, companies always funnel their best resources to advantageous businesses and establish business portfolios in order to create a competitive edge in the markets. This is because companies have to avoid the market risks and guarantee that limited resources are used efficiently.

Under these circumstances, companies have to arrange and plan their business portfolios reasonably and integrate their resources constantly according to market changes. This is a precondition for companies to maintain a superior market position in the world. So, before making a new market strategy, companies have to first assess their current business portfolios, pinpoint the areas that do not fit the market environments and company's resources, and discover and develop growing businesses. Based on these, they have to often adjust their business portfolios and allocate their limited resources to ensure business portfolios adapt to the changing market environments. This is the first step for managers looking to develop new markets, especially for international markets.

In the real world, managers can use a lots of methods to establish their business portfolio and the following methods are often used by multinationals.

BCG matrix

BCG matrix is also called Boston matrix. Created by the Boston Consulting Group in 1970s, BCG is also a very important tool for the international companies to analyze their product structures and investment allocation. Bruce Henderson, the inventor of the model and the creator of the company, believed the companies had to possess various product mixes with different growth rates and market shares if they wanted to win the markets, and that the structure of the business portfolio had to be decided by the balance of the cash flow of the company. In this way, the principle of the BCG is to achieve the balance of the cash flow by integrating and optimizing their various resources.

1. The basic structure of BCG matrix

Every business unit of the company should be put into a two-dimensional matrix chart if you want to use BCG matrix to analyze the business portfolio. The market growth rate and the relative market share are used to describe the current business portfolio. After analyzing the two factors, we can be show which business unit provided the higher potential benefits and which business unit was the resource hopper of the company in this matrix (Chart 7-1).

2. The four types of business units

1) Question mark

Businesses with a lower relative market share but a higher market growth rate. Because the development prospect of this business is not very clear for companies, it is called a question mark. Two situations may occur for this business unit: The first possibility is that, the business unit can improve its market share substantially in a short time and transfer to the star business. Another possibility is that companies may find it

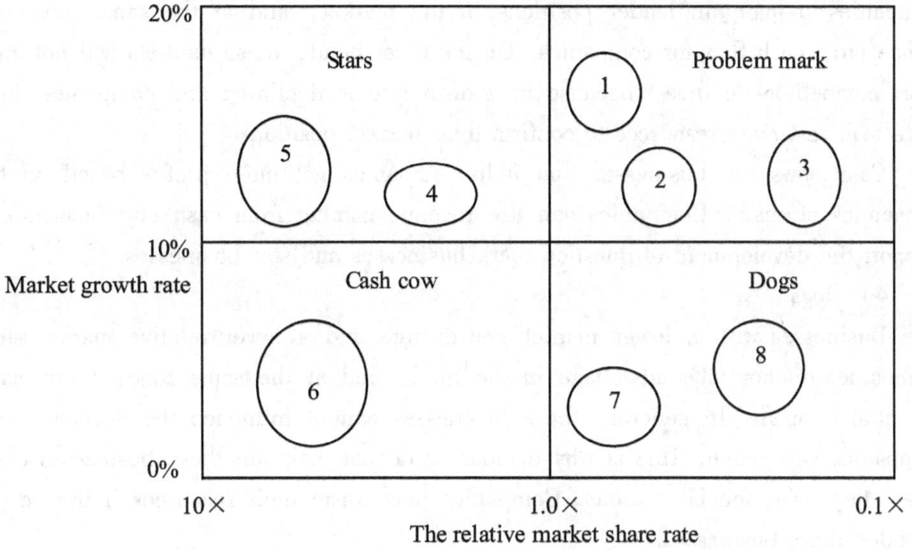

Chart 7-1 BCG matrix

difficult to improve their market shares because of the intense competition or other causes. When confronted with this situation, the company has to decide whether to invest more resources to develop the market or abandon the market to avoid these risks.

Because companies have to face more markets or other problems in this field, the leaders of the company should be cautious and make the effort to study the market before making decisions. The truth is simple: your investment may be lost if you take large risks.

2) Stars

Businesses with a higher market growth rate and a higher relative market share. Star businesses are always the leaders of the market. For companies, star businesses are the best potential businesses and as a result, companies always invest more resources to develop these businesses. However, these businesses will attract more competitors to the field because of their large market potential and clear prospects.

These companies have to invest more resources to maintain their market share and beat their competitors, but at the same time, companies have to maintain higher market growth rate. The result is that star businesses create for and expand large sums of cash from companies simultaneously. They will not become businesse units that make the large and stable profits for companies if companies can not make the business grow rapidly or companies have to face intense competition.

3) Cash cows

Businesses are called cash cows when the market growth rates are below 10% and the companies possess higher relative market share. These businesses will enable companies to maintain leader positions in the market, and at the same time, they create large cash flow for companies. On the other hand, these markets will not attract more competitors to invest because its growth rate is declining and companies do not have to invest more resources to confirm their market positions.

Cash cows are businesses that help companies get more profits based on their economies of scale. Companies can use revenue coming from cash cow businesses to support the development of question mark businesses and star businesses.

4) Dogs

Businesses with a lower market growth rate and a lower relative market share. Companies do not take advantage in the field, and at the same time, their market potential is small. In general, these businesses cannot influence the development of companies very much. This is why companies do not maintain these businesses except when they have special reasons. Companies may waste their resources if they do not abandon these businesses.

In common situations, one strategy business unit will transfer from one matrix to another in its life period, which means that the positions of the market growth rate—relative market share matrix may change in the real world for these special business units. Transfer direction includes: ① an anticlockwise direction, from the question mark to stars, and then to cash cow and dogs; this is the ideal direction for business units; and ② a clockwise direction, from question mark to dogs, or from the stars to question marks. Of course, this is the worse direction for various businesses. So, when the managers analyze the structures of their businesses, they not only have to compare the current matrix with the last matrix, but they also have to make assessments for future change of various businesses and draw up future development tracks for their business units. This is a precondition for them to make the correct investment decisions.

3. Development objectives for strategic business units

1) Development

The purpose of development is to extend business market shares, and sometimes companies even prefer to abandon the current profits for achieving this target. This objective commonly fits the question mark business, because managers have to extend their market share for all of the businesses if they want to help businesses transfer from the question mark matrix to the stars matrix.

2) Maintenance

The purpose of maintenance is to maintain the current market share. This target fits the cash cow businesses. The truth is that only managers can confirm their market share, and they can guarantee the companies get enough cash revenue and warrant the normal operation of companies.

3) Harvests

The purpose of harvests is to get benefits in a short time without considering the future development, This target fits cash cow businesses, in which the growth rate is declining, and partly question mark businesses and dogs businesses.

4) Abandonment

The purpose of abandonment is to transfer company resources to more advantageous businesses to establish the development foundation. This target fits dog businesses or some of the question mark businesses in which there is no better prospect or the cost is higher.

GE matrix

The GE matrix was created by the General Electric Corporation in the 1970s. This matrix overcame the weaknesses of the BCG matrix and has become a new investment mixed analysis method for managers.

1. Two variables of GE matrix

When compared with the BCG matrix, the greatest improvement of the GE matrix is that it uses more indicators to measure the two dimensionalities. Its vertical axis reflects the market attraction with more indicators, and its horizontal axis reflects the competitiveness of the company with more indicators. At the same time, the two dimensionalities of vertical axis and horizontal axis are divided into 3 degrees. Lots of indicators will influence market attraction and company competitiveness, and the extension of assessment factors enable managers to consider questions more comprehensively. The GE matrix helps managers to master real situations correctly and entirely, and this is why the GE matrix is also called the multi-factors investment mix matrix. The following chart gives you an example about factors.

In the real world, managers use a points approach to assess market attraction and company competitiveness for a specific business unit (follow the chart for an example) and the specific contents of this approach include:

(1) Choosing important indicators that influence strength and market attraction of the business units you want to assess.

(2) Assessing the importance of various factors that influence the market attraction and business unit strength, which means you should give the various weights for different indicators. The sum of the weights should equal one.

(3) Deciding the various degrees for market attraction and company competitiveness based on the industry and company situation. For example, using a 1-5rubric in which 1 = there is no attraction, 2 = there is a little attraction, 3 = neutral affection, 4 = there is some attraction, 5 = there is a lot of attraction; For company competitiveness, 1 = extreme competitive disadvantage, 2 = competitive disadvantage,

3 = competitive advantage is same as your competitors, 4 = competitive advantage, 5 = extreme advantage.

(4) To find factor weightings, multiply weight time's degree. Determine the total weightings about market attraction and competitiveness of the business units by summary. A higher score indicates the higher market attraction or competitiveness. Finally, we can put the every strategic business unit on the GE matrix (Table 7-2).

Table 7-2 Market attraction and business strength assessment indicator table

		Weight	Fixed value (1~5)	Score
Market attraction	Total market size	0. 2	4. 00	0. 8
	Annual market growth	0. 2	5. 00	1. 00
	History marginal profit	0. 15	4. 00	0. 6
	Competitors	0. 15	2. 00	3. 00
	Technology requirement	0. 05	3. 00	0. 3
	Inflation	0. 05	3. 00	0. 3
	Energy requirement	0. 05	2. 00	0. 1
	Environment effect	0. 05	1. 00	0. 05
	Talent acquire	0. 1	5. 00	0. 5
	total	1. 00		3. 65
		Weight	Fixed value (1~5)	Score
Competi-veness	Market share	0. 1	4. 00	0. 4
	Width of the product line	0. 15	4. 00	0. 6
	Product quality	0. 1	4. 00	0. 4
	Brand popularity	0. 1	5. 00	0. 5
	Distribution net	0. 05	4. 00	0. 2
	Promotion efficiency	0. 05	5. 00	0. 25
	Production capacity	0. 05	3. 00	0. 15
	Financing capacity	0. 05	2. 00	0. 1
	Unit cost	0. 15	3. 00	0. 45
	Materials supply	0. 05	5. 00	0. 25
	Technology development capacity	0. 05	4. 00	0. 2
	Control level	0. 05	4. 00	0. 2
	Industry experience	0. 05	4. 00	0. 2
	total	1. 00		3.9

2. The three strategic zones and development objectives

According to above chart, we can divide GE matrix into 9 checks and these 9 checks can further be divided into 3 zones.

(1) The green zones—if businesses are in the upper left of the matrix (A, B, C), the market attraction and competitiveness are higher. These zones are called green zones. Of course, these are the ideal zones for companies, and companies should invest more resources to develop businesses that are in green zones. At the same time, they should take various means to improve their market shares to establish and confirm the market foundation.

(2) The yellow zones—if the businesses are in the middle of matrix (D, E, F), the market attraction and competitiveness are medium too. These zones are called yellow zones. Companies should take strategies to maintain their businesses and try their best to improve their market share or competitiveness to transfer these businesses to the green zones.

(3) The red zones—if the businesses are in the bottom right of the matrix (G, H, I), these zones are called the red zones. Market attraction and competitiveness in these zones are all very low. Of course, businesses in these zones are very disappointing for companies. In common situations, companies should take a recovery strategy to arrange their businesses and collect their limited resources to the profitable businesses (Chart 7-2 and Table 7-3).

	strong	middle	weak
high	A	C	D
middle	B	E	H
low	F	G	I

Chart 7-2 GE matrix strategy option

Table 7-3 Competitiveness and countermeasures

		Competitiveness		
		Strong	Middle	Weak
Market attraction	High	Maintain advantage: (1) Develop your business as quickly as possible (2) Collect resources to maintain your advantage	Confirm investment: (1) Challenge to the market leader (2) Improve your strength and shore up weak links	Develop selectively: (1) Collect limited strength (2) Make an effort to overcome your weakness (3) Abandon the business if you cannot see obvious growth
	Middle	Develop selectively: (1) Invest in the most attractive markets (2) Enhance competitiveness (3) Improve production and profit capacity	Choose and maintain: (1) Maintain current investment (2) Transfer investment to the profitable and small risk zones	Limit development and reduction: (1) Seek low risk strategies to develop your business (2) Try your best to reduce investment
	Low	Confirm and adjust: (1) Maintain current revenue (2) Transfer your resources to more attractive units	Maintain current revenue: (1) Maintain your advantage in most of your profitable businesses (2) Upgrade products (3) Try to reduce your investment	Abandon: (1) Seek opportunities to develop new business (2) Reduce fixed costs and avoid investment

Making growth strategies

Companies often have to adjust their business portfolios, because some old business markets may decline and some new business markets will be born as the market develops and changes. On the other hand, the forecast revenue and profit of the current business portfolios may not meet the prospect objectives of the company, which means that there is a "strategic planning gap." Companies have to make up the gap with extending their business portfolios.

In the real world, there are three major methods for companies to extend their business mixes: ① "The intensive growth strategy," or investing and developing in current business zones; ② "The integration growth strategy" or developing businesses related to the major current businesses of companies, or ③ "The diversification growth strategy" or developing businesses that do not relate to the major current businesses.

1. Intensive growth strategy

The basic premise of the intensive growth strategy is to develop market opportunities hiding in the current markets and current products, which mean the companies should increase the revenue, profit rate and market share of the current business units and use the potential of these products and markets adequately to create growth. In practice, it includes four development types.

Current markets	1. market penetration	3. product development
New markets	2. market development	4. diversification

1) Market penetration strategy

In a market penetration strategy companies take countermeasures to increase their revenue and profits in current markets. There are three possibilities if companies take this strategy. First, the companies may increase current consumer purchase frequency. For example, if we lower the price, promotion activities may stimulate old consumers to buy more; Secondly, the companies may use various competitive means to attract new consumers. For example, a company can invest in advertising to attract a competitor's consumers to buy their goods; and finally, holding various public activities to extend market size for the current markets. In general, market penetration strategy is the major mean through which most companies develop their markets. Of course, it is difficult and dangerous because of intense competition.

2) Market development strategy

When companies develop a new market with current products, this strategy is called market development strategy. Under these circumstances, the following preconditions must be met: ① the new markets must have enough demand for the company's products; ② the company's resources, for example, products, management, marketing skill, distribution, logistic, human resources and so forth, must fit the market conditions; and ③ the action to develop new markets must fit the total development strategy of company. The purpose of developing a new market is to increase sales in the new markets and reduce cost to achieve economy of scale. If a domestic market is saturated, new markets exist abroad. This is usually more difficult than market penetration strategy because of the unfamiliar environments.

3) New product developing strategy

This strategy is most difficult for companies, because it involves large sums of resources and the failure probability is very high. Whenever you want to improve your current products, increase the product variety and design, or increase the new product functions, you have to research and develop those products and test the market, and the risk is very high because you can not always control various environments. That is why most of the new products are researched and developed by multinationals, who possess enough resources to develop new products. If they are successful in the market, new products can bring the new markets and large sells and profits. Successful products always can create large market shares for companies and continue for a long time.

2. Integration growth strategy

Integration growth strategy means that companies extend their business to production, supply and sales. The purpose is to control the industry chain and earn more sales and profits. Usually, if a company is very strong in an industry, it can utilize this strategy to achieve its extending target. The precondition is the integration strategy can improve the operation efficiency of company. In practice, there are three methods of integration growth strategy.

1) Forward integration

Forward integration means that companies control production and sale links through acquiring and merging. These specific methods include: ① material suppliers acquiring, manufacturing and distributing through coordination or merging, For example, lots of companies in the gulf countries merger fining plants and gas stations; ② the manufacturers controlling distribution channels with coordination or merging; and ③ wholesalers controlling the distribution channels with merging retailers or to establish their own retail stores.

2) Backward integration

Backward integration means that companies control their own supply system through acquiring or merging. Through this, not only can they get stable products or materials but they also control industry chains and earn more profits. For example, IKEA acquired lots of furniture manufacturers in many countries. The specific methods of this strategy include: ① retailers merging wholesalers; ② wholesalers merging manufacturers; and ③ the manufacturers merging the material suppliers.

3) Horizontal integration

The horizontal integration means that companies acquire or merge a competitor's companies. For example, Lenovo acquired the computer business of IBM in 2009, and Gily bought Volvo in 2010. In the real world, lots of companies use these methods to expand their businesses. With this, not only can they occupy more market share and increase their sales and profits, but also they can reduce their competitors in this way. At the same time, they can get lots of higher quality resources like technology, management, human resource, distribution nets and, most important, customers.

3. Diversification growth strategy

Diversification means that companies invest in other industries to achieve their strategy targets. Usually, if the industry lacks a better market opportunity or other industry possesses more attraction for companies, companies may utilize the diversification strategy to develop their businesses. Note that it is very difficult and very dangerous for companies to use this strategy, because the difference in professions makes one feel worlds apart. If you want to invest in an unfamiliar industry, you have to prepare enough resources and do some serious marketing research. Some companies think the diversification strategy can eliminate business risks. However, lots of companies fail when they use this strategy, because they do not understand the new industry environment. So, it is not a good option for most companies unless the current industry is in crisis. In practice, this strategy includes:

1) Concentric diversification

Concentric diversification means that companies expand their businesses based on the current businesses or products and use current technology and marketing resources to develop a new business or product similar to current businesses or products to attract new consumers and earn more sales and profits. For example, a car manufacturer can produce motorcycle or tractors. Compared with other diversification strategy, the risk of concentric diversification is small because of familiar industry.

2) Horizontal diversification

Sometimes, companies may develop some businesses not related to the current business but find consumers related to both. This is called horizontal diversification. For example, supermarkets open restaurants, bars and beauty shops while maintaining the major business, because all of these items can provide a better service for customers, and improve the sales and profits of supermarkets. In the real world, lots of companies use this method to expand their businesses and get a better effect although the scope is not very large.

3) Comprehensive diversification

If companies develop a business completely not related to the current business, these companies are using a strategy called comprehensive diversification. If it is not necessary, companies will not make a decision. Because it means companies have to abandon current benefits, current products, current markets and other resources, this strategy is really used by companies. Because new companies don't understand the new market environment, the chance of success is very small. That is why most of the world's best-known companies are specialized corporations.

We have discussed various questions about corporate strategy in this chapter. In the real world, corporate strategy is very important for every company, because it is a guideline for companies looking to develop their businesses. It is particularly important for companies looking to expand its marketing internationally because of more complex environments.

Summary

1. Understand the nature of strategy. The word "strategy" derives from the Greece word, originally means "general". It means that someone directs the army with wisdom. Later, this concept was used in various fields like economics, politics and education, generally referring to a far-reaching, significant and decisive plan for an organization.

2. International marketing strategy is the strategy that companies establish for developing the international market and achieving their international business targets. The international marketing strategy is a part of the overall strategy of a company and it is subjected to the overall strategy of company. International marketing strategy is the preferred strategy when companies want to survive and develop in foreign markets. It is established by the marketers based on company resources and external environments.

3. Remember that there are three major methods for companies to extend their business mixes. ① Investing and developing in current business zones, or "intensive growth strategy"; ② Developing businesses related to the major current businesses of companies or "integration growth strategy"; and ③ developing the businesses that do not related to the major current businesses, or "diversification growth strategy".

4. Remember the importance of long-term plan and short-term plan in relation to international marketing. Short-term plans are also called annual plans, and they include annual marketing indicators, area business indicators, product marketing targets and methods, and various marketing means to achieve the above targets. Long-term plans can be divided into 5-years plans, 7-years plans, 10-years plans and even 20-years plans, etc. Long-term plans include long-term marketing targets, growing plans, competition plans and the methods and means to achieve these targets.

5. If multinationals want to make market growth strategies, the international marketers should look for the following preconditions: ① the new markets must have enough demand for company's products; ② the company's resources, such as products, management, marketing skill, distribution, logistic, human resources and so forth, must fit the market conditions; and ③ the action to develop the new markets must fit the total development strategy of the company.

6. Recognize that the entry mode decides the international marketing mode. In practice, entry mode is divided into 3 types: ① export, which includes indirect and direct export; ② foreign investment, which includes taking money and other resources to enter a foreign market to set up a manufacture plant, or signing a long-term contract with a local company with the patent, trade mark, know-how or management skill to cooperate with the local company and get fees; and ③ portfolio, or indirect investment, which means companies can purchase the foreign stocks or bonds to get return.

7. Recognize the value of international marketing strategy, ① in guaranteeing

management will have a clear direction; ② in enhancing adaptability for complex environments; ③ enhancing the stability of marketing actions; and ④ in enhancing the successful possibility of company.

8. Based on the overall company's marketing purpose, the business strategy should pay more attention to two questions: ① how to make the company achieve a better business performance and how to set up competitive advantage in various operation fields, and ② how to plan to use market forces that will influence success and failure of the company in various industries.

9. Based on the content of corporate strategy, the important points of corporate strategy should include following: ① defining the mission of enterprise, especially choosing business fields, consumers and a development orientation that fits the resources of the company; ② selecting strategic business units and make developing plan for the units and defining the different positions for various business units; and ③ making strategies for key business units and making sure the targets of the key business units adapt to the corporate strategy.

10. Understanding the nature of strategy: The word "strategy" is derives from the Greece word, originally meaning "general," a word that meant someone directing the army with wisdom. Later, this concept was used in various fields like economics, politics and education, and generally refers to a far-reaching, significant and decisive plan for organizations.

Questions

1. Explain some purposes for why international companies make international marketing strategies.

2. Why do some people feel that long-term plans are more important than short-term plans?

3. Why do companies like to use the GE matrix to formulate their business strategies?

4. Discuss the failure reasons for Disneyland in Europe.

5. Assume that a Chinese company wants to establish subsidiaries in the U. S., what proposals can you offer?

6. Describe the procedures through which international managers make their international marketing strategies.

7. Is corporate strategy the only type of strategy for international companies? If not, name some others.

8. What materials does a functional strategy include?

9. Business strategies are independent strategies, and all of other strategies should be subjected to it. True or false? Explain.

Chapter 8 Market Assessment and Analysis

Concept preview

After reading this chapter, you should be able to

1. Appreciate: the importance of market assessments and analysis for multinationals.

2. Understand: the methods used to investigate foreign markets.

3. Distinguish: the difference between domestic and international marketing research.

4. Comprehend: the factors which influence international market assessment and analysis.

5. Describe: why marketers take trade fairs and trade missions.

International marketing research helps BMW to sell worldwide

BMW is a unique manufacturer which concentrates on selling fancy cars and motorcycles in the world. It is one of the most successful auto companies of the world, and what's more, it makes one of the most profits in the luxury car and motorcycle manufacturing business. In the 1990s, BMW prepared to carry out its international marketing strategy named "brand globalization and marketing localization." The first step to implement the tactic was doing marketing research. The mission of the marketing research was to establish the ideal market position for BMW in Europe and other related areas.

BMW held many meetings to discuss questions and find out the problems of the various markets and which traits of the brands the consumers would accept in the Europe market. Then, the company designed questionnaires to find out the true demands of the consumers. Not only did these questions include a common "core" for all of the countries, but it also included the materials related to the various countries.

Based on the result of their investigation, the demands of the consumers coming from Austria, Italy, Holland, France and Swiss were divided into three categories:

(1) Similar important traits for all consumers in all countries, which were available in all European markets. The traits included reliability, safety, quality, advanced technology and so forth, and all of the above were called basic requirements by BMW. Cars which did not meet these basic requirements were rejected by the consumers when they made their purchase decisions.

(2) The views about the car standards are very different in various countries. For example, in Holland, the attraction of the car came from the "internal quality" and the consumers paid more attention to the internal allocation of the car. In contrast, Austrians thought the car should show self-confidence and the "car's style is the man" was the most important idea they had in mind when they wanted to buy a car. In Italy, consumers believed that cars should fit the driver's individual style and they paid more attention to the design, appreciation of beauty and motive power. In general, consumers from different countries have various demands although they all live in Europe.

(3) People who are in the same social status always possess the same requirements for cars although they are living in the various countries. According to BMW's investigations, consumers living in various countries and possessing the same or familiar requirements can be divided into 7 categories. Thus, BMW can decide to sell the different cars in a special country.

Successful marketing research established a firm foundation for BMW to carry out its strategy—brand globalization and sales localization. As a result, marketing researches helped the BMW deal with the relationship between their brand and product, brand and communication, product and environment, as well as improve brand position, and enhance its competitiveness. BMW found later that it would not have avoided lots of marketing problems if it had not done its marketing research. For example, some consumers of Holland and Italy were all asked to define unique, but they had very different suggestions for what unique was. BMW put to use this method to develop the North America market and Japanese market, where it enjoyed great success.

8.1 International marketing information and information systems

International marketing information

In the process of taking modern marketing activities, information is regarded as the "nerve centre" of the companies, because if they want to operate in foreign markets, the international companies need more marketing information to compete with the domestic companies. An old axiom says: no news is the good news, but today, it should be changed to no information means no international business. As a matter of fact, lots of international companies fail in the international markets because they lack of information or they did not pay more attention to international marketing research.

International marketing information includes the various data, reference, and intelligence that are related to international marketing activities, especially to some very important market factors. All of the information reflects market actions and environmental changes, as well as market traits and market developmental trends. It is created by a joining of various news, data references and reports relate to the international marketing under the certain time and conditions. Usually, the information is formed by words, data, charts, marks, reports and models etc. Simply put, international information is various news that reflects international marketing traits. Its characteristics include the nature of resources, the nature of temporality and nature of enjoyment.

1. The contents of international marketing information

The contents of international marketing information are very complex and varies widely. In general, international information related to the company's international actions include the international market environmental information, international market product information, international market price information, international market distribution channel information, international market promotion information and international market competition information and so forth.

1) International market environmental information

International market environment information includes information about the economy, politics, society, culture, law, population, technology, nature and other information related to international marketing actions. Specifically, it includes the following:

(1) The economic development level and difference of various countries.

(2) The political developmental trends and trade styles of various countries.

(3) The market segmentation and natural resource situations of various countries.

(4) The trade barriers, especially the tariff and non-tariff barriers in various countries.

(5) The trade agreements, trade practices and exchange controls of various countries.

(6) The limitations to the products in international markets in the field of health, safety, advertisements, price and trade marks, licensing and other bill of requirements of various countries.

(7) The consumer organizations and consumer campaigns in the international market.

(8) The different living styles, values and ideas, folkways, aesthetic standards and ethics based on various cultural backgrounds in various countries.

(9) The different nations, religions, races, geography, age, gender, occupation, education, language, consumer preferences and other cultural traits in various countries.

(10) The different demand traits and social classes in various countries.

(11) The population sizes, population distribution, family structure and population flows in various countries.

(12) The consumer structures and expense styles in various countries.

(13) The industry structures and industry layouts in various countries.

(14) The law of income and expense changes in various countries.

(15) The consumer's income situation and real purchasing power in various countries.

(16) The consumer's deposit and credit situation in various countries.

(17) The price index number, international balance of payment, export and import situations in various countries.

(18) The technological and technology application situation in various countries.

2) International marketing product information

The international marketing product information mainly includes supply and demand, service, quality and preference for products in international markets or target markets. It includes the followings:

(1) The total supply and demand, supply and demand structures, supply and demand characteristics and change trends for the given products in international markets or in the target markets.

(2) The situation regarding the substitute products in international markets or in the target markets.

(3) The situation regarding the propagated demand and derived demand in international markets or in the target markets.

(4) The special requirements to satisfy consumer's demand and causes for consumers to buy your products in international markets or in the target markets.

(5) The requirements and proposals regarding the function, quality, trade mark, package and design for the given products in international markets or in the target markets.

(6) The situation regarding the purchasing customs, purchasing motivations, taboos and preference for the given products in international markets or in the target markets.

(7) The situation regarding potential consumers and potential purchasing power for the given products in international markets or in the target markets.

(8) The situation regarding the product life cycles and development trends for the given products in international markets or in the target markets.

(9) The situation regarding the sale area distributions and area structures for the given products in international markets or in the target markets.

(10) The situation regarding the purchasing objectives, address, time, frequency and manner of the consumers for the given products in international markets or in the target markets.

(11) The situation regarding the new products in international markets or in the target markets.

3) International market price information

The price and the sales revenues are closely related to the profit and loss of the companies. Usually, companies consider their lowest prices based on their cost and profits when they want to enter a new foreign market. That is because they always have to face intense competition, and they have to use penetration strategy to occupy the rival's market shares. They also have to master the following information if they want to take a position in international markets:

(1) The pricing targets and pricing methods for the various companies which produce the same products in international markets or in the target markets.

(2) The total price level in international markets or in the target markets.

(3) The price elasticity and sensitive degree for the price of the consumers in international markets or in the target markets.

(4) The situation and development trends about the substitute product prices and complement product prices in international markets and in the target markets.

(5) The price parity between the given products and other products and the situation regarding the price differences in international markets or in the target markets.

(6) The different reflections for the price of various companies in various segment markets.

(7) The various price strategies and price differences in various product life cycles

for the various companies in international markets or in the target markets.

(8) The added price rate and degree of merchants in international markets or in the target markets from exporting to consumers.

(9) The situation regarding the price leaders, price discrimination and dumping in international markets or in the target markets.

(10) The situation regarding legal rules, price practices and other special rules and requirements related to the price in international markets or in the target markets.

(11) The situation regarding the price trends and price quotations in international markets or in the target markets.

4) The international marketing distribution channel information

The distribution channel information refers to some information about the distribution links, distribution channels and distribution methods. Simply put, it is information regarding marketing channels and physical distribution. Researchers should master the following contents:

(1) The situation regarding distribution channel types and market customs in international markets or in the target markets.

(2) The situation regarding physical distribution methods, costs, advantages and disadvantages in international markets or in the target markets.

(3) The situation regarding the credits, strengths, advantages, disadvantages, effects, services, promotion competition, sales conditions and market position of the middle man in international markets or in the target markets.

(4) The comparison between the product wide range distribution strategies, selection distribution strategies and exclusive distribution strategies in international markets or in the target markets.

(5) The development trends of the distribution channel and middle man in international markets or in the target markets.

5) International marketing promotion information

The international marketing promotion information includes the situation regarding personal selling, advertisements, promotion activities and public relation. Content includes:

(1) The various promotion forms, types and degrees in international markets or in the target markets.

(2) The promotion cost analysis, advantages and disadvantages for personal selling regarding the given markets.

(3) The promotion activity methods, the characteristics and requirements in various markets and the reflection of the consumers and middle man.

(4) The characteristics of the public relation and the experiences and lessons in this field in international markets or in target markets.

(5) The advertising methods, media, art, skills, targets, policies, laws and effects in international markets or in the target markets.

(6) The situation regarding how the middle man helps the manufacturers promote their products in international markets or in the target markets.

(7) The international promotion practices of the international markets or in the target markets.

6) International market competition information

International companies have to overcome the huge pressures coming from their competitors. A lot of the world famous companies will influence the marketing so much, which is why a company has to investigate their international rivals before they enter a foreign market. All of the information about the competitors will help new companies take a position in a new market. The content includes the following information:

(1) Who are your competitors in international markets or in the target markets? Is it direct competition or indirect competition? Where are they from? How about their strength, advantage and disadvantage?

(2) What strategies do your competitors use? Price competition or non-price competition?

(3) The situation regarding the production, sales revenue and market share of your competitors in international markets or in the target markets.

(4) The situation regarding product monopolization in international markets or in the target markets.

(5) The comparison between company images, product reputations, operation strengths, distribution channel controls and market attractions between the competitors in international markets or in the target markets.

(6) The situation regarding the international marketing plans, countermeasures and strategies of your competitors.

(7) Is there an international market opportunity or a blank spare market?

2. How to collect information

1) The principle of collecting

(1) Overall—collecting is decided by the international marketing action, because you can not gain success or avoid mistakes if you cannot master the total situation regarding the international market.

(2) Timely—the information must possess the timeliness. Any information may lose its value if you can not collect it in a timely manner, particularly when you are running an international marketing campaign where the situation changes very quickly.

(3) Correct—of course, all information must be accurate, and this must be basic guarantee for your international marketing decisions.

(4) Suitable—all information must serve the international marketing practice.

Only suitable information can help the marketers to create the correct tactics.

(5) Economy—every marketing research project needs the companies to spend their resources to get the available information. However, you should spend the least amount of resources to get as much information as you possibly can.

2) The source of international marketing information

International market information comes from two sources: the companies themselves, which means that company personnel collect first hand references, or original information themselves. The other source comes from collecting and settling other people's references. This information is called second hand references (Chart 8-1).

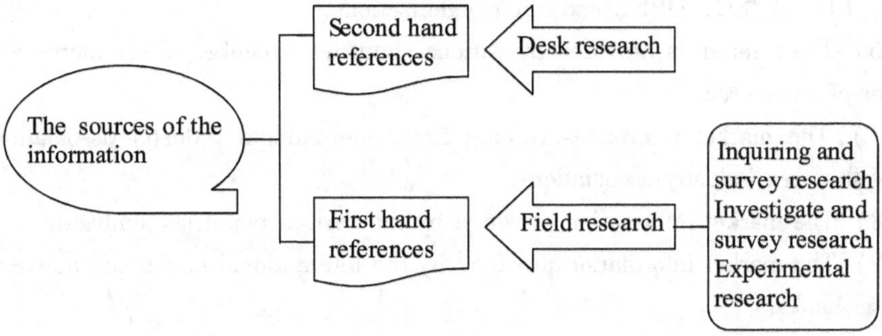

Chart 8-1 The international marketing information sources

Usually, the companies used to take the following methods to get information directly.

(1) The companies appoint their personnel such as technicians, information staff or salespeople to investigate target markets and collect the relevant information.

(2) The companies entrust the economy and trade departments stationed abroad to finish the investigation and collect the information.

(3) The companies entrust people going abroad, especially economics and skilled consultant groups to finish the investigation.

(4) The commercial networks distributed all over the world can provide references about the international markets constantly.

(5) The companies entrust their agents, merchants, importers, wholesalers or other middle man with the task to collect information.

Indirect information sources include:

(1) The various countries' market information collected by the departments station abroad that the native government established in various countries.

(2) The various foreign countries' market information published by the foreign

statistical departments, trade departments and other relative departments.

(3) The various trade data, basic market references about the distribution channels and middle man for the target markets, product and price situations related to the given products provided by native and foreign libraries.

(4) Market information provided by the subordinate departments of United Nations, which include: the United Nations Food and Agricultural Organization; the United Nations Conference on Trade and Development; the United Nations Industrial Development Organization; the International Trade Center; the International monetary fund; the World Bank; the World Trade Organization and so forth.

(5) The references provided by international or area organizations, such as the OECD, EU, APEC, OPEC and other organizations.

(6) The references provided by various countries' chamber of commerce and area chamber of commerce.

(7) The market references coming from international industry associations and some of the area industry associations.

(8) The market information provided by the various countries' embassies.

(9) The market information provided by the international banks and native foreign exchange banks.

(10) The market information provided online.

International marketing information system

1. concept understanding

Marketing information system is the connection made by people, computer and procedures. This system can be used to collect, settle, analyze, and assess marketing information to provide a reasonable foundation for the marketing strategy decision makers. The international marketing system is constructed by computers, people and various software procedures. Its mission is to collect, settle and analyze the external and internal information about the international markets; its purpose is to provide a reasonable foundation for a decision makers; its effect is to provide enough, correct and on time information for the marketing strategy makers. Simply put, it can help the companies make correct decisions in the real world. As a matter of fact, most world famous companies possess an advanced international marketing information system, which is one of the most important reasons why they beat their competitors.

2. The construction of the international marketing information system

Various companies have the different information systems, although the construction is familiar. In common situation, an overall international marketing information system includes an internal report system, an international marketing information system, an international marketing research system and an international marketing analysis system (Chart 8-2).

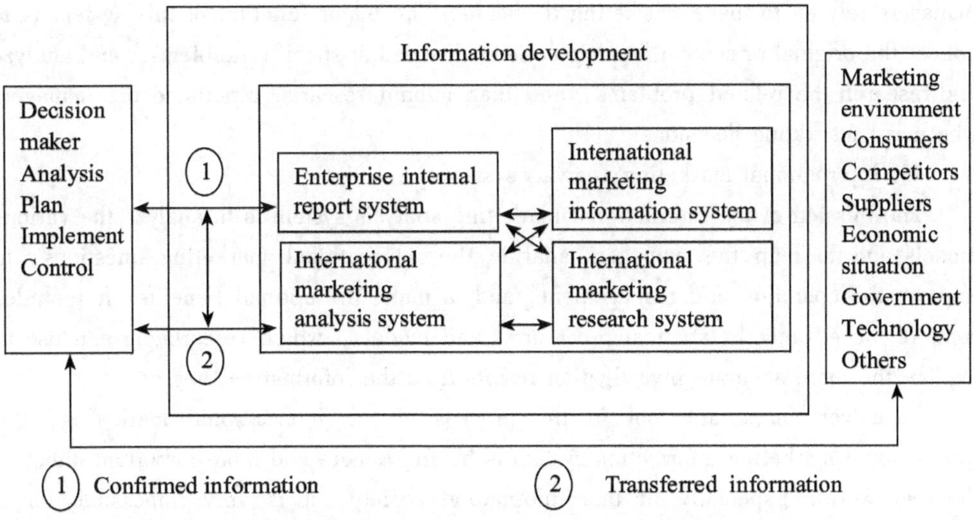

Chart 8-2 Marketing information system

The international marketing information system comes from the information users and ends with the information users. First, decision makers should confirm a range of information, then establish an internal report system, a marketing information system and a marketing research system in their companies, and then via the marketing analysis system settle and analyze the information they get, and finally, transfer the information through the marketing analysis system to the marketing managers based on the forecasting form and forecasting time. The functions of the various systems include:

1) The internal report system of the company

Most marketing managers use an internal report system to get the various data. The system is particularly used in the routine plans, management and control, such as the financial information provided by the financial department; the product information provided by the production department; the store information provided by the storage department and the sales information provided by the marketing department and so forth. All of this information can help decision makers find out marketing opportunities and marketing problems.

2) International marketing information system

Marketing information is the information related to the marketing environment, such as the new laws and rules related to the marketing; social trends; technology innovations; and the situation of competitors and so forth. All of the information will help marketing decision makers establish and adjust their marketing plans.

3) International marketing research system

This is the main body of the international marketing system, and the mission of this system is to collect, assess, settle and transfer the various pieces of information the managers rely on to make marketing decisions. The major function of this system is to collect the original or second hand references directed at specific problems, and analyze and research the related problems, and then submit research reports to the managers who make marketing decisions.

4) International marketing analysis system

The mission of the international marketing analysis system is to analyze the various models and to help the managers analyze the international marketing questions, to improve the operation and management, and to make the optimal benefits. It includes some of the advanced statistical procedures and models, which researchers can use to explore the more accurate investigation results from the information they get.

As a very important tool in the process of the international marketing, the international marketing information system is having a more and more important effect in the real world. Especially in this information society, it is very impossible for a company to experience great success in international marketing if you cannot garner enough marketing information. Advanced information system is a basic guarantee for multinationals who want to develop foreign markets.

8.2 The contents and procedures for international marketing research

International marketing research is a very important means from which multinational managers get enough information about the foreign markets. It is a precondition and foundation for the managers to make their decisions. However, because of more complex environments, it is more difficult compared to domestic marketing research because the contents consist of more materials.

Usually, it is more difficult to do marketing research in developing countries than to do it in developed countries. The causes are very complex. For example, it is more difficult for companies to get correct or enough data in developing countries, and sometimes companies may get incorrect information from the government departments because of political or other causes. As a matter of fact, it is impossible for multinationals to enter all of country's markets. There are enough multinationals who have enough resources to develop all of the markets of the world but some of the markets are not worth entering because of various reasons. This is why companies have to screen markets first before taking any international marketing actions so that only the markets that fit the resources of the companies may enter their lists. Note that marketing research is only used to provide reasons for the decision makers, and it is not the end result.

The first step of the marketing screening process is to determine the basic needs potential. We shall describe this process fully in the next section. Market screening is a modified version of environmental scanning in which the firm identifies markets by using environmental forces to eliminate less desirable markets. Environmental scanning, from which market screening is derived, is a procedure in which a firm scans the world for changes in the environmental forces that might affect it.

For some time, environmental scanning has been used by management during the planning process to provide information about world threats and opportunities. Firms that scan have been shown to outperform those that do not. A study of Fortune 500 firms in 2015 found that 66 percent of the respondents had advanced scanning systems. As you can imagine, increased global competition from the enlarged EU, Japan, the Asian newly industrialized economies, and Asian developing nations will motivate even more managements to scan the world for changes in the international marketing environment.

Market screening assists two different kinds of firms. One type is selling exclusively in the domestic market but believes it might increase sales by expanding into overseas markets. The other firm is already a multinational firm but wants to be certain that changing conditions are not creating markets of which its management is unaware. In both situations, managers require an ordered, relatively fast method of analyzing and assessing over 200 countries and areas to pinpoint the most suitable prospects.

Market screening is a method of market analysis and assessment that permits management to identify a small number of desirable markets by eliminating those judged to be less attractive. This is accomplished by subjecting the countries to a series of screenings based on environmental forces. Although these forces may be placed in any order, the arrangement suggested progresses from the least to most difficult analysis is based on the accessibility and subjectivity of the data. In this way, the least but most efficiency number of market candidates is left for a final through most difficult screening.

Initial screening—basic need potential

An initial screening based on the basic need potential is a logical first step, because if the need is lacking, no reasonable expenditure of effort and money will enable the firm to market its goods or services. For example, the basic need potential of certain goods is dependent on various physical forces, such as climate, topography, or natural resources. If the firm produces air conditioners, the analyst will look for countries with warm climates. Manufacturers of large farm tractors would not consider Switzerland a likely prospect, because of its mountainous terrain, and only countries known to possess gold deposits would be potential customers for gold-dredging equipment.

Generally, producers of specialized industrial materials or equipment experience little difficulty in assessing their basic need potential. The builder of cement kilns, for example, can obtain the names and addresses of cement plants worldwide merely by contacting the Portland Cement Association in Chicago. A list of firms in an industry, often on a worldwide basis, is available either from the industry association or from specialized trade journals.

This is certainly straightforward, but what about the less specialized products of more widespread consumption?

1. Foreign trade and investment

If the nature of goods or services is such that a definite basic need potential cannot be readily established, analysts can learn from the United Nations' International Trade Statistics Yearbook, Volume II, which countries' export and which import their firms' products and the dollar quantities. Furthermore, annual dollar values are given for the past five years, enabling analysts to establish trends for projecting future values. The Yearbook uses the United Nations Standard International Trade Classification system based on 1,312 subgroups identified by five-digit codes. These are combined progressively into 177 groups with three-digit codes, 56 divisions with two-digit codes, to 10 sections with one digit.

For those who want to know if American competitors are already exporting their firm's products and if so, where, analysts can use two U. S. Department of Commerce foreign trade sources. The information on this computer is especially helpful as it gives both units and dollar value, permitting the analyst to calculate the average price of the unit exported. It also lists more countries importing from and exporting to the United States and in addition, how much of the amount exported to each destination passes through each U. S. Customs district. Both sources are available in the Government Documents section of university libraries and in the Department of Commerce district offices.

To help in their search for markets, analysts can obtain information from the nearest Department of Commerce field office numerous studies prepared by various countries' embassies. The Annual Worldwide Industry Reviews and International Market Research Reports also indicate major markets for many products. In addition, the Country Market Surveys indicate products for which there is a good market in a given country.

With the development of the world economy, lots of the countries, especially major trading countries, like China, Japan, America and most European countries publish similar data. For example, the data office of the European Community, Eurostat, publishes an annual External Trade. The Economist, Business International, and other business publications may help you to get more available information about Europe. Many trade associations also publish export data. The yearbook of world economy, published by the Chinese government, has become one of the most important data sources for lots of multinationals who want to study the Chinese market. Companies have to study more references if they want to get correct results.

Notice: the data companies get is just a number, but assessment and analysis are more important for researchers. Companies should pay more attention to the following questions.

2. Imports don't completely measure market potential

Even when a basic need is clearly indicated, most experienced researchers will still investigate market flows to have an idea of the magnitude of present sales.

Management is aware, of course, that imports alone are rarely a measure of full market potential. A myriad of reasons is responsible, among those, a lack of foreign exchange, high prices (duties and markups), and political pressures.

Moreover, import data indicates only that a country has been buying certain products abroad and does not guarantee that it will continue to do so. Management knows that a competitor may decide to produce locally, which, in many markets, will cause imports to cease. Change in a country's political structure may also stop imports, as we saw in the case of Iran, where orders worth billions of dollars were suddenly canceled because of a nuclear problem in 2011. Nevertheless, when there is no local production, import data does enable a firm to know how much is currently being purchased and provide management with an estimate, though conservative, of the immediate market potential at the going price. If local production is being considered and calculations show that goods produced in the country could be sold at a lower price, even without knowing the price elasticity of demand, the firm can reasonably expect to sell more than the quantity being imported.

Companies wanting to know about the amounts and geographic areas of U. S. foreign investment can obtain information at the industry level from certain issues of the Survey of Current Business, which also publishes similar information about foreign investors in the United States. A company can also get references about China from the government work report annually and the reports published by the state statistics bureau of China every quarter.

Second screening—financial and economic forces

After the initial screening, analysts will have a much smaller list of prospects. This list may be further reduced by a second screening based on financial and economic forces. Trends in the rates of inflation, exchange, and interest are among the major financial points of concern. Analysts should consider other financial factors such as credit availability, paying habits of customers, and rates of return on similar investments. Obviously, it should be noted that this screening is not a complete financial analysis, it is a process if the market analysis and assessment discloses that a country has sufficient potential for capital investment.

Economic data can be employed in a number of ways, but two measures of market demand based on them are especially useful. These measures are market indicators and market factors. Other methods for estimating demand depending on economic data are regression analysis, trend analysis, and cluster analysis.

Market indicators

Market indicators are economic data that serving as yardsticks for measuring the relative market strengths of various geographic areas. A well-known American example of this is the Buying Power Index published in the annual "Survey of Buying Power" by Sales & Marketing Management. The purpose of this index is to enable marketers to compare the relativc buying power of countries as well as cities in the United States.

A somewhat similar index for a worldwide scale is published by Cross border Monitor (formerly Business International). This index employs 40 indicators for 117 nations. The indicators include population, GDP, the various categories of private consumption expenditures, and the production or consumption of steel, cement, electricity, and energy. These indicators are weighted and combined to form composite indexes of ① market size, ② market intensity, and ③ market growth.

1) Market size

Market size shows the relative size of each market as a percentage of the total world market. The percentages for each market are obtained by averaging data on overall population (given double weight), urban population, private consumption expenditures, steel consumption, cement and electricity production, and ownership of telephones, cars, and television sets.

The market size index is measurement of the potential market for goods and services. The index is the ratio, expressed in percent, of several consumption and production items for each country compared to the regional total for the same items. Undoubtedly, this is the most important factor for companies, because a larger market size means lots of the marketing opportunities, which is why the Chinese market attracts more international investments.

2) Market intensity

Market intensity measures the degree of concentrated purchasing power the market represents when compared to the world intensity of 100. This is the richness of the market. To produce an index of the relative buying power of the populations of various markets, each country's share of the variables used in the market size index are put on a per capita basis. Car ownership, urban population, and private consumption are doubly weighted. The country's share is expressed as a ratio relative to the regional total of the items with the region total set equal to one. Urban population is doubly weighted because most of the rural population does not participate in the money economy. That means the rural markets are very large when seen from outside, but they are actually very small. It may be more difficult for companies to operate in the real world.

3) Market growth

Market growth is an average of the percentage growth of the following indicators over the past five years: population, steel consumption, electricity production, and ownership of cars, trucks, buses, and television sets.

An analysis of these three indexes will show the international sales manager which major regions and major markets were the fastest growing, what their growth rates were, and which regions and major markets have the highest degree of concentrated purchasing power.

Besides, by comparing the values of the indexes with the sales results of the company's subsidiaries, management can quickly judge their performances. The indexes are also used to set sales targets and to serve as a basis for allocating promotional budgets. Although Euro-monitor does not calculate indexes, it does publish two annuals, European Marketing Data & Statistics and International Data & Statistics, which also provide valuable data. And in China, the government publishes the relative data every quarter and every year. In addition, companies can get this relative data from the industry association or the state statistical bureau.

4) Market factors

Market factors are similar to market indicators, except they tend to correlate highly with the market demand for a given product. If the analyst does not have a factor for that market, he or she can usually use one from the domestic market to get a reasonable approximation. Moreover, an analyst who works for a multinational firm may be able to obtain market factors developed by comparable subsidiaries. To be able to transfer these relationships to the country under study, the analyst must assume that the underlying conditions affecting demands are similar in that market.

The transfer process, done by analogy, works like this: If car registration×1.6 is used to estimate annual tire purchases in the United States, a forecaster who has no market factor for the country under study can use the same 1.6 for that market.

If car registration is 4 million in the new market, then an analyst could forecast that 4 million×1.6 = 6.4 million tires would be sold there. The constant in the country under study may be somewhat different (it usually is), but with this approach, the estimates will be in the right ballpark.

5) Regression analysis

In regression analysis, instead of just using one variable as in the case of market factors, the domestic division utilizes a linear model with several independent variables. For example, in estimating the market potential (MP) for household refrigerators, the marketing manager in the home country may use an equation such as this:

Annual MP = 0.2 marriages + 0.3 divorces + 0.1 housing starts. If there are 500,000 marriages, 300,000 divorces, and 400,000 housing starts in one year, then according to the model, the increase in market potential that year is $0.2 \times 500,000 + 0.3 \times 300,000 + 0.1 \times 400,000 = 230,000$ refrigerators. The analyst, forecasting demand for a new market, may use the domestic model if there are no other data. If sufficient historical data can be obtained locally, she or he may wish to analyze the foreign market by means of regression analysis.

6) Trend analysis

When the historic growth rates of either pertinent economic variables or product imports are known, future growth can be forecasted by means of trend analysis. A time series may be constructed similar to the way that a regression model is made. The arithmetic mean of past growth rates may also be applied to historical data. Caution is advised when using this second method because if the average annual growth rate is applied mechanically, in just a few years, the dependent variable may reach an incredible size. For example, a 5 percent growth rate compounded annually will result in a doubling of the original value in only 15 years.

In as much as trend analysis is based on the assumption that past conditions affecting the dependent variable will remain constant, the analyst will generally modify the outcome to take into account any changes that can be foreseen. Often, there are obvious constraints that will limit upward growth, one of which is the near certainty that competitors will enter the market if large increases in demand continue for along time.

7) Cluster analysis and other multivariable techniques

As multinationals extend their presence to more markets, managers in all functional areas are searching for ways to group countries and geographic regions by common characteristics to simplify their responsibilities. Cluster analysis, for which various computer programs are available, divides objects (market areas, individuals, customers, and other variables) into groups so that the variables within each group are similar. Marketers, for example, use cluster analysis to identify a group of markets where a single promotional approach can be employed; attorneys can use it to group nations according to similarities in certain types of laws; and so forth. Multidimensional scaling, factor analysis, and conjoined analysis are other techniques for examining differences and similarities among markets.

8) Periodic updating

If the estimates are altered significantly in the periodic updating that all long-term forecasts undergo, management may alter the extent of the firm's involvement to fit the new estimates. Fortunately, alternative forms of participation in a market permit the firm to become progressively more involved, with corresponding increases in investment.

Most companies can enter a market in stages, sometimes in this sequence: exporting, establishment of a foreign sales company, local assembly, and finally, manufacturing. Even when the decision is based on whether to produce overseas, management may plan to assemble a combination of imported and domestically produced parts initially and then progress to manufacture more components locally as demand rises. Under this circumstance, managers should often update their relative data to get the correct and latest references about their markets and products. This is the very important precondition for managers who want to master various market factors and make correct marketing decisions. In the real world, lots of multinationals establish their own database to upgrade their data.

Third screening—political and legal forces

The elements of political and legal forces that can eliminate a nation from further company consideration are numerous.

1. Entry barriers

Import restrictions can be positive or negative, depending on whether management is considering exporting (can the firm's products enter the country?) or setting up a foreign plant (will competitive imports be kept out?). If one of management's objectives is 100 percent ownership, will the nation's laws permit it, or is some local participation required? Will the government accept a minority local ownership, or must a minimum of 51 percent of the subsidiary be in the hands of nationals? Are there laws that reserve certain industries for either the government or its citizens? Is the host government demanding that the foreign owner turn over technology to its proposed affiliate that it wishes to keep at the home plant? Perhaps the host government has local content restrictions that the prospective investor considers excessive. There may be a government-owned company that would compete with the proposed plant. Depending on the circumstances and how strongly management wishes to enter the market, any one of these conditions may be sufficient cause for eliminating a nation from further consideration.

2. Profit remittance barriers

When there are no requisites for entry, a nation may still be excluded from consideration if there are, in management's opinion, undue restrictions on the repatriation of earnings. For example, limits linked to the amount of foreign investment or other criteria may be set, or the nation may have a history of inability of providing foreign exchange for profit remittances.

This situation often occurs in developing countries, because these countries lack money, especially foreign exchange. These governments hope to use foreign investment to improve their production, technology, employment and even tax revenue. So, if the market potential is very large, multinationals can consider investing in these countries, otherwise, they should leave the markets before the governments abandon the policy about profit remittance restriction.

3. Other factors

Another factor of serious importance to management is the stability of government policy. Is there continuity in government policy when a new president takes office, for example? What is the political climate like? Is the government stable, or are there cases of infighting among government leaders? How about the public? Is there visible unrest? Do the armed forces have a history of intervention when there are public disturbances? Businesses can adapt to any form of government and thrive as long as the conditions are stable. Remember, instability creates uncertainty, and this complicates planning. An often-heard complaint from businesspeople is the phrase, "They've changed the rules again."

Other concerns of management are tax laws, safety standards, price controls, and the many other factors already examined in the chapters about political and legal forces. No matter how large a nation's potential market is, if its legal and political constraints are unacceptable to management, that nation must be eliminated from further consideration.

Some excellent sources of this kind of information may be found in Financing Foreign Operations, published by the Economist Intelligence Unit; Overseas Business Reports, obtainable from the U. S. Department of Commerce; the Ernst & Young International Series; and Digest of Commercial Laws of the World, published by Oceana.

Fourth screening—sociocultural forces

A screening of the remaining candidates on the basis of sociocultural factors is arduous because these "facts" are highly subjective. An analyst, unless he or she is a specialist in the country, must rely on the opinions of others.

It is possible to hire consultants, but they are expensive. In common situations, small and medium multinationals cannot afford. There are other alternatives, however. For instance, the specialists of various countries' Department of Commerce can provide some assistance, and professional organizations and universities frequently hold seminars to explain the sociocultural aspects of doing business in a particular area or country. Reading Overseas Business Reports (U. S. Department of Commerce), international business publications (Business International and The Economist), and specialized books will augment an analyst's sociocultural knowledge. The use of a checklist of the principal sociocultural components will serve as a reminder of the many factors an analyst must consider in this screening.

After the fourth screening, an analyst should have a list of countries for which an industry demand appears to exist. However, what management really wants to know is which of these countries seem to be the best prospect for the firm's products. A fifth screening based on these competitive forces will help to provide this information.

Fifth screening—competitive forces

In this screening, the analyst examines markets on the basis of competitive forces such as:

(1) The number, size, and financial strength of the competitors.

(2) Their market shares.

(3) Their apparent marketing strategies.

(4) The apparent effectiveness of their promotional programs.

(5) The quality levels of their product lines.

(6) The source of their products—imported or locally produced.

(7) Their pricing policies.

(8) The levels of their after-sales service.

(9) Their distribution channels.

(10) Their coverage of the market.

In management's opinion, countries where strong competitors will make a profitable operation difficult to attain are eliminated unless management ① is following a strategy of being present wherever its global competitors are or ② believes that entering a competitor's home market will distract the competitor's attention from its home market.

Beside the above factors, lots of companies need to consider other problems when they want to take the international marketing research, because various companies have to face different situations and because different companies have different resources and marketing strategies. In general, content should include the following (Chart 8-3).

8.3 Final selection of new markets

An executive of the firm should visit those countries that still appear to be good prospects. Before leaving, this person should review data from the various screenings along with any new information that the researcher can supply. On the basis of this review and his or her experience in making similar domestic decisions, the executive will prepare a list of points on which information must be obtained on arrival. Management will want the facts uncovered by the desk study (the five screenings) to be corroborated and will expect a firsthand report on the market, which will include information on competitive activity and the appraisal of the suitability of the firm's

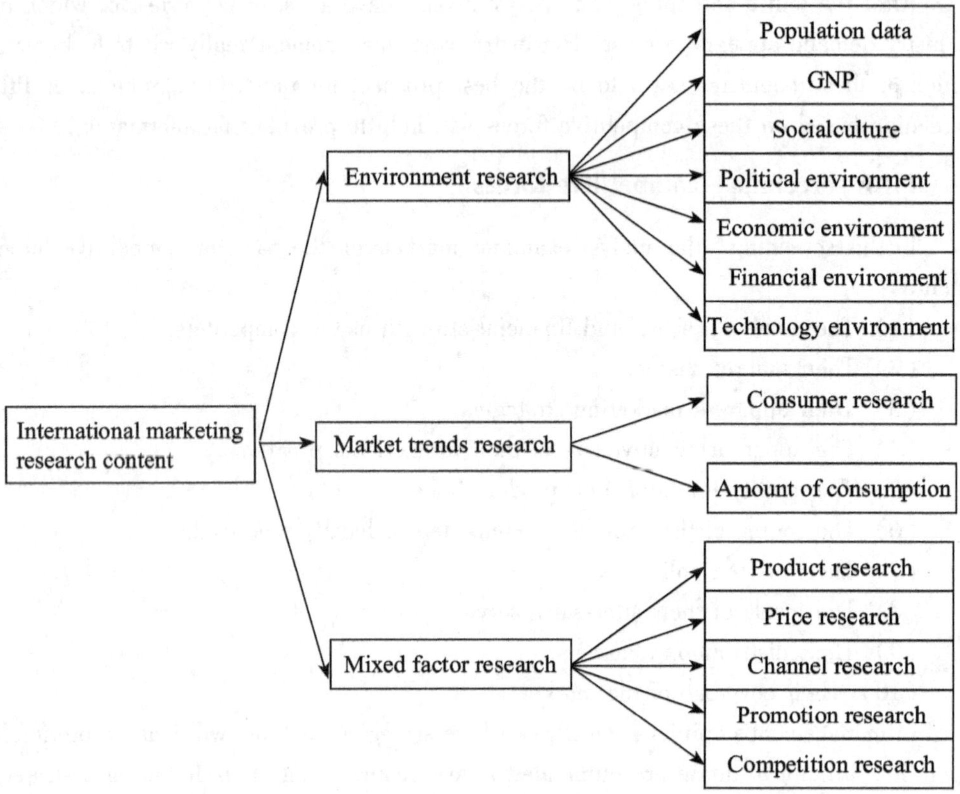

Chart 8-3 Major content included in international marketing research

present marketing mix as well as the availability of ancillary facilities (warehousing, service agencies, media, credit, and so forth).

Field trip

This field trip should not be hurried; as much time should be allotted to this part of the study as would be spent on a similar domestic field trip. Often time can be saved if the executive can join a government-sponsored trade mission or visit a trade fair, because such events attract the kinds of people this person will want to interview.

Government-sponsored trade missions and trade fairs

An important mission of foreign diplomatic ministries, such as the U. S. Department of State and the government department representing industry (the Department of Commerce in the United States), is to promote a nation's foreign trade. This is why commercial officers stationed in U. S. embassies report to both State and Commerce. One of the many means of assisting American firms is to sponsor a trade mission.

When U. S. Department of Commerce trade specialists perceive an overseas market opportunity for an industry, they will organize a trade mission. The purpose is to send a group of executives from different firms in the industry to a country or group of countries to learn firsthand references about the market, meet important customers face to face, and make contacts with people interested in representing their products.

Because of discounted air fares, hotels, and so forth, the cost to the firm is less than what it would pay if it went on its own. Moreover, the impact of a group visit is greater than it is for an individual. Before a mission's arrival, consulate or embassy officials publicize the visit and make contact with local companies they believe are interested. State governments, trade associations, chambers of commerce, and other export-oriented organizations also organize trade missions.

In addition, probably every nation in the world holds a trade fair periodically. Usually, each nation has a specifically marked area where its exhibitors have their own booths staffed by company representatives. Although trade fairs are open to the general public, at certain hours (generally mornings), entrance is limited to businesspeople interested in doing business with the exhibitors.

Although showing products at trade fairs is an ancient sales promotion method, it continues to be effective. Although most trade fairs in developing nations are wide-ranging, with displays of many kinds of products, those in Europe are specialized. Moreover, many of them do not admit the general public. Besides making contact with prospective buyers and agents, most exhibitors use them to learn more about the market. They not only receive feedback from visitors about their exhibits, but they also have the opportunity to observe their competitors in action.

Sometimes local research is required

In many situations, the executive's report will be the final input concerning the information on which the decision is based. Occasionally, however, the proposed human and financial resource commitments are so great that management will insist on gathering data in the potential market rather than depending solely on the desk and field reports. This would undoubtedly be the position of a consumer products manufacturer that envisions entering a large competitive market of an industrialized country. It might also be the recommendation of the executive making the field trip if he or she discovers that market conditions are substantially different from those to which the firm is accustomed. Often, in face-to-face interviews, information is revealed that would never be written. In these situations, research in the local market will not only supply information on market definition and projection but will also assist in the formulation of an effective marketing mix.

Research on the local market

When a firm's research personnel have no experience in the country, management should hire a local research group to do research unless there is a subsidiary in a neighboring country from which a research team can be borrowed. Generally, home country research techniques may be used, although they may need to be adapted to local conditions. It is imperative, therefore, that the person in charge of the project has experience either in that country or in one that is culturally similar and preferably in the same geographic area.

Just as they do at home, researchers will first try to obtain secondary data, but they frequently find that, even in developed nations, they either cannot find what they need or what they encounter is suspect. Fortunately, international agencies, such as the United Nations and the IMF, regularly hold seminars to train government officials in data collection, so that the immediacy and quality of secondary data in some countries are improving.

If secondary data is unavailable, the researchers must collect primary data, and here they may face other complications caused by cultural problems and technical difficulties.

Cultural problems

If the researchers are from one culture and working in another, they may encounter some cultural problems. When they are not proficient in the local language or dialect, the research instrument or respondents' answers must be translated. As we learned in the chapter on sociocultural forces, a number of languages may be spoken in a country, and even in countries where only one language is used, a word's meaning may change from one region to another. As a matter of fact, lots of countries have various official languages.

Other cultural problems plague researchers as they try to collect data. The low level of literacy in many less developed nations also makes the use of mail questionnaires virtually impossible. If a housewife is interviewed in a country where her husband makes the buying decisions, the data obtained from her is worthless. Respondents sometimes refuse to answer questions because of their general distrust of strangers. In other instances, however, the custom of politeness toward everyone will cause respondents to give answers calculated to please the interviewer.

Often, people have practical reasons for not wanting to be interviewed. In some countries, income taxes are based on the apparent worth of individuals as measured by their tangible assets. In such countries, when asked if there is a stereo or TV in household, the respondent may suspect the interviewer of being a tax assessor and refuse to answer. To overcome such a problem, experienced researchers often hire college students as interviewers because their manner of speech and dress correctly identify them for what they are. In general, a company has to understand the local culture first before entering a foreign market to conduct its international marketing research. Unfortunately, lots of the companies are not aware of these issues or they lack enough human resources to finish the job. This is the primary reason why companies fail when they enter international markets.

Technical difficulties

As if cultural problems were not enough, researchers may also encounter technical difficulties. First, updated maps are often unavailable. Streets chosen to be sampled may have three or four different names along their length, and these houses may not be numbered. Telephone surveys can be a formidable undertaking, because in many less developed countries, only the wealthy have telephones. In addition, telephone directories are frequently out of date.

In countries as Brazil and Mexico, researchers often have problems in using their own phones because overloaded circuits make it next to impossible to get a line. Mail surveys can be troublesome too, as mail deliveries within a city may take weeks or are sometimes not even made. The postal service in Italy has been so slow (it takes two weeks for a letter to go from Rome to Milan) that Italian firms have used private couriers to go to Switzerland to dispatch their foreign mail.

Mail questionnaires are not received well in Chile, where the recipient is required to pay the postman for each letter delivered. The response to a mail survey is often low by American standards in countries, like Brazil, where the respondent must go to the post office to mail a letter. To increase returns, firms often offer such premiums such as lottery tickets or product samples to persons who complete a mail questionnaire.

In some developing nations, researchers may also have to obtain governmental permission to conduct interviews and, in some cases, submit questionnaires for prior approval. Some countries prohibit certain kinds of questions. For example, researchers cannot ask Egyptians about the ownership of consumer durables, and in Saudi Arabia, researchers are not permitted to ask questions about nationality.

Research as practiced

The existence of hindrances to marketing research does not mean that it should not be carried out in foreign markets. As you might surmise from the discussion of the availability of secondary data, marketing research is highly developed in industrialized nations, where markets are large and incorrect decisions are costly. Problems like those we have mentioned are prevalent in the developing nations, but they are well known to those who live there. It does not take long for the newcomer to become aware of them either, because longtime residents are quick to point them out.

Analysts tend to do less research and use simpler techniques in these nations, because the firm is in a seller's market in these markets, which means that everything produced can be sold with a minimal effort. Moreover, competition is frequently less intense in developing nations because ① there are fewer competitors and ② management is struggling with problems other than marketing, which keeps them from devoting more time to marketing. Even now in Mexico, an important market for American firms, marketing research is unpopular. When it is done, the preferred method is house-to-house surveying.

Although situations are changing, the most common technique continues to be a combination of trend analysis and querying of knowledgeable persons such as salespeople, channel members, and customers. Researchers then adjust the findings on the basis of subjective considerations.

Although the screening process we have described may appear time consuming, it does assure management that the principal factors have not been overlooked. Because most market-entry decisions can be implemented in stages, the firm can usually make adjustments in time to avoid significant losses when conditions change or if additional information indicates the initial decision was incorrect.

Where do you find this information? When data is difficult to find, but the internet and other departments may be your best sources. The difficulty lies in converting all of this data into information that managers can utilize. For this, the firm needs an international management information system.

Here, we may emphasize the important effect of information system, which closely relates to the management system. The international management information system (IMIS) is an organized, continuous process of gathering, storing, processing, and disseminating information for the purpose of making business decisions. The system's size and complexity can range from a simple filing cabinet in a small firm to a system employing computers to process and store data, as is found in large firms. The means are less important than the end, which is to enable marketing and other managers to use all the sources of information at their disposal. These are:

(1) Internal sources—market analyses, special research reports, and data from company sales, production, financial, and accounting records as reported by foreign subsidiaries, sales representatives, customers, and channel of distribution members.

(2) External sources—reports from governments, trade associations, banks, consultants, customers, and data bases.

Both types of sources can provide data concerning the changes and trends in the uncontrollable environmental variables as well as feedback on the performance of a firm's controllable variables. There is a trend now toward decision support systems, which permit managers to make inquiries and receive specific answers not only from the firm's database, but from external, online databases as well.

8.4 The procedures of the international marketing research

International marketing research is very complex and difficult. However, it is very important for companies to conduct international marketing. Before someone takes a job, he or she should understand the procedures in conducting international marketing research. Although various companies use different methods when they take marketing research, procedures usually include the following.

1. To define research questions

It is very important for the international marketing research team to define research questions. For example, what if sales reduced very quickly in a given foreign market where you were in charge. How would you take approach this problem? As a matter of fact, the answer is very complex, because lots of causes might have lead to this result. For example, it could have been aquality problem, a service problem, an agent problem, an advertising problem or strong competitors' entering the market and so forth. Different reasons may lead to a same result, which means it needs the various solutions. As a researcher, you have to understand what questions you should solve or at least provide correct proposals before you take a research job. Blind research will do nothing except waste the resources of a company.

2. To establish the research plan

The second step of marketing research is to create a careful research plan for your international marketing research. Usually the content of the plans includes the following:

(1) Understanding the objective of the marketing research.

(2) Defining the range of the marketing research.

(3) Dividing the job into several projects.

(4) Defining how to obtain first hand references and secondary data.

(5) Defining marketing research methods.

(6) Creating the marketing research budgets.

(7) Creating a detailed marketing research schedule.

(8) Defining the form of the marketing research report.

3. Carrying out the marketing research plan

If companies need to get the first hand data, they can choose ① to askcompany personnel to take the job; or ② to entrust the specialized research companies to finish the job. In practice, lots of companies use both to carry out their marketing research plan; of course, companies may pay lots of money if they entrust marketing consultants to take the job. However, the quality of your research is most important no matter what methods a company uses, because the research result informs decision makers when they make their marketing strategies. An incorrect result could be a catastrophe for multinationals. This is why lots of famous world companies hire McKinsey to finish these jobs, although it is very expensive.

4. Writing the marketing research report

Because the marketing research report should be submitted to top management of companies and it will influence the decision making process for leaders. The report should be recorded, simple, specific, clear, logical and reasonable. In practice, upper management management prefers that researchers do not give more proposals about the real operation. They also dislike unrealistic results. The marketing research reports should be written skillfully by a writer who possesses a certain degree of cultural mastery as well as understanding the company's strategy and market situation clearly.

Usually, the report includes 3 parts: ① a preface, where you should illustrate the purpose and range of the market research and describe your research methods in a few words; ② the main body, where you should write about the conclusions from marketing research, the methods used to demonstrate the relative questions, describe the details of the investigation and analyze the data you collected, and finally, give your operation proposals to upper managements; ③ and an appendix, which is composed of two parts: the tools, data and references etc. as well as the calculation and settlement result.

Summary

1. Discuss environmental analysis and a modified version, market screening, used for market assessment and analysis. A complete market analysis and assessment as described in this chapter should be conducted by a firm that either is contemplating entering the foreign market for the first time or is already a multinational company that wants to monitor world markets systematically to avoid overlooking marketing opportunities and threats. Most of the data requirement for a foreign decision are the same as those required for a similar domestic decision, although it is likely that additional information about some of the international and foreign environmental forces will be needed.

Essentially, the screening process will consist of examining the various forces in succession and eliminating countries at each step. The sequence of screening is based on ① basic need potential, ② financial and economic forces, ③ political and legal forces, ④ sociocultural forces, ⑤ competitive forces, and ⑥ personal visits.

2. Explain market indicators and market factors. Market indicators are economic data used to measure relative market strengths of countries or geographic areas. Market

factors are economic data that correlate highly with the market demand for a product.

3. Describe the statistical techniques for estimating market demand and grouping similar markets. Some statistical techniques for estimating market demand and grouping similar markets are regression analysis, trend analysis, and cluster analysis.

4. Describe the value to businesspeople of trade missions and trade fairs. Trade missions and trade fairs enable businesspeople to visit a market inexpensively, make sales, obtain overseas representation, and observe competitors' activities.

5. Discuss some of the problems market researchers encounter in foreign markets. Cultural problems, such as a low level of literacy and distrust of strangers, complicate the data-gathering process, as do technical difficulties, such as a lack of maps, telephone directories, and inadequate mail service. These hindrances all may cause your marketing research to fail.

6. Understanding the purpose of an international management information system (IMIS). To provide continuing information on changes in the uncontrollable variables as well as provide feedback on the performance of the firm's controllable variables, many companies have set up international management information systems to gather, store, and use information in an organized manner.

Questions

1. Select a country and a product that you believe your firm can market there. Make a list of the sources of information you will use for each screening.

2. What is the basis for the order of screenings presented in the text?

3. If market data for a country is unobtainable, what readily available data might serve as a substitute?

4. Do a country's imports completely measure the market potential for a product? Why or why not?

5. What are some barriers related to the political and legal forces that may eliminate a country from further consideration?

6. What is the reason for making personal visits to markets that survive the first five screenings?

7. Why should a firm's management consider going on a trade mission or exhibiting in a trade fair important?

8. What are the two principal kinds of complications that researchers face when they collect primary data in a foreign market? Give examples.

9. What do the market size index and the market intensity index tell a researcher?

10. What is the purpose of an international management information system?

Chapter 9 Product Strategy

Concept preview

After reading this chapter, you should be able to

1. Appreciate: the concept of the total product.

2. Understand: how different product strategies influence the result of international marketing.

3. Distinguish: the characteristics of the different periods of the product life cycle.

4. Comprehend: the procedures for developing the new products.

5. Describe: how to overcome the various barriers when you want to introduce your products in foreign markets.

Procter & Gamble, an evolving global corporation

Procter & Gamble, ranked 34 in Fortune's "The World's Largest Corporations" and 12 in its "Largest U. S. Industrial Corporations" obtained $15.9 billion (52 percent of its total sales) from its non-U. S. operations.

As a famous global company, P&G faces higher pressure in most foreign markets than it does in the United States. Many foreign countries have price controls, and there are more competitors in Europe because of the ease of shipping products across borders. For example, in France, P&G competes against Swedish, Danish, and Italian firms in many of its product categories. Commercial TV time, the most efficient way to introduce new products quickly, is limited, and in many countries, such as Belgium, Germany, Italy, and Japan, the use of premiums and gifts for promotion is either banned or severely restricted.

In the 1940s, P&G's strategy was to export its core products to build demand and then establish local sales companies or production facilities. Whether the products were exported or produced locally, they were marketed similarly everywhere. Although those products were not launched with global distribution in mind, (their) new products are. According to Edwin Artzt, P&G's chairman, "If P&G was introducing Pampers today, it would plan to get the product into world markets in five years or less." It took the company 15 years to get them into 70 countries. Now the company tries to introduce products on a worldwide scale early in their development, not after they are established in one market, which gives competitors time to react in all other markets.

Sometimes P&G approaches foreign markets more as a regional market than as a global one. For example, many of its products, such as Camay's smell, Crest's flavor, and Head & Shoulders' formula, are changed to suit the local markets, varying from one region to another, as does the company's marketing strategy. "The idea of moving quickly by taking a piece of technology and implementing it to fit the habits of local markets has taken hold and is leading our operation," said Artzt.

For many years, P&G had a philosophy of employing the same policies and procedures overseas that had been successful in the United States. However, this practice sometimes gave the company problems. In the 1980's, the company rolled out Vizir, based on Liquid Tide, in Europe. What the marketers failed to realize, was that the European washing machines were not equipped to accept liquid detergents. When Vizir was added to a powder dispenser, 20 percent was lost in the bottom of the washer. P&G developed a plastic dispenser that fit into powder dispensers and offered it for free to consumers. One small problem, European washing machines are bolted to the wall. "When we called these women and said we wanted to mail you a liquid dispenser free, just tell us the washer model number, they said, I don't know, the washer is bolted to the wall and I can't see it," explained Artzt. The company finally solved the problem by inventing a reusable ball that sits on top of the clothes and dispenses the liquid. Vizir is now the third-largest-selling detergent in France and has been re-launched in other European countries. Artzt claims, "I think this will go down in history as one of the great all-time rescue jobs."

On the other hand, P&G recycled an ad campaign previously used in the United States when it re-launched Orange Crush in Peru. The TV spot showed a small boy who promises to save his soccer-playing brother's Orange Crush but then succumbs to temptation and drinks it himself. It is credited with playing an important part in a 60 percent sales increase.

To avoid a repetition of the washing machine problem, P&G's present strategy is to first make global plans, next re-plan for each region and then execute the plan locally. It uses autonomous "core teams," composed of representatives of each country in a region, to plan a testing program or a development program for new products and product improvement. These teams recommend products and marketing strategies for the core products (product lines) —soap, toothpaste, diapers, and shampoo. For example, P&G core teams are working on the smell and concentration levels of fabric softeners for different parts of the world.

The opening section illustrates how P&G has changed its marketing strategy from one of using the same procedures and policies overseas that have been proven successful in the United States, to one of making global plans, adjusting them for regions, and then adapting them to satisfying local demands.

Whether a policy or technique is first designed for global use and then adapted for local market differences or, as in the case of the Orange Crush advertisement, the idea comes first from the home country and then is used overseas; marketers must know where to look for possible differences between marketing domestically and marketing internationally. Sometimes the differences are great; at other times, there are no differences.

Certainly there are some strong commonalities. Is it not true that marketers everywhere must ① know their markets, ② develop products or services to satisfy customers' needs, ③ price the products or services so that they are readily acceptable in the market, ④ make them available to the buyers, and ⑤ inform potential customers and persuade them to buy?

Although the basic functions of domestic and international marketing are the same, the international markets served often differ widely because of the great variations in the uncontrollable environmental forces that we examined. Moreover, even the forces we think of as controllable, vary among wide limits. For example, the distribution channels to which the marketer is accustomed are unavailable, certain aspects of the product may be different, the promotional mixes are often dissimilar, and the distinct cost structures may require different prices to be set.

The international marketing manager's task is complex. He or she must frequently plan and control a variety of marketing strategies rather than just one and then coordinate and integrate those strategies into a single marketing program. Even the marketing managers of global firms such as P&G who utilize a single, worldwide strategy must know enough about the uncontrollable variables to be able to make changes in its implementation when necessary.

Both global and multinational marketing managers, like their domestic counterparts, must develop marketing strategies by assessing the firm's potential foreign markets and analyzing many alternative marketing mixes. Their aim is to select target markets that the firm can serve at a profit and to formulate combinations of tactics for product, price, promotion, and distribution channels that will best serve those markets. In the previous chapter, we examined the market assessment and selection process. Starting from this chapter, we shall start to study the formulation of the marketing mix.

As we have indicated above, the marketing mix consists of a set of strategy decisions made in the areas of product, promotion, pricing, and distribution for the purpose of satisfying the customers in a target market. The number of variables included in these four areas is extremely large, making hundreds of combinations possible. Often, the domestic operation has already established a successful marketing mix, and the temptation to follow the same procedures overseas is strong. Yet, as we have seen, important differences between the domestic and foreign environments may make a wholesale transfer of the mix impossible. The questions that the international marketing manager must resolve are: "Can we standardize worldwide? Must we make some changes, or must we formulate a completely different marketing mix?"

9.1 Standardization, adaptation, or completely different

Management would prefer global standardization of the marketing mix—that is, it would prefer to employ the same marketing mix in all of the firm's operations because standardization can produce significant cost savings. If the product sold in the domestic market can be exported, there can be longer production runs, which lower manufacturing costs. Even when the standard product is manufactured overseas, production costs will be less because the extra research and design expense of either adapting domestic products or designing new ones for foreign sales will be avoided.

Generally, R&D is still highly concentrated in the home country. Although some internationals have had overseas research facilities for years and recently global firms have been locating R&D centers in foreign markets. When a firm's R&D is highly concentrated in the home county, the important product changes have to be made there. Thus, foreign and domestic personnel compete for R&D time. Also, a product specification is rarely frozen (look at the minor changes in automobiles in a single model year). Notifying all of the production facilities worldwide about these modifications is difficult enough, but it is much more complex when the product is not internationally standardized.

For many products, both consumer and industrial, that require spare parts for after-sales servicing, and demonstrates why standardization greatly simplifies logistics and acquisition.

If advertising campaigns, promotional materials (catalogs, point-of-purchase displays), and sales training programs can be standardized, then the expensive creative work and artwork need to be done only once. Standardized pricing strategies for multinational firms that source markets from several different foreign subsidiaries avoid the embarrassment of having an important customer receive two distinct quotations for the same product. Although economies of scale are not as readily attainable for standardizing channels of distribution as for the other elements of the marketing mix, there is some gain in efficiency when the international marketing manager can use the same strategy in all markets. In summary, the benefits from standardization of the marketing mix are ① lower costs, ② easier control and coordination from headquarters, and ③ reduction of the time consumed in preparing the marketing plan.

In spite of the advantages of standardization, many firms find it necessary to either modify the present mix or develop a new one. The extent of the changes depends on the type of product (consumer or industrial), the environmental forces, and the degree of market penetration desired by management.

9.2 Product strategy overview

The product is the central focus of the marketing mix. If it fails to satisfy the needs of consumers, no amount of promotion, price cutting, or distribution will persuade the consumers to buy. For example, consumers will not repurchase a detergent if the clothes do not come out as clean as TV commercials say they will. They will not be deceived by false advertisements.

In formulating product strategies, international marketing managers must remember that the product is more than a physical object. The total product includes the customer brand name, accessories, after-sales buys, also includes the physical product, service, warranty, instructions for use, company image, and package. The fact that the total product is purchased often makes it less expensive and easier for an international company to adapt the present product, or even create a new one, without altering its physical characteristics. Different package sizes and promotional messages, for example, can create a totally new product for a distinct market. The relative ease of creating a totally new product without changing the manufacturing process is an important reason that there is more physical product standardization internationally than one might expect.

Total and physical product

Much of the confusion in the ongoing discussion about whether a global firm can have global products results from the discussants not clarifying whether they are referring to the total product, the physical product, or the brand name. For example, Coca-Cola is always offered as an example of a global product, and it is true that the total product and the brand are global. However, the physical product is multinational; its sweetness varies according to local tastes, even in the United States.

Consider two products that Cadbury-Schweppes, the British-based food and soft drink multinational, produces: tonic water and chocolate. The tonic water is a global product physically, but as a total product, it is multinational because people buy it for different reasons. The French drink it straight, and the English mix it with alcohol. Chocolate is neither a global physical product nor a global total product; it is eaten as a snack in some places, put in sandwiches in some places, and eaten as a dessert in other places. Because of strong local preferences, it also varies greatly in taste. So does Nestle instant coffee, which is produced in 200 different blends globally, all of which are sold under the brand name Nescafe, another example of brand name globalization.

Type of product

One important factor that influences the amount of change to be made in a product is its classification as a consumer or industrial product or service. Generally, consumer products require greater adaptation than industrial products to meet the demands of the world market. If the consumer products are high style or the result of a fad, they are especially likely to require changes. We can think of these product types as being on a continuum ranging from insensitive to highly sensitive in the foreign environment.

1. Industrial products

Many highly technical industrial products can be sold unchanged worldwide. Transistors, for example, are used wherever radios are manufactured. Timken advertises that its bearings are interchangeable no matter where produced.

If product changes are required, they may only be cosmetic, such as converting gauges to read in the metric system by pasting a new face on a dial or printing instruction plates in another language. However, many overseas buyers of industrial products, Europeans especially, will not buy American machinery even with cosmetic changes such as dial conversion to metrics. They demand that the machine be made in the metric system to metric measurements. General Electric found out how serious this problem can be when its shipment of electrical goods was refused admission to Saudi Arabia because the electrical cords were six-feet long instead of the required metric standard of two meters (6.6 feet).

Relatively simple adaptations, such as lengthening pedals or changing seat positions, are frequently sufficient to compensate for the physical differences of foreign operators. However, somewhat more drastic modifications in the physical product may be necessary because of two problems that are especially prevalent in developing countries - a tendency to overload equipment and to slight maintenance. These problems are comprehensible to anyone familiar with the cultural and economic forces in the foreign environment. Unlike American children, who grow up owning automobiles and working with tools, the mechanics and operators in many foreign countries rarely have such experience until they enter a training program, which is often on the job.

For example, a bulldozer operator learns that if he pulls a lever and steps on a pedal, his machine will push whatever is in front of it. In the process it is not uncommon to see a bulldozer pushing on some immovable object until the engine fails or a part breaks from the overload. The extraordinary noise coming from the engine makes no impression on the operator.

In another example, despite the careful instructions concerning cleanliness that ball-bearing manufacturers include in the package, one may find a mechanic removing the protective oiled paper leaving the bearing exposed to dust and grime before using it because he may not be able to read. Finally, a very low-paid, uneducated man may be given the responsibility of lubricating equipment worth millions of dollars. He may over grease or miss half of the fittings, and the equipment is destroyed.

To overcome these difficulties, manufacturers such as Caterpillar and Allis-Chalmers have established very thorough training programs wherever their products are sold. Many manufacturers have prepared simple instructions with plenty of pictures to get their message across to persons with limited reading ability. The other alternative is to modify the equipment, perhaps using a simpler bearing system that requires little maintenance. The machine may make more noise and be less efficient, but it runs longer with less maintenance.

Where the technology of even adapted product is too advanced for their customers, manufacturers may market an entirely different product to accomplish the same purpose. A firm that produces electric cash registers in the United States, for example, may be able to earn good profits by marketing a hand-operated model in areas where electricity is unavailable. Products considered absolute in advanced countries are frequently what developing countries need. Furthermore, foreign subsidiaries sometimes find market opportunities for product lines not manufactured by the parent company.

Marketing managers in General Tire's affiliates saw the profit possibilities in selling fan and industrial V-belts in their markets. Although General Tire-USA did not produce them, management obtained the technology for their subsidiaries through licensing agreements with Gates Rubber, a renowned maker of V-belts, so that this totally new product was manufactured in a number of foreign plants.

Occasionally adaptations are necessary to meet local legal requirements, such as those that govern noise, safety, or exhaust emissions. To avoid changing the product, some manufacturers design it to meet the most stringent laws even though it will be over designed for the rest of the markets. In some instances, governments have passed very strict laws to protect a local manufacturer from imports. When this occurs, the company may prefer to design the product to the next most stringent laws and stay out of the first market.

Of course, this is what the government has in mind when it passes the laws. However, words of caution for the company in this situation—test the local manufacturer's product before giving up on the market. On occasion, the local product also has failed to meet the specifications. When confronted with this evidence, the government has to change the laws.

2. Consumer products

Although consumer products generally require greater modification to meet local market requirements than do industrial products, some of them can be sold unchanged to certain market segments. Consumer products of this kind include a number of luxury items, such as large automobiles, sporting equipment, and perfumes. This is because every country in the world contains a market segment that is more similar to the same segment in other countries with respect to economic status, buyer behavior, tastes, and preferences.

This market segment includes the "jet set", foreign-educated and well-traveled citizens, and expatriates. Many products and services foreign to local tastes and preferences have been successfully introduced by first being marketed to these pioneer customers. Gradually, members of other market segments purchase these products and services until consumption becomes widespread.

Before McDonald's and other American fast-food franchisors went abroad, a common complaint among U. S. expatriates was that they could not get a good hamburger. In response, a Brazilian returned from college in the United States and opened a drive-in similar to Dairy Queen in Rio de Janeiro. The first customers were Americans and members of the international set, but before long, the reputation spread and Brazilians became customers.

Thirty years ago, there was only one A&W root beer stand and one Dairy Queen in Mexico City. American expatriates and tourists were the principal customers. Today, many of the American fast-food franchisors are in such cities as Mexico City, Guadalajara, and Monterrey. As an American, when you arrive in Acapulco, the signs of Ponderosa, Kentucky Fried Chicken, and so forth make you think you never left home.

In introducing new products, especially when the goal is immediate market penetration, marketers must be aware that, as they go down the economic and social strata in each country, they will tend to find greater dissimilarities among countries with respect to social and cultural values. Thus in general, it follows that the deeper the immediate market penetration desired, the greater the need for product modification. This does not necessarily mean the physical product must be changed. A modification of one of the other elements of the total product may be sufficient, such as: a different size or color of the package, a change in the brand name, or a new positioning if the product is consumed differently.

Mars faced a drop in Bahrain's imports of candy when it was ready to launch M&Ms. Fortunately, its marketing research discovered that Bahrainis consider the peanut to be a health food, so Mars repositioned its peanut M&Ms. The company was able to turn the hot Gulf climate to its advantage by emphasizing its traditional slogan, "M&Ms melt in your mouth, not in your hand." As you will see later in the next chapter, Mars followed promotional strategy number—same product, different message. Although part of the message, the slogan, remained the same.

Detergent manufacturers were able to achieve deeper market penetration by offering consumers with limited purchasing power smaller packages that are often found only in American laundromats. In humid climates countries, cookies and crackers are packed in metal boxes to preserve both the package and the product.

In general, it is more difficult for you to engage in international marketing if you are producing or operating consumer goods that you have to change or at least modify according to the special situation of the foreign markets. This adaptation strategy is the major countermeasure for you to develop the product in foreign markets. Of course, this means that it needs more resources, especially international marketing talents, to support you to accomplish the job.

3. Services

The marketing of services, sometimes called intangibles, is similar to the marketing of industrial products, in that these products are generally easier to market globally than consumer products are. Andersen Consulting's 24, 598 professionals in their 150 offices in 46 countries, offer worldwide the same kinds of expertise in business strategy that they sell to American clients. Fifty-one percent of the firm's $2. 88 billion revenues came from outside the United States in 2003.

It is true that laws and customs sometimes force providers to alter their products. There are some markets that Manpower, for example, cannot operate in those countries, because private employment agencies are against the law. Accounting laws vary substantially between nations, but Big Eight accounting firms operate globally. Price Waterhouse, for example, has over 400 offices in 118 nations. In 2005, its 7, 200 professionals earned 55 percent of the firm's $1 billion revenues outside the United States. There are worldwide subscribers to Nexis, Mead Corporation's database, one of the fast-growing international computer and data processing industry. Visa, MasterCard, and American Express, with combined billing of over $1 trillion in 2005, are examples of successful companies in the global credit card industry. The physical product may vary slightly because of the local environmental forces, but the total product remains the same.

9.3 The product life cycle and product strategy

The concept and pattern of the product life cycle

For any products, they all have their own life cycles. The process is divided into introduction period, growth period, mature period and decline period. For companies, the market share rate, sales and profit rate are very different in various periods. In most situations, in the introduction period, the sales grow slowly and the profit is always in the negative; when the sales grow very quickly and the profits become positive, the product enters the growth period; if the profits reach the maximum and the sales stop growing, the product enters the mature period; and if the sales and profits reduce very quickly, the product enters the decline period.

The product life cycle can be divided into two types: typical type and atypical type. The typical type includes introduction, growth, mature and decline periods. Its shape is shown in Chart 9-1.

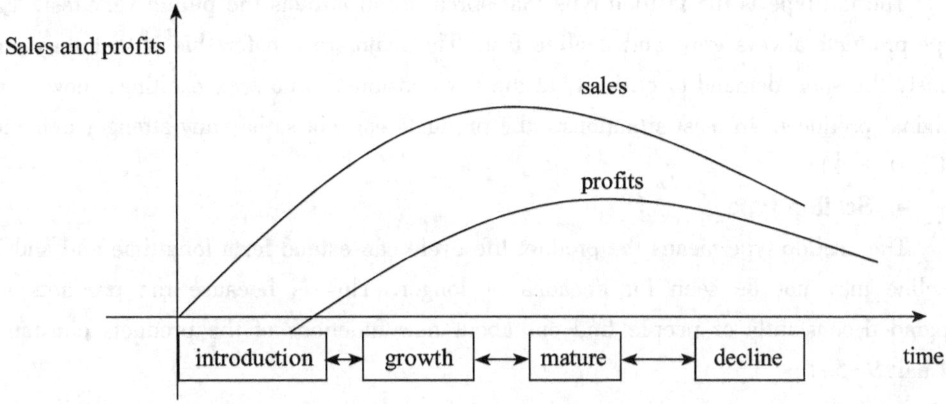

Chart 9-1 Typical product life cycle

The atypical type of the product life cycle period includes the style, the fashion, the fad and the scallop type. The product life cycle period curves of the typical type and atypical type are different.

1. Style type

The products which possess the style type may continue for several generations, and are circulated or re-circulated based on the interest of the consumers. Sometimes they are popular, and sometimes they are not (Chart 9-2).

2. Fashion type

If the products are accepted or welcomed in the special field, they are called fashion products and their product life cycle is called the fashion type. The characteristic of the fashion type is that when the products first enter the markets, only a few people accept them; however, most people will accept them gradually as time goes on. Eventually, the products decline and people begin to take notice of other fashion products (Chart 9-3).

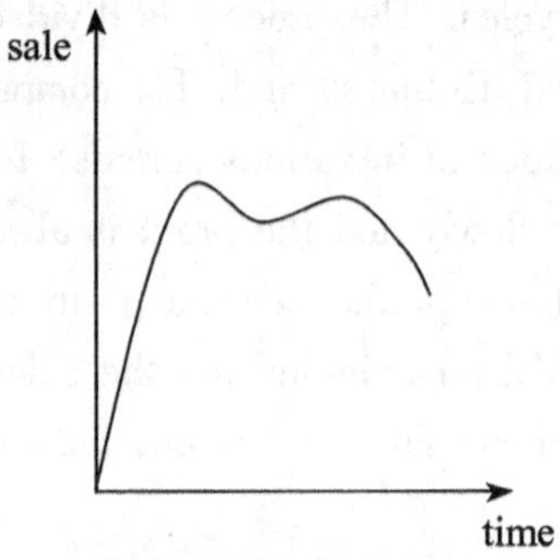

Chart 9-2 Style type

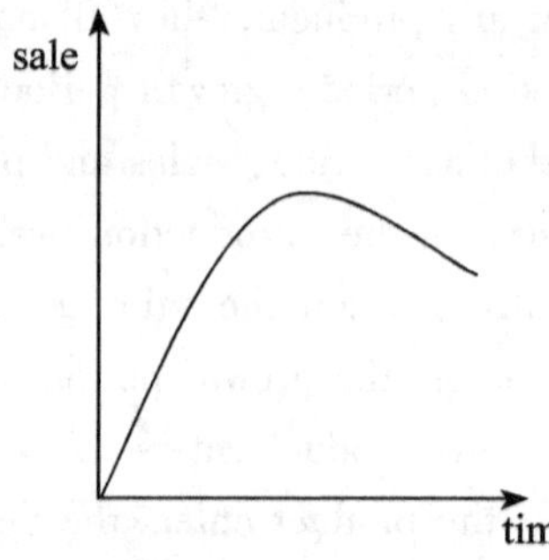

Chart 9-3 Fad type

3. Fad type

The fad type is the fashion type that spreads and attracts the public very fast. Fad type products always grow and decline fast. The major reason for this is that they only satisfy the short demand or curiosity of the few consumers who seek exciting, new, and original products. In most situations, the products can not satisfy any stronger demands (Chart 9-4).

4. Scallop type

The scallop type means the product life cycle can extend for a long time and and its decline may not be seen for decades or longer. This is because the products are upgraded constantly or people find out about new functions of the products constantly (Chart 9-5).

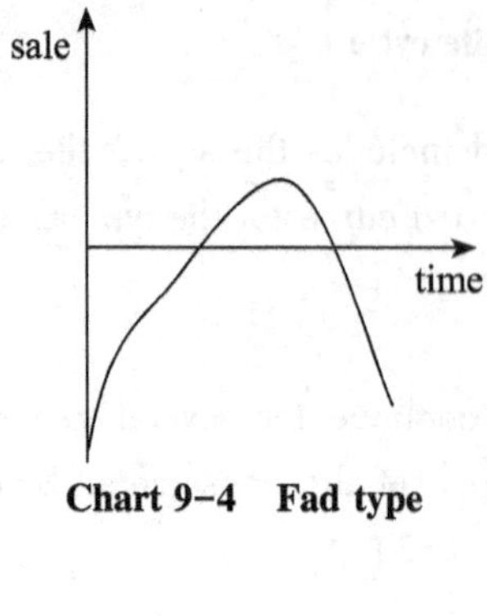

Chart 9-4 Fad type

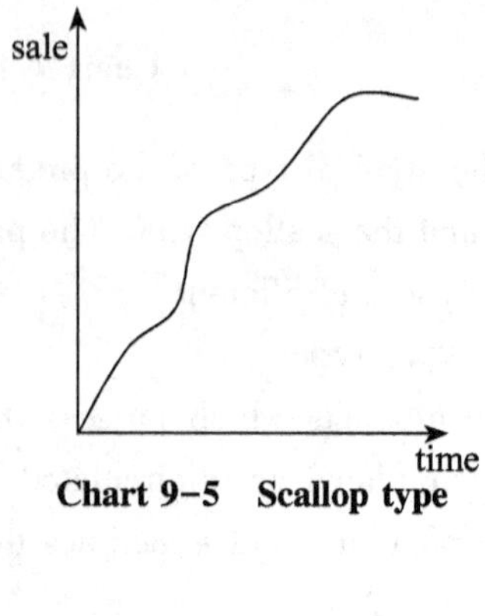

Chart 9-5 Scallop type

For international companies, it is very important to study the product life cycle, especially the same products are always in the different product cycle periods in various countries. Thus, the product life cycle is the foundation for the marketers in creating their product marketing strategy. For example, the product life cycle of the automobile in the U. S. is in the decline period, and in China, it is located in growth period. This is why multinationals utilize various marketing strategies in different markets for the same products.

The significance for the multinationals to utilize the product life cycle theory

The theory of the product life cycle was created by Louis Wells and Raymond Vemon, famous American economists. They divided the product life cycle into three periods: introduction period, growth period, and mature period. Based on the different characteristics of the various periods, multinationals should use different marketing strategies to develop in various markets. For example, in the introduction period, innovation countries can export their products to the developing countries. In the growth period, with technology expanding, some of the developed countries can master the technology and begin the production run. Finally, in the mature period, developing countries master the technology and occupy the markets using lower labor cost while the innovation countries develop new products with their technological advantage.

The importance for multinationals to develop their international markets with the product life cycle is indicated by the following:

(1) Multinationals can constantly adjust their market structure utilizing the different product life cycle periods in various countries, and transfer their market targets in time to expand their product life cycle. The purpose of this is to occupy the international markets for a long time.

(2) Multinationals can adjust their product structure utilizing the product life cycle theory by introducing the new products into the markets, weeding out the futureless products, and speeding to update the products.

(3) Developing countries can draw into the new products produced by the developed countries utilizing the theory of the product life cycle. They can export the products to the original production countries based on the native nature resources and lower labor cost, thus, optimizing their product structure constantly. For example, 30 years ago, most of the Chinese export products were textiles, today over 45% of the high-tech products in the world are exported by China.

The inspiration of the product life cycle theory for China is that the development target for companies is not to be satisfied with only being the acceptor of technology and products developed and produced by developed countries. Chinese companies have to work to create new technologies and products based on the foundation of introducing and assimilating the technologies coming from the developed countries. Furthermore, they must try their best to change the product life cycle in domestic and international markets and promote a native product life cycle to break the control of the foreign counties in order to improve their competitiveness.

9.4 The new product development strategy

With the development of the world economy, science and technology became the most important motive in promoting economic development. Not only did the situation improve the standard of living in various countries, but it also brought about intense competition. Today, the technology life cycle has become shorter and shorter, as a result, the product life cycle is also shorter. Thus, the only way for companies to occupy foreign markets, is to constantly create new products to satisfy the more and more complex demands of consumers. In this sense, the market competition is between new products and is one of the most important reasons why world famous companies can beat their rivals.

How to define the new product

The new product is not a technology concept, but is related to marketing actions. To this extent, the implication of the new product is very large apart from new products emerging because of scientific and technological discovery, they also include other aspects. For example, in the field of production and sales, so long as the function, form or even the package of the products are different from the old products, they are still all the new products. In the field of consumption, the new products provide new benefits or effects and are accepted by consumers in international markets. In summary, if you can provide products which bring a new feeling for consumers, then you are producing or marketing the new products.

Based on the R&D process, the new products can be divided into: branded new products and improved new products.

1. Brand new products

Brand new products are created by utilizing new theory, new technology, and new materials, and possess a new structure and new functions. In general, the products are developed in the world and they can be used to develop the new markets. At the same time, these kinds of new products can change the life-style of people and ask the public to change their consumption ideals and consumption habits. Because it is very difficult to create the new products, the percentage of this kind of new product is very small in practice (only about 10%). The electric light, car, and mobile phone are all examples of new products that were introduced to the markets for the first time.

2. Improved new products

If the companies improve their products in structure, function, quality, color and style based on their old products, even if it just possesses the new characteristic in packaging, they are called improved new products. Because the structure of the improved new products is more reasonable, the function is more complete, and the quality is higher, they can satisfy the various demands of the consumers. Improved new products, which account for about 26% of all new products, are thus easier to create than brand new products.

3. Imitated new products

If the companies imitate products and production created by other domestic or foreign companies, the products are called the new products for those companies. Of course, the legal and technological problems should be solved before you take the method to creat your new products. The most important way to go about utilizing new technology developed by the multinationals is through a license agreement to produce the new products. Because many companies, in developing countries, get more advanced technologies from the multinationals, the imitated new products are widespread in the markets, as a kind of new product. The percentage of imitated new products is about 20%.

4. Series new products

The series new products are products that are furthered developed with a new variety, new color and new specification based on the original product catalogues. Thus, the companies can expand their markets and prevent the competitors from entering their markets. In the real world, many of the multinationals take this kind of new product to develop their markets, especially when they face intense competition. The percentage of this kind of new product is about 26%.

5. Lower cost new products

If a company is able to produce a product whose cost is lower than other, similar products with the same function, that product is called a lower cost product. In most cases, it indicates that the companies reduce the cost by utilizing new science and technology, improving their productive technology or their production efficiency. However, they maintain the original functions of the products. The percentage of the kind of the new products is about 11%.

6. Repositioned new products

If the old products are used to develop new markets, the products are called repositioning new products and account for about 7% of the new products.

R&D strategies for the new products

Only the correct development tactics can guarantee the success for the companies to develop their new products, this is why international managers have to analyze the demand psychology and change trend of their consumers. Some things you may have to consider if you want to develop the new products are: ① energy saving products; ② small and micro products; ③ multi-function products; ④ operating simple products and; ⑤ diversified products.

In general, you can utilize the following strategies when you want to develop your new products.

1. The series new product development strategy

So called series new product development strategy, is about expanding your product line around your original product and developing familiar but different products. This can thus make companies possess various types, specifications and grades of a series of products. For example, based on its brand and technology, Haier developed its refrigerator, television, air conditioner, washing machines and other series products to satisfy the various demands of the consumers.

Because the series products can satisfy various demands of the consumers and the different demands for the same consumers, it can also help the companies expand their market share, increase sales, and strengthen their competitiveness. The series new product development strategy has become a major tactic for companies to develop new products, because not only can it enable the companies to master the market demand, but also it can improve the resource utilizing efficiency of the companies while at the same time saving developing expenditure.

2. The analogy new product development strategy

The analogy new product development strategy indicates methods which the companies transfer their principle, method, skill or ideas in some fields to another field to form new products. In this situation, the managers have to use analogy consideration, draw inferences about other cases, comprehend by analogy, and consider the original technology, workmanship, and materials to analogize the new products. The specific methods of this are:

1) Theory analogy

Theory analogy means analogizing the thinking principle to new fields. For example, using a large-scale socialized production principle to reform the traditional retail industry, the managers created chain store operations. The new operation method thus created the large economic and social benefits in the real world. Although it is not the product innovation, it indeed expanded the markets for the companies.

2) Skill and workmanship analogy

Skill and workmanship means developing the new products based on the original skills and workmanship. For example, Nissin Food invented the instant noodles first, and then instant rice, instant flour, instant porridge and so forth based on the analogy technology and workmanship.

3) Materials analogy

Materials analogy means the companies develop their new products by utilizing the same or familiar materials. For example, after mineral water was introduced, people developed clear water, airspace water, ice tea and vitamin water, etc.

4) Customer tailors new product development strategy

The customer tailor new product development strategy indicates the companies develop or produce the products based on the requirement or even the design of the customers. The products are always very special, and are sometimes unique products in the world. Obviously, the strategy fully reflects the operation idea that, "consumer's demand is the center of marketing," and is the only correct direction for modern companies to develop their new products.

Haier often uses this strategy to achieve success in the market. For example, it developed the "locker plant refrigerator," "refrigerator with the wine bottle shelf," and various color refrigerators designed by the consumers etc. This is why Haier can market its products all over the world and be the first brand of the home appliance in the world.

Companies should possess the following conditions if they want to use this strategy: ① they have to establish the idea "to serve the customers with heart and soul"; and ② they have to establish their own databases to collect and analyze the various demand information coming from the consumers. In time, companies will have the elastic design and production system to develop the individual products for their consumers.

3. Imitated new product development strategy

Imitated new product development strategy is when companies imitate and reform products that other companies developed rapidly and introduced their own new products in the markets. The strategy does not need R&D, comes from the new product development link, and concentrates on imitating the new products introduced by other companies. If the market potential is very large, of course, the companies can share the market benefits with the strategy.

The tactic is called "chasing competition" or "chasing imitation" and though the company does not aim to be the leader of the market, it is also not just pure imitation. The company needs some innovation too because it is impossible for them to occupy the markets for a long time if they just imitate other company's new products. Of course, the strategy not only enables companies to save large sums of R&D expenditure and avoids the market risks, but it also helps companies enter the market successfully by utilizing the new products developed by the market leader. Many companies use this strategy to develop their new products in the practice. Some of the outstanding companies, who were latecomers, may even surpass the former leaders by reforming the new products developed by the market leader. This is why many companies, even the very famous and outstanding companies of the world, use this strategy. And like the Japanese said: "imitation plus reform equal innovation." It is one of the very important reasons why Japanese companies have been able to master so many new products, including the most advanced technologies in the world.

If you want to use this strategy to develop your new products, you have to consider the following points: ① the competitive imitation needs to use forward thinking and reverse thinking synthetically, thus you should look at the system fully and deeply study and analyze the new products in the markets. This means that you should survey special advantages and try to add brilliance to one's present splendor for the enhancement of the new products. At the same time, you should find out the shortages of the new products and try to reform and innovate; ② the competitive imitation requires the companies to possess quick reflecting systems to help avoid losing innovation opportunities.

4. Differentiating new product development strategy

The key of the new development is innovation. If companies can develop the new products according to this principle; they can remain invincible in the market. This is why companies have to consider and compare product difference with other products. Only the new products which possess the distinguished characteristics and impress the consumers can enhance the attraction and competitiveness of the new products.

Besides, any new products that are introduced to the market are accepted from the assessments by consumers. However, it is not easy to introduce products to the markets and persuade consumers to accept them. It requires the managers to study marketing strategies and select the best tactics to expend the markets.

To do this, you can choose two strategies. The first is called the incremental strategy, by which companies enter the major markets or special areas when they expand their new products. The advantage of this tactic is that it can coordinate new product volume, the markets, and is in favor of perfecting new products. In general, it is more reliable for the new products. The disadvantage of the tactic is that the speed of the market expansion is slower, growth rate of earnings is lower and the threats coming from the potential competitors are larger.

The second tactic is called the rushing strategy, which is when companies quickly introduce their new products to all of the markets which the companies hope to occupy. The advantage of this tactic is that the companies can get a higher growth rate of earnings and can effectively prevent competitors from entering the markets. In another words, it can reduce the threats coming from the potential competitors. However, the tactic needs more expenditure to promote the new products and the market risk is very large, because if consumers do not accept the new products, you will suffer heavy losses.

How to develop new products

According to the requirement of the marketing differentiation, managers have to find out the new functions of the new products in order to satisfy the demands of the consumers, as well as have unique and distinctive characteristics. To achieve the goal, you have to take particular methods and obey particular rules when you want to develop the new products.

1. Explore the demand of the consumers and try to find out unique information

The basic function of the new products is to satisfy the demand of the consumers. The demand of the consumers can be divided into realistic demand and potential demand. In practice, the managers should pay attention to the potential demand of the consumers. The realistic demand is known by everyone, and your competitors are therefore producing the products to satisfy the demand, which means the market opportunity is small. The potential demand is the customers' unexpressed demand, which they themselves are sometimes not fully aware of and thus need the marketers to find out and create the new products to satisfy the demands. For example, if you take the long distance bus to travel, how will you solve the problem of using the toilet? The question puzzled lots of people, one Japanese company found out the "demand" and introduced a new product named "paper urine bag" to market and achieved the great success.

The above case indicates that the managers should pay attention to exploring and catching the potential demands when they want to develop new products that are good at promoting consumption. Managers should also create new markets actively and expand the markets by all means. Besides, the new product development needs the inspiration of the product explorers. If you can take information which nobody knows except for you, it is easier for you to develop the new products. For the same reason, you can take old information and integrate it to develop your products. For example, the washing machine, named "big sweet potato", produced by Haier was invented after the company learned that the farmers wash their sweet potatoes in a washing machine. This information led to a new product that brought great success for Haier.

2. Explore the product functions and open up the convenience and science consumption

If companies give old products new functions and occupy the markets again, it is called the strategy to explore the product function. For example, the medicine toothpaste added the function to prevent and cure the odontopathy and the folding umbrella added the function to fold and enable the people to carry it around easily. Companies can even sometimes break out the old consumption habits of consumers and open up the convenience and scientific consumption via the new products. For example, with many governments passing more and more stringent laws aimed at protecting their environments, many disposable products are limited. Thus, some companies found market opportunities to produce portable tableware and portable cups to develop the markets.

3. Develop brim products to satisfy multi-demand of the consumers

Because companies continue to face the more and more intense competition in the markets, brim products are developed by and can occupy the markets for a long time. Brim products collect the multi-industry technologies and satisfy the curiosity of the consumers, making it a very important strategy for the companies to use in order to develop the new products. For example, the paper tablecloth can be used to replace the cloth with paper; the medicine toothpaste not only can clean the tooth but can also cure odontopathy; and the electric pen can satisfy the demand of consumers to write and calculate. Of course, it is not very easy to develop the new products, because it requires companies to have the multi-industry resources, including the technology, management, marketing skill and other outside conditions. Although the border products possess the very wide markets.

4. Use other people's developing advantage to save the resources and tackle key problems

Successful companies always are good at using other companies' advantage to develop their new products. For example, Fujitsu invented the most advanced robot using the technology, equipment, experiment conditions, talent, and capital, and workshop advantages possessed by dozens of domestic and foreign companies. And, through that process, received multi-term patents. This case shows that other people's technology or resources can be used to develop new products. Not only can it improve resource utilizing efficiency of the society, but it can also spread the new technologies and improve the total quality of the company.

Of course, you have to pay if you want to use other people's resources. However, in many situations, it is worthwhile for the companies to use this strategy because if the new products can be developed successfully, the companies can obtain greater benefits. Thus, companies can improve their economic benefits and beat the competitors, as well as save large sums of R&D time and expenditures. They can always introduce the new products in a short time, which is why the technology market has developed so quickly in recent years.

5. Develop the new products for satisfying the curiosity of the consumers

Everyone has innate curiosity for new things. Thus if new products can satisfy the curiosity of consumers, then you can occupy the markets and the products will be welcomed by the consumers. This is a very important point for the companies to consider when they are developing new products. For example in Japan, a new wallet attracted many new consumers because it could change the coins into paper money or change paper money into coins when the consumers opened it. The technology, in fact, is very simple. The companies only had to add several inter layer's in the wallet. Despite the simplicity, it satisfied the curiosity of the consumers.

In general, you have to understand the market before you want to develop new products and pay attention to the fields that your competitors ignored. This is especially true for the small and medium companies, since they have to explore the demand of the consumers more deeply because they do not have enough resources to compete with the larger companies.

6. Break out the thinking frame and create the new demand

Sometimes, new products are always derived from the new thinking or strange ideas. For example, one time, Georgeo Braiasdell found out his friend was lighting his cigarette with an ugly lighter, which sparked an idea to design a lighter that had a beautiful appearance and was convenient to use. His idea was soon realized, and a new lighter with a square frame and hurricane lamp function was designed and produced. This is called the lighter king named Zippo. During the Second World War, the lighter was spread all over the world by the American army and became the most famous lighter brand in the world. This case demonstrates to us, how the value of the whim can be very large, thus requiring managers to survey the details of daily life and in order to discover potential demand of consumers. Because in most situations, consumers are not aware of their demands, even if the products are very important for them.

This means that in general, you have to break out your thinking frame in order to create the new demand in the fast development of the world economy. In fact, lots of the new products including the computer, TV, automobile and so forth all came from human wisdom and exploring the demand of consumers. If you can find out the market opportunities and transfer the market demand into company profits, you can be a successful marketer.

The procedures for the new product development

It is very difficult to develop the new products and may cost large sums of a company's resources. However, companies have to emphasize new product development because they face intense competition and constant change of the consumer demands. Of course, companies have to reduce new product development risks as much as possible.

That means that the new product development should be done through scientific procedure.

1. The new product conception

The new product conception is the design or originality for the new products. It, of course, is not all of the design and originality to be transferred into the new products; however, the more design and originality can help companies get more opportunities to develop new products. It is impossible for companies to develop better and new products if they lack design and originality. However, the first step for you is to define the new product concept before making your new product development plan. And in common situation, new product conception comes from the following:

1) Demand of the consumers

If the consumer is dissatisfied with your products, and offers their suggestions, requirements or hopes, the company will have a very good opportunity to create a new product conception. Therefore, the customers who always complain are the best consumers for the companies because they are the most important resource for the companies to develop new products. If you can not get the available information about the products from your consumers, then you have to study their preference, habit and special requirements before you develop the new products.

2) Originality coming from the scientific and technical personnel

This indicates that the scientific and technical personnel create the new products by utilizing new scientific and technical achievements. In fact, many companies improve product function or quality using this method.

3) The experience and lessons of the competitors

Experience and lessons of competitors indicates that companies can get enlightenment by studying the advantages and disadvantages of the competitor's products and avoiding risks and expenditures in the process of developing new products.

4) The sales people and other internal people

Here, sales people contact the consumers directly every day in order to obtain firsthand data about the demands of the consumers, understand the situation about the competition between company and competitors, and find out the new demand of the consumers or offer the direction of the new product development. According to the statistics, about 60% of new product conception comes from the external and 40% comes from the internal. Of this, (internal source), about half comes from the sales people.

Besides the top management, middle men and the marketing research department can be the sources of the new product development conception. In the real world, you can take many channels to get the information about the new product conception. The key problem to overcome is that you have to be able to understand their value and transfer the concept into profitable products for your company.

2. Screening

Based on the collection of new product conception, companies should consider the following questions:

(1) Whether or not the conceptions adapt to the overall strategy of the company, such as the profit target, sales target, market share target and so forth. This is the precondition for the companies to develop the new products.

(2) Whether or not the conceptions adapt to the company's resources for developing the new products, such as the capital strength, technological ability, and human resource, etc. The truth is simple, any new product development needs companies to invest large sums of resources.

In the real world, the companies should avoid two misunderstandings when they screen a new product conception; one, is abandoning the valuable conceptions and another, is taking unpractical conceptions. Both will bring heavy losses for the companies.

3. Forming and testing the product concept

1) Forming the product concept

After screening the new product conception, companies should transfer the conception into the product concept. This means that they need to describe the new products with words, pictures, models or other forms specifically and clearly. The purpose of this is to establish the image which the consumers can understand and accept. For example, in 1980s, the core product concept of Honda was "to get rid of the machine and chase the hommization." In the 1990's, the company changed its concept to the "quarterback booter wearing the suit", because they wanted to tell consumers that its products possess a strong structure and explosive force and speed just like the booters. At the same time, they also wanted consumers to know that its products possesses a gentle and cultivated appearance which the demonstrated by describing its product characteristics with "open heart", "close contact", "firm and persistent spirit", and "love life". The purpose was to connect the external and internal closely in order to establish a better image of the product in the consumer's heart.

2) Testing the product concept

Testing the product concept means that the companies offer the consumers a product concept described elaborately and let them give the assessment. The purpose is to understand the reflection of the consumers and provide the reason for optimizing the product concept.

3) Establishing the marketing plan

After finishing the product concept formation, the relative personnel of the companies have to study an elementary marketing strategy for introducing the new products. In most situations, the report consists of three parts: ① to describe the size, structure, action, product position, sales, market share, and profits of the target markets; ② to describe the pricing strategy, distribution strategy and the marketing budget in the first year about the new products; and ③ to describe the prospect about the sales, profits and marketing mix in a long term.

4) Business analysis

The business analysis focuses on analyzing the prospect sales, costs and profits about the new products, and to understand whether or not the new products adapt to the company strategy. The top management should assess the sales prospect of the new products based on studying the situation of the target markets and should consider the characteristics of the new products when they make their assessment. At the same time, they should calculate the cost and profit of the new products based on the assessment about the markets. Top management should also meet to discuss these relevant questions with the production, R&D, marketing and financial departments.

5) Product development

In this period, the production department should transfer the product concept into the physical products. In most situations, this period includes a process of trial-manufacture. If the trial-manufacture products fit the below requirements, then it will be known that the new products possess the feasibility in the fields of technology and business. ① In consumers' eyes the new products possess the various traits listed in the product conception; ② the products can develop their functions if the consumers use it regularly; ③ the products can be produced in the range of cost budget. Remember, it is very important for companies to develop the new products. However, it is more important to acknowledge that companies do have to invest large sums of resources including production. Thus, the failure of this stage could mean heavy losses for the companies.

6) Trial marketing

If the top management is satisfied with the result of the trial-manufacture of the new products, then they may promote the new product through trial-marketing and package the new products with the great brand and other marketing means. In the process of new product trial-marketing, not only should the managers take various promotion activities to broadcast the new products to the public and impress the consumers, but they also should contact the future channel members. The trial-marketing stage is the most important for top managers because it is the foundation for making the marketing mix decision. Of course, it is more important, complex and difficult if you focus on international marketing and want to test the foreign markets.

7) Supply the market in quantity

After the successful trail marketing, companies want to supply their new products in quantity, and in the period, the mangers have to answer the following decisions.

(1) When do marketers introduce their new products?

If companies want to introduce their new products to the markets, especially the foreign markets, they have to choose the sweet spot. For example, if the new products are seasonal products, they should be introduced before the peak season; if the new products will influence the sales of the old products, then companies should delay the introduction of their new products; if the new products need improvement or they may be influenced by economic decline, the companies should put off introducing them and so forth.

In general, it is very important for companies to choose the market spot when they want to introduce their new products. Many new products fail just because the company chooses the wrong time to introduce their new products. For example, Sunrise ice tea was the first company to produce ice tea in China, however, after a few years, the company and its products were replaced by other companies like Tianjin Master Kong and unit-president Corporation. Because most of the consumers did not understand and accept ice tea when Sunrise first introduced into the market, they had to spend large sums of money educating and training the consumers. Not only did this waste the resources of the company, but it also developed the market, making it easier for other, rival companies to enter the market.

(2) Where do marketers introduce their new products?

In most situations, companies can choose from a number of markets to introduce their new products in. However, different markets may create varied results for the companies and the key markets are always more significant for the new products. This is why many of the automobile manufactures introduced their new cars in China. Because China has become the largest and most important car market of the world by now, it's market capacity even exceedings the American market.

As a matter of fact, only the key markets can generate enough profits for new products. Of course, various companies have the different market developing tactics and they should choose their proper markets when they introduce their new products based on the marketing strategy and enterprise resources.

(3) Who are the new product consumers?

In the real world, new products are always accepted by the pioneer consumers. These consumers often possess the following traits: ① they always like to try new products and do not mind the price; ② the consumers like to take venture; ③ they may be the big customers for the new products; ④ they are impressed by the new products; ⑤ they may be a leader of a special field and posses great force in that industry.

(4) How to introduce new products?

Of course, companies should establish a detailed and careful marketing plan to introduce their products and strictly control the implementation process. In most situations, the new products should be introduced through the old distribution channels, unless there is no channel in the special markets. This is important because not only can the current channels introduce the new products to the consumers directly, but they can save large sums of money and other resources for the companies. Furthermore, current channels can also help get the new products into the open markets very quickly. This question is, of course, very complex and will be discussed further in subsequent chapters.

Apart from the above questions, remember, it is very important that companies create an effective brand strategy and package strategy, even though these strategies are very complex, they are important for the multinationals. Related questions we have been discussed in previous chapters. If companies want to use international marketing for their products, foreign environments must be studied by the marketers very carefully when they create their product strategies, because all of the various forces, especially the foreign environment forces, may influence the international marketing result.

9.5 Foreign environmental forces

From Chapter 3 to Chapter 6, we extensively examined foreign environmental forces. In this section, the focus and discussion will be limited to a few concrete examples of how some of these forces affect product strategies.

Social and cultural forces

Dissimilar cultural patterns in different markets generally necessitate changes in various products. For instance, worldwide variation in the mundane chore of washing clothes has caused many problems for Procter & Gamble, as mentioned in the opening section. However, it is also troublesome for European appliance makers because of a variety of preferences between different countries. The French want top-loading washing machines, the British want front-loading ones, the Germans insist on high-speed machines that remove most of the moisture in the spin-dry cycle, but the Italians prefer slower spin speeds because they let warm sun do the drying. Thus, Whirlpool must produce a variety of models to satisfy the different market needs. Although after buying the Philips appliance business in 1991, it changed from what was a collection of independent national companies into a European-wide organization that now uses some common platforms. This simplification has allowed the company to produce several models on the same chassis.

Competitors have questioned Whirlpool's drive toward providing a common product mix for Europe. "Whirlpool sees Europe as a uniform market, but we also see the differences in customer demands and needs from country to country," states competitor Bosch-Siemens. However, Whirlpool's CEO argues the national differences are exaggerated: "This business is the same all over the world. There is great opportunity to leverage that sameness."

Although some multinational firms, such as Kodak and Campbell, have been extremely successful in employing the same brand name, label, and colors worldwide, other firms are sometimes surprised to learn they must change to other names, labels, or colors because of cultural differences. Green packages are taboo in the Far East because they remind the public of the dangers and illnesses of the jungle, but gold appears frequently on packages in Latin America because Latin Americans view it as a symbol of quality and prestige. In the Netherlands, blue is considered warm and feminine, but the Swedes consider it masculine and cold.

Procter & Gamble discovered that gold packaging was actually better than silver in Europe after it had launched its Crest Tarter Control Formula in the United Kingdom in a silver box. It was followed two months later by Colgate's equivalent in a gold box. P&G officials sheepishly agreed that Colgate's choice of gold was better than their silver, and explained that they had used silver because that was how the product was packaged in the United States.

Even if the colors can remain the same, instructions on labels, of course, must be translated into the language of the market. Firms selling in areas where two or more languages are spoken, such as Canada or Switzerland, may need to use multilingual labels. Where instructions are not required, as in the case of some consumer or industrial products whose use is well known, there is an advantage of printing the label in the language of the country best known for the product. French labels on perfumes and English labels on industrial goods help to strengthen the product's image.

However, sometimes a perfectly good brand name has to be scrapped because of its unfavorable connotations in another language. For example, in Latin America, a product had to be taken off from the market when the manufacturer found that the name meant "jackass oil", and in the U. S., a Belgian brewery found it was impossible to introduce its Delerium Tremens lager to the country. American authorities told the company that the name was an incitement to drinking. They also said that calling another beer Guillotine was like an American brewery calling its beer "electric chair".

Firms will sometimes choose to not use a perfectly good name because of different meanings associated with that word in foreign markets; which is what happened with the automobile name Nova in Mexico. GM, who produces a car called "Nova", was not able to sell them (the storyteller picks a Spanish-speaking country) because Nova means no va (doesn't go) in Spanish. What was not immediately evident however is was that the two are pronounced very differently; the accent in "Nova" is over the first syllable, whereas the accent for "no va", falls on the second syllable, "va". Therefore, to someone speaking Spanish, the words have very different meanings. Most native Spanish-speaking people connect nova with star, which is probably what General Motors had in mind when they first chose the word. It may be surprising to learn that Pemex, the government-owned oil monopoly that is the exclusive refiner and retailer of gasoline in Mexico, subsequently named its regular gasoline Nova.

Incidentally, an economic constraint to the international standardization of brand names is the refusal of some firms to let a subsidiary put their brand on a locally made product, especially if it fails to meet their quality standards. This may happen because of the inability of the other firm to import the necessary raw materials or because the required production equipment is unavailable.

An important difference in the social forces to which American marketers are not accustomed, is people's preference, in both developed and developing nations, for making daily visits to small neighborhood specialty shops or large, open markets where they can socialize while shopping. More frequent buying permits smaller packages, which is especially important to a shopper who has no automobile in which to carry purchases.

However, this custom is changing in Europe, where a growing sophistication of consumption patterns is demanding the kinds of assortments that only a large store can offer. Shopping frequency is also slowing as European women, especially if employed, are finding that they have less free time than previously. As mentioned in Chapter 5, the solution to this has been the combination of supermarket-discount stores located in the suburbs and ample parking.

A similar situation had been occurring in Mexico, especially after the signing of NAFTA and the lifting of the country's import restrictions. Enormous crowds, anxious to buy at lower prices, showed up at the Wal-Mart and Kmart stores when they first opened in 1993. So many people tried to enter the Monterrey Wal-Mart on opening day that store employees had to bar the doors to control the crowd. However, since the massive peso devaluation, the peso prices of imported American products which had been one of the store's attractions, have risen so high that store attendance has dropped precipitously. Many Mexicans, particularly those living in Monterrey or farther north, may come to shop in the Texas border-city's, Wal-Mart where prices are lower. However as the peso's value continues to fall, this phenomenon is not happening as frequently.

One can easily draw a parallel from this situation to a similar situation that happened in the 1940s in the United States. The same conditions of rising incomes, a growing middle class, and an increasing number of working wives combined to put a premium on the shopper's time. Just like what happened in the United States, supermarkets, mass merchandising, and catalog selling have moved in to fill this need.

Legal forces

Legal forces can be a formidable constraint in the design of product strategies because if the firm fails to adhere to a country's laws governing the product, it will be unable to do business in that country. Laws concerning pollution, consumer protection, and operator safety are being enacted rapidly in many parts of the world and are severely affecting the marketer's freedom to standardize the product mix internationally. For example, American machinery manufacturers exporting to Sweden have found that the operator safety requirements there are even stricter than those required by the Occupational Safety and Health Act (OSHA) in the U. S. Therefore, if they wish to market in Sweden; they must produce a special model. It was previously mentioned that product standards set ostensibly to protect a nation's citizens, can be effective in protecting indigenous industry from foreign competitors.

Laws prohibiting certain classes of imports are extremely common in developing nations, as potential exporters quickly learn when they research the world for markets. Products considered luxuries, as well as products already being manufactured, are among the first to be excluded from importation. However, such laws may also affect local production. As mentioned in the previous section, prohibition of essential raw material imports may require a subsidiary to manufacture a product substantially different from what the parent company produces.

Foods and pharmaceuticals are especially influenced by laws concerning purity and labeling. For example, food products sold in Canada, whether imported or produced locally, are subject to strict rules that require both English and French on the labels as well as metric and inch-pound units. The law even dictates the space permitted between the number and the unit. For example, 16oz. is correct, but 16oz. is not. In another example, the Venezuelan government, in an effort to protect consumers from being overcharged for pharmaceuticals, has decreed that the manufacturer or the importer must affix to the package the maximum retail price at which the product can be sold. Finally, in Saudi Arabia, because of their preoccupation with avoiding food containing pork, the label of any product containing animal fat or meat that is sold in Saudi Arabia must state the kind of animal used or that no swine products were used.

Legal forces may also prevent a worldwide firm from employing its brand name in all of its overseas markets. Managements accustomed to American law, which establishes the right to a brand name by priority in use, may be surprised to learn that in code law countries, a brand belongs to the person who registered it first. Thus, the marketer may go into foreign markets expecting to use the company's long-established brand name only to find that someone else owns it. The name may have been registered by someone who is employing it legitimately for his own products, or it may have been pirated. That is, registered by someone who hopes to profit by selling the name back to the originating firm.

Both reasons prevented Ford from marketing its automobiles under established names in Mexico and Germany. In the case of Mexico, the reason was brand piracy. Ford refused to pay the high price the registrant wanted for the name, so for years the Falcon was known as the Ford 200. The use of the name Mustang by a bicycle manufacturer in Germany was legitimate. The firm was already producing under that name when Ford entered the market.

To avoid Ford's predicament, a firm must register its brand names in every country where it wants to use them or where it might use them in the future. And this must be done rapidly. The Paris Convention grants that a firm which has registered a name in one country, has only six months' priority in registering it elsewhere. To be certain that it has and will have enough names for new products, Unilever, the English-Dutch manufacturer of personal care products, has over 100,000 trademarks registered throughout the world, most of which are not in use but are kept in reserve.

Economic forces

The great disparity in income throughout the world is an important obstacle to worldwide product standardization. Many products from the industrialized countries are simply too expensive for consumers in developing countries. Therefore, if a firm wishes to achieve market penetration in a developing country, it must either simplify the product or produce a different, less costly one.

When Gillette discovered that only 8 percent of Mexican men used shaving cream (the rest use soapy water), it introduced a plastic tube of shaving cream at half the price of its aerosol can. Now more than twice the original percentage of men using shaving cream use the less expensive package, and Gillette has begun selling the tube in other parts of Latin America. Because many Latin American customers can not afford to buy the American-sized packages, the company sells packages of single razor blades and half-ounce packages of Silkience shampoo. Use of the plastic squeeze bottle, "the poor man's aerosol," is common where incomes are low.

Similarly, Hoover saw an opportunity to sell a simple washing machine to Mexicans who could not afford the high-priced, American-type machine. Although Hoover had no American model to simplify, it was able to copy its inexpensive British washer, which became an overnight success.

Economic forces affect product standardization in another way as well. Poor economies often signify poor infrastructure; i. e.: bad roads, lack of sufficient electric power, etc. For example, driving conditions in Mexico required Goodrich to design a tire for cut and bruise resistance rather than for high speed, as in the United States. The tire was so successful that residents in U. S. border towns preferred it to the U. S. product even though its price was higher.

The lack of a constant supply of electricity, another characteristic of poorer countries, has compelled refrigerator manufacturers to supply a gasoline-driven product and office equipment firms to manufacture hand-operated machines. As one would expect, this condition has also provided producers of small diesel standby generators with a ready market. Any users requiring a steady source of power, such as hospitals and theaters, are potential customers.

Market size influences the product mix as well. In poorer countries, the population is not only smaller but also contains large numbers of people who have no intention to purchase anything but the bare necessities of life, thereby making the already small market even smaller. This means that the foreign subsidiary cannot afford to produce as complete a product mix as does the parent company. Most automobile manufacturers will only assemble the least expensive lines and broaden the local product mix by importing, when permitted, luxury cars. All international firms practice this marketing technique whenever possible because a captive foreign sales organization is available to promote the sales of the home organization's exports, and because the revenue derived helps pay the subsidiary's overhead.

Boeing's 737 became the best-selling commercial jet in history partly because its engineers redesigned it for Third World aviation after its initial sales to developed nations dropped off. The runways in developing countries were too short for the original design and, being made of less expensive asphalt rather than concrete, were too soft. By redesigning the wings to allow for shorter takeoffs and landings, and by selling one or two at a time instead of batches of 20 or 30, which airlines in the developed nations order, Boeing built a reputation with developing countries' airlines, which, as they grew, began to buy Boeing's larger planes.

Physical forces

Physical forces, such as climate and terrain, also work against international product standardization. Where heat is intense, gasoline-driven machinery and automobiles must be fitted with larger radiators for extra cooling capacity. Gasoline must also have a higher flash point to prevent vapor locks and stalling.

The heat and high humidity in many parts of the tropics require electrical equipment to be built with extra heavy insulation. Consumer goods that are affected by moisture must be specially packaged to resist its penetration. Thus, one finds pills wrapped individually in foil and baked goods packaged in tin boxes to prevent their degradation by moisture.

High altitudes frequently require product alteration. Food manufacturers have found that they must change their cooking instructions for people who live at high altitudes because at such altitudes it takes much longer to cook and bake. The thinner atmosphere requires producers of cake mixes to include less yeast. Gasoline and diesel motors generate less power at high altitudes, so the manufacturer must often supply a larger engine.

Mountainous terrain implies high-cost highways, so in poorer countries, roads of the good quality are often nonexistent. Trucks traveling on poorer-quality roads need tires with thicker treads and heavy-duty suspensions. Thus, because of the rough ride, packaging must be stronger than that used in the United States. From these examples, it is apparent that even though an unchanged product may be culturally and economically acceptable in a market, the effect of the physical forces alone may be strong enough to require some product modification.

Due to space limitations, it is impossible to examine the influence of every environmental force on foreign product strategies. Sufficient practical examples have been offered above so that these, together with the information contained in the chapters on these forces, will give the reader an idea of their pervasiveness not only in the formulation of the product strategies but also in the design of the entire marketing mix. In fact, a useful guide in the marketing mix preparation is a matrix in which the marketing mix variables are tabulated against the environmental forces.

Summary

1. Appreciate that both global and multinational marketing managers, like their domestic counterparts, must develop marketing strategies by assessing a firm's potential foreign markets and analyzing the many alternative marketing mixes. The aim is to select target markets that the firm can serve at a profit and to formulate combinations of tactics for product, price, promotion, and distribution channels that will best serve those markets. In the previous chapter, we examined the market assessment and selection process; in this chapter, we shall start to study the formulation of the marketing mix.

2. Understand that if the product sold in the domestic market can be exported, there can be longer production runs, which lowers manufacturing costs. Even when the standard product is manufactured overseas, production costs will be less because the extra research and design expense of either adapting domestic products, or designing new ones for foreign sales, will be avoided. The task of keeping many sets of specifications current requires additional, highly paid personnel in the home office.

3. Discuss the various types of products. One important factor that influences the

amount of change to be made in a product is its classification as a consumer or industrial product or service. Generally, consumer products require greater adaptation than industrial products to meet the demands of the world market. If the consumer products are high style or the result of a fad, they are especially likely to require changes.

4. Recognize the importance of the product life cycle for international companies. For any product, there is a specific life cycle. The life cycle process is divided into introduction period, growth period, mature period and decline period, with the characteristics of the different periods varying. International marketers should make their product strategies based on the different periods of product life cycle.

5. Appreciate the concept of new products for international marketers: ① brand new products; ② improved new products; ③ imitated new products; ④ series new products; ⑤ lower cost new products; and ⑥ repositioned new products.

6. Appreciate the principle for developing the new products. Only the correct development tactics can guarantee success for companies to develop their new products, which is why international managers have to analyze the demand psychology and the change trend of their consumers. Some questions that must be considered if you want to develop the new products include the following elements: ① energy saving products; ② small and micro products; ③ multi-function products; ④ operating simple products and; ⑤ diversified products.

7. Recognize the importance of information for developing new products that managers should pay attention to exploring and catching potential demands when developing new products. They should look to create new markets actively and expand the markets by all manner of means.

8. Understand the power of legal and economic forces for products. Legal forces can be a formidable constraint in the design of product strategies because if a firm fails to adhere to a country's laws governing the product, it will be unable to do business in that country. Laws concerning pollution, consumer protection, and operator safety are being enacted rapidly in many parts of the world and are severely affecting the marketer's freedom to standardize the product mix internationally. The great disparity in income throughout the world is another important obstacle to worldwide product standardization. Many products from industrialized countries are simply too expensive for consumers in the developing countries. Therefore, if a firm wishes to achieve market penetration, it must either simplify the product or produce a different, less costly one. This is the most direct effect of the economic forces for the products.

9. Anticipate physical forces, such as climate and terrain, may also work against international product standardization. For example, where heat is intense, gasoline-driven machinery and automobiles must be fitted with larger radiators for extra cooling capacity. Gasoline must also have a higher flash point to prevent vapor locks and

stalling.

Questions

1. Explain some purposes for the international companies to make their product strategies.

2. Why do some people feel that the product standardization strategy is better than other product strategies?

3. Why do the international companies have to make their product plans based on the product life cycle?

4. How do you understand the concept of the total product?

5. Do you think it is possible for a Chinese company to develop a new product in America? Why and how?

6. What are some advantages and disadvantages when you want to carry out your new product development plan in a foreign market?

7. Are legal constraints the only type of obstacle to the product strategy? If not, name some others.

8. Give an example to indicate how the economic forces influence your product strategy.

9. Does the foreigner's purchasing habit influence your product strategies? Explain.

10. If you want to supply the markets with the large number, what questions do you have to consider? And why?

Minicase

The Product Strategies for Nokia

In 1998, the sales of Nokia exceeded Motorola (the largest mobile phone manufacturer at that time), and became the champion in the field of mobile phone. Its marketing slogan "put the network into everyone's pocket," subsequently beat many high-tech giants like Motorola.

Olila, the CEO of Nokia, thought of a new project which was not immediately noticed by the company's top management in 1990. At that time, GSM was not a mature digital mobile phone communication standard in the world. Olila forecasted that it was possible for GSM to become the second generation mobile standard after the analog system. He decided to abandon other traditional products like televisions, papermaking, and rubbers of Nokia and instead turned the company toward the mobile phone and net equipment, which thus became the developing direction of the company. Based on this foundation of GSM, it began to develop the world market with this new mobile phone concept beat all of the rivals and become the industry leader.

By the end of 1993, European countries began to use the GSM as the unified standard of the digital mobile phone. In the meantime, Nokia began to promote its new product—2100 series mobile. The new mobile phone used up-to-date digital communications standards, had a tone quality that was clear and stable, and at the same time, possessed similar characteristics to the mobile phone produced by Motorola'. The original sale target of the 2100 type was 40,000; however, they soon sold over 20 million. Responding to the new circumstances, Ericsson and Motorola began to invest large sums of money in their R&D departments to develop a GSM mobile phone in order to compete with Nokia. However, the market rule that states "first impressions are strongest," gave Nokia's product more notice and enthusiasm than the subsequent products produced by Motorola or Ericsson, even though the facade and boundary of their mobile phones were very outstanding and their technology was more advanced than Nokia in some aspects.

Based on its perfect technology, Nokia competed with its rivals in the fields of innovation speed, design and price. It's slogan was "Mobile phone are not a luxury good for people no longer, it is a fashion finery and easy using tool for people." Nokia introduced a new kind mobile phone every 35 days to the markets its 7100 series mobile phone was the first type mobile phone which support WAP wireless internet agreement in the world.

In order to adapt to the global market, Nokia introduced three kinds of mobile phones which respectively adapted to the three digital communication standards (GSM standard for Europe, TDMA standard for the U. S., PDS standard for Japan). The boundaries of their mobile phones were designed with the various language environments in mind and were based on the various areas. Despite the small changes adapted for each area, all types of the mobile phone maintained the same in facade to show the clear vivid characteristic of Nokia. Until 1998, Nokia was the foremost manufacturer in the world with a market share reaching 22.5% in the global. It became No. 1 in the world, compared to the global market share of Motorola at 19.5% and 15.5% for Ericsson. In China and other emerging markets, Nokia soon became the leader.

Chapter 10 Promotion Strategy

Concept preview

After reading this chapter, you should be able to

1. Appreciate: the concept of promotion and promotional strategy.

2. Understand: how the different promotion strategies influence the result of the international marketing.

3. Distinguish: the characteristics of the different promotion methods.

4. Comprehend: why companies use different promotional methods based on various types of products.

5. Describe: how to overcome the various barriers when you want to promote your products in foreign markets.

Science and technology giants are taking more market shares in the field of on-line advertisement

Today, the international advertising industry is changing quickly with online advertising corroding traditional advertising markets with its unique advantage. For example, its spread ranges the widest of all advertising and is not limited by time and space. Anybody can read the content of advertising so long as he or she is able to get on the internet; something that is impossible for traditional media to achieve. Furthermore, the cost of online advertising is very low, which is its most important advantage compared with the traditional media. Not only can consumers get information about the products they want to buy, but the manufactures can also get feedback about the product from their consumers and adjust or modify their product strategies accordingly. Additionally, compared with traditional media, the expenditure of online advertising is very low and has become the most important promotion means for companies.

Although online advertising has very abundant advertising forms and relative advantages compared with traditional advertising, the providers should still consider how to make the advertisement even more convenient for customers and more beneficial for companies. In the cases, the intense online advertising competition, the most advantageous way to increase profits for advertisers is to constantly improve their innovation ability in the field of science and technology. For example, Google supports and maintains its huge online advertising advantage by utilizing its advantage in advertising smart matching technology. It has become the multi-win model of the industry chain, not only because it provides the biggest platform in the world for hundreds of companies and enables them to get a higher return with lower investment, but it also provides abundant and valuable information to the public.

If you are suspect of online advertising, then it is worth reading the following data. According to Advertising Age, a world-famous magazine, the revenue of internet advertising was $25.5 billion in 2007. The number has been over $51.1 billion in 2012. Furthermore, the revenue of online video advertising was $50 million in 2007, and it has been over $3.8 billion in 2012. The aforementioned data investigation led Microsoft, Google, and Yahoo to use it to their advantage and work to hold the dominant position in this market. For example, Microsoft originally attempted to acquire the online advertising business of Yahoo. However, after Yahoo refused its acquisition, it tried to get part of the stock equity of Yahoo. Google acquired a large online advertiser named Double-Click in order to confirm its market position. With the development of the world economy, more and more companies have used the internet platform to introduce their products. Thus, the advertisers have had to invest more resources in this network if they want to make more profits. Of course, network technology is a key factor for them to maintain and expand their market shares.

According to Advertising Age, traditional advertising is slowing down dramatically while online advertising revenue is increasing quickly. In fact, Yahoo and Google are cooperating to develop more online advertising forms in order to make advertising more interesting to a broader group of people. The data provided by TNS Media Intelligence reveals that the advertising expenditure of traditional media increased 0.6% in 2008. Of this, TV advertising increased 1.7%, magazine advertising increased 0.8% and outdoor advertising increased 2.5%. At the same time, newspaper advertising decreased by 5.2% and radio advertising decreased by 4.5%. Compared to the growth of traditional media, online advertising outpaced all traditional sources and increased by over 8% in 2008. Considering the fast economic development and the huge market potential of China, many market experts proposed that the online advertising of the world will increase over two times in 2012 than in 2008, because the cyber citizens of China will be over 250 million in 2012.

The above data and examples indicate that the new promotional means are changing the layout of international marketing. The specific reasons for using online advertising instead of traditional media include:

1. Search Engines (SE) can improve the efficiency of advertising

Ddata provided by a research institute named eMarketer showed that in 2007, the revenue of the search engine advertising industry was $8.6 billion; and in 2010, the revenue reached $11 billion. Google is the king in this field, with the majority of its revenue of coming from its SE advertising. According to the statistics of eMarketer, in the lucrative search engine field business, Google's market share is 75%, while Yahoo's is only around 9%. The SE advertising of Google is very pure in that the form is different from other companies whose SE advertising attracts consumers with special pictures, animations and games.

The charm of the SE advertising is that it can both attract certain online advertising customers while also providing large amounts of information. For example, if customers search Hanna Montana, they can find out an array of information related to the drama, including tickets to the show, toys, CD players, and other official merchandise.. In summary, consumers can get more information about specific products as long as they input certain key words. This advantage of SE advertising cannot be replaced by any other traditional media.

Furthermore, the business model of SE advertising is very simple. Companies only need to pay certain advertising expenditures to Google or Yahoo, change some relative key words and their company name and product brands will show up in the results of the SE. Once potential customers use SE advertising, they are linked into the manufacturer's network which paid Google or Yahoo. Thus the owners of the SE can make money.

2. Video advertising created larger spaces for the companies

One of the primary difficulties faced by the online image-text advertising was that when it used to introduce products onto the internet, it was difficult for advertisers and publishers to initially accept it because of the depressing, steady state, and excessive commercialization. Since then, videos with complex analysis and fabrication have brought on a fast growth period to the online advertising model. According to eMarketer, the market size of online banner advertising reached $5.9 billion in 2010, and is expected to be over $8 billion in 2012.

As on-line advertising customers become increasingly clever, advertisers have to make their promotion sales more accurate, more creative, and closer to the demands of the consumers. Because network consumers do not like to be led to advertising websites when they are searching the net, PointRoll designed a "mini-website" for their customers so that they can view information published on the "mini-website" instead and do not have to leave the websites they are exploring. Traditional media does not have these functions, which is another very important reason why online advertising has taken a dominant position in advertising market.

3. Social Networking Services (SNS) advertising improved the reputation of companies

Facebook and MySpace provide a better platform for marketers to establish products and company reputation through oral spreading by customers. For example, if one product or service is accepted by private friends of the customers, or the organizations that the customers trust, then the product or service will earn a good reputation. According to data published by eMarketer in 2008, advertisers spent $1.4 billion in social networking service advertising. This number is expected to increase to $2.6 billion in 2012.

Although advertisers maintain a circumspect attitude for social networking services, outside observers have noted that this field is an increasingly important part of online advertising that is growing very quickly. Many observers think that there is only a very small difference between meeting consumer demands and counting their demands.

In general, as a new kind of advertising, online advertising is becoming one of the most important promotion methods for many international companies, thus marketers should pay more attention to this change in promotional means. Of course, this is not to say that other advertising or promotional avenues are useless, In fact, they are still very useful for eliciting various results in various situations. This chapter will discuss questions about how to use various promotional tools to sell products in foreign markets and what questions should be considered when you want to develop the foreign markets with various promotional methods.

10.1 Concept understanding

Promotion, one of the basic elements of the marketing mix, is the communication that secures an understanding between a firm and its public. This is important in order for the firm to bring about favorable buying actions, as well as achieve long-lasting confidence from its customers in the firm's product or services it provides. Note that this definition employs the plural, because the seller's promotional efforts must be directed to more than just the ultimate consumers and the channel of distribution members. Far too often, other publics have been ignored by businesses, not only in China, but in other markets as well. Managements have become aware of the fact that the old advice of always maintaining a low profile in a foreign country is not necessarily the best course of action. Many companies thus since changed this strategy and are now making the general public, special interest groups, and governments aware of their public service activities.

Because promotion both influences and is influenced by other marketing mix variables, it is possible to formulate nine distinct strategies by combining three alternatives: ① marketing the same physical product everywhere, ② adapting the physical product for foreign markets, and ③ designing a different physical product with (a) the same, (b) adapted, or (c) different messages. The following six strategies are most commonly used.

1. Same product—same message

When marketers find that target markets vary little in respect to product use and consumer attitudes, then they can offer the same product and use the same promotional appeals in all markets. Avon, Maiden form, and A. T. Cross all follow this strategy.

2. Same product—different message

In this instance, the same product may satisfy a different need or be used differently, in different places. This means that the product may be left unchanged, but a different message may be required. Honda's campaign, "You meet the nicest people on Honda", appeals to Americans who use their motorcycles as a pleasure vehicle; but in Brazil, Honda stresses economy as it tries to make its product a means of basic transportation.

3. Product adaptation—same message

In cases where the product serves a similar function but is adapted to work in different conditions, the same message is employed with a changed product. For example, in Japan, Lever Brothers puts Lux soap in fancy boxes because much of it is sold for gifts.

4. Product adaptation—message adaptation

In some cases, both the product and the promotional message must be modified for foreign markets. In Latin America, Tang is especially sweetened, pre-mixed, and ready to drink in pouches. Unlike Americans, Latin Americans do not drink it for breakfast. Therefore it is promoted as a drink for mealtime and for throughout the day in Latin America but not for breakfast.

5. Different product—same message

As was pointed out in the discussion of economic forces' influence on product strategies, the potential customers in many markets cannot afford the product as manufactured in the firm's home country. Furthermore, the product may also be too technologically advanced to gain widespread acceptance. To overcome these obstacles, companies have frequently produced a very distinct product for these markets. The previously mentioned low-cost plastic squeeze bottle and inexpensive, manually operated washing machines are two examples of this strategy in practice. The promotional message, however, can be very similar to what is used in the developed countries if the product performs the same functions.

6. Different product for the same use—different message

Frequently, different products require a different message as well. Welding torches as opposed to automatic welding machines, would be sold on the basis of low acquisition cost rather than high output per labor-hour. LDC (less developed countries) governments faced with high unemployment may be persuaded by a message emphasizing the job-creating possibilities of the labor-intensive processes, rather than the labor saving of highly automated machinery.

All of above are basic considerations for you to design your promotional plan when you want to develop a foreign market. However, in the real world, you have to decide what methods you may take. The tools for communicating these messages included in the promotional mix are: advertising, personal selling, sales promotion, public relations, and publicity. Not one of these tools is inherently superior to the others, although circumstances in some situations may dictate that one of them should be emphasized more than the others. Just as in the determination of what product strategies should be used, the composition of the promotional mix will depend on the type of product, the environmental forces, and the amount of market penetration desired.

10.2 Advertising

Of all the promotional mix elements, advertising is the one with the greatest similarities worldwide. This is because most advertising is based on American practices. U. S. ad agencies have greatly aided the global propagation of American techniques as they have followed their domestic customers overseas. Today, the major American agencies are all global, with wholly owned subsidiaries, joint ventures, and working agreements with local agencies. In the latest annual worldwide ranking of the top 50 advertising agencies by income, 23 are American, 14 are Japanese, 4 are French, 3 are British, and 2 are Korean.

Global and regional brands

Manufacturers are increasingly using global or regional brands for a number of reasons:

(1) Cost is often the most cited reason. By producing one TV commercial for use across a region, a firm can save up to 50 percent in the production cost.

(2) There is a better chance of obtaining one regional source to do high-quality work than attempting to find sources in various countries that will work at the same high standard.

(3) Some marketing managers prefer that their companies have a single image throughout a region.

(4) Companies hope to centralize their resources to develop the regional markets.

(5) Global and regional satellite and cable television are becoming available.

Economies of scale are another reason why some firms are emphasizing regional or global standardization of advertising. Coca-Cola, for example, estimates that it saves over $8 million annually in the cost of thinking up new imagery by repeating the same theme everywhere. Texas Instruments, which used to have four different creative approaches in Scandinavia (one per country), now runs similar ads in all four countries it operates in at a savings of $30,000 per commercial.

All the advertising agencies listed above are at least regional, with many global as well. McCann-Erickson Worldwide, part of the interpublic Group, is the world's largest international agency. About 75 percent of its billings come from global marketers such as Coca-Cola, General Motors, Goodyear Tire, Exxon, McDonald's, and L'Oreal. It handles seventeen global accounts, more than any of its competitors; its nearest competitor handles six.

Pan-European accounts, helped by EC 1992, have also been increasing and are estimated to reach $4 billion by 2006. Euro brands for small cars, chocolates, instant coffee, and skin care products already outspend domestic competitors on national television. Furthermore, a good number of advertisers, such as Unisys, Dell Computer, Pirelli, and British American Tobacco, are switching from various domestic agencies to a single agency group for all of Europe. Unilever, the British-Dutch personal care products giant, was producing its Snuggle fabric softener in 13 different formulas, 8 fragrances, and 12 colors just in Europe four years ago. Today, it has only 6 formulas, 2 fragrances, and 2 colors. "International competition has forced companies to rationalize their brands", says the chairman of Grey Advertising.

McCann-American saves money for its multinational clients in Latin America by using regional advertisements. For example one of their clients, Coca-Cola, advertises its global brand in Latin America with commercials designed in one place, usually Venezuela, which are then sent on film to local markets where they are reshot. The local Coca-Cola companies then have the option to add music and indigenous voices. Another regional advertiser, Gillette, uses the same method. With the advent of regional and global media, especially satellite and cable TV, global and regional advertising campaigns have become more feasible for those advertisers that want them. Both of these global brand examples demonstrate how local affiliates are permitted to make changes to regional commercials, thus keeping in line with the slogan of many companies: "Think globally, and act locally."

Availability of media

Satellite TV broadcasters are making it possible for numerous programming networks to provide service for millions of households in dozens of countries. Star TV, TVB, and ABN broadcast programs both in Chinese and English. They also carry cable networks such as Turner, ESPN, HBO, and others with which they reach 3 billion people in Asia. A British satellite TV firm, Sky Broadcasting, transmits programs to European cable companies and directly to homes with satellite dishes. One of the major programming networks using satellite TV broadcasting is CNN, which reaches 78 million households in over 100 countries. MTV calculates its audience to be 210 million people, in 78 countries. Its Asian subsidiary broadcasts in Mandarin and English and the MTV Latino's programs are in Spanish. Fox, Discovery, ESPN, and HBO are other programmers that broadcast internationally and sell time to advertisers. The Middle East Broadcast Center, started in 1992, is the only satellite TV network that broadcasts Western-style news, entertainment, and advertising to Muslim countries in Arabic.

There is also much more international print media available such as the following newspapers: The European, a daily newspaper; the international edition of The Herald Tribune; the Asian and European editions of The Wall Street Journal; and the international editions of the Manchester Guardian and Financial Times. Magazines also garner large international readership such as Reader's Digest which is published in 39 foreign editions. Because all editions of each magazine are written for readers with similar demographics, all editions attract similar advertisers.

Africa is marked by a scarcity of all media. Africa is marked by a scarcity of all media. Only 163 radio stations serve an area and ten countries even have no TV at all. Furthermore, even these numbers are misleading because in many countries, the stations are government owned and noncommercial. Although there are 190 daily newspapers in the 53 African countries, 91 of them are located in only 6 countries. Four countries have no daily paper, and 19 have only one. In this seller's market, an advertiser may find that the newspaper has accepted too many ads for the available space. The solution to this problem by some newspapers' is to use a raffle system to decide which ads will be published!

In Latin America and the Middle East, the opposite situation exists; there are too many newspapers and magazines. The problem in those regions is choosing the right ones for the firm's target market. In which of the 900 newspapers in Brazil, or the 400 in Turkey, should ads be placed? Circulation figures are often greatly exaggerated; therefore advertisers must be careful of the publication's political position in order to avoid associating their firms with the "wrong side", or the side contrary to what the majority of their potential customers believe in.

These problems along with the high illiteracy rate in some nations have forced some advertisers to use other media sources to reach their markets. Cinema advertising is heavily used in many parts of the world, as are billboards. In the Middle East, where media options are limited, videotape ads are rapidly becoming an integral part of the media mix. In order to penetrate this lucrative market, advertisers buy spots on popular video tapes. Thus, films will often have three or four breaks, with six or seven spots each created at the beginning, middle, and end. Three-quarters of households in the United Arab Emirates, Saudi Arabia, and Kuwait have videocassette recorders. Thus, in the first three months after a release, a well-received video tape can draw an audience of 1 million viewers in Saudi Arabia alone.

In a number of less developed countries, automobiles equipped with loudspeakers circulate through the cities announcing products, while street signs are furnished by advertisers to hang their messages on them. In some cases, homeowners can get a free coat of paint by permitting advertisers to put ads on their walls. Where mail delivery is reliable, direct mail is also a powerful medium. One of the most ingenious campaigns ever done in Saudi Arabia, was that of a tea company that gave away thousands of printed prayers with a tea commercial on the other side to pilgrims bound for Mecca.

In summary, some media are available in every country and region. International managers and ad agencies should formulate the proper promotional strategies based on the various situations when they want to promote their products. However, media selection is extremely difficult for international advertising managers who try to standardize their media mix from the home office. This section has only mentioned some of the problems associated with building an effective international marketing campaign. However, from the examples stated, one is still able to appreciate that the variation in media availability is a strong reason for leaving this part of advertising programs to local organizations.

Type of product

Buyers of industrial goods and luxury products usually act from the same motives all over the world. Thus, these products can be advertised using a standardized approach. This enables manufacturers of capital goods, such as General Electric and Caterpillar, to prepare international campaigns that require very little modification in the various markets. Furthermore, as we saw in the previous section, certain consumer goods markets are similar too. However, there is another set of characteristics that also permits firms to use the same appeals and sales arguments worldwide: when the product is low priced, when it is consumed in the same way, and when it is bought for the same reasons. Examples of such products are gasoline, soft drinks, detergents, cosmetics, and airline services. For years, firms such as Exxon (Esso overseas), Coca-Cola, Avon, and Levi Strauss have used this international approach successfully. Generally, the only changes they have had to make are translating the product into the local language and the using indigenous models.

Foreign environmental forces

Like variations in media availability, foreign environmental forces also act as deterrents to the international standardization of advertising. As you may expect, among the most influential of these forces, are the social cultural forces, which were examined in Chapter 5.

A basic cultural decision for that the marketer has to make is whether to position the product as foreign or local; and which way to go often depend on the country, the product type, and the target market. In Germany, for example, consumers are not at all impressed by a carmaker that announces it has American know-how. "After all", reason the Germans, "if so many Americans prefer BMWs and Mercedes over U. S. cars, why shouldn't we?" At the same time, some American products such as bourbon, fast-food restaurants, and blue jeans have had a tremendous impact in Germany and the rest of Europe.

Similarly in Japan and other countries in the Far East, American identity of consumer products enhances their image. The young and the status conscious prefer the casual American look in clothing and seek American labels that identifies the wearer as belonging to the "in group". The influence of the American-style fast-food restaurants on Japanese youth was also emphasized in a survey conducted by the Japanese Ministry of Agriculture. The survey revealed that more than 50 percent of the country's teenagers would rather eat occidental foods than traditional dishes. U. S.-based fast-food restaurants such as McDonald's (Japan's largest restaurant business), Dairy Queen, Mister Donut, and Kentucky Fried Chicken account for half this business. McDonald's alone gross income is over $2 billion annually, more than 10 percent of the company's global sales.

The experience of suppliers in engaging the youth market indicates that this is also an international market segment, much like the market for luxury goods. The director of MTV Europe says, "18-year-olds in Paris have more in common with 18-year-olds in New York than with their own parents. They buy the same products, go to the same movies, listen to the same music, sip the same colas. Global advertising merely works on that premise." Almost all of MTV Europe's 200 advertisers run unified English-language campaigns across its 28-nation broadcast area. This means marketers can formulate global advertising campaigns for these consumers that will require little more than a translation into the local language. Before making the decision concerning local versus foreign identity however, management should check with local personnel on a country-by-country basis.

Just as with communication, the success of advertising will be impossible to achieve if the language is not understood. Thus, translations must be made into the language of the consumers. Unfortunately for the advertiser, almost every language varies from one country to another. A word that may have one meaning in one country may signify something completely different or even vulgar in another, as was illustrated in Chapter 5. In order to avoid translation errors then, experienced advertising managers will use both ① a double translation and ② plenty of illustrations with short copy.

Because a nation's laws generally reflect public opinion, closely allied to cultural forces are legal forces, which exert an extremely pervasive influence on advertising. Just as laws affect media availability, they also restrict the kinds of products that can be advertised and even the copy employed in the advertisements.

American firms, accustomed to using comparative advertising at home, are often surprised to find that legal restrictions on this technique still exist in some markets. Since the early 1990s, Pepsi-Cola has used comparative advertising to compete with Coca-Cola, and wherever possible, Coke has used legal means to stop the ads. Although PepsiCo has won some victories in Japan, Mexico, Malaysia, and 10 countries in Europe, it now wants to use comparative advertising to break Coke's dominance of international cola markets.

In order to do so, the company launched a series of TV commercials in 1995 aimed at testing the comparative advertising laws of 30 countries. The ads presented the competitor's product in a way that was specifically prohibited in some countries as unfair advertising. "We intend to push the envelope on comparative advertising in markets across the world," said the marketing head for Pepsi-Cola International. Germany's comparative advertising law is so strict that Goodyear could not even use its multinational tire campaign that states that nylon tire cord is stronger than steel. Incredibly, the steel wire manufacturers complained of "unfair competition".

Advertisers in Islamic nations have had to be resourceful to avoid censorship. The use of women's photos in advertisements is forbidden unless the models are clearly Western, preferably blondes or redheads. "Erotic" sound effects are also not permitted. For example, a TV soft-drink commercial with a girl licking her lips to show she liked the taste was declared "obscene". In Pakistan, the government decreed that women models could advertise only women's products on TV. They cannot advertise cars or men's cologne, for example.

Globalization versus localization

With so many obstacles to international standardization, what should the approach of the international advertising manager be? The opinion of some experts seems to be that good ideas and good promotions can cross international borders. Robert Trebus, an ad agency executive, believes that far too often businesspeople ask how a product can be sold in Germany without first asking how the firm did it successfully in Sweden. Trebus stated back that, "rarely will a campaign be a success in Sweden without having registered a like success in Greece." He believes too many managers are convinced that to be successful in different markets, they must approach each market differently. The director of multinational accounts at McCann-Erickson also claims that social classes across different countries have shared sensibilities: "A male middle executive in Italy has more in common with a male middle executive in the U.K. than with a farmer in Italy. It is those shared sensibilities that make global branding possible."

This school of thought looks for similarities across segments and countries in order to capitalize on them by providing promotional themes with worldwide appeal—the strategy now followed by many global corporations. A second school of thought however, believes that even though human nature is the same everywhere, it is also true that a Spaniard will remain a Spaniard and a Belgian. Thus, it is preferable to develop separate appeals to take advantage of the differences among customers in different cultures and countries.

Neither purely global nor purely local

You probably have already gathered from this discussion that for most firms, neither a purely global nor a purely local campaign is the best way to handle international advertising. In fact, the president of a large international ad agency stated, "About 15 percent of the multinational companies have global approaches, meaning campaigns will be roughly the same everywhere. Another 15 percent have strictly local approaches. But these two groups are rapidly disappearing into a group we call 'global', meaning advertisers that have developed a common strategy for large regions."

Gillette's pan regional approach

Gillette organized its advertising in the following regional and cultural clusters: pan-Latin America, pan-Middle East, pan-Africa, and pan-Atlantic. The international advertising manager says the arrangement is based on the belief that the company can identify the same needs and buying motives among consumers in regions or countries linked by culture, consumers' habits, and level of market development for their products. Gillette might use the same European-style advertising for Australia and South Africa; but in Asia, it would link developing economies such as the Philippines, Indonesia, Thailand, and Malaysia. It will market the Asian tigers, Singapore, etc., but handle Japan, China, and India separately.

Gillette, which sells 800 products in 200 countries, is trying to approximate a global marketing strategy with its pan regional strategy, while still allowing for regional and national differences. A vice president of Gillette's ad agency, who is also the firm's associate media director, explains Gillette's approach this way: "Our strategy is to develop the best media plans for each country, but then look for pan geographic opportunities to enhance the coverage."

Programmed-management approach

Another middle-ground advertising strategy is what some call the programmed-management approach. In this approach, the home offices and the foreign subsidiaries agree on marketing objectives, after which each puts together a tentative advertising campaign. This is then submitted to the home office for review and suggestions. Next, the campaign is market tested locally, and the results are submitted to the home office, which reviews them and offers comments. The subsidiary then submits a complete campaign to the home office for review. When the home office is satisfied, the budget is approved and the subsidiary begins implementing the campaign. The result may be a highly standardized campaign for all markets or one that has been individualized to the necessary extent to cope with local market conditions. The programmed-management approach gives the home office a chance to standardize those parts of the campaign that may be standardized, but still permits flexibility in responding to different marketing conditions.

How to choose agencies?

When looking to promote products in a foreign market, there are three choices, the domestic agency, local agency or the subsidiaries of the international companies that can help finish the job. However, before making any decisions, it is important to understand the reasons for promoting the product because there are very complex environment factors to consider when taking the job overseas.

(1) Arguments for using the domestic agencies:

A. They are already familiar with the marketer's product and image.

B. They have an existing relationship with management.

C. They may be willing to discount their services in order to receive an opportunity to operate on the international front.

D. They will be able to provide long-term cost savings since domestic and international efforts and staffing are combined.

(2) Arguments against using domestic agencies:

A. They may have no experience with consumer habits in the target market.

B. They may lack the cultural and linguistic skills necessary to reach the new market segment.

C. They may lack the media connections needed to get the best prices.

D. They may be unfamiliar with local laws and politics regarding foreign companies.

(3) Arguments for using the local agencies:

A. They may have strong local political connections and knowledge.

B. They are intimately familiar with the consumer habits of the targeted segments.

C. They share the cultural and linguistic background of the consumer base.

D. They can offer additional input about local standards for product adaptation.

E. They currently operate with all of the necessary media in the local market.

F. They may offer substantial discounts in order to sign up a foreign client.

(4) Arguments against using the local agencies:

A. They may lack the technical sophistication necessary to serve the foreign company.

B. They have little knowledge of the company's image or management style.

C. They have little stake in maintaining the company's international brand equity.

D. They cannot always offer the savings that come from the economies of scale offered by large, global firms.

E. They may attempt to "gouge" the foreign firm with multi-tier pricing.

F. They may be as unfamiliar with the product as local consumers are.

(5) Arguments for using affiliate agency:

A. They already have, or have access to, the level of technical sophistication needed by most international companies.

B. They have the necessary cultural and linguistic skills for the new market.

C. They have local political and media connections.

D. They have a firm grasp of local consumer habits and product needs.

E. They may be able to offer the cost savings associated with large scale operations.

(6) Arguments against using affiliate agency:

A. They usually lack familiarity with the foreign company's domestic market image.

B. They may find it difficult to work with the marketer's management team.

C. They may wish to take their direction from the international agency rather than the marketer.

Media decisions about the international advertisement

In the real world, you can choose various media to advertise your products in a foreign market. However, various media sources has its own characteristics and therefore, it is important to decide which is best adapted to your company and your products.

1. Paper advertising

As an advertising media, paper possesses lots of positive characteristics. For example, some advantages include: extensive spreading, quick reflection, lower expenditures and higher reasonableness, etc. Disadvantages of paper however, include: short contacting time, lower attraction for the consumers, fewer target readers, etc. It is important to be aware that the paper advertising situations of various countries are all very different. For one example, the population of Lebanon is only 1 million, but there are over 210 paper publishers and the average distribution for each publisher is only around 3,500. In contrast, the population of Japan is about 127 million with only 5 nationwide papers. However, the average amount of distribution for each publication is over a million, therefore there is intense competition to carry ads on the papers.

2. Magazine advertising

As an ad media, the advantages of magazine advertising includes: greater professional, longer saving time and greater reliability, etc. The disadvantages of magazine advertising include: longer circle, narrow publishing range and a lack of flexibility. In most countries, many magazines only have the native language edition and therefore find it very difficult to publish in international markets. This is why few multinationals use magazine ads to introduce their products, except to produce greater professional industrial products in international marketing.

3. TV advertising

With the development of the world economy, TV ads have become the most important media for multinationals to introduce their products, especially if they are producing consumer products. The reason is simple, TV ads possess greater advantages than other media because it can not only achieve a visual and oral connection, but it also has a spread range that is very wide, and an ad promotional effect that is very good. This is why many multinationals use TV ads as their primary way of introducing their products in international markets. Of course, the disadvantages should also be considered when using TV media. For example, if the ad time is short and very expensive, then it is very difficult to get the audience's feedback or persuade them to buy. It is also important to be aware of the fact that many governments limit business TV ads, with the limitation sometimes being very rigorous. Not only does the limitation infringe the ad time, but it may also affect the contents and objectives.

4. Radio advertising

The advantages of radio advertising includes: wide range, fast information transmission, lower expenditure, flexible methods, etc. Radio ads can be adapted to less developed countries which tend to have more illiterate populations and fewer televisions. Even in developed countries, many people still listen to the radio in their spare time. The method is similar to one used with food or beverage because the value of the product is lower and the consumers are very large.

5. Outdoor advertising

Outdoor advertising includes things such as: signboards, pictorial posters, neon lights, and bus body's ad, etc. Thead vantages of the outdoor advertising are that they showing the image vividly, they can remain up longer and require lower expenditures. The major drawbacks of using outdoor advertising include: lack of pertinence, single information express form and limited content, and difficultly in assessing the effect of the promotion. Another issue that companies may face is the fact that local governments sometimes limit the position, dimension, and colors of the outdoor advertising. Furthermore, to use outdoor advertising to promote your products requires the company to find room for the new advertising in major business areas buildings. In many places, many of the best locations are already filled with various advertisements. This is especially true in China, America, Japan and Europe where companies are competing to develop these key markets.

6. New media advertising

Compared with traditional media, generalized new media includes "the interactive digital mixed media", such as mobile phone media, IPTV, digital TV, mobile TV, blogs and podcasts. Especially Internet has become the most important media for most multinationals to introduce their products. In general, new media can be divided into two parts ① the digitalization of traditional media, such as electric editions of newspapers and magazines; and ② the new type media, such as the Google, Baidu and TaoBao and so forth.

The greatest advantage of new media is the speed at which it functions while at the same time spreading to more consumers who can then use the net to interact with the business people. However, the broader range and availability of the information may wear out consumers since they are surrounded by such large amounts of information. They may even disregard the information out of boredom. Although there are many issues to study, it must be acknowledged that new media is playing a larger and more important role in the practice or international marketing. Therefore, international managers have to use this new media to develop their markets if they want to occupy enough market shares.

10.3 Personal selling

Along with advertising, personal selling constitutes a principal component of the promotional mix. The importance of this promotional tool as compared to advertising depends to a great extent on the relative costs, the funds available, media availability, and the type of product sold.

Just as in the United States, manufacturers of industrial products rely more on personal selling than advertising to communicate with their overseas markets. However, producers of consumer products may also emphasize personal selling overseas, especially in the developing countries, because salespeople in these countries will often work for less compensation than would be demanded in the developed country. Nonetheless, a newcomer to marketing must be careful to consider all of the expenses in maintaining a salesperson, such as expense items like automobiles and their maintenance (rough treatment on bad roads) which may frequently be three or four times the U. S. cost. Fringe benefits are also commonly stipulated by law, and often comprise a higher percentage of the base wage in other countries.

Marketing managers tend to place greater emphasis on personal selling where commercial TV and radio are unavailable, or where the market is too small to support expensive TV advertising campaigns.

The functions and characteristics of the personal selling

Personal selling for international marketing is used when international companies expatriate their personnel abroad, hire local people, or use a third country's people to contact the present and potential customers in order to persuade them to buy the products produced by the multinational. Personal selling is a widespread practice used by many multinationals that are looking to promote their industrial and consumer products. The method is also used to introduce the products to a middle man.

1. The functions of personal selling in international markets

1) Market research and forecast

The function of personal selling is to collect market information and feedback for companies in order to help the top managers make international marketing decisions. For example, Japanese salespeople always go to the markets to get first hand references about the products, customers, competitors, middle men and other information related to international marketing. Thus, the multinationals can make their decision about new product and new market development based on the information about consumption attitudes and ideas. All of the data will help the companies improve their competitiveness, therefore, not only can the salespeople introduce more products to the consumers, but they also can offer very important information to management. This is an important strategy for multinationals to beat their competitors especially when they are taking international marketing.

2) Expand the markets and deal with relationships with the consumers

Expanding the markets is the most common way that multinationals appoint expatriates or local people in order to find out and visit consumers, train new consumers and maintain the old consumers. Therefore, salespeople must possess knowledge about the products and marketing, understand the developing trend of international markets, and have the ability to develop the markets. This means that they should be good at finding out market opportunities and possessing better professional marketing skills. At the same time, they have to master the operation situation of their consumers, offer the reasonable suggestions for the allocation of the resources to the customers, and supply the products in time. Furthermore, international salespeople have to master the local language, business etiquette, and culture conventions. Thus, in general, salespeople are the bridge and belt for companies to get in contact with the consumers.

3) Transmit and communicate information

One of the most important tasks for salespeople is to introduce their products to consumers and establish better company image and reputation in consumer's mind. Thus, not only do salespeople have to sell their products to consumers and introduce their products to potential consumers, but they also have to transmit information about the products and company to the consumers. At the same time, they can get feedback about the products and the company directly from the consumers. Although companies can get the information through many channels by now, the most accurate information often comes from the salespeople.

4) Sell the products and provide after-sale service

Selling and serving are the most basic functions for salespeople. The specific functions include: free delivery, door installation, consultant service, technology assistance, billing etc. Furthermore, if it is necessary, salespeople have to help customers or middlemen solve financial problems or provide maintenance service. All of the aforementioned jobs need salespeople to be familiar with the business and master the technology. Apart from the marketing skills, the purpose is to offer various selling services for domestic and foreign customers. For example, Japanese salespeople, especially for industrial and durable products salespeople, are all technology experts. They often visit important foreign customers and middlemen, in order to understand their requirements about the products, answer questions, explain various technical questions about the product, and provide economic and technological consulting assistance for the customers. The purpose of this is to let the consumers know what benefits they can get if they purchase their products.

2. The characteristics of personal selling

As the most ancient and most common promotion means, personal selling is an important tool for multinationals to use to promote their products in international markets, although economic development level and wealth vary widely from country to country. This is because lots of the advantages of the personal selling can not be replaced by other promotion methods.

1) Transmitting information is bidirectional

As a kind of information transmitting method, personal selling is bidirectional because salespeople often need to introduce their products to customers when they are first selling their products. At the same time, they can get assessments about the products and companies directly from the customers in the process. Thus, salespeople can quickly come to understand customer's attitude toward the products or services, the situation about the competitors, and market trends, which is an important information source for the company.

2) Diverse selling purposes

In practice, not only do salespeople have to sell their products to consumers utilizing a variety of marketing skills, but they also have to help customers solve various problems by providing after-sale services. These two purposes of the salespeople are interrelated and supplement each other. Furthermore, it is often a precondition for salespeople to serve as advisers to the customers if they want to sell their products to them. Since most products are similar in modern society, if you are unable to provide better service for customers than other countries, you will loss the market.

3) Flexibility of the selling process

Because salespeople can contact consumers directly, they are often able to understand what the reaction of the consumers will be to certain products and can therefore adjust their selling strategies to persuade the consumers to buy. Of course, results will vary from salesperson to salesperson. This is why outstanding salespeople always summarize their experiences and lessons in order to improve their marketing skills. This is especially important if salespeople are working in international markets where they face various complex situations, where it is impossible to apply rigid methods to connect with consumers. Thus, flexible marketing skills are a basic qualification for international product salespeople, who should constantly be studying how to improve their marketing skills and attract their consumers.

4) Promote stronger relationships between the buyers and sellers

Because salespeople are usually in contact with the customers for a long time, they can promote buyers and sellers to establish friendships. A close relationship between the companies and consumers will help encourage consumers to prefer that company's products. These relationships may also facilitate longer-term coordination relations and stable channels of communication between companies and customers. For example, some companies established by Middle Eastern and African countries emphasize friendship between each other and often have a hard time establishing business with the new customers or strangers.

Of course, there are also certain limitations for personal selling. First, since the market spread is small and selling expenditure high, the marketing cost may increase. Second, international marketing requires salespeople to possess certain qualities that enable them to work in more complex environments. Not only must they fit the various culture and customs, but they must also master at least one foreign language. Furthermore, they have to master enough marketing skills that will help them research and develop foreign markets. Because of the requirements to have successful foreign salespeople, multinationals sometimes find it difficult to find the proper people to fulfill the job. Therefore, training becomes the only way to change the situation. However training is always expensive and thus increases the international marketing costs.

Personal selling practices

1. Cases sharing

By and large, the organization of an overseas sales force, sales presentation, and training methods are very similar to those employed in the home country. For example, Avon follows the same plan of person-to-person selling in Venezuela or the Far East as it does in America and is extremely successful. When Avon first entered Mexico, many local experts predicted that its plan would fail because it was thought the Mexican middle-class housewife would be out of the home shopping and playing bridge. Furthermore, the wall around the house would keep the Avon lady from reaching the front door, and when she rang the bell, the maid, as she did with all peddlers, would not let her in. Other American firms had used this approach and had failed for these reasons. However, Avon made small but important changes. For one thing, it mounted a massive advertising campaign to educate Mexicans as to what they could expect from the visits, before sending its salespeople out.

Although the advertisements were the same as those in the United States, the advertising campaign was more extensive because the Mexican housewife had to be taught a new concept. This was not the common door-to-door salesperson that she knew, but a professional, trained to help her look beautiful. Avon recruited educated, middle-class women as representatives and trained them well. They were encouraged to visit their friends, much as Tupperware representatives do. Changing slightly, what was essentially an American plan, to reflect cultural differences, made Avon's entry into the Mexican market an unqualified success. Since entering Mexico in 1990, Avon has built its sales force up to 170, 000, with sales of $370 million every year.

Other firms have also followed their home country approach. Salespeople from pharmaceutical manufacturers, such as Pfizer and Upjohn, introduce their products to physicians, just as they do in the United States. Sales engineers from General Electric and Westinghouse supply their customers with the same kind of information required in America. Salespeople use the same methods of calling on channel members to perform the same tasks of informing middlemen, setting up point-of-purchase displays, and fighting for shelf space as do their American counterparts.

Because of the high costs of a sales call, many firms use telemarketing and direct mail to qualify prospects and make appointments for the sales representatives. As you can imagine, European subsidiaries of American firms, such as Ford, Digital Equipment, and IBM, having learned the advantages of telemarketing from their American counter-parts, use the technique to increase sales. For example, Barbie doll sends her French fans messages in special ink that they can read only under special lights in toy stores where the dolls are sold.

Dell Computer also sells computers in Japan and Europe by mail and telemarketing, even though they were told by the company's vice president for international operations remembers, "In every country, they told us mail orders would not work." There was also a question about Dell's low price in Europe. Dell executives found that European buyers have a long-established prejudice: high price equals good quality, low price means shoddy quality. Yet Dell has surprised its competitors by its success in both markets. Starting in the last half of 1992, the firm's Japanese sales went from 2, 000 to over 35, 000 PCs in 1995. Dell's European sales are 10 times its sales in Japan.

Computerized prospecting, or using computers to analyze customer call patterns to plan customer visits, is another American sales tool adopted by Europeans to reduce the cost of a sales call. This method is very obviously needed because according to a McGraw-Hill survey, the average cost of making a European sales call is $640, and it takes six calls before a sale is made.

2. Recruitment

Recruiting salespeople in foreign countries is at times more difficult than recruiting them in the home country because sales managers frequently have to cope with the stigma attached to selling that exists in some areas (cultural forces). To help overcome this obstacle, salespeople are often given titles that are essentially translations of American titles designed for the same purpose (territory or zone manager).

Another example of the influence cultural forces can have on recruiting is the need to hire salespeople who are culturally acceptable to customers and channel members. This can be difficult and costly in an already small market that is further subdivided into several distinct cultures with different customs and even languages.

In many cases, American firms are aided in their recruitment of salespeople by their reputation for having excellent training programs. These generally come from the home office and are adapted, if necessary, to local conditions. When the product is highly technical, the new employees are often sent to the home office for training. Of course, the opportunity to take such a trip is also an effective recruiting tool.

10.4 Sales promotion

Sales promotion provides an aid for marketing function and includes activities such as the preparation of point-of-purchase displays, contests, premiums, trade show exhibits, cents-off offers, and coupons. Generally, if no separate department exists for these activities, either the advertising or the sales department will perform them.

The international standardization of the sales promotion function is not difficult, because experience has shown that what is successful in China or America generally proves effective overseas. Coupon is a good example of this. Although the United States is the world's leader in coupon, several European markets and Canada are experiencing rapid growth. A recent study reported that consumers in the United Kingdom and Belgium are the most active EU coupon users. In 2010, averages of 17 coupons per household were redeemed in the United Kingdom and 18 per household in Belgium, compared with 77 in the United States and 26 in Canada. In Italy and Spain, only 3 coupons per household were redeemed. Although the number of coupons redeemed was much lower elsewhere, the growth in their use was much higher. In the United Kingdom, for example, there was a 21 percent increase in redemption from 2008 to 2010, the largest increase in the world. In practice, sales promotion is one of the most important promotion means for companies, especially for companies which operate consumer products.

Characteristics and forms of sales promotion

1. Characteristics of sales promotion

1) Substantivity

In sales promotion, companies will contact the consumers directly in order to show their products to the consumers and get feedback from them. Compared with other promotion methods, salespeople can contact their consumers face to face, helping potential consumers to understand the products and persuade them to buy. Many companies use this method to develop their products in practice, especially when they are operating consumer goods. This strategy is more useful if a company is using international marketing in cities with very large populations. In fact, lots of famous companies used this method when first entering the Chinese market. For example, Samsung, Toshiba, Panasonic and other European and American companies used various promotion activities in the Chinese market in order to promote their products and compete with local companies like ChangHong, Haier and TCL etc. Because consumers are contacted directly in this method, the market effect is always better.

2) A stronger impact

Sales promotion can always bring consumers more benefits and have a stronger impact on potential consumers compared with other promotion methods. For example, free trial, gift and prize-giving sales can all increase the purchasing desires of the consumers; this is especially true in developing countries. Of course, not all countries permit companies to use this method in the promotion of all of their products. Therefore it is important to study local regulations before taking action. It is also important to work to avoid any negative effects of this method. For example, the method may weaken brand reputation and excessive sales promotion may lead consumers to suspect the quality or service of the product being promoted.

3) More flexibility

In practice, companies can use a variety of promotion means to advertise their products. They can also use pre-existing forms or the new forms to promote their products based on the various countries situations. As a matter of fact, companies often use different sales promotion forms to develop different markets which are usually decided by the various countries markets. For example, coupons are a very effective promotion tool in America. In China, however, consumers prefer to gift or prize-giving sales.

4) Wholeness

If companies want to achieve the desired effect, sales promotion must be connected with other promotion means as well. For example, companies have to train the salespeople to coordinate the use of both advertising and public relation activities for sales promotion. That means any sales promotion may be subject to the company's broader strategy in product promotion.

2. Forms for sales promotion in international markets

The forms of sales promotion are diverse, and are often used to bolster support for advertising or personal selling. Sales promotion is not only used in developed countries, but is also one of the major methods used by companies working in developing countries as well. In general, common sales promotion forms include the following.

1) Sales promotion directly to consumers including:

(1) Free samples. In many cases, companies will present some products as a gift to the consumers in order to promote their products when they first enter new markets.

The purpose of this is to make the consumers understand the products and establish a better product reputation. The method is very popular in American and European markets.

(2) Coupons. Companies present coupons as a gift to consumers which the consumers can then use to obtain some benefits if they use the coupon to buy the product. In practice, companies may use this method by advertising or mail.

(3) Cash exchange. This means that consumers can ask for the discount after they already bought the product, as long as they use the certain certificates issued by the companies.

(4) Lottery draw. Some companies will use a lottery draw when they are working on promoting their product in the market. The winners who take the activities can get the prize, the purpose of this method is to attract more consumers to take the activities and buy the products.

(5) Transaction stamps. In this case, consumers can get one stamp if they buy one unit product. After reaching a certain number of stamps, the consumer can then exchange the stamps for products or prizes.

(6) Gifts. If consumers buy the product, then the company will give some gifts according to the volume of the purchase.

2) Sales promotion directly to the middle-man including:

(1) Cooperation advertising, in which companies offer detailed references about the product technology and help the dealers train their salespeople. Sometimes it includes the companies helping the dealers design their storefronts.

(2) Discount means that companies give their dealers a price discount or gifts to promote further cooperation with them.

(3) Demonstration means that companies demonstrate their products in dealers' stores or offer a consulting service for consumers, in order to promote the sales of the dealer.

(4) Business meeting and trade fair is when the companies invite the dealers to the industry annual meeting, the technical exchange meeting, and the product fair, in order to transfer information and enhance communication.

(5) Dealers race is when companies use cash, entities, or tourism as the prizes to motivate the dealers to sell more products for them.

3) Sales promotion directly to the salespeople including:

(1) Bonus and profit allocation means whether or not the delers can get certain percentage profits from the manufacturers if they can finish their sale mission. Most companies use this method to promote their products when they are developing their product reputation in new markets.

(2) Sales subsidy is a subsidy given by companies to salespeople who are working

on developing new or difficult markets in order to increase their enthusiasm and energy.

(3) Promotion race is when companies work to improve the enthusiasm and energy of their consumers, in order to promote their products. This can be done by using cash prizes, tourist packages or other material objects.

Specific promotional formats

Direct marketing uses a variety of techniques just like direct mail, door-to-door, coupons, telemarketing, television and radio, and internet to contact potential consumers in the hope of eliciting a direct, measurable, and almost immediate response.

The increased use of computers to gather product preference information on consumers has given rise to a marketing subgroup called "database marketing". Companies sell each other background and contact information about very specific market segments. American Express was a pioneer of this promotional format and has offered information about its membership's buying habits for decades. Internationally, companies track their current consumers' habits in an effort to further segment the customer base. Much of the information for database marketing is pulled from credit card use and consumer response surveys. Such information is usually only available in developed, more technologically equipped economies.

Even small-scale marketers working in very limited markets should track their customer's consumption habits. Computers are by no means required for tracking; even a filing cabinet or a simple Rolodex can be used to create a useful, if less high-tech, database. All of the following forms of direct marketing can make use of customer databases.

1. Direct mail

In this form, a company sends its catalog or "mail piece" directly to the homes or businesses of potential consumers. Mailings are done in a highly targeted fashion and in large numbers and most postal systems worldwide provide a discounted "bull rate" for volume. Direct mailing may be considered successful if it receives merely a 2 percent response rate, therefore, it must be produced as cheaply as the company image will permit. Some markets have been so deluged that effectiveness is increasingly limited. The onslaught has even given way to the nickname "junk mail".

Direct mail requires that the marketer be working in an environment that has an efficient postal system, as both the solicitation and the product will be subjected to the system's efficiency. Although many international delivery systems (such as DHL and FedEx) have improved the level of communication worldwide, they are often far too expensive for the original solicitation. Also required is an efficient way to pay for transactions. Though C. O. D (cash on delivery) is still practiced in some markets, direct mail marketers generally prefer to have their payment made by check or credit or credit card prior to shipment.

Notice: with the rapid development of electronic business, the developed postal system promotes merchandise transaction in China. The total revenue of Alibaba was over 120 billion RMB on November 11th, 2016. And all of the merchandises are posted to consumers directly.

2. Door-to-door

Though associated with a bygone era, the door-to-door sales technique is still used on a regular basis in a variety of markets. Avon cosmetics have made enormous progress in the gigantic emerging markets by sending out swarms of local salespeople to every small village and farming community. Another technique that falls under this category is the use of the "sale party" where friends, neighbors, and business associations are asked to attend a gathering where products are put on display. Amway, another U. S. company, has used this technique to sell its cleaning products for decades around the global. In Japan, Amway was even hired to market consumer products for Sharp Electronic.

However, not every government or society accepts the door-to-door technique or even the selling of products to friends and neighbors. Some localities may even require that each salesperson be licensed as an individual merchant. Local sales tax issues are also a concern. Therefore, marketers must be sure that their supply and distribution lines are efficient before taking orders on the foreign doorstep. As a matter of fact, the technique has disappeared in many countries because of the development of net shops, like e-buy and TaoBao, etc.

3. Coupons

Coupons are vouchers or other documentation that entitles a consumer to discount, a cash rebate, or free add-on products when making a purchase. Sometimes, the coupon goes into effect at the time of purchase; while other times it requires the consumer to contact the producer, after the purchase has been made, to receive the coupon's benefits. In the United State, where coupons are the primary form of sales promotion, large service companies (i. e. "redemption centers") have evolved just to handle the massive volume of vouchers that consumers turn in. Coupons can also take the form of Sweepstakes, another form of coupons, may also be used by directly relating a product to prizes offered, even if it is only in an advertising connection.

These forms of sales promotion, as well as in-store price reductions or gifts, are highly regulated by governments, as they have been frequently linked to consumer fraud. Some countries, such as Germany and Greece, forbid product coupons altogether such as while others such as Brazil, New Zealand, restrict their usage on certain products or limit the value of the benefits. Because regulation on sales promotions is so varied from country to country, international marketers should seek extensive local input before issuing coupons or sweepstakes-type promotions.

4. Telemarketing

Telemarketing is the use of the telephone to contact potential consumers directly, a form of promotion that saw a major growth surge in the 1990s. The immediacy of telemarketing has been both its greatest and least attractive aspect to marketers and to consumers. Many cultures find being solicited at home as a nuisance and telemarketers have seen a rise in regulation—in the form of privacy laws as well as technology, that is meant to thwart their efforts. Despite this, it has not lowered predictions about telemarketing's future growth. In fact, the greatest successes can be found in business-to-business contacts during regular working hours. In these cases, telemarketing is used to identify companies that show some interest in a product and therefore warrant a personal face-to-face sales call. This practice of "qualifying a lead" makes the selling process more efficient, especially where large distances are involved.

Like direct mail, telemarketing depends on having the proper level of infrastructure present. It should be noted that the majority of people on the planet do not currently have access to a telephone; however, there has been explosive growth in telephone infrastructure, especially in Asian emerging markets. Thus, marketers are quick to follow in the wake of these infrastructure projects. Currently, not only do many companies in Europe and the U. S. use international direct dialing as a regular means of establishing customer contact for international business promotion, but many companies in emerging countries, including China, have begun to use this format to develop their oversea markets. The latest developments in "internet telephones" will make telemarketing not only more cost-effective but also less intrusive. All international marketers should give telemarketing a serious consideration in those countries that permit its open usage and where the product's positioning is conducive to such contacts.

5. Television and radio

Whereas telemarketing provides the consumer with an involuntary immediacy, television and radio give the buyer much more control over when and where they will be the subject of promotional efforts. Television offers "shopping channels", with direct viewer feedback as well as "infomercials", in which products are given almost documentary attention for up to thirty minutes, all the while soliciting viewers to phone in their orders. Both of these are quite common in the United States, but satellite networks are quickly increasing their reach in the global broadcasting while many countries lack the necessary level of affluence and infrastructure for widespread television promotion, most countries have substantial radio access.

Despite the advantages of television or radio, there are still some issues associated with their use. For example, television and radio in some countries are under the direct control of local governments, and even satellite broadcasts can be subject to local regulation. Furthermore, most responses to TV/radio promotions are done by telephone, requiring suitable infrastructure and an efficient postal system.

6. The Internet

Internet promotion involves direct contact with consumers via email for the purpose of selling products. This should not be confused with "banners" or cross-link "icons" that appear on many commercial and Internet service provider web pages. Those are more similar to advertising or sponsorship.

Internet promotions combine the feedback speed of telemarketing with a more voluntary consumer contact level (i. e. Promotional email can be deleted from the consumer's electronic mailbox without being read.) Though some internet users were dismayed by the commercial use of the medium, such promotions, as well as extensive advertising, have become common parts of daily cyber-life.

Even tiny companies can afford internet promotion. Like telemarketing, email is a great way to get quality ideas recognized at an international level for business-to-business contacts, before companies begin making expensive trips. Databases of potential customers can be purchased from service companies or assembled from internal records. With the development of network technology and globalization, network marketing has become one of the most important business formats. By now, it is nearly impossible for any multinational to increase profits if they do not utilize network platforms to promote their products. Even for industrial products, network promotion has become the most important guarantee for companies to reach their business goals.

Push versus pull: creating demand and interest

1. Push strategy

A push strategy involves a greater reliance on personal selling and direct contact with consumers. The emphasis here is on allowing advertising to generate interest. Push strategies are most common when the product complex requires a good deal of after-sale-service, and must be marketed in areas where the amount of advertising media is severely limited or too expensive. Thus, these strategies are a common feature in less developed economies or in market segments that place little credibility in advertising. Here, producers and distributors have the challenge of pushing products with little credibility through distribution chains.

2. Pull strategy

Pull strategy techniques are applied when a product is widely used, lacks complexity, when the distribution channel is extensive, and when mass communication media are readily available. This strategy is often used to overcome inefficiencies of long distribution chains, because consumers place pressure on distributors farthest from the producer to deliver the goods or services seen in advertisements. Thus, consumers literally "pull" the products through the channel. In larger markets, such as Europe, China, America and Japan, marketers should consider using a pull strategy for greatest effectiveness only if the other criteria are in place.

In most situations, it is generally easier for a company experienced with push promotions to switch over to pull strategies than the reverse. Marketers facing the process of switching from an advertising-based marketing plan to one centered on direct promotions will require a substantial change in psychology and customer skills. Making sure that the retraining is done before entering the new market.

When marketers are considering transferring sales promotion techniques to other markets, they must consider some cultural and legal constraints as well. The reason international marketing is more complex and difficult than the domestic marketing is because multinational managers have to face different environments which significantly influence the marketing results.

10.5 Environment constraints for international promotion

Legal constraints

Laws concerning sales promotions tend to be more restrictive in other countries than they are in China, the United States or Great Britain. The Belgian, German, and Scandinavian governments are rather negative toward premiums, for example, believing that they distract consumers from considering the merits of the product. Two-for-one offers are prohibited in Sweden and Norway, and although free samples are permitted everywhere, some governments limit their size. Mexico requires special offers and cents-off deals to be approved by a government agency before they can be used.

Every country has its own regulations for promotion that constrain the influence of international marketing directly. This is especially true if the country creates any laws that limit promotions, making the marketing very troublesome for international marketers. After all, the law is the law. It is thus a precondition for international managers to study a country's laws before they take any marketing actions. Although these legal restrictions are bothersome, they have not stopped the use of sales promotions because promotions are seen as one of the best means for the companies to promote the product to the consumer.

Social cultural and economic constraints

Cultural and economic constraints are often even more consequential than legal constraints, making some sales promotion strategies difficult to use. If a premium is to fulfill the objective of being a sales aid for the product, it must be meaningful to the purchaser. A gadget to be used in the kitchen might be valued by an American but will not be particularly attractive to a Latin American with two maids to do the housework. Firms that attach premiums to the outside of packages in less developed countries usually do so just once. Less than a week after the packages are on the shelf, the detached premiums are already being sold in the streets. Putting the prize inside the package is also no guarantee that it will be there when the purchaser takes the package home.

While living in Mexico, an American bought a product that came with a plastic toy as a small premium. When he opened the package at home, there was no toy. Examining the package more closely, he soon found that a small slot had been made in the top, indicating that the toy had been removed before it was even sold. Because labor costs and store revenues are low in the countries, the income from the sales of these premiums provides an extra profit for the retailers.

Contests, raffles, and games, however, have been extremely successful in countries where people love to play the odds. If Latin Americans or the Irish are willing to buy a lottery ticket week after week, hoping to win the grand prize, with odds of 500,000 to 1, why should they not participate in a contest that costs them nothing to enter? Point-of-purchase displays are also well accepted by retailers, though many establishments are so small that there is simply no place to put all of the displays that are offered to them.

Sales promotion is generally not as sophisticated overseas as it is in the domestic countries. Even so, experience indicates that subsidiaries do not make sufficient use of the ideas coming from headquarters. The marketing manager who prepares a well-planned program after studying the constraints of the local markets can therefore expect excellent results from the time and money invested.

Two unsuccessful sales promotions

In 1990s, there were two famous and expensive examples of sales promotions that went wrong: Hoover in the United Kingdom and Pepsi-Cola in the Philippines.

1. Hoover in the U. K.

Hoover's promotional campaign in the 1990s is probably the most disastrous sales promotion attempt in history. In the fall of 1992, the company offered two free air tickets to continental Europe or the United States to anyone spending at least $100 ($150) on Hoover products. In addition, customers spending $300 would also receive free car rental and hotel rooms. Inasmuch as the cheapest pair of tickets costs \$ 500, 200, 000 customers rushed to buy the inexpensive vacuum cleaners for \$ 120. Hoover's mistake was to assume that most people would not collect their tickets after reading the offer's fine print that laid down the conditions about when the flight could be taken and which hotels could be used.

However, so many customers were infuriated about delays in obtaining tickets that Maytag, Hoover's owner, sent a team from the U. S. headquarters to fire the managing director and set up a task force of 250 people to issue the tickets. Maytag also announced that it would take a \$ 30 million charge against profits to pay for the ill-fated promotion. However, it later said that this would actually cost \$ 72. 6 million.

2. Pepsi-Cola in the Philippines

In February 1992, the Pepsi bottler in the Philippines (Pepsi owns 19 percent of the market share) began a promotion called "Number Fever", which would award cash prizes for winning numbers under bottle caps. When the company launched the promotion, it had only 16 percent of the market while Coke had 78 percent. By April however, the promotion had been so successful (Pepsi's market share rose to 23 percent), that the firm extended it to a second stage of an additional five weeks. On May 25, 1992, the winning number, 349, was drawn by computer and announced. Unfortunately, 349 had been printed on 900, 000 caps, half of which carried a 1 million peso (\$ 37, 700) prize. A Pepsi employee discovered the error and tried to withdraw the number, but a news show had already announced it.

Because of the error, the company faced paying winners \$ 18 billion dollars. It quickly suggested an offer of \$ 19 to each person with a 349 cap. Since that time, the company has paid out nearly \$ 10 million. Despite this, many people remain dissatisfied. PepsiCo, anxious to distance itself from the affair, has since stated that the promotion is a local problem. Pepsi's market share, which had gone from 19 percent to 25 percent, plunged down to 16 percent.

10. 6 Public relations

Public relations are where a firm's primary communications occur and where relationships with its various publics, including the governments where it operates, are formed. As lots of economists put it, "Public relation is the marketing of the firm." Although American internationals have had organized public relations programs for many years in the United States, they have paid much less attention to this important function elsewhere.

On the whole, companies have not neglected public-service activities through their foreign subsidiaries; rather, they have failed to inform their publics of what exactly they are doing. For example, Exxon has for years sponsored the study of foreign art students in the United States, and the ITT International Fellowship Program, started in 1973, has already enabled more than 750 students from 54 countries to pursue advanced degrees in the United States and abroad.

Furthermore, many overseas subsidiaries of American firms support public-service activities locally. In Japan, Coca-Cola spends $5 million annually on good works such as programs for children and the handicapped. IBM Japan puts 1 percent of its profits into good works. In 1990, young ballerinas and basic-research scientists were among those receiving $14 million. Eastman Kodak sponsors soccer, and Du Pont, sponsors of golf.

The rising wave of nationalism and anti-multinational feeling in many countries has made it imperative for companies with international operations to improve their communications to non-business publics. This requires them to have more effective public relations programs.

International pharmaceutical manufacturers are often viewed suspiciously by the public in developing nations. On one hand, they are in the business to alleviate suffering, but they are doing it to make it a profit at poor people's expense. Thus, Warner-Lambert, in order to improve its image, began a program in Africa called Tropicare that trains local health care providers in preventive medicine with audiovisual materials. In each country that it operates, the company has organized a commission of experts from national and international health organizations to ensure that the quality of the educational material used in the program is good. The African program was so successful that Warner-Lambert introduced it in Latin America in 1990s.

Tropicare has provided many benefits for both the host countries and the company. It has helped Warner-Lambert enter new markets, subdue criticism of the company's pricing and marketing practices in developing nations, and improve its general image. In addition, developing nations have benefited by having their health providers receive much-needed training.

One of the most vexing problems firms face in their work abroad, is how to deal with critics of their operations and motives. Some try to deflect criticism before it becomes a full-scale attack by holding regularly scheduled meetings where such topics are debated. Others prefer to meet with critics privately, though they might find themselves caught in a never-ending relationship in which the critics continually escalate their demands. This is especially true of single-issue groups, whose existence depends on the continuance of the issue.

A successful strategy employed by some firms is to address the issue without dealing directly with critics and instead work with international or governmental agencies. An alternative approach is for firms to do nothing. If the criticism receives no publicity, it may die from lack of interest. However, bad handling of a situation can have serious repercussions for a firm. An example of a firm that has a very effective public relations strategy is IBM. Its strong lobbying effort convinced EU commissioners that the highly regulated, state-owned telephone and postal organizations are responsible for costly, inefficient phone systems. As a result, partly because of IBM's efforts, one of the main objectives of the EU is to standardize and liberalize telecommunications.

Summary

1. Appreciate the concept of promotion. Promotion, one of the basic elements of the marketing mix, is communication that secures understanding between a firm and its publics in order to bring about favorable buying actions and achieve long-lasting confidence in the firm and the product or service it provides. Note that this definition employs the plural, because the seller's promotional efforts must be directed to more than just the ultimate consumers and the channel of distribution members.

2. Understand the six promotion strategies that are most commonly used. Because promotion both influences and is influenced by other marketing mix variables, it is possible to formulate nine distinct strategies by combining the three alternatives of: ① marketing the same physical product everywhere, ② adapting the physical product for foreign markets, and ③ designing a different physical product with (a) the same, (b) adapted, or (c) different messages.

3. Discuss how to choose your advertising agencies in foreign markets. When a company is looking to promote its products in a foreign market, it can choose the domestic agency, the local agency, or the subsidiaries of the international companies to help finish the job. However, the company must also give good reasons of why it chose before making any decisions. In summary, companies must face very complex environments when taking the job overseas.

4. Recognize the characteristics of various advertising media including: ① paper advertising; ② magazine advertising; ③ TV advertising; ④ radio advertising; ⑤ out-door advertising; and ⑥ new media advertising.

5. Appreciate the functions for personal selling: ① market research and forecast; ② to expand the markets and deal with the relationship with consumers; ③ transmit and communicate information; ④ sell the products and provide after-sale service.

6. Appreciate the concept of sales promotion. Sales promotion provides selling aids for the marketing function and includes activities such as the preparation of point-of-purchase displays, contest, premiums, trade show exhibits, cents-off offers, and coupons. If no separate department exists for these activities, either the advertising or the sales department will perform them.

7. Recognize the characteristics of sales promotion: ① direct; ② stronger impact; ③ greater flexibility; ④ wholeness.

8. Understand the contents of direct marketing. Direct marketing uses a variety of techniques including, direct mail, door-to-door, coupons, telemarketing, television and radio, and the internet, in order to contact potential consumers in the hope of eliciting a direct, measurable and almost immediate response.

9. Anticipate the contents of push strategy. A push strategy involves a greater reliance on personal selling and direct contact with consumers. The emphasis here is on allowing advertising to generate interest. Push strategies are more common when the product is complex, requires a good deal of after-sale-service, and must be marketed in areas where the amount of advertising media is severely limited or too expensive. Thus, these strategies are a common feature in less developed economies or in market segments that place little credibility in advertising. Here, producers and distributors must be able to push products with little credibility through distribution chains.

10. Recognize the significance of understanding how social, cultural, and economic forces influence promotional strategies. The cultural and economic constraints are more consequential than legal constraints and do make some sales promotions difficult to use.

Questions

1. Explain why it is important for international managers to understand legal, cultural, and economic forces when they are creating their promotional strategies in a foreign country.

2. Why do some people feel that personal selling is more important for industrial products than consumer products?

3. List the advantages and disadvantages for sales promotion?

4. How do economic forces influence your media selection in oversea markets?

5. Has the internet become the most important media outlet for international managers to promote their products? Explain.

6. Why do many international marketers choose the local media to serve as their advertising agencies?

7. Are legal forces the only obstacle companies face in promotion? If not, name others.

8. Does the push strategy work in your company, if you are operating consumer products in foreign markets? Why or Why not?

9. Do foreign manufactures prefer to use personal selling or advertising to promote their products in the Chinese market? Why?

Chapter 11 Pricing Strategy

Concept preview

After reading this chapter, you should be able to

1. Appreciate: the significance of pricing strategies for international companies.

2. Understand: why multinationals have to study the host country's environment before they establish their international marketing pricing strategies.

3. Distinguish: the difference between domestic and international pricing strategies.

4. Comprehend: why top managers have to consider various requirements of different departments in companies when they make their pricing strategies.

5. Describe: how various pricing methods influence the marketing result.

The internationalization process for Glanze

At least 50% consumers of the world choose to buy microwave ovens produced by Glanze. In 2007, Glanze sold over 25 million microwave ovens in the global market and had a market share over 50%. With these numbers, it had become the microwave oven R&D center of the world. Furthermore, as the industry leader, its business performance has been far ahead of competitors until today. As the biggest microwave oven manufacture of the world, Glanze first established its scale advantage by buying competitor's production lines and creating a manufacturing center itself. In addition, all of the operations are based on an international vision of optimal management. Especially, its pricing strategy is the most successful in this industry.

1. Establishing a comparative advantage "takes doctrine"

One of the most important reasons Glanze obtained such a high level of success was due to its special method of expanding. At that time, domestic home appliance manufactures always just acquired foreign companies when they developed overseas markets. However, Glanze expanded its business by buying production lines of other famous international brands, a method which has been called "takes doctrine" by managers of Glanze. Qing Deliang, president of Glanze said, "You can take your brand, however, you transfer your production line to me, because the cooperation between us can make the production cost and marketing expenditures reduce drastically."

Liang said, "Several years ago, we had forecasted that the home appliance production base of the world would transfer to Asia, especially China, because the area is good at surviving and developing for the home appliance manufactures with the change of global market layout and the home appliance companies in China rise abruptly. Glanze must capture the opportunity to develop itself and become the biggest production base of the world." Thus, the president of Glanze emphasized the comparative advantage of the Chinese home appliance manufactures.

Although the reason that Glanze first began to use the "take doctrine" was to lower labor costs, it soon became one of its most important sources of comparative advantage. Yu Raochang, vice president, indicated that the company would use top-ranking productivity and top-ranking cost controls in order to combine top-ranking net-sales and top-ranking multinational brands to develop the global market; thus making Glanze the top-ranking company. As Yu Raochang explained, "We take the way to integrate the global resources to achieve our targets, for example, the production cost for unit microwave oven is ¥800 if it is produced in America, we will tell the Americans that they can get ¥400 if they transfer their equipments to us, and the Americans will accept our suggestion, the reason is simple, their total net profit for unit microwave oven is just ¥100. In France, the production time works just 24 hours in a week, however, we can take three shifts to produce according to the situation, which means our working time is 7 times more than that of France. This is why our production cost is far lower than Europeans."

Thus, on one hand, Glanze got the advanced production line for free and was able to expand its production capacity quickly. On the other hand, however, Glanze took over and was able to control overseas markets owned by famous world brands. Glanze created partnerships with competitors by sharing the benefits, helping it save large sums of marketing expenditures and reducing huge pressures to develop the overseas markets. The product quality began to reach an advanced international level because Glanze was able to obtain the latest advanced technologies in the process. Besides, Glanze focused on production and did not have to pay attention to circulation because many foreign importers and dealers asked to sell the microwave ovens produced by Glanze. For example, Carrefour signed a contract with Glanze and authorized Glanze to produce the microwave ovens named "Carrefour." All of the distribution channels helped Glanze develop the market quickly and establish a firm foundation for the company to develop other products like air conditioners, refrigerators, and other home appliance products.

2. A "price butcher" emphasizes the total cost advantage

In 1996, when Glanze reduced its microwave oven prices by 40% the sales increased to 650,000 from 250,000 with the market share reaching 35%. From that time on, it began to establish its dominant position in the field of the microwave oven industry. It was called a "price butcher" because of its reduction of its prices, thus stirring up a "price war".

In response to this, Yu Raochang said, "To reduce the price is our fighter plane, and we will put it in where the markets need." In common business people's eye, it is not the better method to occupy the markets to reduce the price, because it is a double-edge sword, and the precondition for you to hurt your competitors is to hurt yourself first. The better example is the "TV price war" which made all of the domestic manufactures lose in 1995. However, Yu Raochang did not agree the view, he said: "The market position of Wal-Mart came from the small profits but quick turnover, the Japanese and Korean companies took the lower price strategy to develop the European and American markets, especially when we are operating the consumer products, small profits and quick turnover should be the most important price strategy for us to develop the new markets especially for developing the industrialized countries' markets."

The confidence and strength of Glanze in winning a price war was based on its leading advantage in total costs in the scale economy. Therefore, the price war stirred up by Glanze was based on the scale economy. If the scale could be expanded, Glanze would reduce its price. For example, if the company's production capacity reached 3 million, it would reduce its price to the cost of the companies with total production capacity of 2 million, making it difficult for other companies to compete with the lower price.

Yu Raochang, in talking about the company's actions in the price war stated that, "The purpose of Glanze is to destroy the confidence of competitors and let them to understand that in this industry there are markets for the products but there is no any investment value." With this price strategy, Glanze established a doorsill for investors, because they have to invest more money in order to achieve a larger production scale, especially if they want to exceed the profits of Glanze. Otherwise, they will suffer losses. Thus, not only did many investors abandon their investment plan, but many current competitors were also out of the game. Because of these circumstances, more and more famous home appliance manufactures realized that the production scale of Glanze had become a price barrier, making it difficult for them to break the market layout. They came to realize that the best choice for them was to cooperate with Glanze, which is why Glanze was able to use its "take doctrine" strategy.

3. Avoid antitrust with OEM

Qing Deliang said that, "Standing on the shoulders of the giants to develop ourselves," is the first reason for Glanze to be successful through utilizing the OEM strategy in the field of foreign trade. "We are not anxious to establish the brand name, we pay more attention to manufacture." said Qing Deliang. The positioning of Glanze was to be a manufacturing center for famous, global brands and to do OEM for these companies. Thus the positioning of the company was very important so that Glanze could achieve its operation target—become the biggest oven manufacturer of the world in five years. In order to do so, they had to consider antitrust questions. Yu Raochang indicated that Glanze had to pay more attention to anti-dumping, it lost the market in Argentina because its market share was over 70% and in response, the local government began to limit the sale of Glanze products. Because of this, Glanze decided to reduce the market share rate of its own brands in oversea markets and use OEM to improve its market share in foreign markets.

To insist on an OEM strategy did not mean that Glanze did not make any changes, stated Yu Raochang. The major advantage of Glanze was its centralized production costs, however it was very difficult for Glanze to maintain the advantage for a long time, because of the difficulty in beating competitors with a single advantage only. This was especially true if the company wanted to enter international markets quickly and establish their products and company reputation.

Under these circumstances, Glanze offered a "two-leg" development strategy in order to become the top-manufacturer in the world. The core of this strategy was "based on the cost advantage to develop the technology advantage, based on the domestic market to develop the international market." Glanze would construct its "global home appliance manufacture center" and achieve the industry up-grade simultaneously. The specific countermeasures included driving the development of new industries based on advantages in industry resources.

For example, the brand and distribution channels were used to introduce more advanced technologies and expand its cost advantage in the global industry chain, based on an opportunity which foreign manufactures transferred to the domestic. On the other hand, it combined its own brand and famous foreign brands with OEM, using resources, including sale and service nets from the famous foreign brand, to carry its own products to foreign markets. Thus, not only was Glanze able to avoid risks because of development in foreign markets and certain profit spaces, but it could also achieve lower costs by expanding in the fields of production and global market.

Yu Raochang thought that Glanze had integrated the most advanced technologies for producing the microwave oven in the world by using its "take doctrine" strategy and based on the foundation that it should invest more resources in R&D. In 1997, Glanze established its microwave oven R&D center in China and America. Today, the advantage of Glanze is not only reflected in the price, but also in technology.

In a word, Glanze is one of the most successful companies in China. Its successful experience, especially in the field of price strategy, can serve as an example for other domestic companies. Because the price of a product is often the determining factor when a purchase is made, and is always a key to profit, it must also be part of a strategy aimed at seizing market share. Setting a proper price will determine how long any company will stay in the marketplace. When a company practices price competition, it consciously decides to use price as the major means of attracting consumers. It is not unusual for consumers (at both the wholesale and the retail level) to be based entirely on price, regardless of the efforts of the marketer to promote quality or service. In this chapter, questions about how to price products in international markets will be discussed.

11.1 The factors influencing international pricing decisions

Pricing tactics are some of the most important means for multinationals to use in order to take the international competition. However, price is a double-edge sword, and it may be detrimental if price tactics are used in the wrong way. Even if multinationals produce "proper" products and use "proper" promotion strategies to develop the market, and choose "proper" channels to sell their products, all of their efforts will be wasted if the pricing countermeasures do not adapt to local markets. This is particularly true when international managers face different environments in which they have to consider freight, tariff, exchange rate, and political factors. Thus, the pricing process is very complex and difficult in international markets compared with domestic markets.

Under these circumstances, multinationals have to study and master the factors influencing pricing decisions before they create pricing strategies for international companies.

Cost factors

It is very important for multinationals to calculate their costs when they engage in international marketing because in most situations, cost is the lowest bounds of the price. The marketing expenditure of international marketing is more complex than domestic marketing because the cost structure is very different when the products are sold to various countries. Even export products that are produced in domestic markets have different costs. This is because the manufactures have to change the system of weights and measures or power system to adapt to different requirements of various countries, all of which increase costs. The following factors will all influence cost directly:

1. Tariffs

Tariffs are special expenditures for companies to pay when they transport their products to other countries. Not only can tariffs improve the financial income of local governments, but they can also protect domestic markets. This is why it is one of the most widespread trade barriers and will influence product's prices directly.

2. Expenditure for foreign dealers

In most situations, foreign dealers are used to help companies develop their product in foreign markets, especially when using international trade to develop the foreign markets. This means that the company must share its international benefits with local dealers. However, marketing expenditures and profits are different in various countries. For example, it is possible for a company to use direct channels to carry products to the target customers in some countries, using local dealers for the promotion, storage and transportation. In some countries, local dealers may not even take responsibility because there are not enough logistic infrastructures in local markets. Overall, marketing costs are very different because of different market conditions, which is why companies must use different pricing tactics in various countries.

3. Freight and premium

If you are taking international trade, then freight and insurance premiums are very important to take into consideration in regards to your cost structure. The company will therefore have to deal with many multifarious jobs, for example, renting ships, packaging products, loading and unloading, insurance, export and import licenses, and custom clearances. All of the payments will thus increase overall costs and potentially change the product cost structure.

4. Risk cost

In international marketing practice, risk cost includes inflation and exchange rates because of the spacing interval between signing contracts to the delivery of goods. Companies thus have to be willing to risk potential exchange rate or inflation rate changes during this time. International managers have to consider these factors when deciding the product price. Besides reducing risks or transaction obstacles, companies have to replace business credit with bank credit in order to increase operation costs.

Market demand

Cost and demand are the basic factors for companies to consider when determining their product price. This means that companies should consider the demand of consumers while determining the costs with price. It is a very complex process considering the factors that will affect any decisions on pricing tactics because the culture background, nature environment, economic conditions and consumer habits are different in various countries.

For instance, the Japanese prefer bean products produced by Chinese companies. Furthermore, they prefer to pay a higher price on the product because the bean that is produced in north-east China has higher protein content. However, the same bean price is lower in the Finnish market, because companies in Finland buy the bean with the purpose of squeezing out the oil. The bean produced in north-east China does not fit this requirement because of the lower oil content. Therefore, international managers should analyze the specific situations of the markets carefully before making any price decisions.

In addition, consumer's income and the market price flow will influence the demand too. For instance, 20 years ago for most Chinese, it was an extravagant hope to buy a car. Today, however, the Chinese market has become the biggest auto market in the world. This is mostly due to the fact that the income of many Chinese people improved dramatically over the last 20 years. In a similar situation, as the demand for top grade consumer goods increases, the demand for lower grade consumer goods is reduced when income is improved. For products with a larger price elasticity of demand, the proper reducing price can expand demand and improve the total revenue of the companies. Thus, companies should be very careful when they make the decisions about price reductions.

In general, demand is very complex and difficult to control, and therefore requires international management to constantly study local markets.

Market competition

Another factor that influences pricing decisions is market competition because the degree of competition influences price capping. The prices will thus influence market shares directly if companies are producing the same or similar products. In recent years, personal computers produced by HP, Apple, and IBM occupied Japanese markets with their market share increasing quickly, and the price of these companies is 20%～40% lower than NEC. It is for this reason that companies should focus on competitor's change in their price and price strategies in order to respond with effective countermeasures.

11.2 How to price your products

Price is the value of what a consumers exchanges in return for a product. It may take the form of monetary exchange, bartered services, or other goods. The price must be set so that both the consumer and the marketer "profits" by the exchange, if only at a perceptual level. Consumers all over the world consider price a major factor in purchasing decisions, whether they are buying vegetable at the local store, diamond rings, office furniture, or factory machinery. The price is set by the marketer; therefore a major key in controlling the pricing process is the firms' understanding of the targeted consumer's perception of the value of goods.

Consumers must believe that the price is less than or equal to the value they derive from the goods being sold. Marketers can create this belief in the consumer's mind through adjustments to the quality of the goods themselves, the atmospheres in which they are sold, or by promotions.

Based on the above information, pricing is driven by four forces: cost, demand, competition, and risk. Each of these forces can, in its turn, be the main focus of a company's pricing strategy. This is why one can use cost-oriented, demand-oriented and competition-oriented pricing to make pricing decisions. With respect to the risk cost, each pricing method consists of the relative contents.

Cost-oriented pricing

The cost of producing something represents the lowest possible price that a marketer can charge for goods without incurring a loss. However, cost is not as simple as it seems and its full extent can be hidden. Understanding cost in its primary form can assist in explaining what pricing strategies are used.

The basic cost segmentation includes fixed cost and variable cost. Fixed costs are expenditures that do not change, regardless of how much is produced. These include items such as rent, management salaries, depreciation, and property taxes. While these costs remain static for extended periods of time, the fixed cost per unit will decline as production increases. Variable costs are expenditures that change according to the quantity of a company's output. These might include employee wages, materials, transportation, and packaging. The variable cost per unit may actually decrease when production expands as efficiency increases and the savings that come with mass raw material purchasing become evident. Total costs are the sum of all fixed costs and variable costs. Marginal costs are the added costs that occur when a single unit of promotion is added to current levels of production. It only affects variable costs and is used to determine the effectiveness of expanding production and its ultimate effect on pricing. Six cost-oriented pricing schemes are described below.

1. Component cost

This strategy takes a single component of cost and expands it by a standard percentage to arrive at a market price. For example, unit material cost×300% = sale price. That percentage, added by the original producer, is called a markon (as opposed to the markup added by middlemen), and is a very common, if simplistic, pricing scheme. It disregards consumer demand and does not take into account total cost per unit or competitor pricing. Although the method is not often used by most multinationals, it does theoretically serve as a basic pricing method.

2. Cost plus

This strategy adds a profit percentage to the total cost per unit. It is more efficient than the component method because now all costs are considered even though there is still no accounting for demand. The cost plus strategy also relies on costs remaining relatively stable, making large fluctuations difficult to absorb. At the primary producer level, this pricing represents a markon. Middlemen using this strategy to set their sale prices are adding a markup.

3. Average return

In this method, a company adds a fixed amount of profit to its total cost. This amount is then divided by the total number of units to be produced in order to derive the prices. The average return scheme relies on the selling of its entire production run in order to realize profits. As many companies that have used this method have discovered it is impossible to raise prices to recoup profit if demand is lower than projected. Furthermore, discounting further erodes what little profits had been secured by earlier sales transactions.

$$\text{average return} = \frac{\text{total cost of projected unit} + \text{desired profit}}{\text{number of units to be produced}}$$

4. Breakeven

Volume sales can be used to secure profit by figuring the level of unit sales at which revenue (money coming in) equals total costs (money going out). This is the breakeven point. Beyond this point, additional sales represent profit; below this point, all sales will incur a loss. The breakeven point will vary for different prices, projected sales volumes, and variations in competitor prices. Sales forecast can also be experimented with to reach the most favorable prices. Like average return, this method assumes that whatever quantity is produced, will be sold and that the variable costs will remain stable during the production period.

Even when this method is not the scheme ultimately used, it is an effective means of determining where your company stands (and has potential) in a new marketplace.

$$\text{breakeven point} = \frac{\text{total fixed cost}}{\text{price per unit} - \text{variable cost per unit}}$$

5. Margin

Breaking into a new market may require drastic measures to gain market share or recognition. Pricing below total cost—margin pricing—is a method utilized by large and small companies alike. It can be used to quickly grab a piece of a burgeoning market or to drive competitors out. When the former is the goal, a company hopes that long-term efficiencies and gradual price increases will make up for earlier losses. When the latter is the goal, and a company plans on becoming the market leader (if not its sole supplier), it aims to make up losses with long-term volume. This tactic is called "dumping" when it is utilized by international manufacturers which in some economies, is an illegal procedure.

6. Economies of scale

Characteristically, as a company's market share increases (along with its production levels), there is an accompanying increase in the efficiency and a decrease in cost. These economies of scale are brought about by discounts in volume of material purchased and by increased worker productivity. For manufacturing processes, there is typically a 15 percent decrease in per unit costs for every 100 percent increase in production levels. Companies fight for market share as a pricing strategy because the money saved by increased production can be passed along as price reductions, which further increase market share. This is rarely considered for start-up companies, but it is a regular ploy of established companies entering a new market with less efficient competitors.

Demand-oriented pricing

Where cost sets the base for pricing, demand sets the high end for pricing, as consumers often place value on goods far in excess of the costs required to produce them. Gems and precious metals are examples of goods whose prices are set almost entirely by arbitrary demand. Demand can fluctuate wildly, and forecasts of consumer demand are taken on faith (rather than fact) and always as short-term considerations.

Demand, price and supply are closely related and require continual monitoring. In the classic economic principle of supply and demand, as price increases on a steady supply, demand drops. If demand rises and supply is limited, prices increase. If supply increases and demand remains fixed, prices drop. Marketers can manipulate demand to a degree by promotion and have an obvious control over supply. However, it is far easier to tinker with pricing, especially when goods must be produced in advance. Different goods react to price manipulation in different fashions, a phenomenon known as price elasticity of demand. The four main categories of this price-demand relationship are discussed below.

1. Elastic demand

When price is changed by a percentage, demand is changed by a greater percentage. Normally, demand will drop dramatically as price increases and rise sharply as price decreases. However, consumers sometimes interpret price as a quality indicator, in which case demand will actually rise with price increases, as with wine and housing for example. Or, demand may drop with price decreases.

2. Inelastic demand

When price is changed by a percentage, demand is changed by a lesser percentage. The prices of goods that are considered to be necessities or near necessities, like medicine, for example, can absorb very large price increases without affecting demand. Similarly, goods that face a sharp price decrease may see demand change only slightly, as there is a limit to consumption.

3. Unitary demand

When price is changed by a percentage, demand is changed by an equal percentage. Like elastic and inelastic, these two percentages run in opposite directions. Although, it may not always be so for some luxury goods or goods subject to short supply and high demand.

4. Cross demand

When goods are used in conjunction with other products, their price will fluctuate with that of the other product. For instance, as the price of CD-ROM players began to decrease, usage increased, and the demand for music CDs increased.

Determining the price elasticity of demand can be reduced to a formula, but it also requires the marketers to understand how consumers in the target market make decisions. Because of difficulty met by small companies when gathering survey information prior to entering a foreign market, elasticity should not be used for setting initial pricing, only for subsequent changes. A simplified version of the formula is shown below.

$$E=\frac{\text{percentage change in quantity sold}}{\text{percentage change in unit price}}$$

E equals the coefficient of elasticity. If E is greater than one, demand is elastic. If E is less than one, demand is inelastic. Unitary demand exists when $E=1$.

Competitive-oriented pricing

Cost and demand may set the extremes of pricing, but a marketer rarely has a market to himself—at least not for very long. Prices are a matter of recovering costs, meeting demand, and most importantly, responding to the prices of the competition. Some industries, such as auto manufacturers, respond directly to the pricing initiatives of competitors. Others respond to a competitor's price change by increasing their advertising in order to maintain a customer base. Still other industries, such as fast-food operations, respond to competitive pricing by offering consumers a package of goods at discount, in a mix that disguises the marginal profits of the individual goods. A recent trend in pricing is to lower the upfront costs of the product and make up for the reduced price by raising the price on supplies needed to maintain its original purpose. Ink and toner cartridges for computer printers and photocopying machines are a prime example of this trend.

The key to competitive pricing is to keep the consumer from seeing that there is a direct link between your price setting and that of the competition. When consumers are aware of this link, they begin to play one company off another (as regularly occurs when shopping for automobiles). A company that chooses to "hold the line" when a competitor lowers prices must work doubly hard to convince consumers that the product is worth the now-higher price. This may be very difficult if the product was previously positioned head-to-head with the competitor's.

Similarly, discounting and mix-packaging can very often change the consumer's opinion of the value of a product, especially when price changes are dramatic. When price changes are seasonal, price increases are often viewed as "gouging". Many countries in the developing world institute rigid pricing guidelines, or "caps," during holiday seasons to protect against inflation and an angry population. Even in technological societies, companies may be subject to investigation and prosecution if their competitive pricing of certain vital commodities, such as fossil fuel and electrical power, gets to be too extreme or if it seems they are taking advantage of a spike (sudden increase) in demand.

In general, although international companies can choose from a multitude of methods when pricing their products, they should study the market, especially the demand of consumers first. Thus the specific pricing methods should be chosen based on the present situation of the markets.

11.3 Basic pricing strategies for international marketing

Pricing, the third element of marketing mix, is an important and complex consideration in formulating a marketing strategy. Pricing decisions affect other corporate functions, directly determine the firm's gross revenue, and are a major determinant of profits. Because of this, multinationals have to study other factors influencing prices before making their pricing strategy decisions apart from the cost, demand, competition and risk.

Pricing, a controllable variable

Most marketers are aware that effective price setting consists of more than mechanically adding a standard markup to a cost. To obtain the maximum benefits from pricing, management must regard it in the same manner as it does other controllable variables; that is, pricing is one of the marketing mix elements that can be varied to achieve marketing objectives of the firm.

For instance, if the marketer wishes to position a product as a high-quality item, setting a relatively high price will reinforce promotion that emphasizes quality. However, combining a recognizably low price with a promotional emphasis on quality could result in an incongruous pairing that would adversely affect its credibility with the consumer. This is because the low price might be interpreted as the correct price for an inferior product. Pricing can also be a determinant in the choice of middlemen, because if the firm requires a wholesaler to take title, stock, promotion, and delivery of the merchandise, then it must give the wholesaler a much larger trade discount than would be demanded by a broker, whose services are much more limited.

These examples illustrate one of the reasons for complexity of price setting: the interaction of pricing with the other elements of the marketing mix. In addition, two other sets of forces influence this variable: ① interaction between marketing and the other functional areas of the firm and ② environmental forces.

Interaction between marketing and the other functional areas

To illustrate this point, look at the following:

(1) Finance people want prices that are both profitable and conducive to a steady cash flow.

(2) Production supervisors want prices that create large sales volumes, which permit long production runs.

(3) Legal departments worry about possible antitrust violations when different prices are set according to the type of customer.

(4) Tax people are concerned with the effects of prices on tax loads.

(5) Domestic sales managers want export prices to be high enough to avoid having to compete with company products that are purchased for export and then diverted to the domestic market (one aspect of parallel importing).

The marketer must address all of these concerns and as well as consider the impact of the legal and other environmental forces that we have examined.

International standardization

Companies that pursue a policy of unifying corporate pricing procedures worldwide know that pricing faces the same forces that work against international standardization of the other marketing mix components. Pricing for overseas markets is more complex though because management must be concerned with two kinds of pricing: ① foreign national pricing, which is domestic pricing in another country, and ② international pricing for exports.

Foreign national pricing

Many foreign governments, in their fight against inflation, have instituted price controls. The range of the products affected by these price controls varies immensely from country to country. Some governments attempt to control prices on almost everything, while others are more concerned with essential goods. Unfortunately, no agreement exists on what is essential, so in one market the prices of gasoline, food products, tires, and even wearing apparel may be controlled, while in another market, only the prices of staple foods may be fixed. In nations with laws on unfair competition, minimum instead of maximum sales prices may be controlled. German law is so comprehensive that under certain conditions, even premiums and cents-off coupons may be prohibited because they are thought to violate minimum price requirements. The international marketer must therefore be watchful of a recent tendency of many nations, especially European Union members, to open up their markets to price competition by weakening and even abolishing retail price maintenance laws.

Prices can also vary because of appreciable cost differentials on opposite sides of a border. One government may levy higher import duties on imported raw materials or may subsidize public utilities, while another may not. Furthermore, differences in labor legislation will cause labor costs to vary. Competition among local suppliers may be intense in one market, permitting the affiliate to buy inputs at better prices than those paid by an affiliate in another market, which must purchase raw materials from a single supplier, possibly a government monopoly.

Competition on the selling side is also diverse. Frequently, an affiliate in one market will face heavy local competition and be severely limited in the price it can charge, while in a neighboring market, a lack of competitors will allow another affiliate to charge a much higher price. As regional economic groupings reduce trade barriers among members, such opportunities are becoming fewer because firms must meet regional as well as local competition.

One thing European firms cannot do, is agree to fix prices in an effort to limit competition. The EU Commission imposed the largest fines ever under EU competition law, $116.7 million, on 27 European steel companies for price fixing and collaboration. The record fine on a single company was $93 million on Tetra Pak, a Swedish packaging firm, in 1991.

Because a firm, for a number of reasons, does not introduce a new product simultaneously in all markets, the same product will not be in the same stage of the product life cycle everywhere. In markets where it is in the introductory stage, there is an opportunity to charge a high "skimming" price or a low "penetration" price, depending on such factors as market objectives, patent protection, price elasticity of demand, and competition. As the product reaches maturity or the decline stage, the price may be lowered, if doing so permits a satisfactory return. Because life cycles vary among markets, prices will also be different.

International pricing

International pricing involves the setting of prices for goods produced in one country and sold in another. The pricing of exports to unrelated customers falls in this category and will be treated further in the chapter on exporting. A special kind of exporting, intra-corporate sales, is exceedingly common among worldwide companies as they attempt to rationalize production by requiring subsidiaries to specialize in the manufacturing of some products while importing others. Their imports may consist of components that are assembled into the end product, such as engines made in one country that are mounted in car bodies built in another, or they may be finished products imported to complement the product mix of an affiliate. No matter what the end use is, problems exist in setting an intra-corporate price, or transfer price.

Because it is possible for the firm as a whole to gain while both the buying and selling subsidiaries "lose" (receive prices that are lower than would be obtained through an outside transaction), the tendency is for transfer prices to be set at headquarters. The reason for this apparent anomaly is that the company obtains a profit from both the seller and the buyer.

The selling affiliate would like to charge the other subsidiaries the same price it charges all customers, but when combined with transportation costs and import duties, charging such a price may make it impossible for the importing subsidiary to compete in its market. If headquarters dictates that a lower-than-market transfer price be charged, the seller will be unhappy because its profit-and-loss statement suffers. This can be a very real headache to personnel whose promotion bonuses depend on the bottom line.

Both foreign governments and the Chinese government are interested in profits, thus part transfer prices play into the realization of both, because the influence of profits on the amount of taxes paid. American and foreign tax agents have become aware that because of differences in tax structures, a firm can obtain meaningful profits by ordering a subsidiary in a country with high corporate taxes to sell at cost to a subsidiary in a country where corporate taxes are lower. The profit is earned where less income tax is paid, and the company gains.

A recent study by professors at Florida International University found that false invoice prices on American imports, written to avoid U. S. income taxes, could have cost America $28.7 billion in lost tax revenues. Fax machines from Japan billed at $25,000 each, French cordless phones at $4,233 each, and Spanish sand at $1,944 per ton are all examples. Although the data did not identify the firms involved, the researchers found that the largest losses, $4 billion, involved imports from Japan.

The manipulation of transfer prices done for the purpose of reducing income taxes and import duties, or the avoidance of exchange controls, has caused many governments to insist on arm's-length prices; the prices-charged to unrelated customers. Under Section 482 of the Internal Revenue Code, U. S. tax authorities are empowered to reconstruct an intra-corporate transfer price and tax the calculated profits whenever there is reason to suspect that low prices were set for tax evasion.

U. S. tax officials are beginning to crack down on what they claim is rampant cross-border tax fraud by U. S. and Mexican companies. A nine-month study by an IRS team found that tax fraud is estimated to cost the U. S. government hundreds of millions of dollars annually. In one instance, they examined 1,174 tax returns filed by Mexican-controlled firms operating on the American side of the border and found that 70 percent claimed a loss in 2008. Overall, the companies showed a combined rate of return on their assets of negative 17 percent. "You can't stay in business very long losing 17 percent of your assets every year." said the IRS official in charge of the investigation.

Pricing strategy options

All of the above illustrate that multinationals should make their own pricing strategies when they develop foreign markets following pricing strategies according to the company's resources and market conditions.

1. Skim pricing and penetration pricing

Skim pricing means that companies hope to take back their investments with a higher price based on the unique position of their new products in the markets. The typical example of this is Microsoft which used a higher price when it introduced its Windows software. It monopolized the market with the originality of the product and created the new industrial standard, and because it was able to sell its products at a higher price (far exceed the cost) in the global market, it received huge revenues.

Skim pricing fits segment markets in which the elastic demand is small and consumers prefer to pay the higher price to get the products. If the company is the only supplier of these products, it can use this pricing strategy to maximize its profits. However, the higher price and huge profits will attract more companies to invest in the industry, therefore the company may have to consider reducing its prices if competitors enter the industry.

Opposite to skim pricing is penetration pricing which means that companies introduce their products at lower prices in order to get more market shares. It is the most important pricing strategy to use when companies first enter new markets. This is because they have to ingratiate the consumers with lower prices, introduce their products quickly, and establish their brand name in widespread markets in a short time. In general, this is a more realistic pricing strategy for most companies unless they have the unique products.

2. Psychological pricing strategy

Psychological pricing strategy means companies set their prices based on the psychology of the consumers. The strategy includes the following features listed below.

1) Reputation pricing

Reputation pricing is when companies set their product prices higher than congener products, and use psychology to get consumers to admire the famous brands in order to occupy the markets and generate more profits. For example, the price of a Rolex, the most famous watch brand in the world, which is generally over 1 million RMB, is preferred by rich men, and the price of a Land Rover (very famous car brand) may be several million RMB and can attract more people because these products enjoy sky-high reputations throughout the world. The purpose of consumers buying these products is often to flaunt their fortune and satisfy a psychological demand.

Under these circumstances, companies can make large sums of money by using the psychology of the consumers. Of course, the precondition for companies to use this pricing strategy is that they establish the product reputation first. This is why many companies, including Chinese companies, begin to pay more attention to establishing a strong brand image.

2) Mantissa pricing and integer pricing

In many situations, consumers like to accept mantissa pricing, because it generates a feeling that they purchased a quality product cheaply. In western markets, the use of the number "9" in pricing products is very popular. Sometimes you even see several "9's" in a row. The purpose of using the "9" is to hint to the consumer that the price is lower than if the product had been priced with other numbers.

Opposite to mantissa pricing is when some product prices are done with an integer. This strategy is best suited for famous brand products because consumers assess and distinguish the quality based on price. Famous stores and products may especially use this strategy in order to attract consumers and expand their sales. As a matter of fact, in most situations, the consumers do not actually understand the function of the products, thus the use of integer pricing can satisfy their vanity.

3) Custom pricing

Custom pricing is when the price is difficult to change for some products because it has become a custom accepted concept in the consumer's mind. If the companies drop the price, then the consumers may suspect the product quality has decreased, and if the companies raise the price, then the consumers may find issue with the dealers. For example, if the price of an everyday food item rises, then the public will complain, and the government may act in order to maintain social stability. In contrast, if the price of the same food item drops, then the public may suspect its quality. Therefore, companies have to play up to the psychology of the consumer. This is especially true when a company is using international marketing, because various countries' consumers are different and the consumption psychology is complex.

Discounting pricing strategy

Sometimes, in order to encourage customers to pay off payment for goods, buy larger amounts of products, or to increase off season sales, companies may use the discounting pricing strategy. They will provide some favors to the consumers using the following strategies:

1. Cash discount

Cash discount is when companies offer a price discount for customers who pay off the payment of goods in time. For example, "2/10, net 30" indicates that within a payment deadline of 30 days, the companies will give a 2% price discount to customers who pay off their debt in 10 days. In many industries, this method has become an industry custom used to speed up capital turnover and reduce financial expenditures and bad debts.

2. Quantity discount

Quantity discount is when companies give a price discount to quantity buying customers, encouraging them to buy more, because quantity buying can help reduce the production costs and marketing expenditures for the companies.

3. Function discount

Function discount is also a named trade discount. It is the additional price discount that manufactures offer to their middleman, so that the middleman can get the lower price rather than the listed price published by the manufacturers.

4. Season discount

If the customers buy products during the off season, they may also get a price discount. Companies generally use this tactic in order to maintain sales stability.

5. Introduction subsidy

Sometimes manufacturers offer a subsidy to the dealers in order to expand sales. For example, the manufacturers may be in charge of advertising expenditures if dealers can publish the product advertising or construct showcases for products, at the same time, manufacturers often offer certain price in favor of dealers.

Product mix pricing strategy

The product mix pricing strategy is when companies make adjustments to the prices of relative products systematically in order to achieve profit maximize for the product mix based on the relationship of various products. The major strategies of this include:

1. Product line pricing

Product line pricing is when companies change various prices in the same product line according to the role of various products in markets in hopes of achieving total revenue maximization. For example, the function of some products is to solicit consumers, therefore the price is lower, while other products are profit sources and therefore the price is higher. For instance, Panasonic designed five types of color stereo videos with various functions; the price of the simplest type is only $10 while the most complex is $1000.

2. Complement goods pricing

Some products need to integrate other products when they are used. Cameras and film, recorders and tape, contact lens and disinfectant are all examples in which the companies lower prices for the major products (higher value products) while increasing the prices for the auxiliary products (lower value products), thus improving the total sales and profits.

3. Whole set favorable pricing

For some whole set products and service products, companies may lower prices to encourage consumers to buy, expand the sales, and speed up capital turnover. For international giant companies, they often use this pricing strategy in order to develop emerging markets.

Summary

1. Appreciate that price is the value of what consumers exchange in return for products. It may take the form of monetary exchange, bartered services, or other goods. The price must be set so that both the consumer and the marketer "profit" by the exchange, if only at the perceptual level. Consumers worldwide consider price a major factor in purchasing decisions, whether they are buying vegetables at the local store, diamond rings, office furniture, or factory machinery. Since the price of products is set by the marketer, the key to controlling the pricing process is by understanding what the targeted consumer perceives to be the value of the goods.

2. Understand elasticity demand: when price is changed by a percentage, demand is changed by a greater percentage. Normally, demand will drop dramatically as price increases and rise sharply as price decreases. However, consumers sometimes interpret price as a quality indicator, in which case demand may actually rise as prices

increase with products such as wine and housing, or drop with price decreases, with products such as convenience foods and clothing, without any pressure from the supply area.

3. Discuss the various ways to engage in pricing: ① cost-oriented pricing; ② demand-oriented pricing; and ③ competitive-oriented pricing.

4. Recognize breakeven points in which the volume sales can be used to secure profits by figuring the level of unit sales at which revenue (money coming in) equals total costs (money going out). This is the breakeven point. Beyond this point, additional sales represent profit; below this point, all sales will incur a loss. The breakeven point will vary for different products. Projected sales volumes and variations on competitor prices or sales forecast can be experimented with to arrive to the most favorable price. Like average return, this method assumes that whatever quantity is produced will be sold, and that variable costs will remain stable during the production period.

5. Appreciate the significance of price standardization for international companies. Companies that pursue a policy of unifying corporate pricing procedures worldwide know that pricing is acted on by the same forces that work against international standardization of other marketing mix components. Pricing for overseas markets is more complex because management must be concerned with two kinds of pricing: ① foreign national pricing, which is domestic pricing in another country, and ② international pricing for exports.

6. Appreciate the skimming pricing strategy. Skim pricing is when companies hope to earn back their investments with a higher price based on the unique position of their new products in the markets. A good example of this is Microsoft which earned a higher price when it introduced its Windows software, because it monopolized the market with the originality of the product and created a new industrial standard. It was able to sell products at a high price (far exceed the cost) in global market and thus received large revenues.

7. Recognize the importance of the interaction between marketing and other functional areas: ① finance people want prices that are both profitable and conducive to a steady cash flow; ② production supervisors want prices that create large sales volumes, which permit long production runs; ③ legal departments worry about possible antitrust violations when different prices are set according to the type of customer; ④ tax people are concerned with the effects of prices on tax loads; ⑤ domestic sales managers want export prices to be high enough to avoid having to compete with company products that are purchased for export and then diverted to the domestic market (one aspect of parallel importing). The marketer must address all of these concerns and also consider the impact of legal and other environmental forces that we examined.

8. Understand the means of international pricing. International pricing involves the setting of prices for goods produced in one country and sold in another. The pricing of exports to unrelated customers falls in this category and will be treated separately in the chapter on exporting. A special kind of exporting, intra-corporate sales, is exceedingly common among worldwide companies as they attempt to rationalize production by requiring subsidiaries to specialize in the manufacture of some products while importing others.

Questions

1. Explain the reasons why it is important that international managers create their pricing strategies.

2. Why do people feel it is more difficult for marketers to create a pricing strategy for an international company?

3. Why do people think it is very difficult for international managers to standardize their pricing strategies in various markets?

4. What kind of pricing strategies can you choose when you have to face intense competition in foreign markets?

5. Assume you are the manager of a foreign company which manufactures home appliances, can you introduce your products using the skimming strategy in the Chinese market? Explain.

6. What are some advantages and disadvantages for the average return and breakeven pricing methods?

7. Are legal forces the only type of obstacle to international pricing strategy? If not, name some others.

8. Can you use discount pricing to attract consumers in any country? Why or Why not?

9. How does a multinational use intra-cooperate to improve its business achievement? Explain.

Chapter 12 Distribution Strategy

Concept preview

After reading this chapter, you should be able to

1. Appreciate: why it is important for multinationals to establish their own distribution channels in foreign markets.

2. Understand: how different distribution strategies influence international marketing.

3. Distinguish: the characteristics of different distribution channel models.

4. Comprehend: the methods and standards for international managers to choose their channel members.

5. Describe: how to overcome the various barriers when introduce a product in the foreign market with a foreign dealer.

The distribution network, established by Visionary Vehicle for Chery

Many years ago, Visionary Vehicles, an American automobile company, published a distribution plan to make it the primary sales agent for Chery automobile. It planned to change the automobile market layout of North America with price advantages, the better quality cars, and pioneering retail networks.

On March 10th, 2005, Visionary Vehicles appointed Pierre Gagnon, the former CEO of Mitsubishi Motors's North American branch office, to be CEO and sales department chief inspector of Chery automobiles in the North American branch office. He was also appointed to be in charge of managing the distribution business of all of Chery automobile throughout America.

Bricklin, the CEO and founder of Visionary Vehicles, published a distribution plan to sell Chery automobile, disclosing that the company would get 15% revenue.

Because the percentage was 5% higher than the industry average, Bricklin noted that, "Any distributer who has any foresight will not lose an opportunity to make an alliance with China." This decision not only changed the layout of the North-American automobile market, but it also created a large market for Chery and larger profits for Visionary Vehicle. It has been since called the "successful cooperation typical between Chinese and American companies". Since then, one of the most important questions for Chinese companies to evaluate is how to use foreign channel resources to develop overseas markets. The following will demonstrate the specific operational process of this case.

1. The former CEO of Mitsubishi Motor was in charge of sales in the U. S. for Chery automobile

Pierre Gagnon was in charge of setting up distribution headquarters in southern California for Visionary Vehicles. "The cooperation between Chery and Visionary is continuing step by step according to our plan", stated Karn, the vice general manger of Chery auto sales company. From that time on, the distribution plan to sell Chery automobiles began to be implemented.

"Our goal is to radically change the retail style for selling cars and trucks in the American market and re-price luxury cars. Pierre was a very important asset in this process", Bricklin said. Pierre Gagnon had over 20 years' experience in the automobile industry and was considered "the optimal candidate for this position. He will help bring about a new series of luxury cars with an unprecedented auto fair model", Brincklin said.

Before joining Visionary Vehicles, Gagnon was CEO of the North American branch office of Mitsubishi. In September 2003, he was forced to resign because of a failure to introduce certain selling tactics such as, "zero dawn payment, zero interest and pay back in one year" for Mitsubishi. However after his resignation, the sales of Mitsubishi declined, and in February 2005, the sales were down 39.4% compared with the same term in 2004.

"I am looking for the future of automobile industry and Visionary is positioned the top of auto industry wave. It possesses the obvious advantages in the fields of pricing, product and quality, and my mission is to make consumers and dealers maximize benefits. Brincklin's foresight, plus the determination and efficiency of Chery can make this goal possible", said Pierre Gagnon.

Pierre reported to Brincklin and the board of directors directly. He would be in charge of setting up and implementing the distribution net for Chery automobiles. "Visionary will change the North American auto market layout with the Chinese price advantage, better quality cars, and pioneering retail networks", stated Brincklin excitingly.

2. The plan for a "founder group"

The price of the cars exported to America by Chery would be 30% lower compared to European cars. Brincklin indicated that the dealers would get enough cash flow because Chery provided over 15% revenue of the total sales to them and over 250 dealers of Visionary would get the exclusive selling right in various areas for selling Chery autos. Furthermore, he believed that every dealer would be able to sell about 4,000 cars every year.

At the same time however, all of the dealers of Visionary would have to invest $10 million to 15 million in order to get exclusive selling rights to sell Chery cars in the special areas, a fixed proportional equity of Visionary, and the right to set up car exhibitions and sales halls and there is a half mile test drive lane in car exhibition hall.

Brincklin invited the 25 most successful car dealers in America to join the "founder group" of Visionary. The "founder group" would decide the brand name, motorcycle types, engine types and price for Chery autos. They would also be involved in choosing the import time for 10 ~ 15 motorcycle types in future, the decisions on selling procedure for Chery in America, the improvement decisions of the external and internal designs for exhibition halls, and finally they would help recommend 225 other dealers.

In summary of all that it was doing, Brincklin said, "As the first auto company established in twenty-first century America, we are creating a new distribution network and selling system which puts consumers first. Dealers will take part in decisions about the operations of Chery and the Visionary exhibition. It is pioneering work for car distribution."

3. The visionary car exhibition hall

Brincklin published a construction plan for building the retail stores of Visionary Auto Company. The retail stores were designed by Swanke Hayden, a construction designing institute, which designed the Trump Tower in New York, the headquarter office building of IBM, and the Beijing Olympic Hotel. In discussing the exhibition hall Brincklin said that "The Visionary car exhibition hall will establish a new industry frame of reference for North American auto selling. The Visionary exhibition will devote itself to eliminating high pressure selling means when consumers buy cars, therefore allowing for a happier car purchasing process."

Paul Robert, the general market inspector, said, "The Visionary auto exhibition hall will become a very important part of our brand because we are giving our consumers a more pleasant experience when selling our luxury cars."

Rande Dawes, the CEO of the enterprise development and strategy center of the company, said, "Customer retention is decided by consumer demand and quality of selling service. We predict that our customer retention is currently over 40%, a number that traditional."

Brincklin stated that the traditional auto retailers would find out where they ranked compared to their dealers when facing the top-ranking customer service and auto exhibition hall created by Visionary.

Visionary Vehicles and Chery planned to sell over 2 million cars in the U. S. market. One million cars would be produced in Wuhu, Anhui Province of China, and the other 1 million cars would be produced by the joint venture established by both companies.

In 2005, the two companies signed the contract and Visionary got the explosive selling right in North America. In 2006, Visionary introduced 5 types of cars from Chery and in 2007 began to sell them. At the same time, the two companies established a joint venture in America, with Chery taking 60% of the equity.

Visionary invested $200 million to promote the cars produced by Chery in the American market. A New York Investment Company was in charge of financing the job, and if they could reach the sales target—250, 000 cars, then the total sales would be around $2 billion.

Over twenty years ago, Chery was just a small, little known Chinese company, based on the Chinese car market environment. Since then it has quickly become one of the most famous world auto manufacturers. Of course, the most important thing for Chery to achieve is a great business performance that is devoted to both domestic and international markets. Therefore, some of the most important questions for managers to study are how to use external forces to develop markets, particularly for foreign markets. This case provided some general background and will inform further discussion on promotional strategies for developing foreign markets.

While the development of distribution strategies is difficult in a company's home country, it is even more so internationally, where marketing managers must concern themselves with: ① how to get products to foreign markets (exporting) and ② how to distribute those products within each market (foreign distribution). The following section will examine foreign distribution only.

A distribution channel is a route that the product takes when moving from producer to customer. Channels may be simple with few intermediaries or, they may be composed of complex networks with numerous layers of middlemen. Marketers must contend with their domestic marketer distribution to get supplies, as well as with international distribution networks to get their product or service to the foreign market. Once this is done, local distribution inside the target market will have to be considered. In summary, the greater control a marketer has over the distribution channels, the greater the likelihood of success. The amount of control is determined by the factors listed in the subsequent section.

12.1 The factors influencing distribution channels

Cost

Initially, there is a cost to set up the channel, which involves the management labor to locate and negotiate distribution deals. This process can be as lengthy and expensive as finding the consumers for the product. Secondly, maintenance costs on the channel include the cost of internal sales staff, middlemen, and promotional efforts. Finally, other costs to be considered are those associated with transportation, storage, and administration. All costs determined at this level will eventually be passed along to the consumer; therefore, marketers seek to reduce these expenditures whenever possible.

Capital depth

The choice and control of a channel will depend greatly on a marketer's ability to capitalize the process. Some parts of distribution chain may pay for the product as it moves through the channel, in which case the marketer must finance the production. This is true, for instance, of an import distributor that buys a product from a marketer/exporter for eventual resale to local retailers, who have bought it outright for sale to consumers. Each member of the chain receives payment as the channel lengthens and each has very short-term exposure. At other terms, the distribution chain can be lengthy, but no single member (including the producer) receives payment until after the sale to the end-user. This is the case when agents are utilized who only represent (rather than purchase) the products for resale. Even if the agent has better connections than the import distributor and proves to be as better marketing choice, a marketer with little capital may not be able to wait for the extended payment process.

Product line

The type of product under consideration will, of course, greatly influence the method of distribution. Broad product lines attract the distributors, whereas single items are more in the territory of specialist agents. Perishables will, by necessity, require short distribution chains and quick handling. Some consumer products, such as personal care goods, may need more personal selling, while high-tech gear may move from producer to end-user directly, with only a shipper as an intermediary. The per-unit size and price will also have an impact on the availability and choice of members of the chain.

Control requirement

Total control of the distribution channels may not always be necessary, desirable, or even attainable. Each marketer must determine how much control is needed and how much they will accept. With direct sales, a company controls promotion, quality, and price. However, the expense of doing so may be large if it entails the use of separate retail outlets (as is the case with designer clothing stores as opposed to department store retailing). Other times, a company may find that its product requires little care once it has reached its final form. The distributors will therefore be willing to buy the product "up front", rather than after the sale to the end-user (as is the case with companies producing recorded music for worldwide distribution).

Range

The success of product in the marketplace will depend greatly on the size of the area over which it's distributed, also known as its range. Not all products require the same amount of range. Legal services, for instance, may only need to be marketed in urban areas, while a commodity like eggs will need distribution over a much larger area. When seeking an external distributor, agent, or broker, the following should be considered:

(1) Current office location (in order to show the product's focal point).

(2) Previous sales by geographic locale (demonstrates the effect of the effort).

(3) Other accounts (helps determine familiarity with the product type).

Compatibility

Regardless of how stringent a contract is, distribution will not be successful if the producer and the members of the chain do not work together in an efficient manner. Incompatibility may spring from different goals, business practices, or cultures. All of these must be made consistent before any attempt at distribution is made. In the case of goals and practice, a marketer must have them clearly delineated before expecting to find compatible chain members.

Large companies produce guidelines for external members of the distributions chain and make adherence a contractual matter. Smaller companies (with less marketplace power) may not be able to get chain member to sign off on guidelines, but a clear statement of requirements can only help the situation. Other companies (whose products require follow-up service) may choose to work within the confines of "authorized dealerships" to maintain standards. Cultural compatibility can never be the subject of contract or authorization; it must be a matter of tolerance among those that deal most closely with the end-user down to the producer level. Marketers that work for companies that place executives at the top of the organizational pyramid may find this difficult to swallow initially, but such cultural considerations are at the heart of international (maybe more aptly named "intercultural") business.

12. 2 Functions and types of distribution channels

Distribution density

Distribution density refers to the number of sales outlets required to provide adequate range for a product. Density requirements are a direct function of the end-user's purchasing habits. Changes in density needs will ripple through to change other components of the distribution chain. The key to proper density is consumer habit research. A fine example of density and its effect on distribution can be found in the computer industry.

For many years consumers went to computer sales outlets scattered around the globe to look at, compare, and test personal computers prior to purchase. They shopped for computers much in the same way that they shopped for stereo equipment or televisions. Not surprisingly, outlets for these two types of electronic computer goods were also some of the early distributors of computer hardware. Over time, however, consumers became more skilled at computer usage and more knowledgeable about the technology, to the point where they no longer required the assistance of sales personnel or hands-on comparison shopping.

Informed consumers

Changes in consumer skills have altered their buying habits. The latest growth in PC sales is the internet direct sales with companies like Gateway and Dell, which serve customers from remote low-cost locations. Consumers can now review hardware options on-line, order customer-built hardware, and have it shipped directly to their home or office within a matter of days. No retail outlet, no salespeople, no local warehousing—a shrinking distribution chain. For Gateway, distribution density is an assembly plant in South Dakota and cyberspace. (In an extreme example of this new process, crew members of the Mir Spacecraft ordered computer from Gateway via radio, although the delivery details were not immediately made clear.)

While some distribution chains contract, others expand, as in the case with Starbucks Coffee. This one-time coffee roasting company has now taken their "coffee bar" and retailing concepts worldwide, with more than four hundred outlets on three continents. Because the service (coffee brewing) that accompanies the goods (coffee) must be delivered daily and face-to-face, Starbucks must continually open new outlets to reach new customers. Like the fast-food operations that have preceded it, Starbucks must increase its density to acquire market share, with little chance of ever seeing a trend reversal. While some wholesale/retail operators may look to a future of catalog or on-line direct distribution, hospitality operators face ever-expanding density.

Each marketer need consider the density requirements of new markets and the expansion or contraction necessary to thrive there. Technical developments, distributor channel up-grades and competitive moves can all force a company's hand when reviewing the density of the distribution. In general, market share can often be won or lost based entirely on creating the proper distribution density, as product quality and price take a secondary role to access.

Distribution length

Distribution length refers to the number of intermediaries needed to move a product through the marketplace. The expanding density mentioned above does not imply length, as density may utilize very few intermediaries (as is true in the Starbucks). A company may choose to shorten the length of their distribution by setting up a vertical marketing system in which all parts of the chain come under direct control of the producer. There are three types of distribution channel.

(1) Cooperation—the company owns all areas of distribution channel, including shipping and retail outlets.

(2) Contractual—distribution channel members are under long-term contract to the producer and must conform to exacting standards set by that producer.

(3) Administrative—the producer, through dominance in its market segment, overseas all areas of the distribution channel. Members willingly participate, due to the amount of business generated by the producer. Some international companies, such as McDonald's, have taken this a step farther by controlling all areas of their business, including the supply lines, an approach known as vertical integration.

Two companies of one system

Another way to control the length of the distribution chain is through horizontal marketing, wherein two or more companies combine their marketing efforts and their distribution to the benefit of all participants. This is similar to co-branding, but the partnership is also deepened to sharing costs and efficiencies of distribution. A prime example of this can be found in the designer eyewear industry. Clothing designer Giorgio Armani sells a line of prescription eyeglass frame through optometrists and sunglasses through his own retail outlets. Italian frame designer combining the two distribution networks has both expanded market share and reduced promotional cost. The "name" brands, in their turn, have opened market segments formerly closed to them before their marketing went "horizontal".

The additional intermediaries or "lengthening" of the chain can result in a loss of control, which may be damning to some products. It does, however, save the costs of purchasing shipping fleets, retail outlets, and local warehouses, as well as the training of a retail-level sales force. As a general rule, companies whose products require tight quality control have short distribution channels while those with products that are less sensitive can afford (but may not use) longer distribution chains.

Note: During the early stages of establishing a marketing share, the marketer may not be able to control as much of their distribution as they would prefer. Local government edicts may even prevent them from having a hand in any part of the distribution. Still, marketers should always plan their distribution channels and seek any opportunity to make them more efficient.

Logistics

Physical distribution refers to the physical requirements necessary to move a product from producer to end-user. Logistics include export processing, freight forwarding, import processing, warehousing, fulfillment, and just-in-time delivery. On a global scale, logistics can become the most complex issue of market planning. Although logistics are most commonly associated with the movement of goods, services also face similar problems. Logistics can command more than 33 percent of revenues and generally exist outside of a company's "core business". It is not unusual for a company to turn over the problems (and much of the expense) of logistics to external specialists. Efficient logistics is very often one of the most important determining factors.

12.3 Interdependence of distribution decisions

When making decisions about distribution, care must be taken to analyze the interdependence with other marketing mix variables. For example, if the product requires considerable after-sales service, the firm will want to sell through dealers that have facilities, personnel, and capital to purchase equipment and spare parts and to train the service people. This will necessitate using a merchant wholesaler, which will demand a larger trade discount than would an agent because an agent does not perform these functions. Channel decisions are critical because they are long-term decisions; once established, they are far more difficult to change than those made for price, product, and promotion.

International standardization

Although management would prefer to standardize distribution patterns internationally, there are two fundamental constraints in doing so: ① variation in the availability of channel members among the firm's markets and ② inconsistency of the influence of environmental forces. Because of these constraints, international managers have found it best to establish a basic but flexible overall policy. The subsidiaries then implement this policy and design channel strategies to meet local conditions.

Availability of channel members

As a starting point in their channel design, local managers can use the successful distribution system from their domestic operations. Headquarters' support for a policy of employing the same channels worldwide will be especially strong when the entire marketing mix has been built around a particular channel type, such as direct sales force or franchised operators. Avon, Encyclopedia Britannica, and McDonald's are all examples of firms that consider their distribution systems inviolate, so locally there is little latitude in planning channel strategies. However, companies utilizing more common types of middlemen are usually more inclined to grant the local organization greater freedom in channel member selection.

Although a general rule for any firm entering a foreign market is to adapt to available channels rather than create new ones, a number of companies have successfully avoided the traditional channels because of their appalling inefficiencies.

Experienced marketers know they cannot get their products to the consumer by the same retail channel in every country, even in Europe, the differences are substantial. Thus, what is the best way to sell toys in France? A sure outlet is the hypermarket, which sells 36 percent of all toys purchased in France. In Germany, however, the hypermarket accounts for only 15 percent of toy sales. The most important kind of outlet for toys in Germany is independent retailers, which are organized into buying groups. Generally, it is very important for multinationals to choose their distributors and distribution types when they want to develop foreign markets. They have to study the channel options and problems before they make any decisions.

12.4 Channel options and problems

When the distribution system is open to foreign players, there are a variety of methods for accessing. The greatest challenge in trying to distribute in a new market is not always the location of the proper intermediaries but gaining their interest in getting new products to line. Competitors may dissuade local channel members from dealing with a foreign producer because those members may be inconvenient of the foreign producer's viability.

The followings are some common problems that marketers may encounter as well as some options to consider when they want to establish a new position in foreign markets.

Member blockage

When a market has a limited number of distribution choices, the members of that chain can exert a monopolistic force over what enters and succeeds. Marketers may find themselves confronted with one of these "middleman markets" where the consumer is not given choices until the intermediaries have decided "go or no go" on products. This position of power may be the result of natural market dominance, legal edict, or cultural traditions of strong linkage among local producers and intermediaries. Many of the complaints about market entry in Japan stem from this form of distributor blockage.

Competitor's blockage

A more common form of blockage is when a powerful competitor persuades the local distribution network to spurn advances of foreign producers, and as a result, local chain members become threatened with financial ruin if they assist the foreign marketer. Sometimes this type of coercion comes directly from the competitor or through political connections. Such "lucked" markets exist all over the world. Even Microsoft faces continual scrutiny from the U. S. government for its distribution tactics against domestic and foreign competition. Under these circumstances, you can take the following actions to avoid or at least reduce your distribution risks.

1. Legal action

It may be possible to seek legal recourse if distribution is blocked, but only in countries that are signatories to international commercial treaties. This action may be conducted in local courts or in international commercial courts of the World Trade Organization. Besides the enormous expense involved, adverse publicity can result from trying to "sue" your way into a market. Local competitors and distributors are more likely to win local sympathy, so that even if the courts favor the marketer, consumers may reject the product for emotional reasons. Additionally, few countries view foreign producers as something other than the enemy, and not the competitor, and they have little shame about keeping their markets closed and their distribution locked.

2. Diplomatic action

This is the preferred way of attempting to pry open a locked market. It can only function if the marketer and target market have diplomatic relations and there is an embassy or consulate with a commercial component to serve the marketer. Most of the negotiations are conducted out of public view; thus, the emotional levels are kept low. Much of the time when foreign marketers use this method they find that their motives have been greatly misunderstood. Diplomatic action allows all parties involved to clear the air. It can also lay the groundwork for other ventures in the new market.

3. Political action

A producer may find it necessary to remind the target market of the interdependence of the global economy. By using the political structure of their home market, a producer can limit the target's exporting ability, either in a directly related sector or in another segment entirely. United States manufacturers of all sizes regularly lobby their government to restrict products from markets where these same manufacturers experience distributor or competitor blockage. Similarly, all of the trading blocs that were mentioned earlier in the text were partially devised to ensure this type of "fair" trade.

4. Financial action

Blockage is always a matter of money as some party or other is worried about losing customers. Marketers sometimes "buy" their way into a market by underwriting any potential losses a distributor might sustain, or by joint venturing with a potential competitor. In extreme cases, a company may simply buy out the local market competition completely, taking over their facilities and distribution channels.

Lack of infrastructure

Willing distributors, minimal competition, and eager consumers may not be enough to overcome the lack of infrastructure needed to bring specialized goods or services (those requiring high-tech delivery methods) to market. Refrigerated truck fleets, temperature-controlled warehouses, fiber-optic cables, air or eclectic power may be in insufficient quantity, quality, or completely absent in the target market. And sometimes it is important to invest in infrastructure in target markets, which, in practice, is always a combination of public and private efforts.

Marketers may find that their product or project is highly desired but that physical access to consumers is limited. Part of the marketing plan must include an international lobbying effort to secure the proper infrastructure funding. International aid groups and development banks are always the first to approach. Another possibility is to offer a Build-Operate-Transfer plan wherein the marketers finance the infrastructure development necessary for distribution themselves, with an understanding that local governments will buy back the project at a later date while retaining the marketer's right to distribute. Such BOT (build-operate-transfer) projects are generally set up by large global companies. Smaller companies may offer their expertise on behalf of target market governments in order to secure proper funding. Telecommunications gear providers often use this approach when dealing with emerging markets. Setting up proper first-stage financing and installation of infrastructure has allowed Australia's Telstra to secure long-term relationships with many of Southeast Asia's markets and government ministries.

Channel resistance

New products may intimidate local channel members, who may be reluctant to take a chance on an unproven product. Even when the product has shown considerable success elsewhere, local intermediaries may resist adding it to their distribution chain. Marketers can use the following countermeasures to overcome these problems.

1. Co-distribution

A marketer may attempt to distribute its products along with those of anther foreign marketer already operating successfully in the target markets. Kikkoman, the famous soy sauce manufacturer, used this option when its products met resistance during the early 1990s in Mexico. By contracting with successful U. S. food marketer Del Monte, Kikkoman used its existing channels in Mexico, and was therefore able to gain immediate access at a minimal cost.

2. Local labeling

When a company is only interested in marketing its products but not advancing it brand name to the public, it may consider contracting with a local company to place their label on the product prior to distribution. This allows the foreign company immediate access and the local company to link its name to quality goods or service. Many big name Japanese electronics have allowed well-established local brands to re-label their products in order to overcome the resistance of distributors.

3. Local partner

As demonstrated in previous examples, resistance can often be overcome by simply getting involved with the local government. It may take the form of joint-venturing with a local producer or becoming part of the distribution channel. This can be met with varying degrees of another type of resistance to the venture itself in which marketers may find it easier to partner with producers that are not direct competitors or with distributors on the periphery of the main channels.

4. Local buys out

When a marketer buys out a local producer or distributor in order to gain access to distribution, expense is traded for efficiency. The same provisions that apply to local partnering also apply here, with additional advice given to maintain a low profile and keep the local government on your side.

5. Dig new channel

Many times, local distributor resistance can leave foreign marketers no choice but to create their own local channels from scratch. Besides being very expensive, there is a good deal of accompanying risk—but it is usually worth taking. The case of Toys "R" Us is one of the most famous examples of a foreign marketer creating its own highly successful channel in a local market. In the 1990s, after nearly twenty years of institutionalized channel resistance, Japan finally revoked the law that allowed local competitors to give "permission" to companies wishing to open retail stores in excess of five hundred square meters. Toys "R" Us, a proponent of vertical marketing, circumvented the usually thick intermediary layers of Japanese distribution and opened a five thousand square meter retail store in Niigata. As a result, their market share in Niigata in their first year was 50 percent.

12.5 Foreign environmental forces

Environmental differences among markets further increase the difficulty in standardizing distribution channels. Changes caused by cultural forces generally occur over time, but those caused by legal forces can be radical and quick, and can dramatically slow trends down due to cultural demands.

To illustrate, hypermarkets, which are changing distribution patterns in Europe, had a particular impact on France, a nation of small shopkeepers. Originally, there were only 11 hypermarkets in1972. However, the combination of lower prices and one-stop shopping quickly caught on with the French consumer, and 51 hypermarkets were opened in 1973. Manufacturers saw that a quick end to small shopkeepers failed to appreciate their political power. The Royer Law, passed in 1973, gave local urban commissions, often dominated by small merchants, the power to refuse construction permits for supermarkets and hypermarkets. After the law took effect, only 40 percent of the large-store applications were approved.

Although the trend toward more giant stores did not stop, the growth certainly slowed. There were only about 1,000 hypermarkets in 1993 when France's new prime minister announced a freeze on new construction. Both major hypermarket chains immediately complained about the order, even though France's retail sector is saturated and has little room for growth.

Japan's Large Scale Retailers Law, which is very similar to the French law, had also slowed the opening of large retailers. However, because of pressure from Carla Hills, a U.S. trade representative, and the Structural Impediments Initiative (SII) trade talks, the Japanese Ministry of International Trade and Industry suddenly found it could reduce the period that small retailers could block the opening of new stores in their neighborhoods from an incredible 10 years to a maximum of 18 months. This was the breakthrough that foreign retailers needed.

The first large U. S. owned discount store to take advantage of the SII, aimed at prying open new markets for American firms in Japan, was Toys "R" Us. After three years of haggling with Japanese bureaucracy, local vested interests, and heavy, often hostile press coverage, the company opened its first store north of Tokyo. As discussed in Chapter 6, because a revision of Japan's Large Scale Retailer's Law made store opening easier, Toys "R" Us was able to open 16 superstores in only two years.

Another restriction of distribution has been a point of contention in the European Union (EU). Manufacturers have attempted to prevent distributors from selling across national borders, but have been prevented from doing so by the EU Commission invoking antitrust laws. Exclusive distributorships have been permitted, but every time the manufacturer has included a clause prohibiting the distributor from exporting to another EU country, the clause has been stricken from the contract. In effect, a firm that has two factories in the EU with different costs, and thus distinct prices, is practically powerless to prevent products from a lower-cost affiliate competing with its higher-cost products.

Economic differences also make international standardization difficult, although marketers can often adapt to economic changes. In 1960, very little frozen food was sold in France because of consumer's preference for fresh food. However, tight economic conditions forced many housewives to seek employment, and with less time to spend preparing meals, they turned to frozen food. An added attraction of frozen food items was that their prices did not rise as fast as those of fresh foods. The result of this has been that frozen food sales have increased by 10 percent or more a year since 1973.

In Japan, high prices of food also forced women to find jobs because they no longer had time to shop and prepare traditional Japanese foods. They filled their needs by purchasing convenience foods advertised on TV with home delivery, or by going to the more than 50 convenience store chains. The largest of these, 7-Eleven, has over 3,200 licensees, most of whom are former small shopkeepers. Its point-of-sale computer network has eliminated the need for small-scale wholesalers, whose number is already declining all over Japan. Worldwide, marketers are seeing cultural barriers fall as economic conditions force housewives to obtain employment to supplement household income. The premium that outside employers place on their time is leading them to prefer one-stop shopping, labor-saving devices, and convenience foods. The result of all of this has been an upheaval in the way goods are distributed, but American marketers that have U. S. experience as a guide are in a position to make inroads on their foreign competitors, for which this is a new phenomenon.

Can retailing be globalized? Retailers like France's Carrefour, with stores in France, Spain, Brazil, Argentina and the United States, think it can. So do Safeway,

Gucci, Cartier, Benetton, and Toys "R" Us, which have aggressively penetrated markets in Canada, Europe, and Singapore. Kaufhof, the German retailing giant, has 100 shoe stores located in Austria, France, Switzerland, and Germany and is also the leading mail-order shoe retailer in Europe. As Peter Drucker said in 1987, "To maintain a leadership position in any one developed country, a business whether large or small—increasingly has to attain and hold leadership positions in all developed markets worldwide."

Legal requirements

Because the legal requirements for terminating middlemen vary from country to country, the time to think about how to terminate an agreement is before the agreement is even made. Although most countries have no special laws penalizing or precluding the termination of an agreement between the manufacturer and middlemen, some do. In Venezuela, for example, unjustly discharged agents may be entitled to the same severance benefits as discharged employees. In other countries, laws specify high termination compensation related to an agent's longevity, past earnings, goodwill, or "investment" in the product line. Countries with laws making it difficult to terminate agreements include Belgium, Costa Rica, the Netherlands, Norway, and Sweden. In these countries before preparing a contract, management must consult with local attorneys or local correspondents of international law firms in order to begin termination proceedings.

Information sources

Various sources provide information about channels of distribution. The China Department of Commerce, banks, credit agencies, and Chinese chambers of commerce in foreign cities are all good examples. If the names of other companies whose products are being handled by prospective channel members are known, these companies should be contacted. Moreover, the internet can provide large sums of information about distribution channels. These various industry associations are very important information sources for international managers, as well as industry periodicals. Of course, the most accurate information comes from salespeople, channel members, and international marketing research reports.

12.6 Channel selection

Direct or indirect marketing

The first decision that management must make is whether or not to use middlemen, because it frequently has the option of marketing directly to the final user. Sales to original equipment manufacturers (OEMs) and governments are, for the most part, made directly, as are the sales of high-priced industrial products like turbines and locomotives. This is done because the firm is dealing with relatively few customers and transactions but with large dollar value. Even in these cases, export sales may be consummated by local agents if ① management believes this is politically expedient or ② the country's laws demand it.

Other types of industrial products and consumer goods are marketed indirectly. The channel members are selected on the basis of their market coverage, their cost, and their susceptibility to company control. They must also, of course, perform the functions required by management.

Factors influencing channel selection

The factors that influence the selection of market channels may be classified as characteristics of the market, the product, the company, and the middlemen.

1. Market characteristics

Inasmuch as the reason for using channels is to enable the manufacturer to reach its target markets, the obvious place to start in channel selection is at those markets. Which of the available alternatives offer the most adequate coverage? Because of the variance in the target markets, the firm will most likely require multiple channels. Large retailers, governments, and OEMs may be handled by the company sales force or manufacturers' agents, whereas smaller retailers are supplied through wholesalers.

2. Product characteristics

A low-cost product sold in small quantities per transaction generally requires long channels, but if the goods are perishable, short channels are preferable. If the product is highly technical, it may be impossible to obtain knowledgeable middlemen, and the manufacturer will therefore be forced either to sell directly through company-owned distributors or to train independent middlemen. Caterpillar has enjoyed tremendous success in pursuing this second alternative.

3. Company characteristics

A firm that has adequate financial and managerial resources is in a much better position to employ its own sales force or agents than one that is lacking in these areas. A financially weak company must use middlemen that take title to and pay for the goods. If management is inexperienced in selling to certain markets, it must employ middlemen who have that experience.

4. Middlemen's characteristics

Most industrial equipments, large household appliances, and automobiles require considerable after-sales service, and much of the firm's success in marketing depends on it. If the firm is not prepared to provide this service, it cannot use agents. The same is true for warehousing and promotion to the final user. If the firm is unable to perform these functions or perceives a cost advantage in not performing them, then it must select middlemen that will service, warehouse, and promote its products.

It may be that no channel members are available to reach the firm's target markets and perform the desired functions. If there are none, management must decide to ① desist from entering the market, ② select other target markets, or ③ create a new channel. For example, if a frozen-food processor, after studying the available channels, finds that wholesale and retailer cold-storage facilities are nonexistent, then it can either abandon the market or persuade middlemen to acquire the facilities. In a number of overseas markets, firms have purchased the equipment and either rented, leased, or sold it on easy terms to distributors and retailers.

An Italian cheese producer in Brazil not only supplied cold-storage equipment but also established gathering facilities for the dairy farmers. The company sent veterinarians and dairy experts to teach the local dairy farmers how to maintain their herds and increase output. Nestle has similar programs in its developing country markets.

12.7 How to select your teammates

Success may depend on what type of companies a marketer chooses to work with when overcoming the problems of distribution. It is important that the firm choose carefully as the relationship may last a long time and any disharmony may be a big advantage. The following attributes, both financial and personal, should be taken into account when searching out "teammates" for a distribution effort.

1. Connected

Members of the chain should have a wide available network, one that includes not only those resources needed directly for actual distribution but also the political, diplomatic and public relations connections necessary for smooth operation. In international marketing, members of the chain may become political, cultural, and legal intermediaries as well as commercial ones.

2. Financially sound

Distribution is a business, and therefore is likely to face money problems. Just like what was stated above, each member of the chain should be able to prove that they can do what they say they can and that they won't go "belly up" a few months into the contract. Keep in mind that in a new market, your image will be directly linked to the quality of the distribution channel. Particularly, you should notice, in some markets, distributors may be using the prestige of handing a foreign product to leverage financing for other projects. Stay informed about the marketplace to prevent your company's name from being unknowingly used to raise operating funds for channel members.

3. Service oriented

Distribution is a service, and the level of that service must match the marketer's standards. Unless total vertical marketing is achieved, much of the service that consumer sees will be provided by someone out of the producer's direct control. When choosing channel teammates, the marketers should make their standards clear and reasonable for the target market. Distribution, like the product itself, must sometimes be adapted to each specific segment. Rewards for meeting standards, as well as punishment for not meeting them, should be part of the contractual agreement. Even when certification is present, do not assume that your needs and those of the end-user are "understood" by members. Start with quality service and stick with it.

Marketers should take great care to be specific about service levels when distribution channels are limited or when members have been "assigned" to your project by local governments. It may be best to postpone market entry until the status of the channels improves, if assurances on service can not be found. It is not a good idea to try and bring "them up to par" once you have entered the market because by the time you have corrected the distribution problems, the consumer will be elsewhere.

4. Professional

This word means many things in many cultures, but it is only the end-user's culture that matters. Marketing research must reveal what constitutes professional standards in the target market, and that must become the hallmark for local distributors. Accept no less and demand no more. As international marketers, do not apply your market's level of professionalism or attempt to impress it upon the target market, at least initially. You must get used to the local channels and they must get used to you. Unlike service standards, you can afford to wait and you just may learn a thing or two in the meantime.

5. Flexible

Views about contracts vary as greatly as professional standards. However, when a new product enters the marketplace, all members of the channel must be flexible until the "bugs" are worked out. Any intermediaries that show signs of adhering to the "letter of contract" and nothing more should only be used if no alternative is available. So when possible, insert "breaking in periods" with specific starts and ends to let members know that flexibility is not perpetual.

6. Stable

Some members of the chain may not distribute as their core business or may not approach a chosen segment on a regular basis. Marketers can not afford "part-time" channel members. Regular and reliable distribution should be the only kind marketers seek out. International management should note: although stability is most likely found in members that have been in the marketplace for a long period of time, newcomers should not be dismissed out of hand, especially if they embody the right attributes.

7. Eager

Marketers should look for teammates that are excited about distributing products to new markets. Enthusiasm can be contagious; smart marketers know that it filters directly down to consumers. A great deal of consumer resistance can be overcome by the manner and method of the distribution chain. Unlike stability, eagerness is most often found in the newcomer who is not jaded by the vagaries of the marketplace. As movement along the chain approaches those links most directly involved with selling, eagerness will take on greater importance.

Although eagerness is part and parcel of sales, it plays a role in many other aspects of the channel. For instance, many companies choose to ship their products via FedEx just so the deliveries are handled by the global delivery company's enthusiastic drivers.

8. Far-sighted

The international marketplace is full of people who want to make a quick profit. Marketers should learn to avoid them. A new product in a new market may take some time to become profitable. Distribution chain members must be willingly to adhere to the long-term time line of the marketer.

Note: potential members who try to have clauses added to contracts that allow them to easily drop an individual product from an entire line (called "cherry picking"), should instead be encouraged to have shorter initial contracts with an option for extension. Place the burden of performance on the distributor, not the product. If this option is balked at then the firm should look elsewhere.

9. Unbiased

The goal of the distribution channel is to assist producers in getting the product to the consumer—any product, any consumer. Members that demonstrate cultural, ethnic, class, religious or any of the other myriad of negative biases are best left out of the chain. Marketers should interview members of the distribution chain (especially those with customer contact) with as much as time and circumstance allow. This will ensure that they are comfortable with product line and the target consumer base.

Reluctance to deal with "that sort of people" or less-than-subtle remarks about "quality" generally mark potential members as being unable to control their biases; these prejudices will not be lost on consumers.

10. Open

Marketers working on global business discover that each culture sets its own values on openness. At one extreme are the groups that "lay everything on the table", including their personal lives early in a business relationship. At the other end of the spectrum are those cultures that reveal good news easily and can keep the bad news secret, at least until a more private and opportune moment. Neither extreme is necessarily more "honest" than the other; only the timing and level of intimacy are different. What is important is that the marketers learn how to access the level of openness necessary for their business dealings. Much of the needed methodology to achieve this can be uncovered during the cultural research phase.

Though you have applied your research, you may not get the "whole story" from members of the chain unless you have made your requirements known early in the relationship. Keep in mind that 50% of the burden of cultural understanding and honesty is on the distribution chain.

11. Moral

This word is one of the most controversial in all of international marketing. It derives from the Latin "Moralis" which means "custom", and every culture certainly has its own customs. Marketers must look for members that best reflect the level of morality suitable for the marketer and the marketplace. It will most likely be a compromise and concessions will most likely be made. It is not unusual for a marketer to find the level of morality unacceptable (too high as well as too low). If so, look for another market. The same may be true of potential channel members. Unless "the fit" is just right, the relationship will fall in the long run.

Note: morality takes in many of the other attributes stated above. To be successful marketers must maintain the core of their own morality while reshaping those aspects that are less stringent. Just as a product may require minor alterations to make it acceptable to the new market, so too may a moral code. This is not a recommendation for moral indifference, just an acknowledgement that self-righteousness is poor foundation for international marketing.

In general, members of distribution channels may be the only members of the target marketplace with which the marketer will have direct contact. Choose them carefully and treat them well. They will be both your sales force and service representatives. The distribution team will reflect your outlook on the marketplace and determine the level of success or failure. Marketers are coaches as well as managers in this very competitive game.

Summary

1. Understand that the development of distribution strategies is difficult in the home country, and even more so internationally, where marketing managers must concern themselves with two functions: ① Getting the products to foreign markets (exporting) and ② distributing the products within each market (foreign distribution).

2. Appreciate that there is a cost associated with setting up the channel, which requires labor management to locate and negotiate distribution deals—the process that can be as lengthy and expensive as finding the consumers for the product. Secondly, maintenance costs on the channel include the cost of internal sales staff, middlemen, and promotional efforts. The final costs to be considered are those associated with transportation, storage, and administration. All costs determined at this level will eventually be passed along to the consumer; therefore, marketers seek to reduce these expenditures whenever possible.

3. Understand why each marketer must determine how much control is needed and how much they will accept. With direct sales a company controls promotion, quality, and price, but the expense of doing so may be large if it entails the use of separate retail outlets.

4. Appreciate the importance of distribution density. Distribution density refers to the number of sales outlets required to provide adequate range for a product. Density requirements are a direct function of the end-user's purchasing habits. Changes in density needs will ripple through to change other components of the distribution chain. The key to proper density is consumer habit research. A fine example of density and its effect on distribution can be found in the computer industry.

5. Understand the factors influencing the distribution strategies: ① market characteristics; ② product characteristics; ③ company characteristics; and ④ middlemen's characteristics.

6. Understand how legal forces affect distribution strategy. Because the legal requirements for terminating middlemen vary from country to country, the time to think about how to terminate an agreement is before the termination occurs, although most countries have no special laws penalizing or precluding the termination of an agreement between the manufacturer and middlemen.

7. Discuss the standards for the international managers to choose their channel members. Members should be: ① connected; ② financially sound; ③ service oriented; ④ professional; ⑤ flexible; ⑥ stable; ⑦ eager; ⑧ far-sighted; ⑨ unbiased; ⑩ open; and ⑪ moral.

8. Explain it may be that no channel members are available to reach the firm's target markets and perform the desired functions. If there are none, management must

decide to ① desist from entering the market, ② select other target markets, or ③ create a new channel.

9. Understand that although management would prefer to standardize distribution patterns internationally, there are two fundamental constraints on its doing so: ① the variation in the availability of channel members among the firm's markets and ② the inconsistency of the influence of the environmental forces. Because of these constraints, international managers have found it best to establish a basic but flexible overall policy. The subsidiaries then implement this policy and design channel strategies to meet local conditions.

Questions

1. What are the most important factors to influence your international marketing distribution strategies?
2. What future do you see for global distribution?
3. Are there any advantages to standardizing the distribution strategy worldwide? Explain.
4. Why are manufacturers increasing their use of global and regional distribution members?
5. What is the basis for international managers to choose their channel members?
6. Assume you are a manager of an international company, how will you overcome the constraints coming from the foreign channel members?
7. Why is the channel length shorter and shorter?
8. Why must a marketer consider the economic forces when formulating a distribution strategy? Give some examples.
9. Why should the international distribution strategy be stability?

Minicase

U. S. Pharmaceutical of Korea

U. S. Pharmaceutical of Korea (USPK) was formed in 1969. It has one manufacturing plant which is located just outside Seoul, the capital. Although the company distributes its products throughout Korea, 40 percent of its total sales of $ 5 million were made in the capital last year.

There are no governmental restrictions on whom the company can sell to. The only requirement is that the wholesaler, retailer, or end users have a business license and a taxation number. Of the 400 wholesalers in the country, 130 are customers of USPK, accounting for 46 percent of the company's total sales. The company also sells directly to 2, 100 of the country's 10, 000 retailers; these account for 45 percent of total sales. The remaining sales are made directly to high-volume end users, such as hospitals and clinics.

Tom Sloane, marketing manager of USPK, would prefer to make about 90 percent of the company's sales directly to retailers and the remaining 10 percent directly to high-volume users. He believes, however, that this strategy is not possible because there of the abundance of small retailers. Not only is the sale volume per retailer small, but there is also a risk involved in extending credit to them. USPK tends to deal directly with large urban retailers and leaves most of the rural retailers to the wholesalers.

However, the use of wholesalers bothers Sloane for two reasons because: ① he has to give them larger discounts than he gives retailers that buy directly from the firm and ② because of the intense competition (300 pharmaceutical manufacturers in Korea), his wholesalers frequently demand larger discounts as the price for remaining loyal to USPK.

This intense competition affects another aspect of USPK's operations—collecting receivables. USPK has found that many wholesalers collect quickly from retailers but delay paying it. Instead, they invest in ventures that offer high short-term returns. For example, lending to individuals can bring them interest rates of up to 3 percent a month. The company's receivables, meanwhile, range from 75 to 130 days. Wholesalers are also the cause of another problem. Many are understaffed and have to rely on "drug peddlers" for sales. The drug peddler (there are perhaps 4,000 just in Seoul) make most of their money either by cutting the wholesalers' margins (selling at lower than recommended prices) or by bartering USPK's products for other pharmaceuticals. They do this by finding retail outlets where products are sold for less than the printed price. They exchange USPK's products at a discount for other drugs, which they sell to other retail outlets at a profit. As a result, USPK's products end up on retailers' shelves at prices lower than those that the company and its reputable wholesalers are selling them for.

The pharmaceutical industry has made some progress in persuading wholesalers and retailers to adhere to company price lists, but non-adherence is still a serious problem. One issue that manufacturers have not been able to resolve as of yet is the manner in which demands from hospitals and physicians for gifts should be handled.

Sloane believes the industry can do much to solve these problems, although intense competition has thus far kept the pharmaceutical manufacturers from joining together to map out a solution.

1. What should Tom Sloane and U. S. Pharmaceutical of Korea do to improve collections from wholesalers?
2. How would you handle the distribution problem?
3. Can anything be done through firms in the industry to improve the situation?
4. How would you handle the demands for gifts?

Practice Tests Ⅰ

1. Please determine false or truth for the following sentences.

(1) Market factors are similar to market indicators, except they tend to correlate highly with the market demand for a given product. ( )

A. false B. true

(2) Capital, raw material and people are the internal forces for the international companies and they all are uncontrolled. ( )

A. false B. true

(3) International marketing differs from its domestic counterpart in that it involves three environments including domestic, foreign and international instead of one. ( )

A. false B. true

(4) The only way to develop the foreign market is exporting. ( )

A. false B. true

(5) One reason Japan sells more to developing nations than most developed nations do is that it has had an extensive distribution system in these markets. ( )

A. false B. true

(6) If your plans include the construction or purchase of manufacturing plants overseas, you will find that most governments require that you use some local companies as parts suppliers. ( )

A. false B. true

(7) It's the common situation for a country to attempt to stop its local companies from exporting. ( )

A. false B. true

(8) The basic need potential of certain goods is dependent on various physical forces, such as climate, topography, or natural resources. ( )

A. false B. true

(9) If the marketer wishes to position a product as a high-quality item, setting a relatively high price will reinforce promotional emphasis quality. ( )

A. false B. true

(10) Lots of the international managers use the local advertising agencies because they

have an existing relationship with management. (   )

A. false　　B. true

2. Please choose the correct answer and fill in the blanks.

(1) The global firm is one that attempts to (   ) operations in all functional areas but it responds to national market differences when necessary.

A. standardize　　B. adapt　　C. change　　D. adjust

(2) As the managers of the international companies, they always look for the similar rather than different markets to develop, because (   ).

A. they want to develop a new market

B. they want to reduce their cost

C. the similar markets are same as the domestic market

D. it is impossible for them to develop the different market

(3) (   ) are the means by which a government, in the form of a customs office, controls the in-flow of foreign goods across its borders.

A. Export tariffs　　B. Inspections　　C. Quotas　　D. Import tariffs

(4) Lots of governments take the export licensing to limit the international trade, because (   ).

A. they want to protect the domestic market

B. they want to protect the foreign market

C. they want to safeguard the country

D. they want to limit the competitors to enter their markets

(5) (   ) is an arrangement under which a company provides managerial know-how in some or all functional areas to another party for a fee that ranges from 2 percent to 5 percent of sales.

A. Exporting　　B. Management contract

C. Licensing　　D. Franchising

(6) All of the import restrictions for the multinational companies are negative. (   )

A. It is true because the cost of all of the international companies will increase.

B. It is true because all of the international company's competitiveness will be weaken.

C. It is false because some local subsidiaries of the international companies will benefit the import restricts.

D. It is false because the import restrictions will strength the competitiveness of the international companies.

(7) The (   ) is the central focus of the marketing mix.

A. price　　B. promotion

C. distribution channel　　D. product

(8) Lots of international managers use the domestic advertising agencies to develop the

foreign market, because (   ).

A. they are already familiar with the marketer's product and image

B. they may have strong local political connections with the local government

C. they share the culture and linguistic background of the consumer base

D. they are familiar with the local media

(9) (   ) is the one with the greatest similarities worldwide.

A. Personal selling　　B. Promotional sale

C. Advertising　　D. Publicity

(10) The deeper the immediate market penetration desired, the greater must be the product modification. (   )

A. It is true because the companies must meet the local consumer's demand immediately.

B. It is true because the company hopes to occupy the market in future.

C. It is false because the markets are same.

D. It is false because all of the modification will reduce the costs of the company.

3. Please answer the following questions simply.

(1) Why do lots of the governments take the favorable policies to attract the new investment?

(2) Why do some governments take measures to limit the international trade sometimes?

(3) What do you believe makes foreign business activities more complex than purely domestic market?

4. Please answer the following questions and give detailed explanation.

(1) What are the most important reasons of the globalization and why?

(2) Assume you are a marketer and your business is to export oil to other countries. One day, you got bad news that someone made a invention which takes hydrogen from water directly and the test was very successful. Under the circumstance, what will you do and what is the result for you?

(3) Assume you are a boss of an international company, what measures you can take if you intend to extend your business?

(4) Please list some promotional strategies that the international companies most commonly use in the real world and give the reasons.

5. Please make a simple investment plan for your boss because he intends to invest $ 1million to establish a supermarket in America.

Practice Tests Ⅱ

1. Please determine false or true for the following sentences.

(1) The "market" is anywhere that goods or services may be sold or traded. (　　)

A. false　　B. true

(2) As the manager of the international company, he or she must have the domestic vision. (　　)

A. false　　B. true

(3) International marketing differs from its domestic counterpart in that it involves three environments including domestic, foreign and international instead of one. (　　)

A. false　　B. true

(4) The only way to develop a foreign market is foreign investment. (　　)

A. false　　B. true

(5) The domestic environment is composed of all the uncontrollable forces originating in the home country that surround and influence the life and development of the firm. (　　)

A. false　　B. true

(6) The purpose of the foreign direct investment is to obtain a return on the funds invested. (　　)

A. false　　B. true

(7) One of the goals for the governments to establish the tariff and no-tariff barriers is to weaken the competitiveness of the foreign products. (　　)

A. false　　B. true

(8) The development of distribution strategies is difficult in the home country, but it is even more so internationally. (　　)

A. false　　B. true

(9) Physical forces such as climate and terrain also militate against international product standardization. (　　)

A. false　　B. true

(10) All of the consumer products can be sold unchanged to certain market segments. (　　)

A. false B. true

2. Please choose the correct answer and fill in the blanks.

(1) ( ) means one firm will grant to another firm the right to use any kind of expertise and trademarks for one or more of the licensor's products.

A. Export B. Management contract

C. Licensing D. BOT

(2) Managers of the international companies prefer global standardization of marketing mix because ( ).

A. they want to develop a new market

B. they want to reduce their cost

C. the standardization fits most of the markets

D. the standardization is the only way for developing the foreign markets.

(3) The ( ) disasters are engineered by marketer competitors in many cases.

A. advertising B. personal selling

C. public relations D. promotional sale

(4) Lots of companies use the local advertising agencies to develop the foreign markets because ( ).

A. they have little knowledge of the company's image or management style

B. they may have strong local political connection

C. they may attempt to get the better price

D. they have little stake in maintaining the company's international brand.

(5) ( ) promote (s) investment and job creation while protecting domestic manufactures from direct competition.

A. The trade triple B. NAFTA

C. Exporting processing zones D. Franchising

(6) International trade consists mainly of manufactured goods exported by the industrialized nations to the developing nations in return for raw materials. ( )

A. It is true because the industrialized nations mainly produce industrial goods.

B. It is true because the developing nations mainly produce raw materials.

C. It is false because all of the industrialized nations can provide raw materials themselves.

D. It is false because most international trades are taken between the industrialized nations and they exchange the industrial products each other.

(7) Foodstuffs, ( ), and farm animals often have to face the barrier of inspection.

A. medical equipment

B. industrial products

C. consumer products

D. service

(8) Tariffs are subject to much political influence and favoritism. (　　)

A. It is false because business is business, it should not be influenced by the political forces.

B. It is false because all of the governments will benefit the international trade.

C. It is true because all of the governments will consider who will benefit the trade.

D. It is true because all of the governments want to control other country's international trade.

(9) Generally, (　　) require greater adaptation than industrial products to meet the demands of the world market.

A. export products　　B. import products

C. consumer products　　D. service products

(10) The greater disparity in income throughout the world is an important obstacle to worldwide product standardization. (　　)

A. It is true because the consumers of the less developed countries cannot afford to the higher quality products.

B. It is true because all of the products are very expensive in developed countries.

C. It is false because all of the consumers are the same.

D. It is false because the consumers will not be influenced by their income if they prefer the products.

3. Please answer the following questions simply.

(1) When will the international companies prefer a joint venture to a wholly owned subsidiary when making a foreign investment?

(2) Please list some import barriers and give simple explanation.

(3) Why should a firm's management consider going on a trade mission or exhibiting in a trade fair important?

4. Please answer the following questions and give detail explanation.

(1) According to the *Business Week*, what are the characteristics of the famous international companies and why?

(2) Assume you are a marketer and your business is to export the home appliance made in China to America. One day, you got news that RMB increased value substantially. Under the circumstance, what will you do and what is the result for you?

(3) Why do lots of the international companies invest in the foreign markets?

(4) The pricing strategy is decided by only the marketing department of the international company. True or false? Why?

5. Please make a simple marketing research plan for your boss because he intends to invest $1million to establish a restaurant in America.

参考文献

[1] 米歇尔. 国际商务文化. 云红茹，译. 北京：经济科学出版社，2002.
[2] 华盛. 伊朗禁止名人做商业广告. 国际广告，2008（11）：140-144.
[3] 科特勒. 营销管理. 梅汝和，译. 北京：中国人民大学出版社，2001.
[4] 李军. 国际技术与服务贸易. 北京：中国人民大学出版社，2008.
[5] 波特. 竞争战略. 陈晓悦，译. 北京：华夏出版社，1997.
[6] SHIPPEY K C. A short course in international contracts. San Rafael：World Trade Press，1999.
[7] CURRY J E. International marketing. 上海：上海外语教育出版社，2000.
[8] 汤姆森，斯迪克兰德. 战略管理：概念与案例. 段盛华，王智慧，译. 北京：北京大学出版社，2000.
[9] 胡其辉. 市场营销策划. 大连：东北财经大学出版社，1999.
[10] 世界银行. 世界银行发展报告：2009/2010. 北京：中国财政经济出版社，2010.
[11] 世界经济年鉴编辑委员会. 世界经济年鉴：2009/2010. 北京：经济科学出版社，2010.
[12] 甘碧群. 国际市场营销学. 北京：高等教育出版社，2001.
[13] 高鸿业. 西方经济学. 北京：中国人民大学出版社，2000.
[14] 张为付. 国际经济学. 南京：南京大学出版社，2010.
[15] 赵放. 国际营销学. 北京：机械工业出版社，2004.
[16] 佩利. 战略营销. 王海涛，译. 北京：机械工业出版社，2001.
[17] 基根. 全球营销管理. 段志荣，译. 北京：清华大学出版社，2004.
[18] 萨缪尔森，诺德豪斯. 经济学. 肖琛，译. 北京：人民邮电出版社，2004.
[19] 希尔. 国际商务：全球战略竞争. 周健临，译. 北京：中国人民大学出版社，2002.
[20] 赫尔森. 全球营销管理. 刘宝成，译. 北京：中国人民大学出版社，2005.
[21] http://www. wto. org.
[22] http://www. unesco. org.
[23] 克鲁格曼. 战略性贸易政策与新国际经济学. 北京：中国人民大学出版社，2000.

[24] 李尔华. 跨国公司经营与管理. 北京：清华大学出版社，2005.
[25] 谢斯，艾希吉，克里士南. 网络营销. 俞建良，译. 北京：中国人民大学出版社，2005.
[26] 库伦. 跨国管理：战略要径. 赵树峰，译. 北京：机械工业出版社，2003.
[27] 特普斯特拉. 国际营销. 郭国庆，译. 北京：中国人民大学出版社，2006.
[28] 张景智. 国际营销学教程. 北京：对外经济贸易大学出版社，2003.